THE ROAD PAST MANDALAY

A personal narrative

HARPER & BROTHERS

THE ROAD PAST MANDALAY

by John Masters

NEW YORK

Photographs are to be found in a group following page 134.
Maps are to be found on pages 5 and 171.

The drawings at the beginnings of the chapters, by the late Lieutenant
Colonel C. G. Borrowman, except that at Chapter 23, which is by Lieutenant
Colonel R. N. D. Williams, are reproduced from A *History of the 4th
Prince of Wales's Own Gurkha Rifles* by permission of the Trustees of the
4th Gurkha Rifles Private Fund.

FIRST EDITION H–L
LIBRARY OF CONGRESS CATALOG CARD NUMBER: 61–10210

To those who remained on the paths, on the hills.

In the foreword to the first volume of my autobiography, *Bugles and a Tiger*, I wrote: "The purpose of this book . . . is to tell the story of how a schoolboy became a professional soldier of the old Indian Army. In the course of the story I hope to have given an idea of what India was like in those last twilit days of the Indian Empire, and something more than a tourist's view of some of the people who lived there."

The Road Past Mandalay carries the narrative through to the end of the Second World War. Its purpose is to tell the story of how a professional officer of the old Indian Army reached some sort of maturity both as a soldier and a man. Some parts of the story are very unpleasant—so was the war it records; others are almost painfully personal—but this is not a battle diary, this is the story of one man's life. Of death and love I cannot say less with honesty or more with propriety.

There is another difference than that of time between this and the earlier volume. I think most people read *Bugles and a Tiger* for its depiction of a strange and rather romantic kind of life led by a very few. This book, *The Road Past Mandalay*, tells of experiences shared with scores of millions, not yet middle-aged, who have fought in war, have loved, have known separation and discomfort and danger. My story is not unique and I am not a hero, but an ordinary man, and I have written this narrative because I believe that many of you will recognize in it parts of your own life, and know that in writing of myself I have written, also, of you and for you.

As in *Bugles* I warn that this is a factual story but not a history. I have checked every detail as carefully as I can but as I kept no diary and made no notes my memory may sometimes have deceived me. If it has, forgive me.

J.M.

Book One # ACTION, WEST

1 Before dawn, the order reached us: The armored cars of the 13th Lancers were to make a wide outflanking movement into the desert, round the right of the enemy's position defending the small Syrian town of Deir-es-Zor. The 10th Gurkhas were to attack astride the main road. We—the 2nd Battalion of the 4th Gurkhas—were to stay in camp, in reserve, at five minutes' notice for action.

My colonel, Willy Weallens, read the message with a darkening face. He jammed on his hat, abruptly ordered me to follow him, and hurried to Brigade Headquarters. When we were admitted to the brigadier's presence, "Why aren't we leading the assault, sir?" Willy snapped.

The brigadier said that we had been leading for about eight weeks now, and it was someone else's turn. Willy said he didn't see what that had to do with it—sir. The order was a deliberate insult to the 4th Gurkhas. Patiently the brigadier explained the benefits of a system of rotation of duties. Willy fumed visibly. He tugged at the brim of his hat, kicked the sand with the toe of his boot, and looked daggers at the brigadier. Although I didn't know it at the time, since I had never seen a baseball game, Willy was giving a perfect demonstration of how to protest a called strike. The result was the same: we remained in reserve.

The brigadier went forward with his command group. Sulkily Willy waited at the main headquarters, at the rear end of the

3

unreeling field telephone line, and I waited with him. Three or four miles ahead Deir-es-Zor gleamed white on its low hill above the right bank of the Euphrates. The dusty road led straight toward it. To the left a long escarpment of black and gray cliffs marked the southern limit of the arena; the northern limit was the broad, yellow flood of the Euphrates. A neat set-piece battle was about to begin between the Vichy French and their troops, mainly Syrian, who were holding Deir-es-Zor, and the 21st Brigade of the 10th Indian Infantry Division, who intended to capture it. It was early morning on the fourth of July, 1941, and already the temperature had passed one hundred in the shade, but there was no shade, except a strong, yellow, glary kind in the tents. There were only two tents in the whole vast bivouac area. Both were very large and, though of a dull brown color, very conspicuous. One held the Main Dressing Station, full of men wounded in earlier bombing attacks. A large red cross painted on its roof made it more conspicuous still. The other was Brigade Headquarters, where Willy and I waited.

An antiaircraft sentry swung his Bren gun on its mount and peered intently to the west, beyond Deir-es-Zor. Soon I made out nine silver arrows in the sky out there, and diffidently informed Willy that we were about to be bombed again. I added that there were now only two obvious targets in the camp—the two tents. The planes were American-built Martin Maryland medium bombers, provided to the French in the early days of the war in order to fight the Germans, and now being used by Pétain's government against us.

Long dark oblongs formed in the planes' bellies as they opened their bomb bays. They came on in a tight formation of three stepped-up Vs, the sun gleaming on their silver bodies. They looked beautiful, and I stepped down into the nearest slit trench. A score of Bren guns began to rattle, and tracer streamed up in long, lovely curves against the blue sky. Directly overhead bombs fell from the bays in a glittering shower. The whistling rose to a multitudinous shriek, the explosions roared, eruptions of earth marched in long parallel lines across the camp. Two bombs fell directly into the Main Dressing Station, killing twenty of the men who lay awaiting evacuation to base hospitals. The Martins wheeled slowly above the sun.

Map illustrating Book One—ACTION WEST

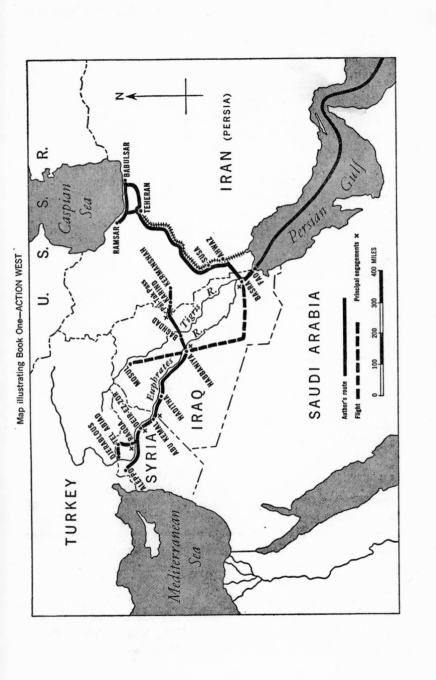

"This will be for us, sir," I said. I huddled well down into the trench but watched the bombers, for by now I could judge to within a few yards just where bombs would land. When the shining bombs left the black bays, I knew that Willy and I were for it. I dived flat in the trench and lay on my face, my arms crossed on the back of my head. Round the angle of the L-shaped trench Willy did the same. Or I presume he did. He might have thought the pilots up there could see him, and then he would have remained standing, or begun to read a book.

The scream of the bombs grew louder. Suddenly the ground jumped. A huge force lifted and shook me and the trench and the whole earth in which the trench had been dug, moving everything bodily upward and sideways. Thick yellow earth clogged my mouth and nostrils and I began to choke. A sharp pain on the left cheek of my buttocks forced the earth out of my mouth in a yell.

The thunder of the bombs died away. Through the cloud of settling earth I heard Willy's voice. "Are you hit, Jack?" I put my hand on my wound, and yelled again. Willy was bending over me with a look of terrible anxiety on his face.

I thought, what a gentleman you are, colonel dear, and scrambled to my feet. I held out my hand. In the palm lay a still hot .303 bullet, one of ours. Fired at the Martins by a Bren gun, it had become red-hot in its passage through the air, and fallen precisely onto my arse as I cowered in the trench, burning a small hole in my trousers and in me. At the same time a 250-pound bomb had fallen about ten feet from my end of the trench. Willy and I were standing in the trench at the rim of the crater it had formed. The force of the explosion had bodily shifted the whole trench, so that it now lay several degrees off its previous line.

The telephone buzzed. The brigadier at the other end ordered us to advance a certain distance behind the 10th Gurkhas, well closed up and in tight control, ready to repel counterattacks or to exploit success. A couple of orders, and we moved off astride the road. I could hear small-arms fire from the direction of Deir-es-Zor. Something went bang, sharp but not very loud, close to my feet. Some dust rose, but very little. Still slightly deafened and dazed by the bombing, I had no idea what it was, and could not summon the interest to find out. Several more bangs followed. I plodded on.

Willy, a few paces to my left, looked at me with an approving smile. "That's the way, Jack! Set an example. . . . You're a good cool one."

Another bang, and another puff of dust rose between me and the nearest rifleman. "What is that, sir?" I asked Willy.

His expression changed. He said crossly, "Shells, you ass! We're being shelled by French 75s from the edge of the town up there. You are wet behind the ears, aren't you?"

My knees began to ache with the effort of keeping up that steady, nonchalant plod. I was being shelled, for the first time in my life. By French 75s. The master gun of World War I. Could fire twenty rounds a minute, effective range eight thousand yards, weight of shell thirteen pounds, lethal zone of the burst about—I looked at the next puff of dust, which rose almost between a rifleman's legs—about two feet, apparently. We continued to advance.

Willy was angry with himself at having shown emotion on my behalf—twice now, for he knew I'd seen his anxiety in the trench—and insisted that this wasn't real shelling. The famous French 75 was a mere peashooter. *Bang bang.*

I said I'd rather be shelled than bombed, any day. *Bang.* A small hole appeared in the wide brim of my Gurkha hat. Willy shouted, "You wait—(*bang*)—until you've really been shelled—(*bang*). You don't know—(*bang*)—what you're talking about."

Bang!

His words, and their accompaniment, will serve as a proper introduction to this narrative.

I was twenty-six years old and my substantive rank was lieutenant, though the expansion of the war had made me a temporary captain. Born in Calcutta of a family that had even then served for four generations in India, I was educated at Wellington and the Royal Military College, Sandhurst, in England; on August 30, 1934, received a second lieutenant's commission in His Majesty's Land Forces; and immediately went out to serve as one of the small band of British regular officers in the Indian Army.

The British Army, where both officers and men were British, also had large forces in India. In the Indian Army all the en-

listed men were Indian; the officers were British, in slow process
of being replaced by Indians.

Since I must use the names throughout this book, I had better
explain here that in the Indian Army we had, besides officers
who held the King's Commission, others who held their commission from the Viceroy of India. These latter were always men
who had risen through the ranks, and so were of the same caste
and tribe as the enlisted men—in our case, Gurkhas. They ranked,
in order, below second lieutenants as follows: *subadar major* (only
one in a battalion: the colonel's right-hand man and adviser in
all matters relating to Gurkha customs, religion, and morale);
subadar (commanded a platoon, or was second-in-command of a
company); *jemadar* (commanded a platoon). They were all saluted, held powers of discipline and punishment, and were called
sahib. The noncommissioned ranks were: *havildar major* (first
sergeant, sergeant major); *havildar* (sergeant); *naik* or *amaldar*
(corporal); *lance naik* (lance corporal). The plain private soldier
was usually called *sepoy*, but all Gurkha regiments were Rifles
(this is an old distinction without any practical modern difference,
though a potent factor in esprit de corps), so our soldiers were
called Riflemen.

Of Gurkhas, what can I say that will compress the knowledge
of fourteen years, and all the love and admiration it gave me,
into a few sentences? Their homeland is Nepal, the small country
sandwiched along the Himalayas between India and Tibet. They
are of Mongol extraction; small and sturdy in stature; mountain
men all; endowed with an inborn honesty toward life that gives
them perfect self-confidence, without any need for swashbuckling
or boasting; as fond of pranks as of discipline; cheerful under the
worst conditions—especially under the worst conditions; brave,
courteous . . . well, you get the idea: I thought highly of the
men with whom it was my privilege to serve.

The regiment I joined in 1935 was the 4th Prince of Wales's
Own Gurkha Rifles, in the 2nd Battalion. During four years of
"peace" with it I fought in two campaigns on India's North West
Frontier, shot a tiger and two snipe, attended the usual professional schools, had a great many love affairs, learned something
about my profession, crossed the United States on a long fur-
lough, and added four years to my age. Of all this, of the gaiety

and the grimness, of the hard processes of learning and the wild abandon of young men, of the atmosphere of that India, I have tried to tell something in *Bugles and a Tiger*, referred to in the foreword.

To me, and to the battalion, war came on September 3, 1939, in the little Indian outpost of Loralai, near the Afghan border. By then I was the adjutant.

2 We were a battalion of regulars, who had marched and fought and played together for five, ten, twenty-five years. We did not remain that way for long. War expansion began at once, and we had to send hundreds of men away to form the cores of new battalions, training depots, and the like. We filled the vacant places in the enlisted ranks with raw recruits and rusty reservists, and, among the officers, with tea planters, coffee planters, junior tycoons from the great merchant houses of Calcutta and Bombay, and boys just out of school. Most of them had done some weekend soldiering with the Auxiliary Force, but they had much to learn and an unknown but certainly short time to learn it in. My time was spent wrestling like Laocoön with promotion rolls, equipment states, company strengths, hospital reports, and training programs.

One day I looked up to find a tall young Indian standing in my office. He wore an ill-fitting uniform, a cheerful smile, and the badges of a lieutenant of the Indian Medical Service. I frowned ferociously. No one is supposed to smile in the office of an adjutant. The young man said his name was Dutt, and that he had been posted as our medical officer. This was a shock, as in those days all King's Commissioned officers in a Gurkha battalion were British. Still, we would have to make the best of it. I pulled an officer's record sheet toward me, and asked, "Name?"

"Dutt," he said. "I just told you."

"Rank?"

"Lieutenant, I.M.S."

"Christian names?"

"None."

I put down the pen and stared at him. "I am very busy," I began coldly. "And . . ."

"I am not a Christian," he said with a triumphant beam, "so how can I have Christian names? I am Hindu, and my full name is Santa Padhaya Dutt, if that is what you want to know."

I stared at the paper as though it had bitten me. "Christian name" is, in English-English, the normal phrase for "first name." I realized suddenly that it was not a mere phrase, it meant exactly what it said. The point had never arisen before. Times were changing. There was a war on. Oh, well . . . I silently quoted one of my colonel's pet phrases—"Worse things happen at sea."

"Have you seen the colonel yet?" I asked the doctor.

"No, I am looking forward to that pleasure," he said.

"Wait here . . ." I began, then the colonel's voice called me from his office next door.

Lieutenant Colonel W. R. W. Weallens sat in the big chair behind his desk looking at a small oblong of pasteboard. His expression was much like that of an insulted bloodhound. Since this was normal with him, I did not become alarmed.

"Have you seen one of these?" he asked.

"Yes, sir," I said. It was a calling card, still a required item of an officer's equipment in 1940. The inscription, in the correct copperplate print, said, *Mr. R. L. H. Werner,* and, on the line below, *4th Prince of Wales's Own Gurkha Rifles.* The form was correct, I knew, because I had written out for each of the new officers exactly what he must have printed on his card, taking special care to point out that *Wales* was not a plural and that therefore it was *Wales's,* not *Wales',* a common but disastrous solecism.

Willy said, "Emergency Commissioned officers cannot be members of the regiment. They're only attached from the General List. That's what they should have printed on their cards."

I looked at him with awe, exasperation, and affection. Twenty years older than I, he had been passed over for command some

years earlier, and sent to work out his time for pension in the
Publications Department at Delhi. Before that, during a short
spell of service together in 1936 and 1937, he had shown sharp
distaste for me, my dress, attitude, morals, and shade of hair, a
distaste which I had returned by poorly concealed insubordination, for I was then a second lieutenant and he a senior major.
In 1940 the powers pulled him out of Publications, where he was
dying of shame, and gave him all that he had ever asked of life
—command of his own battalion, of his own regiment, in war.

When he reached Loralai he found that I was the adjutant,
his chief staff officer and personal confidant. But our experiences
in the intervening years had chastened both of us, and though
he could have fired me at any moment, we got on well from the
start. Military comradeship grew into something much more
as he realized that though I was a mannerless little blighter of
the Jazz Age I loved the regiment and the Gurkhas as much as he
did. For my part I soon understood that he was not an ignorant
old curmudgeon but a brave and honest Edwardian gentleman,
suffering from a needless complex about his capacity as a soldier.
The complex was caused by the fact that he had never attended
the Staff College, for higher military instruction, and I noted
that, too.

Now we stared at each other across the slip of pasteboard. I
wanted to say, "Times have changed. Calling cards don't matter
any more, still less what's written on them." I wanted to give
him a lecture on the relative importance of efficiency and correct
form in time of war. But none of that would be any use. There
was a way, though. I must mention the 4th Gurkhas.

I said, "Very well, sir. I'll tell them to get new ones printed.
. . . But if any of them win the V.C. while they're with us, I
suppose we'll have to say that it wasn't a 4th Gurkha who won
it, only some chap on the General List."

Willy glared at me, his lips tight. Slowly his wonderful smile,
a little prim, a little uncertain, transformed his face. "Get out,"
he said.

"Yes, sir," I said. "Our medical officer's arrived. Lieutenant
Santa Padhaya Dutt. I think he's going to be a good egg."

"I wonder if he knows Colonel Dabholkar," Willy said eagerly.
He jumped to his feet. "Doc Dabholkar was the best doctor in

action we ever had. I remember in '16 . . . Send him in!" Before I'd left the room he was greeting young Dutt with outstretched hand, as happy and open as a boy.

"Goddamn it," I muttered, when the door closed behind them. "Goddamn it, when will I ever learn how complicated people are?"

They moved us a couple of hundred miles down the frontier to Quetta, where we practiced even harder to fit ourselves for the war already raging in the Libyan Desert. We were soon trained to a hair, but we lacked a number of items of equipment then considered essential for a well-dressed battalion about to take part in a battle. Gas masks, motorcycles, and most of our trucks we had, also mosquito nets, but we did not have enough Bren guns, and no antitank rifles at all. Day and night a small squadron of officers and noncoms blockaded the local arsenal, howling for two-inch mortars, of which we were supposed to have sixteen and had none; and three-inch mortars, of which we were supposed to have six and had two; and Bren-gun carriers, the little tracked semiarmored vehicles on which much of our tactics was based, of which we had none.

All our indents for these items were returned "N.A." (not available). Roger Werner, lately a tea planter and now our Transport Officer, muttered, "Do they expect us to fight the Germans with our bare hands?"

The regulars laughed sardonically, and I said, "My boy, the Army Estimates must be reduced!"

The regulars were still, just, in a majority. Between us and the E.C.O.s (Emergency Commissioned Officers) there was very little of that friction which had added so greatly to the unpleasantness of the first war. Both sides had learned a lot since 1914. Regulars no longer thought it funny to refer to E.C.O.s as "temporary gentlemen," nor to subject them to humiliating lessons in deportment. On their part, the E.C.O.s realized that our collective name was not Blimp, that we knew our craft, and intended to teach it to them, thoroughly and quickly, for the common good. The E.C.O.s' only fault was a marked distaste for the chores of administration. They had volunteered to fight, not to count shirts and weigh rice. Tactics, map reading, shooting—to these they bent their energies with enthusiasm, but a lesson on the laws of

evidence met glum, almost surly faces; and an order to spend four
hours double-checking the next-of-kin rolls caused mutinous
grumbles—"Why can't the company clerk do it?" We answered,
"Because these are your men, not his." As the months passed
even these disagreements vanished and we settled down, one with
another, and formed a new entity—the wartime regular battalion.

In England my father, ten years since retired as a lieutenant
colonel, crept about the Devon hills with tin hat and rifle as
commander of the Uplyme Home Guard. The Germans dropped
bombs on the peaceful fields and Spitfires dropped empty shell
cases on the street.

In Cyrenaica, General Wavell inflicted a crushing defeat on the
Italians. The 4th Indian Division led the assault. Indian troops
were in action and *we* were not. Willy's face became a symphony
of woe. There was only one ray of light: no other Gurkha battalion had yet beaten us into battle.

In the evenings my duties would often take me down to his big
bungalow on Queen's Road with papers and orders and messages.
His wife Biddy treated me, and indeed all the other subalterns, as
though we were still hungry overgrown schoolboys, plying us with
cake and a wonderful motherly sympathy, embracing but unde-
manding, that was also having its effect in softening Willy's
temperament. (They had not been married long.) Willy himself
always caused me deep embarrassment on these visits. Brusque
and even curt on parade, as soon as he reached his home he became a plain gentleman, and a host. The fact that I was far his
junior and his adjutant made no difference. When I arrived he
helped me out of my greatcoat—in winter Quetta is as cold as
Montana. When I fumbled for a cigarette he was halfway across
the room with a match. When I left he hurried ahead to open
the car door for me. The next morning, full of affection, I'd greet
him with a salute and a smile; his face would always be cold and
set. "The Quarterguard turned out like a pack of sailors to me
just now. And what's Tumbahadur doing at the . . . ?"

We lived and moved in a peculiarly uncommitted atmosphere.
No one knew when we would reach the big war, or exactly where,
so we couldn't tie ourselves to that. The frontier stretched away
to the north—but we'd left that. England was being bombed,
There Was a War On, men were dying on two continents—but

the girls and wives and grass widows here in Quetta still wore long dresses to the club dances, and all of us changed into mess kit for dinner, and into dinner jackets to go to the club, and the girls and wives and grass widows were very gay, and we organized picnics up the Hanna Valley, and games of charades and sardines, and someone found a camera by the Hanna Lake and handed it to a shop to be developed so that they might know whose it was, and the pictures showed many respectable ladies and gentlemen prancing about with no clothes on at all, in suggestive or plain copulatory attitudes; and we danced in the club and dined in beautiful drawing rooms and flirted in dark gardens, and it was all a game except when suddenly it wasn't, when the satin skin moved differently under your hand and the low voices, your own among them, tried to ward off with jokes the unexpected assault of love, unexpected and unwanted because earlier that day you had already been caught in the same way, when the clacking roar of machine-gun bullets dipped suddenly close on the field firing range, and war showed its face, violent and demanding, behind the play of the maneuvers.

On parade in the winter mornings the Khojak wind blew through all our clothes, so that we felt as naked as the Pan Prancers of Hanna, and we marched and maneuvered in the snow, and came back sweaty and dirty to hot baths and the formalities of the mess. At Christmas we formed bands of waits and went singing carols down the long straight cantonment roads where the senior officers lived with their wives and families just as they had done before the war; and when we went to the flicks we wore high, padded felt boots and sweaters and took rugs, too, to spread over our knees and legs, under which hands were held and silent promises made. In the Gurkha Officers' Mess *Subadar Major* Sahabir reigned, and we went often to drink *raksi* and dance the *jaunris* there, because soon it would all be different; more exciting, perhaps, but different. And chaps in the right sort of uniform would still put their monocles in their eye and look slowly up and down chaps in the wrong sort of uniform, and take the monocle out and turn away, without saying a word. . . .

The wheels of Delhi turned, our number fell. They sent us over a thousand miles south, by rail, to Poona, and warned us that our division was earmarked for Malaya, since the Japanese were making threatening faces in that direction. We threw away our Desert Warfare manuals, indented for Jungle Warfare Training pamphlets instead, and set out to find some jungle. Steel helmets we received, and camouflage netting for them, but no two-inch or three-inch mortars. N.A.

Once a week Ronny Smith, Roger Werner, "Shirley" Temple and I would borrow a couple of nurses from the local hospital and take them out for a picnic ten miles up the river. The sun sank, turning the water pink and then dark violet; we played my portable phonograph on the bank, ate curry puffs and drank a can or two of beer, if we could find it, and returned in the dark to Poona. The next morning half the officers were at the arsenal again. We felt like firemen trying to find our shoes and socks while the alarm jangled ever louder and more hysterically in our ears.

In March, my cousin Marjorie, twenty-two years of age, newly married, dancing in London with her husband, a fighter pilot in the Royal Air Force, died under German bombs dropped into the Café de Paris.

In April, 1941, the powers took us out of the division that was due for Malaya and ordered us to Iraq to defend that country against possible German attack. Mr. Hopkins, President Roosevelt's special envoy, went to Iraq a little later and remarked to a British general, "The Persian Gulf is the arsehole of the world, and Basra is eighty miles up it." It was to this exact spot we were now to be sent, as a form of military enema.

I didn't know much about Iraq but I did know it was mostly desert. We threw away the Jungle Warfare pamphlets and began a search for the Desert Warfare series. Before we found them we entrained for Bombay and boarded the troopship *Devonshire*, which at once eased out into mid-channel—and dropped her anchor. We waited.

What were we waiting for? The Indian Ocean was full of submarines. A German pocket battleship was loose off the East Coast of Africa. We were waiting to form a convoy.

None of this was true. We were waiting while the quartermasters went ashore to Bombay Arsenal. They came back with the rest of our Bren magazines, our first-line reserve of shell dressings, and four two-inch mortars, complete with ammunition. The launches rocked alongside the gangway while fatigue parties of

Gurkhas manhandled the awkward sacks onto the jury platform and into the ship, singing as they worked. But there were
no three-inch mortars and no Bren-gun carriers. N.A.

Still, all our rifles were clean-bright and slightly oiled, our
bayonets sandblasted and matt-black so that they would not
catch the light in night attacks, and our spirits rode high. The
ship's siren boomed thrillingly, imperiously. We were off!

Nothing happened. The captain had been calling to his mate.
We waited a day or two more in the stream, studying the Yacht
Club through field glasses to see if we could recognize the slack-
ers drinking on the terrace there, and, what was much more
interesting in India, recognize the women they were drinking
with. We grappled with the British sailors' inability to understand
the administrative necessities of Gurkha soldiers. The food was
not good nor were there proper places where it could be cooked.
The Gurkhas, as usual, smiled through conditions which would
have made some troops mutiny. Willy tramped rapidly up and
down the decks, inspecting everything many times over.

One evening he sent for me to come to his cabin, where he told
me abruptly that he thought we might have to make an opposed
landing. At least we should be ready to do so.

This was ludicrous. We were going to Basra in fulfillment
of a treaty pledge to protect Iraq should its recent independence
be threatened by anyone; and it was certainly being threatened
by Germany; or shortly would be. It was strictly a standard troop-
ing movement. Nothing had been loaded or packed for an assault
landing, which would have wasted valuable space in the ship.
Willy listened glumly, and at last agreed that he was probably
worrying over nothing. He almost admitted aloud that he worried
too much; and I almost gave him an encouraging clap on the
back. Our talk ended in one of his quick smiles, and he said, "Oh,
well, worse things happen at sea."

We set sail, several ships protected by an armed merchant
cruiser. We had an uneventful trip to the mouth of the Persian
Gulf, except for the arguments that developed when Santa Padhaya Dutt said blandly that he wasn't fighting to maintain England's rule over India, only to insure that it was not replaced by
Germany's. It must be remembered that British officers of Gurkha
battalions, spending most of their time protecting India's frontiers
against tribal raids, lived a life far removed from the turmoil of

Indian or world politics. Dutt was regarded as something of an eccentric, not for his nationalism but because he knew about the matter at all and was interested in it. The rest of us had simply shut the whole thing out of our minds. When the time came, someone would tell us to go home; meanwhile we had a job to do. But all Englishmen love an eccentric and Dutt became very popular.

As we entered the Persian Gulf the temperature stood at 110, the humidity at 100 per cent. I was sitting in a deck chair, reading. A wild scream shocked me out of my book. A panting engine-room lascar, his eyes rolling, dashed out of the steel door beside me, ran across the deck, vaulted the rail, and leaped into the sea forty feet below. I rushed to the side, hardly believing my eyes. I felt so hot that, although it appeared that a lascar had become deranged, it might just as easily have been me. But there he was, fast drifting astern, and someone had already thrown him a life-belt. "Man overboard," I croaked. The second time it came out better, in a full seamanlike bellow.

We picked him up eventually, but he died of heatstroke. I don't know what the temperature in the engine room was at that moment, but I stoked for an hour in very similar conditions when first going out to India in 1934, and the temperature then had been 149 degrees Fahrenheit.

I returned to my reading. Willy's orderly appeared and said, "*Colonel sahib salaam bhanchha.*" What now? I followed him. Willy was in his cabin. His worried frown had disappeared. "We're going to make an assault landing," he said. He spared himself the pleasure of giving me even a grin.

Jesus Christ. No assault landing craft, only the ship's lifeboats. No covering fire, except from the armed merchant cruiser. No rehearsal. No communication channels. Where in hell was the reserve ammunition packed? The mortar bombs? Who was responsible for this bloody mess, anyway? I swore to myself that I would never believe a senior formation's order again. Any troops I was responsible for would in future travel loaded and ready for action, however uncomfortable we were, however much space we took up, whatever orders I had to disobey.

The company commanders arrived and Willy explained what had happened. Some weeks earlier an Iraqi politician, Rashid Ali, had, with three others, formed a cabal and overthrown the government. The Golden Square, as the cabal called itself, was pro-Hitler. They had just informed England that Iraq did not need to be helped, since she was not threatened by anyone, except indeed the force now steaming from India to her assistance. She would resist the landing of that force, and would get help wherever she could. This obviously meant the Germans, who had recently conquered Greece. German bomber squadrons were already on their way to Iraq.

We steamed on. The brigade staff issued orders for the landing, detailing the various waves of assault, and the lifeboats allotted to each. I suballotted them to our companies, under Willy's direction, and soon found my cabin full of the same mass of paper that I thought I had left behind in Poona. The riflemen clambered cheerfully in and out of the lifeboats, armed, if not to the teeth, at least to the waist. We thought that we would not meet very heavy opposition, since the bulk of the Iraqi Army was upcountry near Baghdad. The enemy at Basra would be mostly armed police, who had already attacked the nearby R.A.F. base.

Just before we reached the mouth of the Shatt al Arab, the name by which the combined streams of the Tigris and Euphrates are known after their junction, we had a final rehearsal. The riflemen thought it a huge joke, and I was inclined to agree with them, though not so sure who was supposed to laugh. Some of these men, my men, were going to die, needlessly, because of some bloody fool's over optimism. Willy clapped me on the back and said, "It'll be all right on the night, Jack."

I retired to my cabin. Five minutes later Willy's orderly arrived. *"Colonel sahib salaam bhanchha."*

Willy showed me a copy of a signal that had just come in: *"Deflate balloon. Dock area in our hands."*

I began to cheer up. Willy looked ready to cry. We landed late in the afternoon at the Basra docks, without fireworks, and marched into a grove of palm trees that stretched along the side of a road close to the river. The 2/4th Gurkhas had reached a theater of war, preceded only—among Gurkha battalions—by the 2/7th, of 20 Brigade and that, as Willy pointed out, was pure bad luck.

3 Under the palms we lay in a marsh, the stifling air full of mosquitoes, and no one could find any drinking water. From the depths of the huddled city so close to us we heard occasional single shots, sudden bursts of machine-gun fire, and a few heavier crumping explosions. No one told us what it was all about so Willy doubled sentries and kept one company, in rotation, standing to arms throughout the night. In the morning we found that the commotion had been caused by the 2/7th Gurkhas fighting their way into the old city to give us all more elbow room. They had located a strong post held by a few Iraqi regulars, and the brigadier ordered us to support them in an attack. Willy and I drove into the narrow, stinking alleys to co-ordinate details with their colonel. We found him in a battered police station his battalion had captured during the night. He looked tired but cheerful and he had a peculiar gleam in his eye.

"Morning, Willy," he said as we arrived, and then at once, "Do you know where our two-inch and three-inch mortars are? The ones that were N.A. all over India? . . . The Iraqi Army has them."

This turned out to be true. The British government had been supplying Iraq and other "allies" with modern arms, leaving none for the regular battalions of the Indian Army, a force which even Mr. Churchill came to learn was of more value to our cause than the Arab conscripts now busily supporting the Golden Square's Nazi-inspired revolution.

We put in a brisk attack, alongside the 2/7th Gurkhas, more to get at our mortars than out of any pique at the enemy, who fired a few shots and fled. We settled down to hold Basra until more troops came, to release us for operations farther upcountry.

We took over another police station for our headquarters, and spread the companies throughout the city. One company the colonel placed near a date-processing factory, if that is the right word to describe rows of old women, their teeth reduced to two, who expertly ripped the pits out of the dates (with the fanglike pair of teeth) at the rate of about a hundred a minute. Dates had become a prominent part of our ration, and they were excellent, but now we looked at them with near-nausea. Dutt assured us that the sugar content of the date is so high that no germ can survive in it for more than a few hours. He said that cholera, typhoid, and other disease bacilli had been massively injected into dates, with no result. We believed him. We had to; we were damned hungry.

One section of our Vickers machine guns Willy placed on the flat roof of a big house near the river, where they had a good view down several streets. As we left the building after our preliminary reconnaissance Willy turned to me with his brow furrowed. "Jack, do you know what I believe that house to be?"

"It's a brothel," I said.

Willy was racked with anxiety. Did the house really offer the best field of fire available in that part of Basra? Would the girls tarnish the innocence of the young machine-gun officer, who must go through their quarters every time he went up to the roof to inspect the guns and the sentries? He told me to keep an eye on the situation. I saluted briskly and said, "Yes, sir!"

Later inspections convinced me that Peter McDowall's morals were in no danger, yet. We had only been out of India a week, and the youngest "girl" was a charitable forty. In the harsh Arabian morning charity was absent and I would have said nearer sixty. But, talking with the madam and some of the tarts over a cup of tea, I learned that there might be a security danger. Nearly all the women were enemy aliens, or had originated in countries now under Hitler's dominion. Most of them were fair-skinned, and even those who weren't insisted that they were not "stinking Arabs," but Yugoslavs, Bulgarians, Hungarians, or—most often—Rumanians. Their histories showed a common pattern, a Grand Tour in reverse, which had imposed itself the moment they set out for the glamorous Orient. In their twenties the pimps shipped them to Cairo or Tripoli or Beirut. Ten years or so profitable labor followed in those fine cities; but little of the profits stuck to the women's fingers. Sagging charms and lined faces forced the next move—to Istanbul, Baghdad, Alexandria, or Aleppo, for another five or ten years, with possibilities of a side trip to Teheran. The routes from there to the end of the road were various, just as one can travel from New York to Los Angeles by an almost infinite variety of ways; but the end itself was always the same—this brothel in Basra.

However, we were not unfortunate whores but a battalion of Gurkha Rifles, and we were supposed to be making that Grand Tour in the opposite direction. It was time to get moving.

Since our moves for the rest of the summer took us through the Middle East like the writhings of a demented snake, I will summarize them here. First, needing more elbow room in and around Basra, we pushed the Iraqis back until they could no longer even threaten the port and the base that was already beginning to build up round it.

That done, we flew to the center of the country, and helped chase away the Iraqis attacking a treaty-held British airfield at Habbaniyah, not far from Baghdad.

The Habbaniyah-Baghdad area thus became, as it were, our launching pad. From it we made three boomerang-like sallies. First, in June, we went to Mosul, in the extreme north of Iraq, held that until conditions quietened—and returned to Habbaniyah.

Sally Two, in July and August, saw us hurtling northwest into Syria, almost as far as Aleppo and the Mediterranean—then back to Habbaniyah.

Sally Three, in August, September, and October, launched us northeast into Iran—then back to Baghdad.

That was the "large picture." From the worm's-eye view of an infantryman, this is what it looked like. . . .

The spring flooding of the great rivers had begun. All the flat lands had become one huge lake, with isolated clumps of palms showing where the villages stood on higher ground. The road to the sea ran along a narrow embankment, overarched with date palms, the yellow sweep of the river on one side, the still floods on the other. Fifteen miles to the west the ridge of Shaiba, where the R.A.F. had a base, stood out of the waters, and was safely held. South along the same ridge, our patrols found no enemy as far as Sinbad's Tower.

Basra itself was split and crisscrossed by creeks and canals and water channels, all now full. In the city they ran full of garbage and dhows and house scows, under the tottering, blind brick walls. Black-veiled women watched from dark corners, and dead dogs and babies and the entrails of donkeys swelled and stank in them under the glare of the sun. North a little, beyond the limits of the city, the creeks ran in tortured loops through palm and scrub and thickets of jungle. All these we searched, in narrow canoe-like boats commandeered for the purpose.

Once I went out with a boat patrol. For hours we paddled stealthily through a maze of channels, with never a view except down the shadowed waterways. We saw nothing until, near five o'clock, another boat appeared round a bend a hundred yards ahead. We challenged; it turned, heeling over under the frantic efforts of the two Arabs in it, and fled. The Bren gunner crouched uncomfortably in the bow of our canoe opened fire, but after he had fired three long bursts, the boat rocking with our efforts to gain speed, the canoe ahead vanished. We never found it again, and had a hard job finding ourselves, as we were moderately lost. When we eventually got back, I reported our adventure.

Willy had a peculiar look in his eye. "Show me where you were on the map," he said.

I examined the map. I really had no idea. "Somewhere round here," I said.

"And which direction were you firing in?"

The sun had been on my right, the shadows going from right to left across the creek. "About southeast," I said.

Willy rolled up the map. "Divisional headquarters is standing-to in the Airport Hotel," he said happily. "Those chair-borne blighters have all been crouched under their desks since five o'clock, when someone put three long machine-gun bursts through the windows."

"Any casualties?" I asked politely.

"Unfortunately, no," Willy said. "I'll tell them they can stand down now. And look where you're firing in future."

Continuing to probe north, we found the roads and the flooded land clear as far as a creek and a bridge that emptied into the Shatt-al-Arab seven miles up, at Habib Shawi. These the enemy held.

We reconnoitered in force. On the approach march I saw a young rifleman beginning to sway from side to side in the ranks. His comrades tried to support him but he fell away from them and walked into one of the row of palms beside the road. The column marched on, and he had cannoned off several more trees and fallen down before help could reach him. His face was suffused, his eyes bulging out. This was heatstroke, and though Dutt sent him back at once, he died.

Later, during the assault we ran into accurate machine-gun fire aimed down the road. There was no advance, no cover, and no escape, except by swimming. Three men were killed, and we retreated.

A few days later we tried again, in a combined operation with the Navy. The captain of the Australian sloop *Yarra* put on Arab dress, and with two similarly disguised petty officers sailed up the Shatt in the dusk in an Arab boat, until they were opposite the Habib Shawi creek. Here they took soundings, discovered that the center of the resistance was a big house just north of the creek, and silently dropped back downriver. If we loaded a couple of companies into the *Yarra* and a felucca tied alongside it, we could assault the position from the river.

A conference was held to discuss fire support. The guns of the *Yarra* could fire over our heads as we assaulted the Big House. Good. And our own artillery could support us from its positions near the airfield. Good. Then we would advance again up the road. But where could the artillery officers find an elevated observation post from which to direct their fire after we had taken the Big House?

"From the roof of the Big House itself," Willy said impatiently.

The captain of the *Yarra* shook his head. He pointed out that three four-inch naval guns would have been firing at it from four hundred yards or so, for ten minutes. The Big House would be a pitiful little heap of smoking wreckage. Willy bit his lip. How could he have overlooked such an obvious factor? He recovered himself.

"Cotton wool for the ears?" he asked.

The captain nodded. "Good idea. For anyone close to our guns."

For their observation post the artillery cut down a telegraph pole, equipped it with guy ropes, steps, and a platform on top. It looked very dangerous, and was hell to load onto the *Yarra*. Finally we got it on board, where it lay along the upper deck like a giant, shorn Christmas tree, and everyone stumbled over it in the dark. We reinforced the deck with sandbags to stand the shock of recoil and placed our three-inch mortars up there, with machine guns between them. At two A.M. we sailed, while the rest of the battalion moved up to attack by the old route, to hold the enemy's attention to the road.

Twenty minutes before dawn our assaulting companies were ready in the ship's launch and the rowing boats. Willy and I stood in a corner of the bridge, where a dim blue light shone on the captain's strong jaw and curly black cheek whiskers. Light spread across the great yellow river, sihouetting us for the enemy, who were to our west. Out of the river mist rose a slender forest of palm trees and, just visible among them, the flat roof of the Big House.

H-hour.

A long, furious burst of Bren-gun fire, from the Habib Shawi bridge, broke the ghostly peace. From the south I heard the dull *bom-bom-bo-bom* of our howitzers, and began to count. The seconds ticked away, Bren and rifle fire increased around the creek and bridge, and now the enemy were firing back. The howitzer shells arrived and burst accurately around the Big House. The diversionary attack had started.

On the *Yarra* the captain picked up his speaking tube to the guns. "Target, bearing red nine-oh." Below me, just over the lip of the low bridge, the four-inch guns swung around toward the land. The captain barked, "Shoot!" I put my hands over my ears, already well plugged with cotton wool. Nothing happened.

Willy's mouth opened and shut. I took the cotton wool plugs out of my ears and leaned over to hear what he was saying. Loud buzzers buzzed twice all over the ship, and the guns went off in my ear with an appallingly loud crack.

"When they say 'Shoot' they fire electrically when the roll is steady. That's what the buzzer means," Willy bellowed into my aching ear. The guns fired again.

I gathered my wits and turned to watch the results of the shelling. The high-velocity shells, designed to pierce armor-plated warships at ranges of five miles, screamed straight toward the Big House, so close. Usually they hit a palm tree and ricocheted off into the dawn sky, fizzing with incandescence, headed for Arabia Deserta. By the time the gunfire had to be called off, when our assaulting boats touched the bank, several palm trees had been severely wounded.

On the bank our men, led by Beetle Lowis, broke into a run. Rifle and automatic fire increased, and a volley of grenades exploded in or near the house. Then the enemy fled northward up the road, but they had killed six of ours and six Madras sappers, all in the diversionary force.

Willy and I went ashore and hurried up to the roof of the Big House. I noted that H.M.A.S. *Yarra* had bored one small hole through a corner of the upper wall, in addition to savaging the palm trees. The artillery observers disgustedly threw their telegraph pole into the river and joined us. Looking northward we saw many small round wicker boats being launched onto the inland floods which stretched away over the horizon. The artillery officer was through by radio to the guns. I urged him to hurry up and open fire. Willy had his binoculars to his eyes. He lowered them. "Wait!" he said. "There may be women and children in those boats, too." As the boats were setting out from a concealed village up there, it was quite possible. The gunner and I were stern young men, racked with efficiency, and whether or not the boats contained women and children, they certainly contained enemy soldiers. I said so to the colonel. Willy looked at the boats another long time, but they were already too far for any such details to be made out. He spoke to the gunner, "Don't fire on those boats." He turned away, his shoulders hunched.

Disgustedly I went about my job. I hoped Willy would think back to this next time we engaged these enemy and stood afterward among our dead. Then later I thought, Damn it, it's rather wonderful to know a man who would really rather be killed than do anything in the least dishonorable; and I tried to show him I thought he was right, but he remained unconsoled because his character had prevented him doing what a real ball-of-fire soldier would have done.

We marched back to Basra. Dutt had collected our dead in some underground tunnels which dotted the edge of the airfield, for what purpose I never discovered. There lay *Jemadar* Sakas, my old friend, soaking wet where the machine-gun bullets had thrown his body, on instant death, into the flood water. *Subadar Major* Sahabir and I went through his pockets for papers and valuables, and when we opened his mess tin there was nothing but a soggy piece of bread, and the face gray and wet in death. The colonel appointed an even older friend, 6573 *Havildar* Sarbdhan Bura to take Sakasbahadur's place in command of the Pioneer Platoon. We cleaned the mud out of our weapons, retold the story of the battle, and wondered—what next?

Three hundred miles north, on the right bank of the Euphrates, the Royal Air Force had a big airfield and base at Habbaniyah. The previous year the generals in charge of the Iraqi Army had come to their British allies and asked advice about the annual maneuvers. What did their British allies and friends think the Iraqi Army ought to be practicing in these troubled times? The British replied with modest candor that they had no idea. The Iraqis, one of whom later became a member of the Golden Square, said that, as a matter of fact, they themselves *did* have an idea. Suppose the Germans were to seize the airfield at Habbaniyah. The Iraqi Army, helped by whatever troops their British allies could send, would certainly have to seize it back again. It might therefore be a sound idea if the maneuvers consisted of a mock attack on Habbaniyah. Good idea, the British said, *jolly* good.

The maneuvers were held. The Iraqi Army's generalship was

studied carefully, errors in planning and execution were pointed out to them, and a good deal of information given about the defenses of the base. By the end of the conferences the Iraqi generals were in possession of a plan, guaranteed by the British—indeed, made up by them—which would capture Habbaniyah Air Base.

This plan the Iraqi Army, on the orders of the Golden Square, now put into effect. It did not succeed, because they had not reckoned with the heroism of the Royal Air Force crews, who took off in training aircraft on a field actually under close-range artillery fire; on the tough fighting of a British regular battalion flown in from Karachi; on the leadership of Colonel Ouvry Roberts; nor, above all, on the fanatical courage of the Assyrian Levies. (The R.A.F. employed several thousand locally enlisted Levies, so called, to guard its establishments in Iraq; a high proportion of these were Christian Assyrians. In their most earnest prayers the Assyrians could never ask for anything better than a chance to get at the Arabs who had systematically massacred them for so long.)

Habbaniyah held, but it was having a hard time. The Germans had moved bomber squadrons into Mosul, in the north, and fighters into Baghdad itself, both within comfortable range. We moved up to reinforce Habbaniyah, so that the defense could be turned into attack.

Our A Company went at once. In succeeding days the rest of us followed, in mixed flights of Vickers Valencias and Douglas DC-2s. My turn came. None of the Gurkhas in my aircraft had flown before, so I gave them a short lecture on the safety of modern flying machines, explained the purpose of the paper bags, and urged them on no account to stand up or rush about inside the aircraft once we had taken off, however fearsome they found the experience. We emplaned, armed to the tonsils now, and loaded down with extra rations, maps, and all the paraphernalia of war.

We took off. I had concealed from the riflemen that this was only my second flight. I was by no means accustomed to, or particularly appreciative of, these twentieth-century fear-ecstasies, when the door shuts with a hollow and decisive thud, when the inanimate seat suddenly presses hard into the small of the back, one's center of gravity squats lower to the ground and the whole of one's life is left behind by the rapid acceleration. . . .

We skimmed the palm trees, crossed the network of canals, and the Big House, out over the flood waters where the wicker boats had fled from the fight. I wiped my forehead and looked round at the faithful soldiery with a reassuring grin. They were all asleep.

We turned west to avoid Messerschmitt fighters that might be looking for us on the direct route up the river, and for an hour headed into the desert that stretches from the Shatt-al-Arab to the Jordan. The sun was low in the west and the light slanted flat across the desert, so that the smallest rise or depression threw long, obvious shadows. Marks that stood only an inch or two above the rock and sand, or might even have been below it, showed the clear ground plan of houses and roads and cities, all long vanished. I forgot the Messerschmitts and the war, and for two hours, until the light failed, stared down at the faded, hurrying cinematograph of ancient civilizations. Here a wide road had run straight as a lance across the desert from north to south. (From where to where, though? Roman? Arab? Chaldean? I searched my map, and could learn nothing.) Here had been a walled city, every street clearly defined, and something that looked as if it might have been a reservoir outside the walls. . . . Here two roads crossed in the emptiness and there had been a house or temple at the junction. What was that thin straight line, a single mark only, running into the hazy southeast? Darkness came, and took back the past.

Soon we slanted down to land, in total darkness, nothing visible below. At the last moment, when the throttled-back hush of the engines only accentuated the rush of air over the wing surfaces, lights sprang up to mark the runway. We touched down and taxied to the dispersal point. Yawning, I began to gather my belongings. The door opened and a face appeared. "Out, quick!"

"What's the hurry?" I asked.

"We're being bombed."

I dashed up and down awakening the Gurkhas and we stumbled out into the stifling embrace of the heat. Two bombs fell at the other end of the runway—*crash, crash*—and the drone of engines filled the night above. On the ground all the lights had gone out again.

"All right, Jack?"

"Yes, sir."

Willy was there, and gave me a marked chart showing me where to send the companies as they came in. Guides from A Company waited in slit trenches under the hangar walls. The droning and crashes and crumps continued as German Heinkels from Mosul flew leisurely back and forth above us. About two in the morning they went home. Willy and I, our backs to a hangar at the edge of the airfield ate dates and dry army biscuits, washed them down with whisky and tepid, musty water and, later, tried to sleep, but it was too hot.

The other troops, assisted by our A Company, now attacked east toward Baghdad, fifty miles away. We pushed west, up the Euphrates, to protect the back door. The temperature increased steadily. In the early afternoons, on the shadeless desert, it always reached above 120. We had several more cases of heatstroke.

One of these occurred in a platoon that was at the time on the farther side of the river, and I happened to be in the boat that brought him back to hospital. It was Paramdhoj, a small un-excitable man of thirteen years' service. I hardly recognized him, not so much from any change in his physical appearance as in his manner. He was on the edge of delirium and under extreme nervous strain. He could hardly lie still and all the time his hands and feet and head jigged and kicked sideways, and his eyeballs rolled. He kept plucking, too, at his fly and muttering the Gur-khali word for "urine" or "urinate." I remembered something Dutt had told me, that the inability to urinate, though the victim des-perately desired to, was one of the worst agonies of heatstroke. We lifted Paramdhoj up and got his trousers and loincloth off. The stretcher bearers held him while I splashed water over his genitals and made encouraging noises, as though putting a baby on the pot—an art of which I had no experience. Gurkhas have a very strong taboo against complete nakedness, even among other men, but it is their genius to adapt custom to environment, and no face in the boat showed any feeling except a desire to give Paramdhoj some relief. At last he succeeded, almost weeping for joy, and at once the near-delirium seemed to leave him, though he was exhausted.

Another relieving force arrived, having traveled across the desert from Palestine. It contained some Household Cavalry, who normally stand guard duty in Whitehall, splendid in long black boots, steel breastplates, and nodding plumes, but the majority were Yeomanry (National Guard Cavalry). The major general in command was of course a regular, a cavalryman, and his first name was George. Normally this would have been a piece of information of little practical use to his subordinate officers or men, but Yeomanry were something special. At the general's final inspection before the division left England for war, he had asked one of the Yeomanry colonels whether everything was in order. The colonel replied, "Oh, I think so, George." The general gently pressed for details—ammunition? Vehicles? Noncoms' training? Gas masks? The colonel scratched his head and said, "Dash it, I don't know about any of that, George . . . but we've got forty dozen of champagne, well crated, and the pack of foxhounds is in fine fettle."

George now took over command of all land forces from Colonel Roberts. John Strickland, of our A Company, had the privilege of sitting in at one of his first conferences, and surreptitiously noted down a conversation that ran as follows:

The General:	"Well, I think we should send a patrol up the Euphrates for fifty miles or so, to make sure no one's lying up in the desert out there."
One of his Yeomanry colonels:	"Good idea, George."
The General:	"From your regiment, I thought, Harry. About a troop, with a couple of guns, eh?"
The Colonel:	"Oh, yes, George . . . I think I'll send Charles."
	(horror in his face) "Charles? *Charles?* Do you think he'll go?"

We learned later that though Second Lieutenant Charles was distinctly vexed at being sent on such a piddling mission, he did finally agree to go, since George and Harry seemed to set so much store on it.

They were delightful people. My own favorite story about them concerns an early inspection, by the general, of one of the regiments. The Yeomanry colonel, going down the line introducing his officers, stopped before one captain, and said, "This is Captain . . . Captain . . ." He shook his head, snapped his fingers and cried genially, "Memory like a sieve! I'll be forgetting the names of me hounds next."

In the meantime the King's Own, the Levies, and our A Company had captured the Euphrates crossing at Falluja in a smart, fierce fight. The road to Baghdad lay open. George, Harry, Charles, Rodney, Cecil, and the rest climbed into their vehicles and thundered east, leaving us to garrison Habbaniyah. Willy strode up and down glaring at the sand. He whipped round on me. "They have no right to leave us here. We got here first. Rank favoritism."

He did not cheer up until we got orders to fly to Mosul, three hundred miles farther north. The Golden Square had fled, and the Iraqi Army, overawed by the pack of foxhounds and the height of the Life Guardsmen, signed an instrument of surrender in Baghdad; but there was no knowing whether the garrison commanders in the rest of the country would adhere to it. Mosul we had to have at once, to prevent the German bombers using it; but the very presence of the bombers would stiffen any resolve the local commander might have to fight on. So we were to fly to Mosul. When we got there we were either (1) to take it over or (2) to capture it, according to circumstances.

We landed in unarmed transport planes under the muzzles of twenty antiaircraft guns and a score of field guns, all at point-blank range, no one (including the men behind the guns) being sure whether the triggers would be pulled or not. My bladder had become a small tight knot during the flight and the only way I could keep it from exploding as we landed was to rush down the aisle, waking up Gurkhas and yelling at them, "We're *there!* We're coming in! Prepare for action!" Two Hurricanes circled overhead, the Gurkhas tumbled sleepily out of the planes. *Subadar Major* Sahabir looked round and grunted, "Bad climate." No one fired a shot.

After a time we returned to Habbaniyah. The battalion went by truck but I was not with them, for a case of athlete's foot went bad on me, and Willy had ordered me into hospital. For a time the doctors looked as if they were going to cut my foot off. Finally they painted it purple instead and released me. I flew down in a Valencia against a strong headwind, on a burning hot day. The air over the desert heaved with a thick, visible turbulence and as the aircraft, which could only just qualify as a heavier-than-air machine, bumped and floated south with its two mighty engines (about 200 hp) at full throttle, I watched an old gentleman on a camel five hundred feet below us. He also was heading south, and I watched him for a long, long time. At one moment I saw that he was passing us, and made ready to complain to the R.A.F., but we were turning, and it was an optical illusion—but only just.

Outside Habbaniyah the battalion gathered, now all together again for the first time since we had left Basra. We had completed Sally One.

4 We lived in tents beside a lake over the ridge from Habbaniyah. Naturally we had no amenities, except millions of huge, soft-bodied, squashy flying insects that got into our tea, our food, our beds, and made a jelly under our feet; but the R.A.F. inside the air base had a fine club, with walls and a roof and chairs and all, and they had real female nurses, and a swimming pool. We junior officers organized a sortie.

The sandbags had been removed from the club windows and the blackout lessened; it was now merely stifling. On arrival we deployed at the far end of the bar and, after a few drinks, began to sing the German national anthem. The R.A.F. officers, and officers of other regiments, began to look at us in a marked manner. We sang louder, and between verses we agreed that we didn't deserve to win the war; we were decadent and effete; we didn't want to fight our German friends; we liked them; besides, we were frightened. Roger Werner, who always carried things farther than was necessary, said he wouldn't fight *anyone*. The R.A.F. edged along the bar toward us, many a fist doubled, many a top tunic button undone in the Battle-of-Britain tradition. The rest of the Army seemed to be against us too, and those faces that I could see were an unhealthy shade of violet. (We learned later that most of the other Army officers in the bar came from a British regiment which had recently broken and run away under heavy Italian bombing in Abyssinia. This was an unhappy coincidence.)

Just before the rush began the nearest warriors heard the words we were singing to the grand old tune:

Ours is not a happy household, no one laughs or ever smiles,
Mine's a dismal occupation, crushing ice for father's piles.
Jane the under housemaid vomits every morning just at eight,
To the horror of the butler, who's the author of her fate.

We began the second verse:

Sister Sue has just aborted for the forty-second time.
Uncle James has been deported for a most unusual crime. . . .

The honest faces lit up with pleasure, drinks appeared before us, and we were kept busy teaching them the words. Soon, when they were all singing, we sneaked out, found and collected all the four nurses then available in Habbaniyah, and took them to the swimming pool. There we ate sandwiches, drank whisky straight from the bottle, sang, and later lay down in a row in the road in underpants (men) and bathing suits (women)—lady, gent, lady, gent— our Vernon Betts on one end without a nurse, because he was married. Then we kissed the girls good night and good-by, and drove back to our camp and the flying insects. War was rather a lark.

Training continued. On night driving practice two fifteen-hundredweight trucks, crawling one behind the other, drove over a thirty-foot cliff at the edge of camp, the second landing perfectly on top of the first in an early example of vertical parking. The trucks were undamaged, as of course were the Gurkhas in them.

We met our new divisional commander, Major General Bill Slim, late of the 6th Gurkhas. He had just been promoted to us from a brigade on the Abyssinian front, where, we heard, his preferred command position was within whispering range of his leading riflemen, and where he had received a burst of machine-gun bullets fired into his rear elevation by an Italian aircraft. So far we had hardly been conscious of any formation larger than the 21st Brigade, of which our battalion was a part. To impress on us that the 21st Brigade in its turn was part of something larger, the 10th Indian Infantry Division, Slim gathered together all his of-

ficers then available in Habbaniyah and, in an R.A.F. hangar,
lectured us on his doctrine of war.

This is a sensible and necessary thing to do, since a good division functions as an extension of the mind and will of its commander; but it is also a very tricky thing to succeed with. All the
regulars in his audience had received many such lectures in their
time, and, in the majority of cases, had gone away with the impression that their general was a pompous old blatherskite.

The quiet that fell in the hangar when Bill Slim entered was
not, therefore, entirely of awed expectation. It was, in part, a
judicial hush. We waited.

Slim was squarely built, with a heavy, slightly undershot jaw
and short, graying hair. He began to speak, slowly and simply,
with no affectation. He told us first that we had done a good job
in the Iraqi campaign. But no one could call that a very serious
business. He had already seen enough of our fighting spirit and
our technical competence to know that we needed little teaching
there. What he wanted to do was to prepare us, practically and
above all mentally, for the heavier fighting that we must soon
meet.

By now he had our whole attention. He talked a bit about matters that still needed attention—road discipline, defense against
air attack, battle drills to speed up the execution of orders. . . .
Then he began to talk about the nature of modern war, of what it
was really like when you engaged an enemy as determined, as
numerous, and perhaps better armed than yourselves. Then, he
said, tactics and strategy, important though they have been and
still are, become less central. Situations develop which no tactical
or strategical move can alter. . . .

"We make the best plans we can, gentlemen, and train our
wills to hold steadfastly to them in the face of adversity, and yet
to be flexible to change them when events show them to be unsound, or to take advantage of an opportunity that unfolds during
the battle itself. We have already trained our men to the highest
possible level of skill with their weapons and in their use of
minor tactics. But in the end every important battle develops
to a point where there is no real control by senior commanders.
Each soldier feels himself to be alone. Discipline may have got
him to the place where he is, and discipline may hold him there

—for a time. Co-operation with other men in the same situation can help him to move forward. Self-preservation will make him defend himself to the death, if there is no other way. But what makes him go on, alone, determined to break the will of the enemy opposite him, is morale. Pride in himself as an independent thinking man, who knows why he's there, and what he's doing. Absolute confidence that the best has been done for him, and that his fate is now in his own hands. The dominant feeling of the battlefield is loneliness, gentlemen, and morale, only morale, individual morale as a foundation under training and discipline, will bring victory."

I went back to our camp in a thoughtful mood. Slim's sort of battle wouldn't be much of a lark, after all.

Far to the west General Wavell, Commander in Chief in the Middle East, asked Dentz, the Vichy-French governor of Syria, for an assurance that he would not permit any German infiltration into that country. Dentz refused. We could not afford to leave it at that, since Syria's borders touched the Mediterranean, also Palestine, Iraq, and Turkey. A German dominance there might easily have rocked Turkey off its neutrality, on the wrong side. Wavell ordered Syria to be taken over, by attacks from Palestine and Iraq.

A few days later, at the end of June, 1941, our 21st Brigade moved up the Euphrates toward the Syrian border. We moved in column, all in trucks, along a blinding road, no more than a whiter glare in the desert. The earth shimmered and heaved, at first only in the distance, then closer and closer until sometimes the trucks in front of me took on the distorted shapes of animals, or vanished altogether. I felt heatstroke closing in on me. The dust billowed up now and I began to choke. My thirst increased until I could not identify the seat of it, for it was general all over my body. Swaying in the front of the truck, waves of heat crawling inside me, I held desperately to the discipline that would not allow us to touch our water bottles until a fresh supply was at hand. Naru my orderly, the driver, and the two signalers in the truck with me were suffering too, but apparently not so severely. Naru tried to make me drink from his bottle. The wind blew steadily into our faces, at forty miles an hour and a hundred and forty degrees. The sweeping desert blurred and I thought, What a way to die. I wondered if I looked like little Manibahadur, who died stumbling amongst the palm trees. Now I saw palms, and the swaying, jumping hovels of an Arab village. An oasis . . . but it would not save me. We had to keep going. The truck slowed and I muttered to the driver, "Keep distance."

But Willy was there, and he had stopped the whole convoy. The Arabs were selling watermelons. We bought all they had, and slowly, luxuriously, during that hour-long halt, I felt myself clawing back, with the juice of the melon in my mouth and the tips cold against my ears, from the edge of a dark, hot pit that had been outside and inside my brain.

We drove on and in the afternoon bivouacked among orchards and scrub at Haditha, around an oil company's pumping station.

On June 28 we advanced again, and at noon crossed the frontier into Syria. The wind blew as hard and hot as ever, and we bivouacked at Abu Kemal on the bank of the Euphrates. In the late afternoon the French reacted, and we saw the Martin bombers for the first time. A heavy bombing attack came in as we were digging our slit trenches. When it was over we had suffered our first casualties from the air, and *Jemadar* Sarbdhan Bura, who had just replaced Sakas in command of the Pioneer Platoon, who had been my "grandfather" when I was training the recruits in 1938, who was quiet and shy and brave, with a small mandarin mustache drooping over the corners of his mouth—Sarbdhan lay in the main dressing station, wounded. Dutt told us that it was serious, and *Subadar Major* Sahabir and I went in to see him. He lay on the operating table, silent, and there was no mark on him except a tiny hole in his side, high up under his armpit, and a tear in one corner of his brown eye. He put out his hand and I held it tight. Sahabir asked him if it hurt, and he said, "Yes, sahib." We told him he'd feel better tomorrow; then they put him out and operated, and he died during the night.

The next morning, having slept fairly well once the parade of my hours with Sarbdhan had passed before my memory, I heard Naru speaking in my ear. "Five o'clock, sahib." I opened my eyes, but it was pitch dark. As first light was about 4:00 A.M., I knew he must be wrong. I told him so, and he repeated, "Five o'clock, sahib." He began to shake me, and I couldn't even see the shape of him, or his hand. "It's pitch-dark," I said irritably. "I'm not going to get up."

"It's day," he said.

I sat up with a jerk and put my own hand close before my eyes. Nothing. My God, I had gone blind in the night! A moment of panic held me stiff and still, then I cautiously felt my eyelids. They were tight shut. Probing along I found why. My eyelashes and lids had become fastened firmly together by a rough cement, formed as the tear ducts squeezed out tears all night in a vain attempt to cleanse the dust and inflammation of the two previous days' drive into the furnace wind. At last, by breaking off pieces of the cement, usually with the eyelashes enclosed, I got them open. Ten minutes' work with soap and water, and Willy again had an adjutant.

We drove on, widely spread over the desert as a protection against bombing attacks. We found our way by the road, when we saw it, by the oil pipe line to Tripoli, when we were near it, and by guesswork. The maps were masterpieces, and must have been made on the assumption that only an enemy could possibly need to use them, for they were rather like inanimate poker players, giving as little information as possible, and that misleading. One, that covered four thousand square miles, showed the Euphrates in one corner, in another corner a village with a query beside it, and —over all the rest—the word *Unsurveyed*.

The Martins bombed us as often as they could fly back to Aleppo, refuel, and get at us again. We drove on, past and between towering columns of black smoke, where trucks burned on the seething desert. The only planes we had which were capable of attacking the Martin were four Hurricanes back at Habbaniyah, but they did not come. Aerial bombardment is an unnerving business in the open desert, and when no reply is seen to be made it is bad for morale, particularly when you have recently left the pilots sitting in comfortable quarters with iced drinks and pretty girls and you are driving into a sandstorm, half-crazy with thirst, suffering from a crick in the neck.

For the fourth time a formation of Martins came in from the northwest, at about eight thousand feet—nine of them in their usual three tight Vs. Two black dots appeared in the southeast. Crouched on the burning sand I pointed up and shouted to those

Gurkhas within earshot, "Hurricanes! Now watch!" The Hurricane was at the height of its fame, after the Battle of Britain.
Remembering my fright as I lay on the sand, or drove on in the
truck while the bombs screamed down, unable to do anything except direct the fire of the Bren guns, I badly wanted to see some of
those impervious silver Martins join us in our dusty element, and
rapidly.

We watched eagerly as the dots closed, and swooped down to
attack from astern. The faint roar of multiple machine guns
echoed down to us from the high sky, like the simultaneous tearing of many strips of calico. A black tree root grew from the
leading Hurricane's wing, turned red, expanded. The Hurricane
turned lazily on its side and plunged toward the earth. A moment
later the second Hurricane followed it.

The Gurkhas avoided my eye, and I theirs. The pilots had
died, and we'd bloody well have to put up with the consequences,
as they had. We continued the advance. Dust storms increased,
cohesion was lost, and for a couple of hours our *Blitzkrieg* advance
was led by Dutt and the cook trucks. In this unorthodox formation we reached bivouac in front of Deir-es-Zor. The armored
cars of the 13th Lancers, thrusting crossly past our cooks, reported
that the place was held in strength. We prepared to attack.

The Martins came with increasing insolence and exactitude.
One Indian noncombatant cook of Brigade Headquarters couldn't
take it and ran away. We found his headless, mutilated body
tangled in the reeds by the river the next morning. The Arabs
had done us the service of underlining that discipline must hold
fast against natural fear. Two Madrassi signalers also decided that
they had had enough, but since they were determined in their
fear, and had a vehicle, they succeeded in reaching Basra, 550
miles to the rear. There was considerable confusion everywhere
in those days and I believe they got gasoline by saying they were
carrying urgent dispatches.

By now we had established the routines of this life. We slept
in or on the edge of holes dug in the soil, and usually avoided
the few buildings we came across, first because they made bombing targets, second because they were always full of fleas. There
was an officers' mess tent. Sometimes we used it, sometimes not,
depending on the weather and the threat from the air. Usually

all officers ate in mess, but in two shifts, so that a single bomb would not wipe us all out. Whether we put up the tent or not, two long trenches were always dug first. We sat in them, using the earth in the middle as a table; and at night the mess staff slept in them. When we were in physical contact with the enemy, officers ate with their companies, but this upset the rationing arrangements—we could only draw a dozen British rations, and it was not always feasible to send to each company the proportion of this which its one or two officers would be entitled to—as in the case of a leg of lamb, for instance.

Our transport moved in two echelons. A Echelon, consisting of things that we needed for fighting—water, reserve ammunition, picks and shovels, some barbed wire, the medical aid post—actually traveled with the battalion, and was under the command of the *subadar major*. B Echelon—roughly speaking, cooks and clerks—followed behind, those of all three battalions usually moving together, escorted and under brigade orders. As soon as B Echelon came up the head clerk opened the back flaps of the three-ton truck which contained the battalion main office, the signalers hooked up the field telephone wires, and we were in business. There might be a battle tomorrow, but today someone had to read Army Instructions and Force Orders, note that Division wanted the names of all officers with legal experience, note that Mark VII ammunition over three years old was to be exchanged, telephone the brigade major and tell him we needed more maps. Someone had to indent for rations, someone else had to say where they were to be delivered—at some time the following afternoon, when no one could know where we would be.

Rations, ammunition, supply . . . it was a complex business and I realized I didn't know enough about it. The vast desert enclosed us, rimmed to the south there by the escarpment that marked the farthest limit of the river valley. The Euphrates ran beside us, but men drinking from it, or even putting a foot into it, were liable to get bilharzia, cholera, dysentery, and numerous varieties of worms. (One ingenious type entered through the sole of the foot and later emerged elsewhere, causing an ulcer but only sticking its head out to drink when the part was placed in water. To get rid of the worm it had to be enticed out by being put near water, then its head quickly wrapped round a

match. Slowly and slowly, a little at a time, you twined the worm
out on the match, but it took days, for if the worm was broken,
that part left in the body would still live.)

So all water had to be chlorinated. Where did the chlorine
come from? And some of the food we ate came from Basra, some
from Baghdad, some from India, some from England; how did
exactly 843 rations arrive at a map reference in this empty desert
just when we needed it? Ammunition . . . How could anyone
know whether our artillery was going to fire ten shells today, or
a thousand? It made quite a difference—some fifteen tons, or
five fully loaded trucks; yet whatever was shot off had to be replaced in the caissons at once. At this very moment the attack
on Deir-es-Zor, as we all knew, hinged on gasoline. General Slim
wanted to send the 13th Lancers right round the back of the town
in a large sweep, while the infantry attacked from in front; but
there was hardly enough gasoline even to let the armored cars
reach Deir-es-Zor straight up the main road. We heard that Slim
had ordered the emptying of every other vehicle in the division to
give the Lancers the range he wanted for the battle; and it was
true, because we had to empty our own tanks, protesting bitterly.
If the attack failed we would all be stranded. My God, what
a decision to have to make! Obviously, I must learn a great deal
about such things before I could really wield these forces, with
whose tactical employment I was quite familiar.

Sometimes there was a rum ration. Sometimes a beer convoy
caught up with us, but that was rare. Every Sunday I wrote to
my parents, a friend or two, and some girls. I began to feel restless. The war was an enormous, overshadowing, moving monster,
far bigger than I had imagined it would be. I was twenty-six and a
half, and beginning, suddenly, to feel my age.

We captured Deir-es-Zor, with few casualties, in the attack
already described. Here I first actually saw the enemy, for when
we arrived, the Lancers had already collected quite a number of
prisoners in an open place outside the town. There were not many
French among them—those had mostly pulled out and made a
getaway, including some Marines and Foreign Legionnaires. Staying behind were Syrians and half-and-halfs, like a cheerful warrant
officer who, when I asked him whether he was French, replied
"Un peu, mon capitaine." They were smallish men, not at all

romantic-looking in their ill-fitting uniforms, and were obviously glad it was over. The warrant officer volunteered to accompany us as interpreter and guide, and we put him in the care of Sahabir, who soon made him understand that the wrath of a *subadar major* was a good deal more painful than death by burning, so we did not worry about any possibility of treachery on his part.

As soon as we were dug into bivouac Willy settled his hat firmly on his head and marched off to brigade headquarters. Now it was the 2/4th's turn to lead the advance again, he said. Brigadier Weld had to be quite peremptory before he convinced Willy that there was not going to be any advance the following day.

The day after that, though, the sun shone, and Willy took off his hat—a rare event, as he was sensitive about his increasing baldness. With the 13th Lancers and a battery of field guns under Willy's command, we were to cross the Euphrates, advance across the desert on the left bank (this desert is called the Djezireh), and capture the French-held fort and town at Raqqa, eighty miles west.

In the predawn dark of the following day the armored cars rumbled over the narrow bridge, where I waited at a control post with a telephone set. The colonel and the battalion came, and I joined them. Once across the bridge we turned left, and as the light grew, headed west into the rolling brown grass sea of the Djezireh. Every hour we halted, to rest and check vehicles. Every hour the Lancers of the advanced guard reported back where they were, and Willy sent them the simple message that cavalry like best to receive—*HOA*, or Hack On, Algy. The sun climbed and the antiaircraft sentries, bouncing about in the back of each truck, took a firmer grip of the arched supports that usually held the covers, but the canvas had all been removed so that each man could use his weapons against the expected air attacks. They did not come.

Willy had appointed me map reader and guide of the main body. I carried out this duty by judging which of the many tracks across the grass looked most used, for I thought that anyone moving through the Djezireh here had nowhere but Raqqa to go to, once we had passed another road which led due north to Ain Arous. There the map showed a stream as entering the Euphrates; and sure enough we came to it, and crossed it, though

we saw no road, and from then on I rapped out orders with
nonchalant confidence, not bothering to look at the map. Willy
said I was a genius with a map, and I said, "Thank you, sir."

Early in the afternoon the 13th Lancers, miles ahead of us,
sent back word that Raqqa was clear of the enemy, but only just.
They had very recently left. By then we were advancing in a
magnificent rhythm, one troop of field guns with trails down
ready to fire, the other roaring at full speed through the middle of
the column to take up the next position, and the battalion motoring steadily on in long spread lines. At last we drove into a
narrow street which seemed to have been visited by raving luna-
tics. We knew better, for we had already seen something of this
at the Haditha pumping station. This was the work of the noble
Arabs, but this time against their own people, for Raqqa was a
purely Arab community. In the street broken glass lay inches deep
among paper, books, ink, food, smashed wood, torn cotton goods
and charred clothing; all destroyed, as far as we could see, for the
sheer lust of destruction. This particular specimen was the work
of an armed band led by a man called Fawzi Kawakji, whom we
were to meet again.

We deployed into defensive positions and spent most of the
night digging in. Before we went to sleep Naru and I were the
joint owners of a very fine, deep, and narrow trench just outside
the barrack building where Willy had established his headquarters,
over my protests that it would draw bombs.

The next morning, just after stand-down, idly glancing up
from some paper work, I saw a Hurricane approaching low across
the desert—another, another. . . . There weren't that many Hurricanes east of Suez! I leaped for the trench, blowing my whistle.

They were French Morane fighters, tearing in at three hundred
miles an hour, twenty feet above the desert, six of them in line
ahead. All round the whistles went, men dived for cover. The
lead plane opened fire when almost directly over me and I heard
a multigun fighter, close to, for the first time. It is not a long-
drawn sound, like a machine gun's, which can at a pinch be represented by *ratatatatatatatat*. The guns have a rate of fire of 1,300
rounds a minute each, as against 650 for the ground gun, and
there are six or eight of them. The sound of this weapon firing

at you is a single, enormously loud CRRRRRRRUMP, and in
those two seconds three hundred bullets have crashed by. The
sound hangs in the air behind the plane, and if you are watching
it closely as it fires you can see it check momentarily in mid-air,
while gray smoke flickers along the leading edge of the wing.
Then, as it pulls up its nose to climb away the hail of empty
cases and brass links falls out of the wings, but are only seen if
the light is at the right angle. CRRRRRRUMP.

By now two Bren guns were at them—four, five, six—twenty.
The racket grew to formidable dimensions. The Moranes went for
the armored cars dispersed along the river and in the orchards
the other side of town. The armored cars fired back with their
turret machine guns. Everyone fired. As each Morane finished
his first attack it turned its nose straight to the sky and climbed
away under full power. At about fifteen hundred feet they fanned
out right, left, right, left, alternately, and swooped down in six
different, lovely parabolas to attack again. It was beautiful, and
also a good target, so it deserved the attention it got. Converging
streams of tracer from all over Raqqa formed a tent over my
head, the apex around the plane that was nearing the top of
its power climb. CRRRRRRRUMP! The ground a hundred yards
from me boiled momentarily and was still. CRRRRRRRUMP!
"Shirley" Temple was bathing in the river, his revolver strapped
round his naked body. He danced about in the shallows, firing at
them, but they ignored him.

They vanished. We listened cautiously, the sentries scanning
the air, everyone else busy refilling magazines. Time for breakfast.

They came again at midday, and at dusk. The next morning
they returned at dawn, only four of them now. At midday we
again heard the sound of aircraft engines. In a flash everyone was
at his post, and ready. Two twin-engined planes appeared from
the west and came in with single front guns firing. This was
nothing, and the return fire of twenty Bren guns lashed up at
them. They roared low overhead, bullets ripping into their bellies,
and dropped about twenty small bombs in our B Company area,
damaging no one. They swung round and came in again. More
bombs, more machine-gun fire from the nose. As one of them
wheeled, a few hundred yards out over the desert, I distinctly

saw the R.A.F. roundels on its side. It leaped to my mind, and to
Willy's at the same time, that from their shape they could only
be Blenheims, a British light bomber.

"Cease fire!" the colonel yelled.

The nearest man to me was a machine gunner who had got a
Vickers gun loosened on its tripod so that it would make an
effective antiaircraft weapon. The Blenheim came in, our machine
gunner took a good lead and pressed the buttons, while the aircraft's fire ripped somewhere over our heads.

"Cease fire!" I bellowed at the machine gunner. "Ours, ours!"

"Why's he firing at us, then?" the gunner asked politely, swinging round and sending a hundred rounds up the Blenheim's arse.

A little later two battered Blenheims landed at Mosul and reported a successful raid on the French at Tel Abiad, some sixty
miles to the north of Raqqa. By then the radio waves were boiling with furious signals from Willy. Next day we heard that the
officer responsible for the error had been removed from command
of his flight. Willy looked sick with worry. He didn't want the
chap to suffer for an honest mistake. Dashed brave attack they'd
put in, really.

I made two mental notes to add to the many I was accumulat-
ing through the campaign: (1) A loaded warplane is like a pregnant woman. When its time comes, it is under a compulsion to
drop its burden, however unsuitable the circumstances. (2) Airmen, though splendid at finding their way to Gosnau-Feldkirchen
in night, fog, and rain, cannot tell Raqqa from New York in
broad daylight. Some soldiers were inclined to believe that no
airman's brain functions at all under three thousand feet, but I
thought this was an oversimplification.

The Vichy forces in the Djezireh were now hemmed in between the Turkish border and the curve of the Euphrates. Intelligence reports that they were pulling out westward were confirmed
by a squadron of spahis, which rode in out of the desert and
surrendered to us. Willy paced up and down in a fever. We ought
to get north, get across the line of their retreat, cut them off.
. . . Tel Abiad, a fort on the frontier sixty miles due north of us,
that's where we should go. But we had positive orders from
brigade not to move beyond Raqqa. Radio communication had
broken down. Willy sent a message back to Deir-es-Zor by truck,

explaining his thoughts and urgently asking permission to leave a small garrison in Raqqa and, with the rest, move on to Tel Abiad. In case the reply was favorable, we made everything ready for an instant start.

It was. Again Willy appointed me the pathfinder, and this time it was really difficult. The bright moonlight threw a gauzy curtain over the desert, everything looked the same, and the map was even more secretive than usual. *Jemadar* Amarsing, the *jemadar adjutant*, stood on the running board beside me with a shaded flashlight, and the driver held a steady speed. I counted minutes, took bearings, jumped out to look at hazy, obscured tracks crossing and recrossing each other, jumped back in again, the figures dancing a fandango in my head and all around the low growl of the engines in the dark. Sixty miles to go.

We came upon a wider track, which seemed to be going in the right direction. I ordered the driver to follow it, holding his speed at 12 mph, and Amarsing to watch the compass heading.

The battalion rolled remorselessly on to its objective through the moonlight. Everyone except drivers, sentries, and officers was asleep, jammed against each other in the trucks as they rocked and jolted forward. I felt very good. This was the war morale of the old regular army to which I belonged. We had called the Germans every sort of name before September 3, 1939. They were murderers, liars, Nazis, blond beasts, Huns, Boches. After that date these words were never used, and that was a relief. It is too much mental strain to hate anyone for a long time and besides, it warps the judgment. The Germans became the *dushman*, the enemy. Once you had said *dushman* you had said all that was necessary. *Dushman* were to be killed in the most efficient manner possible. Of the French we had spoken very differently even a month ago. Now they too, sadly, had become *dushman*.

We rolled on. After four and a half hours someone fired at us from close ahead. The advance stopped and one company went forward on foot. The firing continued, but it was very light, and nonautomatic. But where the hell was it coming from? We ought to be near a little village at the head of the slope down to Tel Abiad; but we might have run into Tel Abiad itself. If so, I was out in my calculations, and had led the force too close to the enemy for comfortable deployment.

Working forward, Willy and I reached a house, and saw more rooftops silhouetted against the night sky beyond. That was an Arab village, not a town, still less a *Beau Geste* fort such as we knew there was at Tel Abiad. Good. Willy was saying something to me and I turned. "What was that, sir?" A few bullets whacked by, not close.

"No. I'll go," he said, and walked out across the open space between us and C Company, who were deploying to attack. I swore silently. Damn Willy! He must have asked me to deliver some message to the men across there, where the occasional bullet smacked past, sounding very loud in the night; and then he'd realized that he was asking me to do something dangerous. "No officer orders a man to do anything which he is not willing to do himself." Damned old fool. I walked out into the open space and waited there until he returned a minute later. A couple of bullets passed but I was pretty sure no one could see me, still less deliberately aim at me.

"Get under cover!" Willy snapped.

I told him that in future I would be pleased if he'd allow me to do my job. A brisk argument began between us, behind the wall in the darkness, until an armored car came and told us that the firing was from nervous Arab villagers, who had now seen that we were not raiders, and had come out in peace; and it was the right village. Through our warrant-officer interpreter, we learned that the fleeing French forces had passed westward through Tel Abiad the previous day. We had missed them. The advance continued.

In Tel Abiad we settled down in and around the fort, which did indeed look like a movie set for *Beau Geste*, a little walled fort dominating a huddled town and packed orchards—the desert all around. The wine in the cellar was good, but the inscriptions chalked over the walls were sour. *Wait, dirty English bastards, until the Germans come. We run away now, so will you, soon.* I love France, and it made sad reading, in a way sadder than the actual fighting, and that was tragic enough.

The Moranes found us as I was inspecting the trenches and barbed-wire barricades round the little hill on which the fort stood. I jumped for cover as they came in—CRRRRRRUMP! There was a horrible smell about in that deep trench, horrible

and unmistakable. Not to put too fine a point on it—shit. I examined myself cautiously. No, I was not that frightened. Beside
me Naru took calm aim with his rifle and I joined him with my
revolver. The Moranes went home and the sharp, clean smell of
cordite blew away, leaving us to the other. We were standing in
six inches of human ordure. The trenches, sited and dug for the
outer defense of the fort, had in fact been used as latrines. The
subtle French had had their revenge.

That evening Willy and I were studying the map, preparing
orders for a small force to be sent west to the Euphrates, when it
really penetrated my mind that the railway line running across
the flat desert there, a few hundred yards north, was the frontier
between Syria and neutral Turkey. The large building on the hill
a mile beyond, therefore, must be in Turkey; and it looked like
a barracks. I suggested that during the night we take some of our
trucks out of the orchards where we had tried to hide them, and
place them, well scattered, along the edge of the railway line.
Willy looked sharply at me, then grinned, and gave me the
order to go ahead.

We moved half a dozen of the most battered three-tonners and
arranged them in the open. Willy moved our headquarters the
other way, into the orchard, for the fort made a perfect bomb
trap.

Morane fighters came the next morning. Since they attacked
from the southwest, firing into the orchards and at the fort walls
as they came, and then rocketing skyward, they did not see the
vehicles in the open. They saw us in the orchard, though, and
once again I found myself peering out of a hole in the ground,
half-blinded with dust, listening to the CRRRRRRRUMP,
CRRUMP of their machine guns.

I looked right, and there, standing in an open field, I saw two
riflemen of B Company. They had been moving their Bren gun,
on its antiaircraft mount, from one site to another when the
attack came in. The Moranes were not firing at us now, but at
them. Unhurriedly the two Gurkhas set up the tripod. One took
the gun, the other stood ready with the reserve magazines. The
fighters screamed down on them—CRRRRRRUMP. The Bren
began to fire back. I began to cry with pride. The earth boiled
round and behind the two men, both nineteen years old, and

they stood there, completely in the open, upright, and always sending that thin stream of fire back at the multigun monsters. This was what we were fighting with, and by God, this was what we were fighting for, too—survival, and self-respect, a refusal to be terrified by sheer force. The attacks continued for five minutes, and the last plane climbed away very slowly, black smoke pouring from its engine nacelle. Riflemen Deba and Ghanbahadur picked up gun and tripod and marched on to their new position.

Two hours later the Martins came. They saw the vehicles carelessly left in the open. They swung round at about six thousand feet, just out of range of our small arms, as they well knew, and began their bomb run. They were certainly very near the frontier; they had to be. They had hardly settled into the bomb run before black balls of heavy antiaircraft fire burst under the lead plane's nose. It jumped violently in the air and for a moment I thought it was gone. Then it dived sharply down and to the left and the formation broke up, pursued by vicious and accurate fire from the heavy A.A. guns which we did not have, but the Turks did. Again, one of the planes was sinking and on fire when they disappeared in the west. Willy gave me a wink and ordered me, the next day, to acquaint the Turkish commander opposite that British forces had temporarily occupied this part of Syria.

The next morning, about eleven o'clock, I polished my boots, cleaned myself up, remembering that I was a sort of ambassador from His Majesty as well as from the regiment, called the *jemadar adjutant* and Naru, inspected them, and went down to the railway station. The stationmaster did not understand my French, and sent for the schoolmaster, who arrived in ten minutes. The schoolmaster sent a message up to the Turkish barracks. Soon an elderly Turkish lieutenant arrived, and introduced himself. His name sounded like Ekmek Kedaifi. We saluted each other a great deal. I gave him Willy's message and he bowed. I assured him of British friendship, and that we would on no account transgress Turkish neutrality as the French aircraft had done yesterday. His heavy eyelids drooped. He sent for beer, and we drank several bottles, almost red-hot. He told me a dirty story in Turkish. The schoolmaster, giggling hysterically, translated it into French, and I put it into Gurkhali for Amarsing. Naru had decided an ambassador needed a footman and stood behind my chair at attention through-

out, leaping forward to light my cigarettes, sucking his teeth with
unnecessary deference, and generally giving the impression that I
was a field marshal in disguise, or perhaps the Duke of Kent. It
was time to drink the health of the Turkish president, of Mustafa
Kemal, King George VI, Colonel Weallens, Lieutenant Ekmek
Kedaifi, Captain Masters, *Jemadar* Amarsing, and the schoolmaster. The Martins came back and the A.A. guns from the fort
opened fire on them, *boom boom*, the aircraft this time being, by
my calculations, two miles inside Syria. The lieutenant clapped his
hands and the old English custom of drinking Benedictine before
lunch, with the temperature at 120 in the shade, was respectfully
observed. I returned to the fort.

At the fort, hell was breaking loose. Brigade headquarters at
Deir-es-Zor had sent us an urgent signal. It was indecipherable—
literally: they were using a cipher which they had not issued to
us. After many repeats they sent the message in clear. Fawzi
Kawakji, with several hundred raiders and some French artillery,
was attacking the small garrison we had left behind in Raqqa.
The situation was critical and we were to return there forthwith.

Immediately afterward a message came in from Raqqa itself.
It was in clear, and reported that the situation was in hand. I
hurried to our set and ordered the operator at Raqqa to call an
officer to his set immediately. No officer came. Communication
went out.

Now what? Was the "good" message from Raqqa genuine? Or
had Fawzi overrun the place and forced a signaler to send it, a
pistol at his back? Would Willy be justified in disregarding
brigade's direct orders to return to Raqqa? At the same time the
small force we had sent west to the Euphrates reported it had
driven the French there across the river at Djérablous, and with
some reinforcement could probably cross the river itself; then it
would find an open road to Aleppo, to the airfields those damned
Martins and Moranes came from, even to the sea. Damascus had
already fallen. A stroke like this might end the campaign. Almost
any risk was worth while to achieve it.

But we had very little gasoline. We could not send reinforcements to both Djérablous and Raqqa. Which?

This was the fog of war, indeed. I suddenly remembered Slim's
heavy, serious face—"The dominant feeling of the battlefield is

loneliness." Now Willy was alone, and no one could help him, for the decision was his.

He decided to go back to Raqqa, but he hated doing it, and remained in a sulfurously bad temper for the next three days. When we reached Raqqa we found that the situation had been critical for a time, but the garrison had beaten off two determined attacks and all was well.

The French asked for an armistice, and the campaign was over. Slim congratulated Willy handsomely. (Later, he wrote in his official dispatch: ". . . There were instances of drive and initiative, notably that of the column sent to intercept the French retreating from the northeast of Syria, which boldly and at great speed covered 200 miles from Deir-es-Zor and drove the enemy across the Euphrates at Djérablous.")

Willy almost smiled, then the corners of his mouth drooped. "We ought to have gone on, Jack."

We hung around for two or three weeks more, and I took leave to go to Aleppo. It was full of Australians, whores, and Military Police, in about equal proportions, and after two days I came home to the battalion.

Early in August we drove back down the desert road to Habbaniyah. Sally Two was over. We cleaned ourselves and our weapons, and waited expectantly.

5 The country to the east of Iraq is Iran. It contained oil (mainly in the hands of the Anglo-Iranian Oil Company) that was vital to the Allied war; but the Nazis were steadily infiltrating it with aid and influence, abetted by Shah Reza Khan Pahlevi, a fine old fascist dictator himself. He had risen through the ranks of a Russian-trained Persian Cossack brigade, finally became Prime Minister, and in 1925 deposed the then shah and assumed the job himself. Now the British and Soviet governments delivered him an ultimatum: get rid of the Nazis—or else.

The invincible German Army was battering at the gates of the Caucasus, only two hundred miles north of Iran. The Shah thumbed his nose at the ultimatum.

Mr. Churchill's first reaction, a very proper one, was to decree that "Iran" sounded too much like "Iraq," and that the British would in future refer to the country by its ancient and usual Western name of "Persia" (from one of the Iranian provinces, Fars). Mr. Churchill pointed out that the Swiss call their country Schweiz or La Confédération Helvétique, and the Germans call theirs Deutschland, but that does not mean the English-speaking world has to follow suit.

Secondly, the name of a town inside Persia, but not far from Iraq, was changed from the confusing Araq to Sultanabad. These necessary preparations having been made, we invaded the country.

We moved east through Baghdad, across the Tigris, and east

again. Now, late in August, the heat was worse than ever as our long convoys drove across the stony plains that slope gradually up out of the valley of the Tigris toward Persia. The rest of the division moved smoothly enough, but the progress of the 2/4th Gurkhas was jerky. Willy had been here in 1917 and 1918 as a young subaltern, with this same battalion of this same regiment, but fighting against the Turks. While I drove, he scanned the ground through field glasses, muttering, "Nye's company was held up there, by that old *karez*. D'you see it, Jack?"

"Yes, sir."

"There! We halted there. Durgan was wounded, and . . . wait a minute, I think that's the line. . . . Stop here."

"The convoy, sir . . ."

But we stopped. Behind us, the whole convoy stopped. Willy jumped out and darted off, followed by his orderly. It was a good place for a lunch halt anyway, and I ate chupatties in the thin shade of a thorn bush. Willy disappeared in the heat haze. I sent a motorcyclist down the column to fetch the only other man who had been with the battalion in that campaign of twenty-four years before—*Bhisti* Hira Sing. Willy returned and talked happily with Hira Sing for the rest of the halt time. I was glad that Willy was happy, but felt quietly amused too—as though those ancient battles meant anything now! (But I think I can show you every hole I slept in, and the exact spot where every bomb fell near me, during these campaigns I am writing about; and would be delighted to do so.)

Ahead, mountains loomed above the haze and everyone's heart became a little lighter. We had seen nothing higher than a hillock since leaving Quetta six months before, and we were mountain men. The Persian escarpment rising there in front of us was in fact the western face of the same high plateau, covering all Persia, Afghanistan, and Baluchistan, on which Quetta stood— one thousand six hundred miles away—guarding the eastern escarpment.

Already smelling the cool air, and sensing flowers, we crossed the frontier at Sar-i-Pul Zuhab. A few miles more and we harbored for the night amid scenes of utter confusion, due to a breakdown in the military policing and the narrowness of the roads, which would hardly take one of the big quads that towed the field guns, let alone the monsters in charge of the six-inch howitzers. I lay in my hole, wrapped happily in my greatcoat, praying only that the Persians also would stay in bed, as no one knew for sure where one of our companies was, and the transport area looked like the General Motors parking lot—a bomber's dream. Late in the night a message from the sentries awakened me. There was a fire. I struggled up and saw that the mountain behind us was ablaze. For a short time the flames formed a bright, yellow heart on the mountainside, and the wind brought me the smell of smoke, and sage, and thyme. Then, as the center burned out, the fire advanced outward in spreading red ripples. It was beautiful, but no one knew whether it had been done by accident or on purpose, or, if so, why.

In the morning we advanced cautiously up the road toward Kermanshah, 150 miles away. Soon we found ourselves at the foot of the Pai-Tak Pass, where the road climbs three thousand feet in zigzags and hairpin bends. Intelligence said the Persian Army was holding the crest in strength. The 4th Gurkhas, as vanguard, moved on astride the road in battle formation. A few heavy shells rumbled over from somewhere behind the pass, but landed far to our left. I saw that here, too, the mountainsides were ominously blackened. Willy guessed that the Persians had been ranging their artillery on all likely routes of advance. It was an unpleasant thought. We would certainly have to send flanking attacks around the pass once we had contacted and pinned the enemy frontally, and every vale and draw and gorge would be ranged in to a yard by those bloody howitzers. They were big, the shells bursting with tremendous authority. Our own howitzers began a slow fire and a short Bren burst from in front made us think we had made contact. But no, it was one of our own men shooting another by mistake, not seriously.

A khaki sedan appeared, coming down to us from the direction of the pass. The leading riflemen dropped and prepared to open fire. But the car was obviously unarmed and flying a red divisional flag from the radiator cap. It stopped beside us and General Slim got out. "How the hell did he get past us?" I muttered. Willy hurried forward. "Morning, Willy," the general said. "There's nothing until you get round the fourth hairpin. They've got an antitank gun there." There was a large hole through the back of the car body.

Slim climbed back into his car, we saluted, and he drove on. The pace of our advance quickened. By evening we were well up the slopes and had made desultory contact. At dawn we attacked; but there was no one there. The Persians had gone. Since the Pai-Tak was the strongest defensive position between the Iraqi frontier and Teheran, over four hundred miles ahead, it was clear that they would not fight much longer.

We crossed the pass and entered a wide, high valley. The light had the same opal quality I remembered from Arizona, and good days after rain in Baluchistan. Water ran cold in the streams that flowed down from the hillsides, and the colors were pale gray, pale green, and violet from the wild flowers growing among the rocks. The villages stood close against the hills, with clear water dashing through them under the mulberry trees, and the walls were washed white or pink or pale yellow.

On the road we passed travelers—the war wasn't serious enough for them to be refugees—moving on foot or in ancient donkey carts. The women were swathed in nondescript Oriental garments, but the men wore trousers, bright coats in many colors, with brass buttons, and a variety of caps, alike only in being non-Oriental. We learned that the Shah had determined, like Mustafa Kemal in Turkey, to westernize his people. He had forbidden the wearing of the traditional clothes, or turban, or fez. The secondhand clothes dealers of Europe and, particularly, the U.S.A. had seen their opportunity and jumped in with both feet. The most conspicuous of the men in the first group was wearing a brown derby and a long blue coat with the crested buttons of a hotel in Cincinnati. Another wore a pageboy's short jacket, the buttons mostly missing, and a doorman's peaked cap from Piccadilly.

Noon that day found us eating our rations in an orchard where the hill sloped down and we had a long view to distant hills and, beyond them, the peaks of jagged mountains. We were to continue our advance at 1400 hours. But we did not, for a signal came that the Persians had surrendered. The lunch turned into a party. We found some of our beer and whisky ration and, joined

by anybody who happened to be traveling on the road, sang and
ate and drank till late at night.

We settled down to make a camp near Karind, and train for
whatever might befall us next. We had started the great war for
democracy by invading three neutral countries against the wishes
of their inhabitants or, at least, of their governments. The supply
of opponents was now running out. Surely our next move must
be the big one—to the Western Desert, to fight Rommel.

We swung around the valley and the mountains in progressively
more ambitious training exercises. We learned that it was safe
to leave anything, anywhere, in Persia. There was no pilfering, at
least on the highways. If there was, the Shah's police cut the
offender's hand off; or, if no offender could be accurately identified, they cut off the right hands of several prominent citizens
in nearby villages. The Persian regulars drifted back into their
garrisons, and when they saw them coming the villagers fled, or
hid in their houses. We found out about that too, when we returned to a village around which we had been exercising a day
or two earlier, and found it a heap of smoking rubble, the inhabitants scattering hopelessly across the wide country with their
belongings on donkeys. The village had been backward in paying
its taxes. For centuries Persia has consisted of a small number of
immensely rich and ruthless men and a large number on the edge
of starvation. We were invaders, but the huge majority of the
people only wished we would stay, and overturn the country's
whole polity, so that they could breathe.

We turned round and round in our camp, like a dog settling for
the night, and pushed it into a shape to please us, and soon believed we owned this place as home. The partridge and quail
volleyed across the hillsides, and in the tiny villages, where the
people did not hide when they saw *us* coming, we sat and ate
huge flat loaves of Persian bread, and drank red wine. The pretty,
dark-haired girl washing clothes in the stream showed her awareness of us, in the liquid look from the corner of her eye and the
low, slow stare, like a bullfighter's *veronica*, as she passed to her
house, carrying the clothes on her head. In Shahabad there was
a restaurant where we ate meals of saffron rice and lamb; in
Kermanshah there were shaded gardens such as pleased Omar;

beyond, high on the rock cliffs of a mighty gorge, a man had written, two thousand five hundred years earlier: "I AM CHOSROES, KING OF KINGS."

Across the Caucasus the Germans still pounded forward, and just north of us lay the country of the Kurds. These famous people were a prime object of persecution from the three countries in whose territories their ancient land now lies—Turkey, Iraq, and Persia. They did not like to pay taxes, especially as what did not stick to official fingers was largely used to pay for an army big enough to keep them in order. The Kurds have a fierce national and race pride, and detest their nominal rulers, particularly the Persians and Iraqis—the Kurds in Turkey are few—and, above all, they want to be united, and to rule themselves as one people. This is true now, and it was true in 1941. Now it is Soviet agents, then it was Germans among them, promising them freedom and autonomy if they would help the Cause when the time came. In 1941 the time would be the advance of German columns south through Persia, onto the oil fields.

We were ordered to reconnoiter routes through which the Germans might advance, report on their feasibility and make recommendations for their defense. So one day I set out with three trucks, half a platoon of Gurkhas, and a Persian lieutenant as interpreter, to explore a valley about thirty miles north of Karind.

The first evening we reached the end of a rugged but just motorable track, camped by the bank of the stream, set our sentries and went to sleep. In the morning the Persian said we could go no farther. The valley was impassable. I examined the country ahead through field glasses, and saw that it would soon become difficult, indeed; but the Germans were very competent chaps in the use of armored and motorized columns, and we must go forward until we—and hence, the Germans—found it absolutely impassable. The Persian had been smoking since first light and there was something funny about his eyes. My *subadar*, Sukdeo, said curtly, "Opium."

We went on, the Persian now unable to control the trembling of his body and arms. He was supposed to sit in the front of the truck with me, but he gave me the jitters and I ordered him into the back. The cart track narrowed and became a footpath. The

mountainside steepened until we were grinding forward in low
gear at three miles an hour, steeply tilted, about halfway up a
severe slope. Below us the slope soon turned into a cliff, falling
sheer for two hundred feet into the gorge of the torrent. The
mountains rose higher and higher, and far up the sides the
Kurdish villages gleamed in the sun. It was a most impressive
place, with something of the half-sunny, half-murderous atmosphere of Glencoe. Finally the vehicles could go no farther. I
stopped, left guards, and with a few men went forward on foot. I
also had to leave the Persian officer, as he was almost unconscious
from fear and drugs.

Two hours on the cliffside, or among huge boulders on a dangerous slope, convinced me that there was no possibility of the
Germans moving armor through here lightly. It could be done—
anything can be done, given the resources of a major power in a
major war—but it could not be done easily or by surprise. We
need only note that the valley existed, and keep it under observation.

A few Kurds, long-striding, armed with long rifles, and reminding me very much of the Pathans of India's North West Frontier,
came down from a high ridge toward us, slowly at first, then faster
as I waited for them. Glancing round at the savage grandeur of
the place, I knew that rifles were covering us from those flat-
roofed houses, or from behind those rocks perched on the mountain walls.

The Kurds chatted easily—we could not understand each other
—and happily smoked a cigarette with me. I made them understand we would like fresh fruit, fresh meat, whatever they had,
and they returned to the trucks with me. There I called for the
Persian lieutenant, since I needed him to interpret. He did not
appear. Sukdeo went and dragged him out from his hiding place
inside the truck.

The reason for his fear became obvious. As soon as they saw
him the Kurds' brows drew down in an angry glare. They stalked
forward and began to curse and swear at the lieutenant. He shook
his head, stuttered something and leaned against the truck, arms
outspread. The Kurds became angrier. They pointed up the hill,
down the valley. One made a motion of cutting his throat, then
of dashing something to the ground. I do not know exactly what

he was saying, but I guess he was reminding the Persian, or accusing him, of having cut children's throats and dashed them to the ground. It may have been this particular man they were accusing—Persians are famous for their subtle humor, and his seniors were quite capable of the macabre joke of sending him off to the scene of some outrage he had committed—or it may have been the Persian Army as a whole.

I attempted to quieten the two Kurds. They took no notice. One of them shouted up the hill to the village above us. The other fumbled with the bolt of his rifle, almost slavering at the mouth with rage and foreseen revenge. About twenty men, all armed, tumbled out of the village. I told the Persian to shout to them to stay where they were, at peril, and ordered Sukdeo to open fire if they came any closer. The rattle of the bolts, the single purposeful jerk with which the Bren gunner cocked his gun, and the sudden disappearance of the Gurkhas into hidden action positions made the Kurds realize that other people besides themselves and their prey had parts in this drama.

The Kurds turned to me, pointed at the lieutenant, and intimated quite clearly that they would like to cut his throat. If I'd just hand him over it wouldn't take a minute and then we could get on with buying the fruit. I wished I could accede to their wishes. The officers of the Persian Army, from what I had seen, were a disgrace to the title, and I would have loved to spend the night carousing in that mountain eyrie with these proud, bold Kurds.

But I had to say no. One of the Kurds waved his arm excitedly and someone up the hill must have started a downward movement, for a short burst from the Bren gun made me turn my head. The twenty Kurds were scurrying back, and no one had been hurt. I noted the Bren gunner's name for extra practice and lit a cigarette.

The work of the patrol was done, and I ought to go back. On the other hand, I ought not to be forced back. On the *third* hand, this valley probably held about two hundred Kurdish fighting men, all armed, and it would be silly to get ourselves massacred with no compensating gain, sillier still to put the Kurds against us. There was no doubt who was master of the situation now. I was. Any solution I chose to impose now would be of my own volition. Later, that might not be true—very little later, if those white and gray dots scurrying across the farther mountain meant what I knew well that they did mean.

I shook hands with the Kurds, who gave me a puzzled smile in answer to mine. I took their rifles and laid them down beside the track a few yards off. I ordered Sukdeo to put the Persian lieutenant back into the truck, but to use his pistol to do it, with the maximum of violence. Sukdeo drew his pistol and jammed it into the Persian's stomach. The Kurds broke into expectant smiles. Sukdeo threw the lieutenant into the truck and jumped in after him, waving the pistol. I wagged my finger warningly at the Kurds, the riflemen ran up, and we drove away. Then I took off my Gurkha hat and wiped my forehead.

Dussehra, the greatest festival of the Hindu year, came at this time. In peace, and in India, we would have bought a buffalo for each company and another for the battalion as a whole; and scores of chickens and male goats, all to be sacrificially executed by single blows of a kukri, the curved, heavy-bladed Gurkha knife. Here we could find only goats, and not too many of them; but the atmosphere was the same, and somehow our quartermaster had collected enough rum, so we danced and sang round the camp-fires under the loom of the Persian mountains, and ate a huge meal of rice and lentils and chupatties and curried goat, and by dawn were escorted back to our own tents by small troops of reeling, solicitous riflemen, who undressed us and put us to bed.

It grew very cold at night, and we wore greatcoats under our blankets, inside the tents. What next, what next? Winter in Persia—or battle in Libya? Snow over all this valley in front of us, perhaps a trip to Teheran, roaring fires in the inns at Kermanshah and Shahabad—or the camouflaged loom of a German Mark III tank coming out of the sunset?

The orders came to return to Iraq. We were for the Western Desert. We wound down the Pai-Tak Pass, through the tortuous streets and over the narrow bridge at Sar-i-Pul Zuhab, and on west. We went into camp in open country just west of Baghdad, and began to reorganize for the desert. We had completed Sally Three.

The minarets of the great mosque of Al Kadhimain rose out of the morning mist above the Tigris. The wild duck were on the marshes and it was good weather.

Willy's orderly came to me. "*Colonel sahib salaam bhanchha.*"
Willy said abruptly, "I've nominated you for the next Staff
College course at Quetta. It begins in February. I've also been
ordered to find an officer for temporary staff duty with Headquarters, Lines of Communication Area, in Basra. I'm going to
send you. It will help you to learn something before you go to
Quetta. . . . I shall be sorry to lose you."

The battalion, my battalion, the 2nd Battalion, 4th Prince of
Wales's Own Gurkha Rifles, lay encamped around us. For seven
years I had had no other home. I knew every man by number, rank,
and name. Hundreds I knew by personality, in barrack and in
battle—but not as well as they knew me. These men, this spirit
which I had played my part in forming, were going at last to the
big war.

I wanted to go, and I wanted to stay. Only at the Staff College
could I learn to be a better soldier. But the regiment—Naru, and
young Dean, and Balbir; Aiman, Amarsing, Sukdeo, Roger Werner,
Willy himself.

"Sir . . ." I began.

Willy said, "I have given an order."

Later we said good-by. I did not think I would ever again have
the privilege of serving such a good man, nor ever be so peculiarly fitted to fill special needs in another's life. Willy felt himself
cut off from our generation, and it was true; but through the close
association between him and myself he had come to understand
something about all of us. Now he could communicate. As for me,
I hope that what I have already written, and what follows, will
make clear the debt I owe him. He had no children, and I am
sure that, if he had, he would have been horrified to have his son
turn out like me, but the relationship between us had grown into
something of the sort.

"I'll miss you," he said again, and I thought, Christ, I'll miss
you.

We parted. That evening I jolted south in the narrow-gauge
train from Baghdad West, in a sleeper bound for Basra.

Three brisk campaigns completed. Quite a lot learned, very
little damage suffered. I was going away from it all. And what,
precisely, was I going away from? From the crack of the field guns
ranging on Deir-es-Zor? From the murmurous night on the

Djezireh, the truck engines rumbling and grumbling and the moon bright? No, all that had, for the moment, utterly vanished. As usual, it was people who remained. People, and something of nature's marvels, through which it had been our lot to travel, armed. Willy's face and expression were so clear before me that I found it hard to convince myself he was not in the compartment with me. Roger Werner was there, too, a rather bogus frown lightly creasing his forehead, put there because the situation was grim, the trucks had run out of fuel, something had broken down that shouldn't, and he was responsible, and he knew he ought to look worried to please Willy, so he did; but he wasn't really worried because, really, nothing at all worried him. Temple, Whittall, John Strickland, Beetle Lowis were there; and, filling the whole memory, the Gurkhas.

There they were, and yet I couldn't pick out a single face unless I deliberately tried. Naru—appear! Yes, here he is, round of face, cupid bow lips, shaven head, soft eyes, shy smile. Narbahadur Gurung . . . heavy, lined face, powerful jaw, deep cracked voice, shambling walk, power in every line . . . The Gurkhas were individuals, but they were also the regiment, and above that they were The Gurkhas, and they had this unique quality of being a character while still in the mass, of remaining absolutely single, not composite, though ranked in hundreds. I heard them singing among the tents at Karind, and the soft throb of the *madals* we took with us wherever we went. I saw them kneeling round a burning truck, looking upward, the round Mongolian faces full of unexpected angles and the rifles aimed at the coppery sky, dark flames behind and a tower of black smoke beyond. I smelt the cardamom seeds they chewed to keep themselves from thirst.

I saw spread lines of trucks moving across an empty, hot dawn, and the driver beside me, eyes already raw and red and dry, and the riflemen sitting in the back, handkerchiefs across their mouths, and the sun coming up behind, a huge red ball momentarily rolling along the hard rim of the desert.

I began to feel miserable. Good-by, good-by, good-by, the words kept running through my head.

I must snap out of this. Think, man, think. Your tour as adjutant was nearly up and even in peacetime you'd have had to leave the regiment for two or three years, because that's the custom.

You're sad because the time has come to grow up. This is the end of an era in your life. Don't look back, look ahead. You will return to the regiment, but not as a subaltern, not as a young man, even if you go back in six months' time. You may laugh more than you ever have, but you'll never laugh as lightly again. In military terms you are about to become a field officer; in civilian language, a responsible adult.

I went to sleep, and awoke in the morning to be served tea at Ur of the Chaldees.

Interlude

6 *With a Jug of Wine, a Loaf of Bread but no Thou—being the narrative of a brief and unarmed digression into Persia.*

Basra, on longer and closer acquaintance, proved to be all that Mr. Hopkins had said about it. At the beginning of December, weary of the everlasting flatness, the great muddy river, the unvarying heat and the diverse smells, I took ten days' leave. Persia was by far the most beautiful and most interesting country within reach; and there I went.

The first stage was Ahwaz, in south Persia. To reach it I crossed the Shatt al Arab on the bridge of boats (which was removed before every flood season, and replaced after), and then motored ninety miles across a flat desert. Ahwaz lies on the Karun River, which is there tidal, and contains some of the world's hungriest sharks. During the August invasion three Indian sepoys, washing clothes in the river, standing in water only up to their knees, were taken by sharks which their comrades on the bank could see wriggling toward them across the mud flats, dorsal fins and most of their backs out of the water.

At Ahwaz I caught the Trans-Persian Express. For three hours we chugged northward across a stony plain, the mountains invisible. We passed Susa, where the Persian King Shapur II held the Roman Emperor Valerian prisoner for many years (from A.D. 260). At Andimishk the locomotives were doubled and we

began to climb. From the kitchen car the attendants brought me
a magnificent meal of saffron rice, chicken and Persian red wine.
I ate and drank, alone in the big compartment, while twilight fell
on the crags and the locomotives ahead labored upward, their
exhausts thundering in the canyon. We wound round and
round and in and out and up and up. We crossed and recrossed
ourselves, and tied corkscrew knots with our own tail light.
We ground along ledges two thousand feet above narrow torrents,
clanked over high steel bridges, bellowed through long tunnels. At
last, long after it was totally dark, the train stopped and I got
out to stretch my legs.

An icy wind blew down the platform and I rushed back for my
greatcoat. The heat and the flies of the low country had vanished,
and reality. A genie from *The Thousand and One Nights* had projected me into a spy movie and I had a part to play. The long train,
its lights gleaming, stood in a high, narrow valley. The moon
glittered on snow peaks to east and west. Half a dozen Persian
officers strolled up and down in their long German-pattern greatcoats and high-fronted Nazi hats, their boots crunching in the
snow. A heavily veiled woman, wearing a mink coat, stood outside a sleeping car talking to a small fat man who was smoking
a cigarette in a long holder. Two sentries stood against the bulk
of the locomotives, their bayonets faintly gleaming.

I joined the walkers, my collar turned high. In a dark corner
outside the station building I lit a cigarette, the small yellow glow
illuminating my face. I looked at my watch, and then scanned
the sky. The Persian officers looked at me and then nervously
at the sky.

It began to snow, a locomotive gave a low, mournful scream.
I walked back to my compartment slowly, giving the veiled lady
a long, level stare.

Early next morning we rolled into Teheran station, and I remembered that someone had told me to look at the ceiling of the
concourse. Swedish contractors had built the railroad itself, but a
German firm had done this station. As I stared up, the decoration
on the ceiling appeared at first to be purely geometrical, in imita-
tion of the old Persian manner. As I looked, the fine pattern leaped
to my eye: it was all swastikas.

I found a cheap hotel and began to explore the city. I did not find it very interesting. Parts of it resemble Paris, parts Basra. As in the rest of the country, a few immensely rich people, in immensely shiny cars, moved about among a multitude in rags. In the bar of one of the more ornate hotels I saw a group of American officers and tried to make friends, but they were as aloof as the traditional Englishman in a railway carriage. Nothing personal, I was given to feel, just that their position here was semisecret, and as officers of a neutral country they couldn't afford to get too pally with the British.

In a sleazy night club I almost became the owner of a Rumanian dancer. She was not very pretty, she was forty, and her story, which saddened me immensely, was probably untrue in all material particulars. I didn't mind then, and I don't now. I'd much rather be had for a sucker than go through life with my hand over my wallet. From the lady I bought several dances, and for her several drinks. Late at night, a tear in her eye, she whispered that I was kind, generous, handsome, brave, well born, rich, and exceptionally virile. Could I not take her back to Basra with me? She would cook, and sew, and clean my room. If any silly old general should ask what she was doing there, she would say she was my sister.

I thought of Willy. I thought of my commander in Basra, Major General George de la Poer Beresford. I had found some nice nurses in Basra, but they represented, in the long run, more expense than Sonya the Rumanian would, and there was besides so much running after to be done, so long and involved a game to play, and the game itself, once so exhilarating, had become something of a bore.

Still, it wouldn't do. I gave Sonya fifty rupees. She knew it was no good, really, and took the money with a nod and word of thanks, and I returned to my hotel but not, for a long time, to sleep. Sonya's attractiveness, I realized, did not lie in her face or her availability. I was restless, restless to settle—not to become a cabbage, but to establish a human relationship that would be my new and permanent home (the regiment had reached the Western Desert), from which I would work, play, travel; inside which, always, there would be love and a kind of active calm, like an ocean under a long swell.

The next night I took a taxi and went out to the Darband Hotel,

which stands on the southern slope of the Elburz Mountains,
ten miles out of Teheran and nearly two thousand feet above the
city. Here the rich men and the embassies have summer homes and
swimming pools; but now it was midwinter, snow lay everywhere,
and snow was falling. I walked up from the road, across steep
terraces, toward a row of tall doors and windows. Light poured
out onto the snow and the drifting flakes. I put my nose to the
glass and looked in—crystal chandeliers, thick carpets, men and
women in full evening dress with wine glasses in their hands.
They were all Persians, and I learned later that one of them was
the new Shah's sister.

I stood in the snow, shivering in my worn khaki and low shoes,
and thought sardonically, V*ae victis*—Woe to the conquered.
Then I thought, I daren't face that lot, they'll look at me as
though I'm something the cat brought in. Then I pushed open
the doors, letting in a blast of freezing air, and went in, and
walked straight through the glittering crowd toward the bar. A
tall Persian officer in the Prussian uniform that never failed to
annoy me did not get out of my way. I had no monocle but I
knew how to do it well enough. The trick is not to imply that
there's anything wrong with the man himself, but that his clothes
fill you with wonder. Before my eyes had reached his knees he
stepped aside.

I awoke next morning determined to leave Teheran. More
restless than ever, I could think of no other solution than to keep
traveling. Earlier I had visited an Assyrian family, relatives of a
sergeant in the R.A.F. Levies in Iraq. Besides giving me much
underground information about Persian oppression against the
various tribal groups in the country, they had urged me to visit
Mazanderan, a province lying on the Caspian Sea, north of the
Elburz Range. It was very beautiful, very different, they said.

I went to the British Embassy to get the necessary permit. Passing through the gates in the high wall I entered Arnold's Rugby,
with rooks cawing in immemorial elms and chestnut trees spreading their gaunt branches across graveled paths; and there was a big
gray English country house, and a smell of tea and crumpets in
the counselor's study. I strained my eyes to see Tom Brown,
my ears to hear distant cries of "Play up, School"; but it was Persia, and the military attaché was doubtful.

The Caspian coast lay in the occupation zone of our Russian Allies, and our Russian Allies did not like their British Allies visiting it. After much telephoning the attaché said he could not give me any proper authorization, but merely a *laissez-passer*, telling the world who I was and inviting it to let me pass. He wrote it out and handed it to me, saying, "I don't suppose this will do you any good. For God's sake wear uniform all the time, so that they can't shoot you as a spy. Not according to the Geneva Convention, anyway," he added.

At Irantour, the monopolistic Persian travel agency, I hired a Dodge sedan, with chauffeur, to take me on a three-day excursion through Mazanderan. The next day we set out, heading first for Babulsar, said to be a seaside resort in the southeastern corner of the Caspian.

Until early in the afternoon we ran east through a wild, desolate, and stony country of plain and mountain, thoroughly typical of all that I had so far seen of Persia. Then we crossed a low saddle and began the long northward descent to the Caspian. The short grass and herbs of the pass gave place to pines, and those to oaks. The stream running narrow and cold between its sedgy banks grew wider, and made a hollow roaring sound, and cows appeared in the small fields. The houses took on a European look, and in fading light we passed through villages that might have been in Switzerland, complete to cowbells and half-timbering. Night fell, and the Dodge wound on and down. It began to rain as, at last, we reached the flat land, and still we had twenty miles to go. I sat in a state of high tension, expecting to overrun a Russian guard post and get shot—but we saw no Russians. Then we lost our way, and it was ten o'clock before we drew up before a large building, where no light showed.

"It has been shut for the winter," my driver said gloomily in his poor French; but he got out and rang the bell. After a long time standing there in the slanting rain under the dark wall, the door opened. . . . I heard Beethoven's Hammerklavier Sonata. Subdued pink light glowed on polished furniture, a luxurious carpet. The Swiss manager and his wife greeted me with practiced, tactful courtesy.

I was the only guest, and enjoyed an excellent meal at a small table with my host and hostess. Where were the nearest Russians? In Babulsar village, just up the road—hadn't I seen them? . . . How were they behaving? Very well. They had just shot two of their men for making advances to a Persian girl. After dinner and a long talk about the sad state of the world, and the wonders of Persia in peacetime, I went up to my room.

The pretty chambermaid was hanging around, dusting a picture, though it was late. Remembering the Russians, I stood a long way off from her and said in a neutral voice, in French, "I would like to be called at six, please. That is all." She nodded pleasantly, lay down on the bed, and hauled up her skirt.

The next day the chauffeur drove me east along the shore of the Caspian, bound for Ramsar. Rain fell continuously, clouds hung low overhead, and on my right hand tall waves rolled steep and gray against a desolate, sandy shore. It looked and felt like the North Sea. This is Central Asia, I repeated. Over there is Krasnovodsk, where the battalion fought the Bolsheviki in 1919; and beyond that is the forbidden city of Khiva, where Burnaby made his great ride in 1879; and beyond that the Kara-Kum, the Black Desert; and Merv, Samarkand, Balkh, Bukhara . . . but flights of wild duck swept low along the wave crests and the wind blew sharp and cold and salt. To the left, across marshy meadows where cows grazed, there were heavy, dark trees, and mountains soaring into the cloud base. Again I had to repeat, to reassure myself, I am in Central Asia, and those forests are full of Chinese pheasants, huge, thick-haired Caspian tigers.

At lunchtime, near a small village, two Russian sentries stopped us. They were very alike, quite short, bullet heads, cropped hair, blue eyes in pallid faces, high Slavic cheekbones, very young. I sat back, fumbling for my *laissez-passer*. The soldier on the left leaned in and spoke to the driver, one word only, the commonest word in the Soviet language, "*Propusk?*"

The driver produced his Russian pass. The soldier peered at it for some time, but with unfocused eyes, and I will swear that he could not read. Then he gave it back and waved the driver on. We engaged gear and left them. I felt like protesting. The sentries had not only not asked for my pass, they had not seen me.

A little later a large car came tearing toward us along the road, a flag whipping furiously from the radiator cap. "Russian general," I said to the driver. "Give him room." We pulled well over and the car raced past, hurling its bow wave of mud and water all over us; but the flag it flew was the Stars and Stripes. The American Ambassador, I thought. Very odd; and what is he in such a hurry about? It was December 8, 1941.

At Ramsar a hotel stood on a shelf of the Elburz Mountains, two miles from the shore and several hundred feet up. It was a model hydro of the old school—a huge building leprous with turrets, buttresses, and towers, its gardens convoluted with high hedges, paved walks, and labyrinths. In every nook groups of statuary writhed and postured. In one arbor Venus clasped her hands across her pudenda, while a stag at bay backed into her side, two small naked boys peed over her feet, and, from a perch just above the stag's head, a pelican surveyed her fanny with stony disapproval. Inside the hotel were miles of passages, a hundred wide flights of creaky stairs, and God knows how many marble rooms with tall, dusty windows, but, of course, no other guests.

Behind the hotel, though, a sulfur spring gushed out of the mountain into a formal bathhouse, and there I enjoyed a hot, evil-smelling, and relaxing tub. And at the foot of the garden the old Shah had built a little summer palace. It was very small, square, one-storied, and built throughout of the finest, matched Meshed marble; it had a corrugated-iron roof. In the bathroom the fittings were of pure gold and the finest porcelain; the cedar doors had cheap brass handles and gimcrack bolts. On the bedroom floor, wall to wall, lay a carpet of gray and blue that shimmered and lived, as a living thing, under the feet, and was worth eight thousand dollars as it lay; on the walls hung garish reproductions of the worst kind of nineteenth-century Italian Romanticist "art."

After dinner I found the chambermaid, as pretty as the one at Babulsar, hanging around my room, dusting something. I stood a long way off from her and said, in French, "I would like a call at six, please. That is all." She gave me a look as sulfurous as the afternoon's bath and left the room, slamming the door.

The next day we headed south. It was a long, long climb, nearly seventy miles—out of heavy trees and orchards, through pines in swirling cloud, in a driving blizzard past a long procession of Bactrian camels winding up, the camelmen huddled against the storm and our wheels slipping on the edge of gigantic drops, out at last onto the high plain, into pale clear sunlight, and dry air, and running water and mulberries and the color-washed houses of the Persian plateau.

In Teheran I again met the American officers. They greeted me effusively. We were allies. I thought they had become deranged until they told me about Pearl Harbor. Understanding now why the Ambassador had been in such a hurry, I bade them welcome to the war—and welcome to it.

The next day, heavily loaded with smoked salmon, good red wine at twenty cents a bottle, and five pounds of excellent black caviar at fifty cents a pound, I took the train back to Ahwaz and Basra. Three weeks later I sailed for Karachi.

Book Two **CHANGING COURSE**

7 After three weeks' waiting in Karachi I took the train to Quetta, for the Staff College. At dawn the next morning, on a day in February, 1942, I pulled up the blinds of my compartment. We had just surmounted the long climb over the Bolan Pass and were running out onto the plateau by Spezand. Snow covered the mountain Chiltan opposite, from its eleven thousand foot crest to its foot in the plain. The light struck pale and diamond-sharp, bringing bare slopes forty miles away as close as the frost-covered blades of sage grass beside the track. Twenty thousand volts crackled through me and I could smell each clump of thyme, feel each granule of snow on Chiltan. The line curved gradually to the right, and the wheels clacked faster over the rail joints. "Quetta, here I come," I whispered.

It was an excitement of challenge, for the Staff College really mattered. I was going there not only to learn staff duties, but to fit myself for the higher command of troops. All in all, there was no more important phase of a professional soldier's career, except command in battle. If I failed here I would have to show extraordinary qualities of leadership and intelligence to re-establish my military reputation; but I would be unlikely to get opportunities to show any such thing, for the powers would not post me back to regimental duty; they would simply give me inferior staff jobs well away from the battlefield.

And Quetta itself, now so close ahead . . . Capital of British

Baluchistan, the encyclopedia informed anyone who wanted to know. A variation of the word *kwat-kot*, signifying fortress. (Come now, mind your language there, *Britannica*.). . . 536 miles by rail north of Karachi; 5,500 feet above sea level. Pop.: 60,000 odd. (Not so damned odd, *Britannica*; just Baluchi tribesmen and army types.) Largely destroyed by earthquake May 31, 1935. Ringed by mountains. Standing eighty miles back from the Afghan frontier. A garrison town. Probably very hot in summer and very cold in winter. A dull place, the encyclopedia hinted.

It was right and wrong. The physical description was correct enough, especially the bit about the cold. The pass leading to Afghanistan is called the Khojak, and a diabolically cold, dry wind often blew in over it, chapping lips and freezing ears and drying the skin so that women poured olive oil into their bath water; and I had seen men and girls in Saint-Moritz clothes skiing down the wide avenues, and a string of camels coming slowly up in the opposite direction, snow on their heavy, supercilious eyelids, and the dark mountains towering out of the slanting snow above them all.

But Quetta was not dull. It was electric. Something in the air produced pregnancy in the childless, nymphomania in the frigid, larceny in the respectable, and scandals of wonderful variety. . . .

There was the Musical Beds Scandal of the mid-1930s, when four officers in a remote outpost had passed three wives around in a year-long orgy—the odd man out, a week at a time, doing all the military work.

There was the Bhoosa Scandal. Bhoosa is chopped, dried straw, usually baled, used for fodder for the army's mules and horses, and the scandal was too complicated to explain here, but it involved two sets of scales, one accurate and one inaccurate, and midnight openings and illegal substitutions among the bhoosa stacks. And the Coal Scandal, when a quartermaster sergeant sold government coal to the local cinema proprietors (what they did with it I cannot imagine; they certainly didn't heat their movie houses), and pocketed the proceeds. And the Car Scandal, involving a chap who registered and insured an old heap as the military vehicle he was entitled to, and got a receipt for a new car, and bought a race horse, and won many races and much money with it. And a girl with unruly hair and disposition, known as the Pas-

sionate Haystack; and another as the Lilo (a form of inflatable
rubber mattress); and another as the Sofa Cobra. There was a
Vice Queen who collected other ladies' husbands and cut a notch
in her bedstead for every conquest. No one knew why the bed
was still standing.

And a major who leaned forward with a choked grunt at a
ceremonial dinner party and hauled out of its shell the left breast
of the lady sitting across the table from him. And another who
applied for short leave, paid his debts, handed over his job to a
brother officer, and shot himself. (His colonel had twice warned
him about homosexual advances toward the troops, and told him
that the next time he'd go to court martial. The third time had
arrived.)

And there were hailstorms of stunning violence, when donkeys
lay dead in the streets and camels lay stunned at the edge of
the surrounding desert. And flash floods that swept away trucks,
guns, and men, if they were caught in the usually dry river beds.
And frequent earthquakes. And tremendous chukar shoots on the
mountains, duck shoots far to the west, skiing, jackal hunts with
the pack of foxhounds, point-to-point races, a race course with
regular meetings. And the Staff College.

In 1940, when I'd been there with the battalion, the pace was
hot enough. Now, from what I'd heard, it was frenetic. Urgently
the government had pulled up a long, little-used strategic railroad, for the scrap metal. Then the Germans attacked Russia.
Only Persia and Afghanistan stood between the Nazi Beast and
the Brightest Jewel in the British Crown. Urgently the government was relaying the strategic railroad. The peacetime garrison
had gone to war, leaving their families. From all over India other
abandoned women were sent to Quetta for the duration. Good
girls grew lonely, naughty girls grew naughtier. As fast as regiments left in one direction, others arrived, thundered west, and
began digging defenses against the expected coming of the Germans. The war against Japan began and Singapore fell. General
Auchinleck, known to the entire army as the Auk, ordered that
officers must put away their mess kits and dinner jackets for the
duration, and wear uniform all the time. The war had reached
India.

The Staff College course, which used to last two years, had

been cut to five and a half months, but with very little reduction
in the syllabus. I would have to work hard, I saw; but I was
damned if I'd let them run me into the ground. I would make it a
point of honor to attend every single dance night at the club—
they took place on Wednesdays and Saturdays. I would throw a
party in my room every Sunday night, alternately Beethoven-and-
beer and Beiderbecke-and-beer, as I had done in 1940. Brow fur-
rowing and midnight oil were for others; I owed my regiment
a certain nonchalance, a to-hell-with-it air. . . .

The train drew into Quetta station. A tall officer stood on the
platform, watching it pull in. His tunic was of a peculiarly dark
shade of khaki barathea, his shirt even darker. He stood in an
aristocratic stoop, his feet at what appeared to be an impossible
angle to each other, and his face wore an expression of great ennui.
I leaped out of the train and slapped him on the back. "Maitland," I cried. "My God, we haven't met since we came out together in the *Nevasa* in '34, have we? And what's this?" I fingered
his tunic. "Have you joined the Coldstream?" (By then I had
recognized the very dark khaki as that affected by H.M. Foot
Guards when uncouth circumstances force them to get out of
their red coats.)

Captain Maitland France of the Frontier Force Rifles, Indian
Army, examined his fingernails. "No," he said, "I just prefer the
shade." Maitland always liked to choose a good pose, and stick to
it.

Then the man he was waiting for came up, and it turned out
that they were both for the course, too, so we shared a taxi up
to the Staff College at the far end of Quetta.

As soon as I had settled into the quarter allotted to me—study,
tiny bedroom, bathroom—I looked at the list of students on the
course. Several I knew personally—Paddy Massey of Hodson's
Horse; Beetle Lowis of my own regiment; Philip Mortimer, who
had led that squadron of the 13th Lancers through the Syrian
campaign at our side; Mohammed Usman of the Baluchis; Goff
Hamilton of the Guides, who'd earned a D.S.O. as a second lieutenant, twenty years of age, by commanding his battalion through
a scorching day of frontier battle, all the other officers killed or
wounded, with a bullet through his stomach; a score of others.
The total was about ninety. The average age appeared to be just

over thirty. Nearly all were temporary captains, like myself; a couple of lieutenants, a couple of majors. . . . This was going to be good. This was going to be tremendous!

It was like starting at the Royal Military College, Sandhurst, again. There was a hushed pause lasting through the first week-end, during which they gave us books, tables of organization and equipment, and a hundred pamphlets. The bulletin board blossomed with charts dividing us into syndicates, and allotting us to halls of study, or classrooms as we more humbly called them. Our teachers introduced themselves. All lieutenant colonels (local), they were known as the Directing Staff, or D.S. Very nice. They weren't going to teach us, only direct the natural flow of our energetic minds. Ha!

Alone in my room, the night before the course began, I collected my wits. When I left the battalion I had been like a boy leaving home to seek his fortune in the great world, his belongings wrapped in a bundle on a stick. There was nothing in the bundle but a little experience and a little knowledge, picked up here and there. But the world of the army was large and confusing. I had better open my bundle, examine its contents, and make sure that I knew, at least, how to use what I had. . . .

Armies exist to further by force or the threat of force civil policies which cannot be furthered by any other means. In a democracy an army is not, and ought not to be, self-activating. It functions only at the will of the people, indeed, as the will of the people, expressed through constitutional forms. (That much I'd learned at Sandhurst.)

An army is divided into two main groups—arms and services. The arms kill the enemy. The services supply the arms with all that they need to fight, and tidy up behind them.

There are really only three arms—infantry, who fight on foot; artillery, who throw shells from a distance; and cavalry or their modern successors, armored troops, who fight while mounted on a horse or in an armored vehicle. In addition, two services, though they do not actually kill the enemy, work so far forward in the battle area, and are so integral to the battle, that they are considered to be arms—that is, engineers and signals. (About all these I knew a fair amount, at least at the forward, business end.)

There are many, many services. For example—supply, transport, medical, ordnance, repair of electrical and mechanical implements, legal, pay, chaplains, graves registrations, salvage, police, hygiene and sanitation, financial, government of territories captured from the enemy . . . and . . . and . . . (I knew vaguely what each of these did, but I had no idea how they did it. I graded myself "ignorant" about the services.)

Organization—an army looks like a gigantic pyramid. At the summit stands a representative of the civil government and, grouped close enough round him to hear what he has to tell them, a few generals and field marshals—who stand on the shoulders of more lieutenant generals; who stand on the shoulders of still more major generals, and so down to the mass of private soldiers, who support everyone else. (But Bill Slim and my own battle experience has taught me that the army is also an inverted pyramid, the broad brass base at the top, and the whole balanced on a single fine point—the will, skill, and discipline of the individual soldier.)

How the ordinary blocks in which fighting formations are built up, I knew well enough—from the single man to the section of ten men, the platoon of three or four sections, the company of three or four platoons . . . up past battalion, brigade, division, corps, army, army group.

What about the staff? I had heard and stored away in my memory several definitions of it: *"The staff is a bloody nuisance, inefficient where it isn't actually crooked." "The staff exists in order to deprive the 2/4th Gurkhas of their rights."* (This was, naturally, Willy's opinion.) *"The function of the staff is to so foul up operations, by giving contradictory orders and misreading their maps, that wars will be prolonged to a point where every staff officer has become a general."* (A fairly common view.)

Well, all right, perhaps that's what it sometimes is—but what ought it to be? The army is a huge and incredibly complicated machine. The drive that causes it to function efficiently, all parts in a single cause, is the chain of command. At the very top and the very bottom the orders given are simple. President or Prime Minister says, "Destroy Vichy French control of Syria so that I can hand it over to the Free French." A couple of hundred links down the chain Naik Banbahadur Thapa says to his seven men, "Charge!" Between these two extremes the orders become considerably more complicated. Who decided Naik Banbahadur should

charge that particular hillock, and made sure no one else was charging it at the same time, from the opposite direction? Who supplied
him with ammunition (made three thousand miles away in Calcutta), in the right quantities and at the right time? Who saw that
he was fed, who cured the bellyache he had yesterday, who put his
pay in his pocket? The staff! Well, no, not actually. The commanders decided what must be achieved; the services actually did the
various jobs; the staff co-ordinated the whole and prepared the
detailed instructions. So, if the chain of command drove the army,
then the staff might be defined as its lubrication. (I felt a little
better. I could see myself as a drop of oil.)

What did I know about the staff? . . . Broadly speaking, all
the problems that an army faces come under three headings. Two
of these headings would still apply if it were not an army but a
collection of civilians, as, say, a city or a province. Those two are
—the problem of people, and the problem of things.

Under "people": People would still have to be paid, policed,
promoted, fired, taken to court, imprisoned, pensioned, adjudged
sick or well, and so on. All this is the responsibility of the branch
of the staff which our army calls G-1. The British called it the
Adjutant General's Branch, or A.

Under "things": Civilians, like soldiers, must have clothes, food,
tools, transport, plumbing, garages. This we call G-4 and the
British the Quartermaster General's Branch, or Q. (They also had
an Ordnance Branch mixed in here, but I'll omit that.)

The third sort of problem, however, arises only because these
men are not civilians. These are the problems to do with fighting
—how to attack that, how to defend this, how many rounds of
ammunition will be required to capture the other, how to know
what the enemy are doing, how to circumvent them. This, everything that arises from the fact that the army's job is war, the
British placed under the General Staff, or G.S., which included
both Operations (what our forces do) and Intelligence (what the
enemy do). The U.S. Army divides it into G-3 (Operations) and
G-2 (Intelligence).

Obviously, the G.S. branch is the most important, and also
must be the prime mover, since it is no use the Q people sending
rations to Rome if the G.S. are attacking Paris. But the other
branches are far more than deferential housekeepers. The G.S.

can plan the most gorgeous battle that ever was, but it will result in an even more gorgeous snafu unless they have made certain that Q can bring up the required ammunition, and that A can fit their columns into the available road space. The three branches must always work in close co-operation, and always as a part of their commander's will, not as a separate entity.

It appeared that the staff officer must have two loyalties. First, to his commander: his function is to help the commander exercise command, no more and no less. Second, to the troops: it is his duty to point out, if he can, how a job can be better or less expensively done, in terms of money, lives, or time.

Amen.

I seemed to know something after all. Whistling nonchalantly, I opened a drawer of my desk, and found that the man who had had the room on the previous course had left behind a specimen of his work. It was a huge square of graph paper, labeled "*Movement Diagram, Appendix K to 4 Ind Inf Div O.O. 36.*" Diagonal bands, in several colors, crossed it in all directions, and lines and lines of fine writing surrounded it. Obviously many people had worked for hours to produce it. I couldn't make head or tail of it. I had never seen such a thing in my life; and it was covered in pungent comments by another hand, all in red ink, which said, "Careless" and "No" and "Didn't you read the order?" and "Not again!" and "Your slovenly planning has now caused seven accidents on this move. Murderer."

Slowly I burned the graph in the grate and went to bed. As Willy had said to me outside Deir-es-Zor, I was still very wet behind the ears, in terms of this new and enlarged world.

Work began. Our main task of the first two weeks was to learn about the War Establishments of every unit and formation an army could possibly dream up. These twenty- and thirty-page pamphlets, each one devoted to a single type of unit, contained the information which was the raw material of staff problems. Most of us already knew how an infantry battalion was organized and armed. But what about a Casualty Clearing Station? How many Advanced Dressing Stations was it equipped to handle, and how many casualties could it hold at one time? We all knew that an armored regiment could move itself in its own vehicles, but could a Graves Registration Unit? If now, how many extra vehicles, and of what type, would it need? What about a Field

Radiological Laboratory, a Mobile Laundry, a Heavy Repair Detachment? . . . Our overwrought brains began to invent units—
what about a Carrier Pigeon Squadron; a Parachute Brothel,
Type A (50-tail); a Map Falsification Section of the Royal Engineers; a Mobile Rationalization Troop of the Royal Propaganda
Corps; a Base Girdle Filling Detachment of the Women's Auxiliary Corps?

There were thousands of different types of units, and those
students who tried to learn the details of each one by heart were
already headed for a nervous breakdown. The only way to survive
was to know where to find the right pamphlet, and to learn your
way about the tables themselves, carefully developing an eye to
spot the parenthetical notes that studded the long list of ranks
and figures, thus:

$$\text{Cooks, Indian Troops, Grade III} \qquad 6 \ (\text{ff})$$

Now you looked up (ff) several pages farther on, and found:

$$(\text{ff}) \qquad 5 \text{ if unit is serving out of India.}$$

The D.S. gave us exercises to test our new learning. We were
to submit the ration return for a force composed as follows.
There followed an Order of Battle of the damned oddest force
I never hope to see collected in one place for any purpose whatever. At the end Dick Bryers had achieved a ration strength of
6709, while my solution was 6710, and the D.S. red ink spread
heavily over the page because I'd missed Note (xz) attached to
a naik of the Indian Disinfestation Section, where it stated clearly
that the naik would remain at advanced base among the first reinforcements and would therefore NOT take the field. "Careless," the D.S. red ink snapped. It was their favorite word.

Then they told us to get our miscellaneous force on the move.
How many vehicles did it have? Back to the War Establishments . . .

Captain Mohammed Usman, known as the Apeman from our
Sandhurst days together, leaned back more indolently in his
chair. He was appallingly ugly, with long swinging arms and
a shambling gait, and the softest, most beautiful voice I have
ever heard in a man. He said, "One thing . . . where is this force
going?"

"What does that matter?" the D.S. asked. "That's not part of
the question."

"I'd like to know all, all the same," Usman said. "Because if this collection of odds and sods is going toward the enemy, I'm damned if I'm going with it."

Grinning and more relaxed, we returned to the problem . . . 746 vehicles, wasn't it? But the force had to take 9 days' rations with it, plus sufficient petrol, oil, and lubricants (or P.O.L.) to have 200 miles' radius of action when it got to its destination, 80 miles away. Count the ration strength again—6709, wasn't it? At 3 lbs. per man per day that comes to 20,127 lbs. per day, 181,143 lbs. for 9 days, or 27 three-ton trucks. Add them to the 746, makes 773. Now the P.O.L. . . . but remember that the trucks carrying rations and P.O.L. will themselves need more P.O.L., and their drivers will need more rations. Approximate figures are no good for the Staff College; they've got to be exact, down to the pound. The British are not going to have another Crimea, when cases of left-footed boots were loaded into ships on top of ammunition that did not fit any gun in the theater.

The column finally works out at 866 vehicles. At normal dispersion, against light air threat, of 40 v.t.m. (vehicles to the mile), that will take . . .

My mind wandered back to a long sandy beach, where small red crabs ran about in thousands on the edge of the curling sea, scuttling sideways into their holes as you approached, their claws held up in a perfect offensive-defensive attitude; and the long, long, lovely and naked legs stretched out beside me in the sand, the hand laid affectionately in mine, the soft American voice, a little sleepy in the hot, deserted afternoon: "You were here as a little boy? On this same beach? How lovely." That was Karachi, during the three weeks I waited there before the course began. She was a wonderful girl and I knew she would marry me if I asked her. A schoolteacher. Well, our Wilfrid Oldham always did say that the 4th Gurkhas married schoolteachers or barmaids. But the truth was that she wasn't a girl; she was eleven years older than I. Could it work? Was it not really as hopeless as Sonya? All the same, what a wife she'd make, what a gentle, loving personality she . . .

"If you'd care to join us now—" the D.S.'s voice was solicitous—"we'll go on to the next problem."

I sat up with a start, looking alert. But it wasn't me. At the end of the table Captain Tim Bromilow of Hodson's Horse was fast asleep in his chair. The D.S. repeated his invitation, louder. Tim awoke and said smartly, "I agree with Bryers."

There were numerous syndicate discussions. In the previous two or three days we had read a many-paged document, with diagrams, prepared by the D.S. and mimeographed on white paper, setting out the theory and practice of organizing the Lines of Communication in an overseas theater of war. Now we would discuss it in our syndicates, each composed of seven or eight students under a D.S.

Our D.S. turned to Bulgy Leach, a rotund artillery captain. "Leach, what's the underlying principle?"

Bulgy said, "No one's got to look back over his shoulder. The chap in contact with the enemy mustn't have to go back and get *anything*, it's all got to be brought forward and put ready beside him. But I can tell you that in Eritrea sometimes . . ." By the time he had finished, the D.S. didn't have to point to another speaker, for Dick Bryers and I both had something to say in contradiction of Bulgy, and of each other. The D.S. sat back, occasionally throwing in a question to control the flow of speculation and comment. We had come from every corner of the empire, and between us had taken part in almost every battle so far fought during the war. We held opinions, each necessarily based on our own experience. The D.S. had to see that we did not try to impose a general solution from a particular knowledge, and that the principles of the subject were brought out and thoroughly understood.

"Bromilow, what do you think?" the D.S. said.

Tim said, "I agree with Masters." His eyelids drooped and he glanced at his watch. With an effort he finished his statement. "Masters worked on an L. of C., didn't he?"

The D.S. sighed wearily and turned to me. "Even our Sleeping Beauties are sometimes wiser than the wise men. We've covered the theory pretty well and I think it would be a good idea if we heard something about what it's actually like in a Lines of Communication Headquarters. Tell us."

After a brief pause to collect my thoughts, I began.

The day I arrived at Basra, in the humble capacity of General Staff Officer Grade 3, I asked my immediate boss, Major Joe

Trotter, what the general's name was. "Squeaky George," he said absently. "Come on, and I'll introduce you." In his office Squeaky George, his back to us, wearing an old fur coat of his wife's, was examining a huge map of the Basra docks. After giving me a keen look and muttering, "Plenty of work" (he did have a high squeaky voice), he turned to Joe, said, "Come on," and dashed out to inspect something. Alone, I went to the General Staff office and began to find out what units we had in the area and what they were doing. Problems started descending at once, of a kind I'd never had to face before. For example:

Here is a message from Q Branch, informing the General Staff that three ships have arrived simultaneously from India, and asking in what order they are to be unloaded. They attach manifests of the three ships. I read the manifests. The first ship contains forty Bren-gun carriers, and I know that every battalion in the country is howling for them. This must be the first. But wait— the next contains a heavy A.A. battery, which is needed right here in Basra, for we are within reach of long-range German bombers from several spots. And the third ship contains a five-hundred-bed base hospital. I know that two hundred men are being held forward of Baghdad in Casualty Clearing Stations, waiting for this hospital. What on earth is the right answer here? No one tells me. I make a decision and await execution. No one protests. Next.

This is more serious. Some dastard fired five shots at a supply convoy yesterday, at map reference 109456, Sheet A 58, quarter-inch to the mile. Find the map. Find the spot. Seventy miles up the road to Baghdad, out in the desert . . . Should we provide escorts to every convoy? Out of the question. We don't have the men. Ah, what about that armored car regiment due for Baghdad? I might order it to carry out a sweep of the area on its way north? Have to send some police with them, to interpret and arrest if need be. But first I must pass the message to my opposite number in Intelligence for any information he has or can get about Arab bands in the area. When he replies, draft an order. This one will have to go through Joe and be approved by the general. And it is urgent, because the armored cars are moving tomorrow evening. Next.

A scrawl from Squeaky George. "GS—Civ pol anxious re Maqil.

Hotbed R.A. adherents. Str tps available area IS," *and his initials.*
Translation first: "To the General Staff: The civil police are
anxious about Maqil (a section of Basra), which is a hotbed of
Rashid Ali adherents. The troops available for internal security
in that section are to be strengthened." I experience utter gloom.
There are no troops available. . . . But what about that antiair-
craft battery which we decided to unload in the second ship,
starting in three days' time? Someone decided long ago that, when
that battery came, at least two guns were to be sited right there,
on the northern edge of Maqil. That's about fifty men. All men
not actually guarding the guns can be organized into riot squads,
because it is very unlikely that Rashid Ali's pals will be milling
about the streets during an air raid. Draft a reply accordingly,
attach to the file with a marked map, take to Joe's desk. . . .

I developed a facility in drafting orders, answers, and questions.
I also developed a permanent, dull, throbbing headache, known
as Staff Migraine. My shoulders stooped and I cowered, where
once I had carried myself like a man. And yet—there was a power
complex. Sitting at the center of affairs, or so it seemed, I caught
myself thinking that a few lines from me and twenty thousand
men would have to get up at five in the morning to do physical
training. What a picture! The power of a staff officer dizzied me;
and then I thought of Naru, my orderly, now back with a rifle
company, somewhere in the Western Desert. If he were in this
Area, he would have to get up at five, perhaps when he had just
come off sentry. So I tried consciously to think of Naru, and the
effect on him of whatever I did, and reflected again that Bill
Slim was a great man.

Why did I cower, then? Well, imagine this youngish captain,
writing away at his desk, wondering whether the general will
notice that the new air-raid trenches around headquarters aren't
ready yet. (No men. No excuse.) The door opens and a lieutenant
colonel of the Royal Indian Army Service Corps storms in. Joe
Trotter is out with the general. The G.3 (Intelligence) is drink-
ing tea with the police lieutenant, but not here. I am the General
Staff, all of it.

The colonel slaps a large folio of paper down on the table.
"How the hell can my men issue ninety tons of rations per day
and spend six hours on the rifle range—one getting there, one get-

*ting back, and four hours' shooting?" The words are not out of
his mouth when another Service Corps colonel joins him, this
one waving the appendix to the same folio, wherein his transport company is ordered to provide trucks on such and such days
to take men to and from the rifle range, which is out in the desert
beyond Shaiba. The two colonels shout in chorus, "Do you bloody
Staff twerps, sitting on your backsides in the office, realize. . . ?"*

*Mustn't lose my nerve. They are Service Corps, I am the
General Staff. Furthermore, I am an infantryman, and I've been
into battle. But I am a Staff officer. Mustn't annoy them. Drop
of oil, that's me. Squeaky George has approved these orders. His
actual words were, "They'll all yell bloody murder. I don't care
a damn. Every man in this Area will be proficient in firing his
weapon, digging trenches, and throwing grenades. And be physically fit to march fifteen miles, under load, in any weather. This
is a theater of war, damn it."*

*It would not be tactful to pass this to the colonels in exactly
the way it was given to me. Instead I must soothe them. Give a
little here, take a little somewhere else. The threat of the general
is always behind me. I know it, and they know it, but I must not
use that threat except in real emergencies. I am a drop of oil.
I am a drop of oil. . . .*

*The colonels are dealt with. It turned out that we had picked
the worst possible time of day for the shooting practice. I changed
the times and all was well.*

*My temporarily straightened shoulders return to their defensive
hunch. A red-faced major is at the door. More complaints.*

*Next, the clerk tells me that two officers from an artillery regi-
ment staging through Basra want to see me about the area allotted for their camp. They look very purposeful and one of them,
a captain like myself, is enormous. He stares at me with brows
bent. I push back my chair. I've had enough. If he feels like that
about it, he can bloody well sit in this bloody chair and I'll take
command of his bloody battery and we'll see who makes the bigger balls-up.*

*The big captain leans forward. "You're Jack Masters, aren't
you?"*

I purse my lips. "I think so," I answer warily.

He said, "I was at Wellington with you, in the Orange. You beat me once, for eating on Turf."

I look at him more closely. He is simpering. I stand up slowly, feeling my stature increase almost audibly. "Oh, yes," I say, "though I don't think I remember you."

"Oh, you wouldn't," he says quickly.

I shrug. "Now, about this camp area. What's the trouble? I'm sure we can fix it."

"Oh, yes," the captain breathes reverently; and we do.

That was the turning point. I began to enjoy the work, and when Joe left I was made G.2 in his place. (The General Staff grades were 3rd (captain), 2nd (major) and 1st (lieutenant colonel), abbreviated as G.3, G.2, and G.1, respectively; above that the ranks were self-evident, e.g., brigadier, General Staff). When my occasions took me to the area where we had sited our machine guns just after our first arrival, a traffic jam developed while the madam and half a dozen strumpets hurried out of the brothel to greet me, carrying a pot of tea and crying that all the girls remembered me, and when was I coming back to give them again so much pleasure. . . .

"You seem to have had an interesting time," the D.S. said drily. "A valuable experience, too. Wake up, Bromilow. You're going to stand me a sherry."

We began to know each other, not merely as names and faces, pet jokes and capacities for whisky, but as quick or slow workers, accurate or careless, plodding or imaginative. Syndicates changed occasionally, and for every exercise the D.S. allotted us different jobs, to widen our experience and to enable them to judge how we measured up to the different responsibilities; but we always did each exercise collectively as a syndicate and the leader for that exercise had to get his fellows to agree on a solution (with no power of command to force them to), see that they did their work (with no power to punish them if they didn't), and assume responsibility for all that they produced, whether or not he had had time to check it himself. At the same time he remembered, if he was wise, that the course was going to last five months, the war longer still, and his life in the army, he hoped, a good deal longer than that. It was not a good idea, on any grounds, to

threaten and browbeat your contemporaries in the hope of im-
proving your own marks. It was a still worse idea to polish the
D.S.'s apples, or go bum-sucking, as the English call it in their
homely Chaucerian way. The D.S. were extraordinarily acute at
seeing through such fakers, and the students were even better.

"Arsehole Bill," Usman drawled over a predinner drink—refer-
ring to an industrious apple-polisher—"is going to get a Second
Grade job, and that'll finish him." Second Grade was the highest
we could hope for on first appointment; and Usman turned out
to be precisely right, for it was Arsehole Bill's wife who sat up
till three and four every morning, retyping and polishing his syndicate's work; the man himself didn't have it.

Our two alcoholics, one British and one Indian, sat through
the increasing pandemonium in a genial haze. Bingo Fink, a
Wodehousian character who had not wanted to come on the
course in the first place, and had no intention of becoming a
general, attended a few lectures wearing Burmese dress instead
of uniform, and kept asking the D.S. to help him take more interest in the beastly war.

Quetta began to have its tangential influence. A bachelor student
fell in love with a married student's wife and moved into the
married household, where they could thrash out their problems
in privacy. Another, awaiting a divorce, brought up the girl he
was going to marry, and somehow managed to live with her. A
dozen other affairs, of varying legality, began to flourish. Scores
of the ladies of Quetta had joined the WAC (I)—Women's
Auxiliary Corps, India—as privates, corporals, and sergeants, mainly
to be employed as typists and clerks in the several headquarters,
and, if we went downtown during the day, we would be embarrassed to receive smart salutes from our dancing partners of
the previous evening, then gorgeous in silk and tulle, now wearing
rather unattractive khaki drill. In their short, tight skirts—since
the WAC high command refused to allow them to wear trousers—
the ladies had to bicycle miles to work, before sunup, against the
Khojak wind. At a cocktail party one red-faced dame, colonel's
wife, huntin' type, and WAC corporal, bellowed confidentially
to me, "It's bloody awful! First thing I do when I reach the
office is go to the lav and thaw the icicles off it."

I myself, in pursuance of my policy of nonchalance, went regularly to the club. Every Saturday and Wednesday evening, the War Establishments thrown into the shelves, the fountain pen filled and the pencils sharpened against the morrow, I climbed on my bicycle, pedaled it out onto the road, turned left, and hoped there would be no traffic to interrupt the three-mile freewheel.

Left turn, and there I was. The first week I saw no other member of the Staff College, neither D.S. nor student. Then gradually they began to make an appearance until, at the end of a month nearly everyone was there on Saturdays, and a considerable number on Wednesdays.

Nonchalant, that was the word for me. After all, I had been here in 1940–41, and several ladies I had known well then were still here. I danced, I played, I bicycled slowly back up the long hill to the Staff College at all hours of the morning, the wide avenues deserted, the lamps falling painfully back and winter fading, in the dulled edge of the Khojak wind, in the blossoms on the trees, in the scent of spring itself in the newly watered gardens.

Nonchalant; in control of my environment; mastering the work of the course—even the movement graphs and how to make them I now knew, and the red ink on my work often expressed a grudging admiration; looking forward to a good posting at the end of it all; easy among old friends, making new ones; twenty-seven and a half years old.

Every few dances, each club night, they had a Paul Jones. The women formed a circle in the center, the men outside. The band played a march and the two circles rotated in contrary directions. The music stopped and each gentleman danced with the lady then opposite him. Three minutes—thank you—reform the circles —begin again. I usually joined in the Paul Jones; searching, I suppose, but not aware of it; in any case, finding nothing, politely taking what came.

She was in one of those Paul Joneses. She had noticed the thin captain with the big nose and the black badges of a Gurkha Rifle Regiment. She never used to join the Paul Jones, but she did that night, willing the music to stop when she was opposite him, but it never did.

And there was a friend who kept telling her about someone

*called Jack Masters. She really ought to meet him. She and he
would have so much in common. The friend was so enthusiastic
about the fellow that she knew she would hate his guts. But if
the friend insisted, well, why didn't he ask this Jack Masters to
his birthday party, to which she was already invited?*

Basil Knott rang me on the telephone. He was an engineer
who had been in Loralai with us in 1939–40, of saturnine appearance, interested in classical music, a keen and flexible mind, a
good friend. "Come to my birthday party. Next Saturday at the
club. Dinner first, then the dance. Only half a dozen others."
I had no commitment and I liked Basil very much. "Yes.
Thanks."

I strolled nonchalantly into the Snake Pit—the club sitting
room—that Saturday evening and looked round. I saw Basil and
his party around a table on the right, near the fireplace, and
moved forward. One of the women in the party was looking at
me with an expression of utter astonishment. She was about
five feet five inches, a good figure, with wonderful green-brown
eyes, classically set. She was wearing a flowered silk dress in a
pattern of dark red roses on a dark green background. Her hair
was a bit of a mess. She managed to control her surprise, but
by then we were looking straight at each other, and it had
happened.

8 Out of the night, out of nowhere, the lightning's hour was upon us. Just how much hurt it would cause her or me I could not guess. She wore a wedding ring.

At the Staff College we were working more and more in the open, traveling miles into the surrounding country and there trying to solve, on the ground, problems of attack, defense, approach, and withdrawal. It rained on us, it hailed, the wind blew away our maps and papers, the sun scorched us, still our groups dotted the shadeless desert or huddled together on the barren ridges. We sited bases and headquarters and minefields. We Appreciated the Situation (Object, Factors, Courses open to the enemy, Courses open to us, Plan); we issued orders (Information, Intention, Method, Administration, Intercommunication, Acknowledge). The D.S. gave us White Papers to read, guided us with surreptitious help from their private Green Papers, and, when each exercise was over, informed us of the Correct Answer, on Pink Paper. We usually disagreed with the Pink Paper, sometimes violently, and sometimes in such concert that we could have been charged with mutiny; but the D.S. wearily explained that really there was never any single Correct Answer in war. This answer was as good as their collective brains and experience had been able to think up, and anyway we'd got to take it, otherwise we'd have no common ground from which to proceed to the next question. Every two or three days would find an officer

*thankfully stuffing his syndicate's answer—sometimes fifty pages
of typing and graphs—into the D.S. pigeonhole; and another
anxiously pulling out the one we'd done a few days earlier, now
poxed with red ink.*

*Some of the exercises, such as the Attack Series, lasted a week.
It began with the usual general study of the subject, and continued with discussion. Then the exercises came, one after another, setting a continuous series of problems as our imaginary
force advanced, made contact, reconnoitered, attacked, consoli-
dated, was counterattacked, broke through, and pursued the enemy. We crawled up gullies, we stared through our binoculars, we
marked maps, estimated casualties, organized transport, chose ration points, salvaged tanks, buried the dead, treated the wounded.
All those peculiar units which had bothered us so much at the
beginning of the course were becoming an orchestra under our
hands.*

*Arsehole Bill was leading the syndicate the last day of that
series, and had to give out verbal orders. He glared at us as though
expecting us to fall on our knees. He bellowed his orders in a
voice that would certainly have been heard by the enemy if they
had been where the exercise said they were. The Apeman beside
me kept putting his little finger in his ear to clean out imaginary
wax, and wincing whenever the voice rose above its usual bellow.*

*Maitland France muttered, "In the Guards, they just give orders
in a normal voice. Nothing more is necessary, between gentlemen.
This fellow's proper niche is corporal major."*

*"Any questions?" Arsehole Bill finished, in the usual formula.
Bulgy Leach, ten feet from him, bawled at the top of his voice,
"Yes. Why are you shouting?"*

*The Defense Series began. We drove out to Chaman, for the
earlier problems of this series were based on the defenses that had
actually been built against the coming of the Germans. It had
rained the day before, and on the way out we passed through a
wide, high valley four or five miles long. The rain had turned it
into a flaming yellow sea of goldenrod. We got there and debussed.
Situation I . . . Problem I. Solutions here in one and a half
hours, that is, at . . . 1100 hours. Any questions? That's all,
gentlemen.*

I went for a walk, alone, on the mountain Chiltan. Climbing

steadily up the long slope, the rock hard under my nailed boots, the sweat pouring down my face and making my gray shirt heavy and black as I forced myself on, faster and faster. The valley spread out below me, the distant peaks rose above the confining walls, but I saw nothing but the sharp stones and the crushed herbs.

Barbara had not leaped out of a happy marriage at the sight of me but, rather, acknowledged that her marriage, in its solemn meaning, had ceased to exist; and she told me that her husband agreed. She was unhappy and bitter. At this time, walking on Chiltan, and for long afterward, I held strongly partisan feelings about her situation, as I was bound to do. I am a great deal older now. I have seen the failure of too many marriages, and warmed my hands before a few glowing successes, and in every case have thought and examined and wondered, and never found any logic, for marriage is as mysterious as life or fire. I know only that there is no objective existence to it. It cannot be studied from the outside and conclusions drawn, for it lives only inside itself, and what is presented to the observer or the listener bears only the relationship of a distorted shadow to the reality inside. There is no right and no wrong; there is no truth and no falsehood, neither wronged husband nor betrayed wife. There is only marriage, which is a mystical union, and when the partners to it cease to know that they are one flesh, when the mystical sense goes, there is no marriage. There is instead a practical problem, with a hundred factors pressing on the mind and the emotions. What to do? To pretend, to fight? To stay, to go? To deaden the senses or quicken them? To think of the children, who must be loved, or think of the mystery, which must be refound, without which there is no love? To die, to live?

All this will be a part of the consciousness of some of my readers, to others will be strange, not to be understood, perhaps sinful. In any case, there is no more explaining to be done. Nor can I say more about love for here, too, you know what you know. We loved, and there's an end.

Her husband was not away at the war, but there in Quetta with her. She had two young children. I had met them too, and loved them, and she was their mother, and there was nothing unnatural about her. The Court of St. James's, slowly reacting to

Wally Simpson, had recently announced that officers who became involved in divorce would be ordered to show cause why they should not be called upon to resign their commissions. No man is complete without a pride in his job, his craft, his art. Soldiering was all to me. I had no other training, skill, or aptitude, as far as I knew. Every day the horizon was broadening and greater vistas becoming apparent to my view. Now in the vivid glare of this sudden lightning I saw for the first time a different kind of happiness, which I had never known, not even what it would be like, knowing only that I needed it. With it, inseparable from it, I saw fretful and frustrated years in some trade or profession foreign to my nature. Sandhurst gave no college degree, and every passing day was equipping me with a more specialized skill in the one role that I would not be permitted to take—the command of armies.

And love was not enough, particularly not this sudden overwhelming kind. What did we really know of each other? What sort of future could be based solely on an instant certainty? (Yet I knew that it could be.) But it must be shown, proved to the hilt, that for us, for everyone concerned, there was no other solution. The Staff College course was hardly halfway through yet. There would be time, to see more of her, to show her what kind of a man I was, to find out what lay behind her green eyes.

I reached a high ridge—not the crest, it was too far—and at once began the long descent. I felt better. It was impossible not to know that the Staff College approved of me. The higher they climb, the harder they fall, I reflected with a certain grim amusement. I appeared to be climbing fast and far.

We progressed to War Games. The D.S. divided the student body into two sides, one representing Us and the other the Enemy. They gave each side a separate set of rooms, the controlling staff another, and laid yards and yards of telephone wire so that the umpires could tell each side whatever they would in reality have experienced from actions taken by the other side. War Games were always souped up far beyond anything that could happen in real life, because there were no live troops to move and because our precious time must not be wasted. A movement that would actually take an hour was adjudged finished in ten minutes—so we, preparing orders to be given upon the move's completion, had only ten minutes instead of sixty to do it.

More than anything else the War Games reproduced the pressures of battle. Telephones rang and radio sets buzzed all the time, panting messengers dashed in with cipher messages that couldn't be deciphered (I remembered Raqqa and kept very calm). . . . Here is a report of heavy shelling on Point X. What can that mean? Is it a preliminary to an enemy attack on that sector? But, damn it, we sent strong patrols out two miles ahead of our line there, only two hours ago, and they (the D.S.) reported no enemy contacted. . . . Another signal: Tanks and infantry are advancing toward Point Y, from the EAST repeat EAST. That's impossible! No it isn't. It's our own 254 Brigade, moving into position for the counterattack due to start in twenty minutes.

The D.S. taps Dick Bryers, our "general," on the shoulder and informs him with a grin that he's dead. Dick, who is in the middle of giving me some instructions, groans convincingly and heads for the mess, licking his lips. I'm the G.2 (Ops.)—got to tell Bogey Sen to come in at once to take temporary command of the division, find the G.1, inform Corps. . . . "But what killed my good general?" I ask the D.S.

"Sniping, from Hill 45," he says. "It's about time you thought of asking that."

Quite: though I would have known in real life, since Dick practically died in my arms. Sniping from Hill 45, at Divisional H.Q., eh? They've sent a patrol through to harass us. Mustn't be harassed. Tell the G.3 to warn the rest of Headquarters. Tell Jimmy to clear the hill at once, with tanks, and this time bloody well see that he keeps it clear. . . .

Sunday evenings, a dozen men and women gathered in my room. They sat on the floor, beer mugs in hand, and even the evenings of jazz passed in pleasant somnolence. Beethoven nights brought a real calm to settle upon us from the silent mountains, and heads sank quietly, and eyes closed, and men and women touched hands while the music poured out, distorted but tremendous, from my old wind-up phonograph, which had come out to India with me in 1934, as new as I, and been hauled across America and round the world with me, and seen a hundred bivouacs, a dozen battles.

After midnight, and time to end. We rose painfully, cramped from long hours in one position, and sighed and shook ourselves like dogs coming out of water. Then, as they tossed back the last of the beer: "What time's the bumf for Exercise Parrot going to be in our lockers tomorrow, Jack?" One week ended, another beginning.

The Vice Queen came once to a Beethoven night, uninvited, but she had heard about them from somewhere, and afterward issued me an outrageously unsubtle invitation before pouring herself out of the door. Paddy Massey put his monocle in his eye, helped Leigh to her feet, and looked at me. "Don't go, Jack," he said. "McNie's still searching for the last chap." Major McNie was the gynecological specialist.

Usually, when Barbara came, someone else had brought her in his car, but I always took her home on my bicycle, she sitting on the cross bar in the way my brother Alex used to sit years before, when, as boys, we bicycled across Wiltshire and Dorsetshire. It was easy going downhill, for her extra weight made us roll ever faster down the long slopes, the fresh night wind blowing her hair all over my face; but uphill, working for two instead of one, always anxious lest she fall and hurt herself, made hard, straining work.

In the desert my battalion, and the rest of the brigade, vanished on the night of June 6, in the Battle of the Cauldron, overwhelmed by German panzers. Dutt won a Military Cross for gallantry. Willy, walking calmly up and down our lines with the tanks and machine guns firing at him, was miraculously unhurt, and taken prisoner. So was Naru. So was Roger Werner.

My parents telegraphed me from England that my brother Alex had been reported missing in the first battles in Malaya.

Here in India my favorite aunt, my mother's favorite sister, died of a broken heart just over a year after her daughter Marjorie had been killed in the Café de Paris. I began to wish the course would end. It was time I got back into battle.

But we were already going as fast as we could. We embarked on the most complex of all studies, Combined Operations, and in its most complex form, that is, landing a large force on a hostile shore a considerable distance from the home base. In the syndicate rooms we worked out manifests and load tables. We put eighteen thousand men, with their guns and tanks and trucks, into twelve ships for a long sea voyage, all the loads in the right place, in the right order. We made out assault landing tables, operation orders, administrative instructions, tide and current tables, and "going" maps of the interior. We arranged covering fire with the Navy and strategic and tactical support with the Air Force. We made detailed plans to feed the civil populace, control traffic, collect refugees, repair port installations, take over rail-roads, issue money, and—by far the worst—we arranged com-munications.

For this the whole course and all the D.S. gathered in the cen-tral model room. We sat all around in banked rows, the floor space occupied by a great cloth model showing the enemy shore which we were assaulting, a segment of sea with ship models arranged on it, and model aircraft hanging from the ceiling. The various syndicates, one by one, began to string up colored rib-bons, each representing one channel of communication—ship to ship, ship to shore, ship to aircraft, ship to base, aircraft to base, one beach to another, between forward and rear parties, between beach and aircraft. It required so many channels that we almost ran out of the allotted frequencies. The colored ribbons multi-plied until . . . it defies description.

We staggered out into the sunlight, heads swimming and dull pains at the base of the medulla oblongata. Why hadn't we taken up some simple study, like, say multidimensional geometry?

"We did it, though," I said exultantly to Paddy Massey. "What'll you have?"

"I am a man of simple tastes," he said. "The best is good enough for me. A Bristol Cream . . . Yes, we did it."

We, the students of the 5th War Course, had done it. The D.S. had taught us, but we'd done it. Therefore we could do it in real life. Many of us did, two years later, for it was in these classrooms and their equivalents in England and America, that D-day was made possible.

The Staff College Ball came. Barbara and I danced together and drank champagne together under the heavy shadows sur-rounding us, for we were both nearly frantic with love, and op-pressed by the decisions that we must make, sooner or later. About one o'clock in the morning several of us left the lights and the awnings set up on the lawn and walked together up the Hanna road. Without warning she caught my hand in one of hers, lifted her heavy skirt with the other, and began to run, running up the dusty road in her high heels. The others ran with us, all suddenly laughing and shouting to each other, what a wonderful thing, to run under the moon shadow of Murdar; but soon we left them all behind and ran on alone together until we heard nothing in the valley but the sound of our own breathing.

The day of our reports came. Joe Lentaigne of my regiment had told me all about this five years before, when he returned from the Camberley Staff College. "You go into the Commandant's office," he said, his eyes gleaming and his Irish grin predatory, "and you can't see a thing. It's pitch-black in there, the curtains drawn. Pitch-black! Except a bright light in the far corner, shining straight down onto something white, and square, set out on a high lectern with a green cloth on it. That's your report. A voice speaks from the gloom, and you start a bloody mile, 'Lentaigne, read your report,' it says. It's Gort, the Commandant, sitting behind his desk right beside you, but you haven't seen him in the dark. You stumble across the carpet, your legs trembling so that you have to hold onto the lectern to support yourself."

It was something like that, too. The drawn curtains were a typical Lentaigne curlicue, and I could see our Commandant, Geoff Evans, quite clearly as I went in; but there was the high desk, and a square of white paper on it. Brigadier Evans said, "There's your report, Masters. Read it." I crept across, steadied myself, and began to read.

"This officer has the manners of an organ grinder and the morals of his monkey. I am unable to report on his work as he has done none. . . ."

No, that was a famous report of legend, which had been running through my brain as I came in. I opened my eyes and began again.

"This officer . . ."

I read on with cautious amazement. Initiative . . . drive . . . ability to work with others . . . The military virtues lay like confetti all over the page. It was by far the best report I had ever had, and suddenly I half-smiled, thinking, "The higher they climb . . ."

I straightened. "Sign it," Geoff said. I did so. "Sit down," he said. I sat down in the chair opposite his desk.

"That's your official report," he said. "That's what we think of you, officially. There are three other points, though. They're not the kind of thing one puts in a Staff College report, because that's going to affect you for the rest of your service, while these are not basic matters, we hope, but can be put right by you yourself, if you've got the guts and the ability to profit by your own mistakes. First, you don't take enough trouble over your dress. *I* don't care a damn, but there are plenty of people who do. Whether they're right or wrong you're giving yourself an unnecessary handicap if you don't take the trouble to dress neatly and correctly at all times. Second, you don't give enough attention to the minutiae of staff duties. The right abbreviations, the right forms, are not just subjects for satire, as you sometimes seem to think. They're meant to take all possible strain out of understanding what the message or order means, by dropping tumblers into the mind of the man who's reading it. If you use a different form, he's got to think about sorting out your meaning. That's all right for a novel, but not for a military operation order, to be read by an exhausted man in a hole in the ground. Thirdly, you are an extremely opinionated young man. Your contemporaries don't mind, for the reasons given in that report. Also, because they can argue with you and you can argue back, and you have a perfect right to press your opinions against theirs. Your seniors do mind, because they cannot get down and argue with you as man to man, at least not in public, and because they are sometimes talking from experience, something felt and grown into their military knowledge, rather than from the actual facts or some apparently logical theory. . . ." He stood up, smiling. "You seem to have enjoyed yourself here, Masters."

I thought a moment, and said, "I don't believe I've ever enjoyed anything more."

He said, "Good luck," and put out his hand.

Maitland France was waiting outside. "How did it go?" he muttered, as he straightened his faultless tie and flicked a spot off his spotless tunic. "All right," I said. Maitland was one man they'd never reprimand for careless dress. I went to my quarter, put on the *Eroica*, and stretched my legs.

Dress? Well, I'd do my best, but in spite of my admiration for Geoff, I couldn't regard the subject as of the first importance. A slighting view of staff duties? Fair enough, though it would be sad never to be able to laugh at all those correct forms again. Opinionated? Hum. Look it up in the dictionary. "Of stubborn adherence to one's own opinions." Hum. Or, as one might say if one agreed with those opinions, "determined, tenacious"—why, those very adjectives had been floating round in the report. There was something important here. Was it not true that every quality had certain defects built into it? Determination—opinionatedness, obstinacy. Drive—insensitivity. Love—possessiveness.

To some extent, perhaps, but not wholly, not universally. I had met men who were firm without being dictatorial, sympathetic without being mawkish. I would try to follow their example.

We received our postings. Bingo Fink, who had an intimate knowledge of Burma, where the war now raged, they sent to the Middle East. A few other square pegs were faithfully fitted into round holes. Several of us were posted to the 7th Indian Infantry Division, then training in northern India. My new job was Brigade Major of the 114th Indian Infantry Brigade in that division.

I said good-by to Barbara, or au revoir. Neither of us knew which. Her mind was made up, but she must show nothing, expect nothing. She had met a man and fallen in love. He was going away. The children remained, the technical fact of marriage remained. The mountains remained; nothing had been settled; God had not spoken out of a cloud, and she was a woman and a mother.

For my part, I knew that I must go away, saying no more than had been said already. When we are unhappy we do not see even facts straight, let alone the shifting evanescent emotions. In a few weeks she might know that the sheer marvel of our hours, of our instant knowledge and affection and passion, had been no more than the tinsel of an affair; or, at the most, a man feeling pity for her, and thankful to go free.

She came to the station to see me off, and stood where Maitland France had stood, to watch the train pull out. The wheels clacked faster over the rail joints. I lay on the berth, staring at the ceiling, seeing nothing but her face, until at last I fell asleep.

9 Two days later, dozing on sacks of rice in the back of a ration truck, I arrived at 114 Brigade's camp at Bakarial at 2 A.M. The next morning, early, I took a quick look around before reporting to the brigadier. Hundreds of brown-dyed tents spread over low hills dotted with pine trees. Higher ridges to the north hid the peaks of the great mountains—we were due south of Nanga Parbat, and less than eighty miles from it—but the morning air had a Himalayan freshness, and my new job thrilled me and I ate a large breakfast.

Afterward, in my tent, I found my orderly waiting. Since they knew I was a Gurkha they had given me a soldier from the one Gurkha battalion in the brigade, the 4/5th—a thin young man, Rifleman Daljit Thapa. He was smart and alert, and carried himself well, and the sight of his Mongolian face made me want to embrace him. I had been too long away from him and his peerless like. Later, I found him shortening the chin strap of my broad-brimmed Gurkha hat. I took it from him, pointed to the huge black metal roman IV on the left side, and said in Gurkhali, "I am only a humble black man from the 4th Gurkhas, where we wear our chin straps on the point of the chin, not, like you gentlemen of the Royal, under the lower lip. Leave it alone! And let me see these boots of mine *really* clean—not 5th Gurkha clean, but 4th Gurkha clean, for I am about to report to the brigadier-sahib. Do you understand, O one pubic hair?"

Daljit grinned in delight, then quickly remembered that I was a stranger here. I might have learned that idiomatic Gurkhali by a trick, and not really be an officer of the Gurkha Brigade at all. His face resumed its alert, unsmiling passivity.

I dressed carefully, determined to make a good impression. Brigadiers are not called "general" in the British service because, technically, they do not rate the grade. A general is so called because he is in "general command" of troops, that is, he commands troops of all arms and services; the smallest formation which permanently embodies all arms is the division, commanded by a major general. Below that the brigades (or U.S. regiments) are of infantry only, of artillery only, etc.; hence their commander is a brigadier of infantry, of artillery—not a brigadier general.

But never mind whether brigadiers were or were not generals. For some time to come they would loom large in my life, and they came in all shapes and sizes. What would this one be like? There were brigadiers who could not see the trees for the wood. There were brigadiers who could not see the wood for the trees, who allowed no detail to escape them, provided it was insignificant enough. Such as a famous brigadier of cavalry, who liked to snoop. One day, a squadron sergeant major of the British cavalry regiment in his brigade, seeing him on the prowl in the regimental lines, carried out the normal drill for unexpected visits by senior commanders; that is, he sent a man running by back ways to warn his colonel, and himself shadowed the brigadier at a distance. The brigadier entered a stable and began peering under the horses' hoofs and tails. At length he opened a feed bin and tasted a piece of grain. The stable sentry came up and heard him mumbling, "Very poor." He tasted another piece. "Very bad. Burned out. Dried. Poisonous!" Here the stable sentry intervened with the mournful politeness of the old regular. "I wouldn't eat any more of that stuff if I was you, sir. That's stable sweepings, and them black bits is rat shit."

When properly dressed I went to the office—a collection of large tents—and reported myself. Brigadier Michael Rookherst Roberts, late 10th Gurkha Rifles, was friendly without being effusive. He shook my hand, said a few words, and the interview was over. Well, he couldn't afford to unbutton until he knew whether I'd measure up to the job.

After three hectic days of handing over accounts, files, funds, books, secret documents, ciphers, confidential papers, arms, ammunition, keys, all of which had to be checked and signed for, my predecessor went his way. He was a charming Indian of great diplomatic gifts and a splendidly Edwardian manner of living. We had to indent for a whole railroad boxcar to carry away his kit to his new post—that is, of course, merely the bare necessities he had with him in this rough camp. His large car drove away down the dusty road and I heaved a sigh mixed of relief, anticipation, and anxiety.

Then I sent my shirts to the darzee, and he brought them back himself, the three stars removed from each shoulder and replaced by a single, black silhouetted crown. Having given the darzee the customary tip I reflected whether I should go to the office first, or visit the 4/5th Gurkhas. The latter, I decided. Might as well get it over with. Besides, it would be fun to see whether their promotion customs were the same as in my own regiment. I went down to their lines, and passed their Quarterguard. Yesterday the two sentries would have saluted me by shouldering arms and tapping the rifle sling. Tomorrow they would salute me, since I was now a field officer, by presenting arms. Today, if I knew Gurkhas, they would not salute me at all.

They stood there like wooden dummies, staring straight ahead, not seeing me. I called the guard commander and blasted him to Basra and back for inefficiency, idleness, insubordination, and mutiny. I demanded the guard book, seized a pencil, and wrote. The entire guard stood around me at rigid attention. When I had written, I tore out the sheet and handed it to the guard commander. I snapped, "Show that to your . . . canteen naik." It was an order for one tot of rum for each member of the guard. The guard commander saluted, the sentries presented arms, they all burst out in wide grins.

I was a major. I was the Brigade Major. It was a Second Grade appointment on the General Staff, the best of all of them. Corps and Army swarmed with G.2s, who licked stamps and seldom came closer than twenty miles to a living, breathing soldier. Division owned two G.2s, but they had a G.1 over them. At brigade the G.2 was called the brigade major, and he was in a humble way the chief of staff. Besides being responsible for all General Staff matters he commanded Brigade Headquarters, as such, and was thus also responsible for the training, discipline, and administration of everything and everyone in it (except the brigadier!). The only other staff officer, the staff captain, was responsible for A and Q matters.

Being formally invested with the job, I turned my attention to the real core of my work—the brigadier. Michael Roberts was about forty-eight then, and I had met him once, three years earlier, when I had taken his beautiful young daughter Valentine out to a dance in Quetta. I thanked heaven that I had behaved like a gentleman on that occasion. Now I learned that the brigadier was inordinately fit, that he had a quick brain, and that he knew his own mind. So far, so good, for the life of a staff officer whose commander does not know, and will not decide what to do, is hell on earth.

But after a week or two it became clear that Michael Roberts, in addition to knowing his own job, also knew mine. There is nothing laid down about what a commander shall or shall not do. He can do anything he likes, and very often not only can but should encroach on the affairs of his subordinates. I thought that the space the brigadier left me was cramped. Chris Lane (the staff captain) and I were learning how he liked things done, and we ought to be able to see that they were done that way. He should be able to say to us, "I want to move the brigade about ten miles tomorrow, carrying out a withdrawal exercise on the way—and back the next day, carrying out an advanced guard exercise," and then go off to ruminate or read a book or inspect socks, confident that a complete, sound plan for the moves and the exercises would be ready for his approval within a few hours.

I knew, therefore, what I wanted to achieve, but it is not wise simply to tell a regular brigadier of the Indian Army to move over in the bed. The opportunity came one evening, after I had been in the job about a month, when he and I were sitting in his office tent after a day of paper work. Michael said he intended to run a big exercise—three or four days. The tactics should not be complicated. He wanted to hammer home just two basic principles—physical fitness and tactical mobility away from motorable roads. He talked on while I asked questions, threw in suggestions, and tried to remember all that he said, without making notes.

Dinnertime came and the brigadier picked up his hat. "I'll make out a draft scheme tomorrow," he said, "and you can whip it into shape." I saluted and went to mess. But afterward I returned to the headquarters tent, and drafted an exercise such as he had in mind. Then I called Chris and warned the G.S. clerks to stand by for midnight. By then Chris and I had the orders written out in full, complete with all the logistical appendices and annexures. At two in the morning the head clerk brought me the cut stencils, with one copy actually run off. The copy I placed on the brigadier's table with the relevant maps, marked, beside it, and a penciled note: "For approval."

About ten o'clock Michael called me in and, smiling, handed me the papers. "All right," he said, "I may be a brigadier, but I'm not a bloody fool. Carry on, Jack," and put on his hat and left the office; but I put on mine and went with him, for my people knew what they had to do and I did not intend to sit on their necks any more than I intended the brigadier to sit on mine.

With Exercise Minden began a good and, for me, fruitful relationship. Just as a chef dislikes cooking for a man who does not care what kind of food he gets, so a staff officer dislikes working for a commander who is easily satisfied. Michael did not nag, but he did not overlook mistakes either, and when he praised some piece of headquarters work, we felt that we had earned a reward worth the effort we had put into earning it.

Michael was the second commander to whom I had been chief of staff, or its nearest Indian Army equivalent. Before the war ended I was to hold such an appointment twice more; and also to command a battalion, a brigade, and—momentarily—a division. You have read, and will read more in this book, of what "I" did, or said, or ordered. The "I" is inevitable, because this is an autobiography, but you should understand very clearly the difference between the "doing" of a staff officer, even a chief of staff, and the "doing" of a commander, even of one so lowly as a lieutenant in command of a platoon.

This difference is best illuminated by a tale told about Field

Marshal von Hindenburg. At the Battle of Tannenberg, fought in September, 1914, the Germans crushingly defeated the Russians. Hindenburg, the German commander in chief, was its Hero.

Or was he? It began to be heard in military circles that the plan of battle had been devised in every particular by Hindenburg's Chief of Staff, Major General Ludendorff. Opinion veered to the view that Ludendorff was the real Hero of Tannenberg.

Or was he? It began to be heard in military circles that the plan of battle had been devised in every particular by a certain Captain Hauptmann of the Operations Section of the General Staff. Hauptmann was the Hero of Tannenberg.

Years after the war a lady (only a woman would have dared) asked Hindenburg what was the truth of the matter. Who, *really*, had won Tannenberg? The old field marshal rumbled, "Madam, I do not know who won the battle of Tannenberg. I only know who would have lost it."

The weeks passed. The training exercises lengthened and grew in severity. We were bound for the Western Desert and I was eager to go. No premonition haunted me. . . . The names and faces became real people. Chris Lane had an enormous fund of good temper, and the ability to humor me out of my fits of military ferocity. I drove the headquarters hard, determined to see that they could move and fight and do their job as well as any battalion. I took them out on long exercises, and at the beginning everything went wrong, and Michael came, watched for an hour, and went away without a word. As I have said, he was a good man to work for. But a tiny flaw developed in our beautiful relationship. . . .

An old Indian proverb divides mankind into three classes, according to how they attend to their natural functions, that is, *itifaqan* (by chance), *hazri ke bad* (after breakfast), or *bara faja* (very early, at sparrow-fart, as the army says). The proverb implies that a man's general character corresponds to his category in this rather specialized area, and there is probably something in it, though I don't think it is precisely what Stonewall Jackson meant when he said, "Give me three-o'clock-in-the-morning men." Michael was a *bara faja*, as I discovered on an overnight move, when he got up long before dawn and headed for the latrine tent. His footsteps awoke me, I leaped up in my khaki pajamas, notebook and flashlight ready, and asked him what I could do.

"Not even the most efficient brigade major in the world could do this for me," he growled. Next time I did not leap up, but I always awoke, and could seldom get back to sleep.

Nearly three months had passed since I left Quetta. Barbara kept writing that she was well, and the children well. On a brief visit to Rawalpindi I ran into a portly lieutenant recently down from Quetta. (He was an actor in peacetime, and recently achieved some fame as Friar Tuck in the Robin Hood TV series.) He told me that she was not well at all, but suffering from dysentery.

Returning to Bakarial I made up my mind. Brigade Headquarters was in good shape, because it knew what the purpose of its existence was. I felt a compelling necessity to be as sure of my own purpose as were these abstract yet living organisms, the battalion, the regiment, the brigade, to which I had devoted my life. I could gallop into an affair with the reckless dash of a hussar but marriage was serious, and imposed caution, wisdom, clear thinking, clear seeing, and, above all, honesty.

I wrote to her, asking her if she wanted to come on a two-week walk with me in the Himalayas. She telegraphed, yes. Then I asked the brigadier for leave, and told him I intended to spend it trekking up the nearby Kunhar Valley toward Nanga Parbat and the Babusar Pass.

Michael said, "Certainly. You know the trout season's over?"

I told him I was not going fishing, or hunting.

10 The immensely high crest line of the Himalaya is cut by a series of passes, thinly spaced among the tremendous peaks. Elsewhere in the world, passes have often been the focal points of war, but not here. The Himalaya is too big for war. Conquest, and tides of history, have swept into India over its shallow western frontier, or across the sea. There have been fights in plenty, struggles between hill rulers for women or land or pride, but when the *shirr* of the arrows ceased and the clangor of the swords died, the mountains remained. It was not an author's whim that placed Shangri-la here, for in the Himalaya many have found their own Shangri-la, some through contemplation, some through striving.

There is nothing so remote, so calm with the calmness of original creation, as the side of a Himalayan mountain toward evening. To watch the night climb out of the valley onto the snows, to look across windless depths to far ice walls and farther heights, the gold of the snow turning to a pure cold blue as the light dies; to turn then, and see a yellow light spring faint from a shepherd's hut miles down in the darkness—these are the rewards, after the day's work. And the work also carries its own rewards, for we must climb through forests of oak, to pine, to fir, to juniper, to the short springy grass of the high alps; through hanging gardens, past slanting miles of wild flowers, and meadows smoky blue at noon against the sweeping desolation of stone and scree.

Here the metallic, iridescent Himalayan pheasant soars out over the abyss, partridges whirr and rocket down the slope on short wings, a lammergeier drifts along the cliff face two thousand feet below our path, the sun on his wings; two thousand feet above, the coneys crouch under the lichen-covered rocks. Always we move among humanity—free-striding men, boys with reed pipes guarding their flocks, veiled women, whose dark eyes now smile at my companion, because she too is a woman, and they can see that she is in love.

Reward and toil, inextricably joined—the stones sharp under our feet, the brutal cold of thigh-deep fords, the vertigo of tilted grass slopes sliding mile on mile away from the clinging track, sudden bitter winds that lash the pass, the running sweat of noon, salt in our eyes and salt in our mouth, the fierce sun on open rock. We relearn the elemental harmonies; to breathe easily, and step with a delicate rhythm; to sleep smoothly in flowers and grass, hard and yielding-firm like our muscles; to rise with the sun and eat by the fire.

I met her at Rawalpindi. She looked haggard and tired, but her dysentery had stopped the day she left Quetta. She had left the children there with their father and the ayah; but when she returned, she was taking them and separating from her husband. She could stand the strain no longer.

The motor road ended at Balakot, three thousand feet above sea level on the right bank of the Kunhar. From there we set out on foot—Barbara, myself, four men in charge of the three ponies that carried our stores, food, and bedding, and Daljit in charge of the four men. We had a few cans of meat, but the staples of our diet were to be ordinary Gurkha rations—rice, chupatties (discs of unleavened bread made from whole wheat flour), and dal (a kind of lentil stew).

The first day we climbed four thousand feet to the Forest Rest House at Kund. It is a short walk in miles, but a tiring one, and for Barbara's sake I would have preferred a lesser climb; but that was the nearest Rest House, and I had to get her out of the hot valley at once.

We took a long rest halfway up, a little shy with each other, alone together for the first time. Daljit and the ponymen were an hour ahead. An old tribesman came down the steep, followed at a respectful distance by his old wife. They sat down, the man in the shade of the same mulberry tree where we were, the woman farther off. After the formal Pashto greetings the old man asked us where we were going. I told him. Was the mem-sahib not tired? A little. It was a long climb, and the sun was hot, and there was no water. Indeed, that was true. The mem-sahib appeared thin. Yes, she had been sick.

Almost absently, without looking at her, his gnarled hands went out and rested on Barbara's bare legs, near the ankle. I started, her eyes caught mine in a moment of panic. His hands started massaging gently, then more firmly, more strongly. She winced as his sure fingers kneaded painful muscles. Addressing me, he said, "It hurts, but it is good." He continued unhurriedly as far as her knees, where the edge of the short skirt lay.

"If there is need of more, that one will do it," he said, jerking his head in the direction of his silent watching wife. Barbara smiled at him. "I feel much better." We thanked them, and went on.

We both felt better, much better, and when the slope eased, we walked hand in hand. We were in the mountains, among mountain people.

The particular fades into the general, the incident into the whole. Every afternoon we came upon the Forest Rest House which was that day's destination. Some stood high on the ridge, some close beside the loud river. Four or five times a year the District Forest Officer passed through on his tours of inspection, but now there was no one. The rooms smelled of wood smoke, and flowers grew in a small fenced garden, and there was a caretaker who came up from the village, two or five miles away, when he saw the smoke from the chimney. We built a big fire in the grate, for a mountain chill always fell as soon as the sun sank behind the Black Mountains to the west. The curtains drawn, we ate huge plates of rice and dal with our fingers, and drank a tot of rum with sweet cocoa and milk. At night the wind roared across the roof of the world, and we lay alone under its eaves, for the horses were silent in the stable and Daljit and the ponymen slept. In the mornings, the pale light spread across the floor, and Daljit came smiling with mugs of cocoa. "Six o'clock, sahib."

Once, having lost our way, we did not reach a Rest House, but slept on the veranda of a tiny village school. In the morning forty men and women and countless children gathered to watch us dress. An hour later on the road, I began to itch and, lifting my shirt, saw a rash of fleabites covering all my skin. Barbara's too. We reached the Rest House very early, but stopped; and spread out a sheet on the lawn, took two bars of soap and a basin of water, damped the soap, and set to work. First we took off all our clothes and put on bathing suits. Then, one by one, we placed everything we possessed on the sheet, and searched it for fleas. When we saw one, we dabbed the bar of soap onto it, it stuck, and we killed it between the thumb nails. Some we caught in the seams of the garments, some leaped out onto the white sheet, where we could easily see them. At last we were able to change into disinfested clothes, take off the swim suits and search them. By then we had been at it four hours. Over three hundred fleas killed, half a dozen missing, no wounded, no prisoners.

Winter sharpened the wind that blew down the river. Sheep and shepherds prepared to move down to warmer levels. Each day the snow clouds sat lower overhead as we climbed up toward them, yet still autumn covered the valley in glory.

The river ran pale green and silver, cold and noisy-shallow over the stones beside us. Across the water the leaves of a line of poplars on a grass bank had turned pale and dark yellow. Behind them the mountain started climbing—first a band of yellow and and red and brown and green and crimson, mottled, splashed, streaked, scattered with golden chestnut trees and scarlet berries; above, a band of dark, dark firs, their unbroken ranks cut at the top as by a ruler; another band of thinning birch and juniper; a band of gray rock, scree, and short grass; at last—snow, ice, and full dark clouds low above. The sun leaped over the ridge behind and in one blinding moment burnished the river and the mountain, the trees and the snow.

On the ninth day, a cut in the left wall of the valley showed where a side stream entered the Kunhar from the east. I studied the map. The stream seemed to have its source in a lake five or six miles up the gorge. From the lake there ought to be a good view of the 18,500-foot mountain Malika Parbat, which the valley walls hid from our view down here. Telling the ponymen to go on to the next Rest House, we turned up the side stream. Daljit came with us.

The stream tumbled down steeply and our climb, against it,

was abrupt, slow, and very beautiful in the morning. Three hours later we reached the lake and stood close together, silent. The mountains ringed the lake on two sides, their snow-covered flanks sweeping straight down into the water. Beyond, snow clouds drifted across the face of Malika Parbat, and a glacier ended at a beach of stones near the water's edge. The water was black, dark, and still. There were no birds, no grass, and no trees, yet driftwood, bleached white and twisted into the stark shapes of an ocean shore, littered the beach.

We collected wood, lit a fire, and made cocoa. The snow clouds sank lower, and for a few minutes surrounded us, so that the fire became a blur and then an orange ball in the swirling vapor, and then disappeared. The cloud lifted and we saw Daljit looming like a dim giant beyond the fire, facing us.

He asked me, "Which way lies my home in Nepal, sahib?" I pointed to the southeast. Daljit took two chupatties from his mess tin and went a little apart to the edge of the water. He stood there two or three minutes, head up, looking into the snow and the livid gleam of sun above in the southeast, then laid his chupatties on a flat stone by the edge of the water and returned to us.

We started back, stiffly at first, then faster, our nailed boots crunching steadily on the wet rock. It is a gift from God, the sensual satisfaction of that uncompromising work-sound—stone on steel. We forded the stream just below the cleft where it left the lake and started its plunge down to the Kunhar. We leaned into the ridge separating us from the valley, two thousand feet of wet grass and black rock. Scattered pines clung insecurely to the steep face, the plash of water died down behind us, and heavy wisps of gray vapor drifted across the ridge. It began to snow. Big soft flakes hissed down and mantled Barbara's hair and Daljit's broad-brimmed hat. We passed over the ridge and the snow clouds stayed behind, hanging over the lake and the glacier. The sun shone and we went straight down the ridge, off the grass, into the pines and down at last to the river and the Rest House.

There had been no recurrence of her dysentery and after the first two days, when I held to a slow pace, she had kept pressing me to go faster. Her color had returned, now overlaid with sun and windburn, and she looked wonderful. While we drank a glass of rum by the fire, waiting for the rice to cook, I said, "You look as fit as a flea now. That dysentery cleared up quickly."

She gave me an odd glance, hesitated, and said, "The doctor could never find anything, you know. No bacilli, no amoebae. The fourth time I went down with it he didn't even try. He just asked me whether I was happy. When I told him, he said I had to go away for a time, at once, otherwise he wouldn't be responsible for my life."

A memory crossed my mind. Something about Quetta being cut off because of floods on the Indus. It had not registered at the time, because she had already wired me that she was coming. Now, "How did you get out?" I asked her.

She told me. Her sister (whose marriage was also breaking up at that time) had been staying with her, but wanted to return to Bombay. Barbara had no difficulty in getting leave from the WACs—but was forbidden to leave Quetta. No one was allowed to, except on urgent military business. Whereupon they set out, with one servant. Twelve hours in the train brought them down from the Baluchistan plateau to the edge of the floods. The servant went off and found a tonga which would take them on between arms of the great flood to a point where, it was alleged, they might find a boat to cross the Indus proper. A tonga is a two-wheeled cart, pulled by a single horse, usually very bony and underfed. It has some sort of springs, but you would never believe it, even on a dead smooth road. In this they covered twenty-four miles in the extreme heat, through a barren country dotted with isolated villages. In some of them the people all seemed to be waving banners and beating drums. It was the time of Gandhi's biggest nonviolent civil disobedience campaign, during which several thousand people were murdered—nearly all Indians—policemen set on fire, and trains derailed. This part of the journey, along a heavily rutted dirt road, in choking dust, took six hours.

The two women reached the edge of the river, even here far over its banks, found a dhow, and continued. The boat contained, besides them, two Indian peasant families with their carts and oxen. The Indians noticed immediately that the fare for an ox was twelve annas, while the fare for a mem-sahib was eight annas. The statement of this theme, and the working out of all possible humorous variations and cadenzas upon it, cheerfully occupied the two-and-a-half-hour crossing to dry land on the far side. Here they found a bus to take them eight miles to Rohri, where there was a military rest camp. The bus decanted them in the middle of the teeming Rohri bazaar, among the angry "Quit India" signs, but, as was general in India, with rare and bloody exceptions (who knows whether he's born to be an exception?) they met the utmost courtesy, and took another tonga to the rest camp. The colonel in charge first threatened to put Barbara under arrest; then gave them a quarter where they spent an hour getting clean, took them out to dinner, and begged them to give him all the information they could about the boats and dhows on the Indus. He was supposed to commandeer them all, to get supplies through to Quetta, but many were—as the women had just proved—being used for illicit trade. Next day Barbara came on in the train.

When she finished, I felt limp. "Wouldn't it have been a good idea to tell me about this before?" I said.

"You didn't ask me."

"What would you have done if there had been no boats? If they had arrested you and sent you back?"

She looked straight at me, as in the moment of our first meeting. "I'd have got here."

After supper I walked out along the river bank under the hunter's moon. It seemed to me that my questions were answered. The solutions had not come from weighing and balancing and deciding, nor by the use of logic and skill and experience, such as I used in my profession. I had passed nine days with Barbara, a woman, Daljit, a Gurkha soldier—and the mountains. My life, my love, my work were all here, and the answers had taken shape out of that union.

First—it is better to travel than to arrive. The thought of becoming General Sir John Masters was attractive, more so the vista of responsibility, the work I could achieve. But supposing I learned that to become a general I must give up service with Gurkhas. I would not do it, because the wonder of living lay not in the abstractions of command, as such, but in a direct personal relationship with men like Daljit. No goal, no ultimate point of arrival, was worth the sacrifice of each successive "now."

Duty I knew, and ambition I knew. I would bend my course

for the sake of duty; but for the sake of ambition, not one inch. The delight in each day, the lyrical enjoyment of each hour, these I must not sacrifice, or even risk.

It is better to travel than to arrive; but in marriage a wife is not only a companion, she is also the journey itself, and the goal. I would travel with Barbara, if she would accept me. Four years earlier I had walked beside another Himalayan river at night and wished that I could find a woman with whom to share the capacity for love that then seemed to overwhelm me; but there was no such woman, not then, not there. Now I had found her, and seen her on the mountain and in the storm, and she had walked beside me against the whistling wind, and rested with me among the wild flowers. Together we had watched eagles, and in another place we had shared Beethoven, champagne, and the subtle partnership of the dance.

I walked quickly back to the Rest House, and took her hand, and asked her to marry me. She said, "Yes."

I said, "Wait." Carefully I listed the difficulties we would face, the decisions that might or must come, many of them hard for me and harder for her. I warned her that if she said Yes, I would turn back for nothing, nothing at all, nor must she. The moment for turning back was now. I spoke with unnecessary brutality, telling her that if she had hopes of becoming Lady Masters, she had better think again. I had no money and did not expect to inherit any. Her children, the two wonderful kids who had crawled over me in Quetta, would become involved.

She began to cry. "Do you think I don't know all this?" she said. "I am sure. I have always been sure. Do you think I'd be here if I wasn't?"

Then I asked her again if she would marry me, and again she said, "Yes."

Winter marched down the valley in a blizzard, and with it snow-draped men of the Frontier Constabulary, returning to the plains from their summer vigil on the Babusar Pass. Soon no one would be able to move in the upper Kunhar until April. Behind the Constabulary followed a long string of camels, and a small group of Powindah nomads re-entering India from Central Asia. We went down with them, down from the snow and the sleet into the October sunshine of the lower valley, and parted.

11 As soon as I got back, I told Michael Roberts that I was about to become involved in a divorce. He said, "You bloody young fool!" and then invited me to tell him as much as I cared to about it. I tried to explain to him what had come to me in the Kunhar. He listened carefully, and when I had finished, sat a minute looking past me, out of the open tent flap, where his orderly sat on a bench within earshot. He said slowly, "You're not a bloody young fool. A happy marriage is worth anything. Certainly this—" he indicated the red band on his hat—"ten times over. Well, keep me informed and I might be able to be of some help to you. Come and have a drink."

Barbara returned north a month later, with her children, and got herself a job with the General Staff at Army headquarters in Rawalpindi. (One sort of WAC, mostly consisting of army wives, could be employed only in the place where they lived, or chose to live.) In the next two months we saw each other twice, one day each time. The division's training and preparation came to a peak. By the end of December we stood ready for the Western Desert.

In January they sent us to the Central Provinces and told us to train for jungle warfare. We were going to fight the Japanese, not the Germans. Alamein, and the continuing westward advance into Libya and Tunisia, had totally altered the strategical situation. The prospect of action receded another three or four months.

I became impatient. For God's sake, I cried, let me live in peace
with Barbara, or get into battle, not this betwixt and between
half-existence.

The troop trains clanked south through the sharp, cold-
weather days. The great snow peaks slid slowly below the northern horizon. . . . Chhindwara, around which we made our jungle
camps, is a small town near the center of what is now called
Madhya Pradesh. It is a rolling country of trap rock, forested in
sal and dwarf teak, very hot and dry in the summer, sunny and
fresh in January and February. The jungles are full of game—
wild pig, deer of several kinds, including the lordly sambar, bear,
leopard, and tiger. It is the country of Kipling's *Jungle Books*,
and the maps on which we worked showed the Seeonee Hills and
the Wainganga River not far to the east of us. Every time I
found myself alone in the jungle with Daljit—reconnoitering a
site for a bombing range, studying ground for an exercise—I expected to see Mowgli trotting through the thin trees toward me,
Bagheera at his heels and Kaa coming fast behind, the flat head
raised and the unwinking eyes fastened on me. What a superb
understanding of India Kipling had! If only he had understood
Indians one-tenth as well.

January, February, the shirt hot on my back even in the dap-
pled jungle shade, the rivers dwindling in their rocky courses and a
layer of dust dulling the sheen of the leaves. I got a cable from
my father, telling me that my brother Alex, missing in Malaya for
over a year, was a prisoner in Japanese hands.

March, the sun striking like a bludgeon between the eyes
and the throat parched and the hot stars glowing in a violet sky.
Late at night, in mess, a dour Scots lieutenant suddenly groaned,
laid his head in his arms on the table and mumbled, "Ah, I love
women's brrreasts so much I wish I had a pair myself."

In Rawalpindi Barbara was learning Pashto, in order to be
able to concoct codes for use by Pathan secret agents. A parachute captain, boy friend of a woman she knew, tried to rape her
when the other woman became periodically *hors de combat*.
She'd had enough of Rawalpindi, and would soon go to Bombay,
to live with her sister.

April: the full coppery-gray bowl of the hot weather pressing
relentlessly down, a mango shower so strong that it rather overdid

its mission. Half the mango trees in the province were stripped bare of fruit before it was over.

May: and Michael said to me, one evening, "We're about ready. Do you want fourteen days?"

The fighting in the Arakan, where we would almost certainly go, was of a peculiarly grim and dreadful kind, unalloyed by any sort of romance, peripheral pleasure, or, so far, the taste of victory. The climate was bloody, the terrain worse, and the British generalship to be set on a par with New Orleans, Passchendaele and the blockheaded stupidities of the Boer War.

All this we of the 7th Indian Division intended to alter, but it would be a hard, murderous business. I thankfully accepted Michael's offer and, with Daljit, set off at once for Bombay, where Barbara had recently arrived.

We went immediately to a cabin at Juhu, the beach fifteen miles north of Bombay. It was a sultry day, the sky the color of dull iron, and distant rumblings of thunder. We lay on the sand in the dusk while Daljit, dressed in his loincloth and underpants, dubiously examined the Kala Pani, the mighty Black Water about which he had heard so much, but never seen.

Barbara told me there was not going to be any easy divorce. Her husband had refused it. I thought unhappily, Now what? We would not turn back, that was certain. I knew of at least two other officers in the same situation, who had struggled painfully along for years, now and then obtaining a bungalow through the generosity of a station commander, but usually living apart from their "wives" and always liable to snubs and social ostracism. Others, I knew, had left the service, the country, and, in many cases, the Empire.

I was about to go into action, but security orders did not permit me to tell Barbara this. I suggested that, for the time being, we might simply accept the situation, doing and saying nothing to embitter it, in case—

"In case what?" she interrupted, and I could not answer, for I meant, in case I were to be killed. It is a hard world for a woman with two young children and no money.

She said, "I want to bear a child of yours."

I saw by her face that she knew I was going back into action. But where I had thought to protect her position, such as it was, she wanted to burn her boats. She also meant just what she said, for I do not think any woman feels that love is whole or complete until she has conceived and ripened its fruit. She implied as much now, for when I began to protest that it seemed a hard thing to bring a child into our uncertain future, she said, a little impatiently, "If you were a woman, you'd understand."

Daljit came up the sand, saluted, and reported that the water in the Kala Pani tasted unpleasantly salty. In fact, it was undrinkable. The Kala Pani was a great waste of space.

That night another mango shower found me. This one struck at midnight, when Daljit awakened me. Coconuts, he said, were falling on the roof and he feared the oil lamp might be knocked over and set the hut on fire. Daljit, like all Gurkhas, had a strong penchant for meiosis. Actually, the coconuts were driving through the palm-leaved hut like shells, and screaming on across the beach and out to sea, to sink passing ships, for all I knew; and the wind ripped off the tops of the trees—huge fronds, full bunches of fruit, trunks two feet thick, and all—and hurled them after the individual nuts. Then the rain began, and poured without let through the creaking, shell-torn structure. The three of us scrambled along the beach to the nearest concrete house, hurling ourselves to the sand in the fitful lightning flashes to avoid the coconuts that howled past, or bust at our heels. It was much worse than the French 75s at Deir-es-Zor.

In the morning I told Barbara that Bombay, for all its luxury, was a little too explosive for me, and suggested that five days' traveling and seven days in the Kunhar Valley would be more restful than twelve days here. She agreed with delight, Daljit smiled, and that night we took the Frontier Mail for Rawalpindi. But first I visited my lawyers and made a will, leaving all that I possessed to Barbara; and turned my bank account into a joint account, which she could draw on. And thought, What a ridiculous thing to do, really, to gallop off to war leaving a woman with two thousand rupees (about four hundred dollars) and, probably, a baby.

On the third afternoon we were again climbing the long slope from Balakot. The air freshened as we climbed, peonies carpeted the earth under the deodars, and spring flowers covered the upland meadows in wild, sweet disarray.

For two days we walked along the ridges. On the third night, at three A.M., Daljit knocked on the bedroom door. *"Tar ayo,"* he said. I stumbled out and found a tired messenger from the telegraph office at Balakot. The telegram was from Brigade Headquarters, and it ordered me to report back to Chhindwara at once. Obviously, the move to the front had been accelerated. We were off.

Barbara and I parted at Delhi.

When I reached Chhindwara, I found that the brigade had gone, leaving only its rear elements, which were due to move within the week. I also found a sealed envelope addressed to me in the brigadier's handwriting. I opened it. It contained two pieces of paper.

The first was a short order from the Military Secretary at G.H.Q., posting Lieutenant (War-Sustantive Captain and Temporary Major) J. Masters, 4 G.R., as Brigade Major of the 111th Indian Infantry Brigade. He would report forthwith to the brigade at Ghatera, Central Provinces.

The second was a letter from Michael. The commander of 111 Brigade, he had learned, was Joe Lentaigne of my own regiment, who had apparently asked for me by name. Joe's brigade had a mysterious and top secret mission, something to do with long-range penetration. Joe Lentaigne was a _____ and a _____ and a _____, and he, Michael, had made every effort to have the posting canceled, pointing out that he and I had worked like hell for ten months to make a team out of this headquarters. It was sheer lunacy to break up the team now, just when we were going into action. G.H.Q. had offered him any officer he wanted from the army list to replace me; but they had refused to change the orders. He was sorry, very sorry. . . .

My first feeling was of surprise. Why? Then, as I realized that 111 was a newly raised formation and would therefore require training, came exasperation. This was too much. Always a bridesmaid, never a bride. I was being used as a pawn in some Olympian game of snakes and ladders. For a moment I considered protesting the order myself; but if Michael had failed, I could not hope to succeed; and I was a professional, with a deep distaste for questioning orders. I had given too many myself not to know that there are usually reasons which the toad under the harrow cannot be aware of.

Curiosity returned. What was Joe Lentaigne up to now, that he had the necessary *piston* to get a B.M. out of a brigade actually moving up to the front? In the first Burma campaign, as a lieutenant colonel in command of the 1st Battalion of our regiment, he had done brilliantly, leading the battalion like a tiger, personally heading half a dozen bayonet charges, time and again saving the battalion and damaging the Japanese through that long, painful retreat by his quick thinking and aggressive actions. For reward he had earned an immediate Distinguished Service Order, and command of a brigade on the Assam front. He was a tall Irishman, now about forty-three, and I sufficiently resembled him in looks so that when I first joined the regiment the Gurkhas had called me *Syano Lantin Sahib*, "Lentaigne Junior."

Brilliant, unorthodox, quick, wonderful sense of humor (as a second lieutenant, in 1918, he sent forged messages to Brigade Headquarters announcing the imminent arrival of an Elephant Troop, sending the staff into an absolute frenzy as they tried to find the appropriate manuals on the care and feeding of elephants). . . . Long Range Penetration, eh? Had I not heard rumors of another brigade, 77 its number was, commanded by a mysterious chap called Wingate, supposed to be experimenting in that field? Wasn't 77 actually behind the Japanese lines in Burma now, but running into trouble? H'm.

And Ghatera? At last I found it in Bradshaw's *Indian Railway Guide;* a station on a cross-country line in the jungles north of the Nerbudda River. From Chhindwara I could reach it direct in six hours—but first I had to go all the way across India, find 114 Brigade, collect the rest of my kit, hand over to my successor, whoever he might be, and return. I'd be traveling for a week more, and I'd have to say good-by to 114 Brigade, collectively and severally. I'd better check my supply of Alka-Seltzer. Barbara would be pleased though, unless she ever learned what I had got into now. Long Range Penetration sounded interesting, but dangerous.

12 The train came late to the junction and I missed the connection. After some argument the stationmaster permitted me to board the footplate of a freight train. In this fashion, jolting and groaning through the June afternoon, I headed for Ghatera. The countryside streamed with water. It lay in lakes on the fields, and shone under the canopy of the jungle, and swirled deep and brown under the reverberant iron bridges. The black smoke drifted away across the bright green of standing crops, across the huddled villages where women crouched in the doorways and narrow trails, deep in mud, went from nowhere to a darker, danker nowhere beyond.

"Ghatera," the engineer said contemptuously, and the old locomotive wheezed to a stop.

Joe Lentaigne was surprised to see me, but he was a quick man to recover himself, and said, "Where the hell have you been all this time?"

I began to explain but he interrupted me, "Have you seen the new American cars? Jeeps. We've got two. They're the caterpillar's spats." It was only four years since I had visited the United States, and I winced. Joe noticed nothing, but hurried out, myself following. A Gurkha rifleman outside the tent saw us coming and scrambled quickly into the back seat of the small open car waiting there. Joe leaped into the driver's seat and I only just got in beside him before we were off. His eyes gleamed with enlarged, diabolic energy behind his spectacles as he turned to me. I noticed that the Burma campaign had lost him all his front teeth, except for a single upward jutting fang in the lower left corner. "Four-wheel drive!" he barked. "High and low gear ratios." He flung the floorboard levers backward and forward. The motor whined and roared, the car jumped, teeth flew off the cogs. Joe's long jaw stuck out in a fierce grin, armed with the single fang; his beak nose curved down to meet his jaw; the wide-brimmed Gurkha hat, worn forward on his head, rested on top of his spectacles.

We dashed down a bullock cart track, with tents visible in the trees to the left. Wheeling left at full speed we plunged down a jungle path hardly wide enough to take the jeep. Tree roots and large stones stuck out everywhere. I half-stood in the seat, crying, "Sir!" Joe grinned fiercely. "She loves it. You watch. Most wonderful vehicle ever invented!" We bounded a foot in the air, landed heavily, the springs groaning. A metallic crash behind me made me turn my head and I saw the Gurkha, Joe's orderly, a Thompson submachine gun strapped around him, once more fly into the air, his hands holding onto the back of my seat and no expression visible on his face—or was he actually laughing?

After we had covered some ten miles through the jungles, nearly bogged ourselves twice, tried to climb a boulder just too big for us and instead had to roll it out of the way, the three of us sweating and heaving for twenty minutes, we came to a metaled road, and headed back toward camp at a reasonable speed. Joe handed over the wheel to me and lit a cigarette.

"We're a Long Range Penetration brigade," he said abruptly. "Two battalions—1st Cameronians, under Gillespie, and 4/9th Gurkhas, under Morris. Know him?" I shook my head. "We're organized on the same principle as Wingate's 77 Brigade, each battalion into two columns. I've been experimenting around a bit. It's an unwieldy organization, inflexible. Wingate's just out of Burma, so we'll be getting some practical tips soon. He's an odd bird, Wingate."

For the remainder of the ride, and far into the evening, Joe explained the background of our role.

After the disasters in Malaya and Burma an unusually talented artillery officer, Orde Wingate, had thought out a way to show the Japanese, and our own troops, that we too could use the jungle. The method, based on the work of the Long Range Desert Group in Egypt, was to pass well-armed forces—not guerrillas—through the enemy front, and operate against his less-protected lines of communication. The Commander in Chief in India at that time was Field Marshal Wavell, who already knew and had used Wingate in similar off-beat enterprises in Palestine and Abyssinia. He agreed to give the plan a trial. So 77 Brigade was formed, under Wingate, for the specific task of Long Range Penetration. In February, 1943, having organized his force into small columns of about four hundred men each, each column capable of functioning independently, Wingate passed through our lines on the Assam front, passed through the Japanese lines—there was plenty of room in the jungle if one avoided the main routes—and began operations against the Japanese communications two hundred miles inside Burma.

The force blew up railroad bridges, ambushed road convoys, and attacked isolated Japanese posts. Their supplies they received by air from India, C-47s flying in to points given by radio and there dropping food and ammunition over the fires which the columns lit in jungle clearings. Soon the Japanese reacted, and sent troops into the jungle after the columns. Finally they trapped the force in the great bend of the Shweli River and caused it to break up. For the last month the remnants of 77 Brigade had been working their ways back to India in parties of all sizes from single men to whole columns. They had lost one-third of their strength.

Before Wingate came out, even before he met defeat, Wavell saw that whatever the final outcome of the attempt, Long Range Penetration was a great morale raiser and could be a valuable adjunct to more orthodox operations. He therefore ordered the formation of a second Long Range Penetration group—111 Indian Infantry Brigade—and selected Joe Lentaigne for command of it. Joe had asked for me as his brigade major.

My interest and excitement quickened. What was our role, exactly? Joe said, "Not allotted yet, in detail. But we've got to be ready by November. We're going to carry out another raid of the same sort as Wingate's. Meanwhile, I suppose, 77 Brigade will refit, and go in again when we've had enough. . . . The strain on the men is going to be enormous. If they try to keep an L.R.P. brigade in the field for more than three months at the outside, they're asking for trouble. . . . Wingate's had a hell of a good idea in this. The man's a genius in some ways—but of course he's made mistakes, and we've got to do better. We've got to think for ourselves, as well as learn from his experience. There's no morale-raising in L.R.P. if you lose thirty-five per cent of your force. We must achieve more, and lose less. Good training, good morale. We'll do it."

He pointed to the device of a snarling leopard's head on his sleeve. "That's us," he said. "Pack of hungry leopards. Wingate chose a *chinthe* for his lot."

"What's a *chinthe?*"

"The lion-headed dragon that sits outside all Burmese pagodas," Joe said. "Supposed to be the only living thing, in the Buddhist religion, that is permitted to use force—to guard the sacred pagodas, of course. People are pronouncing it *chindit* for some reason, and that's what Wingate's people are being called—Chindits. The Leopards and the Chindits. But the Leopards," he grinned at me fiendishly, "are going to wipe the eye of the Chindits."

The whisky bottle passed again in the little tent. My mind raced. . . . Obviously we could not carry heavy guns. It would have to be air support instead of artillery. Supplies and ammunition down from the air, yes. But casualties out?

"We'll have to leave them in a friendly village," Joe said. "And sometimes clear a strip long enough for Dakotas (C-47s)."

O.K., I thought, but in that case we can afford very few casualties. No force will retain its morale for long if it is continually leaving its wounded to die in the jungle or to be sheltered by villagers, who will certainly, sooner or later, be visited by the Japanese.

Radio sets . . . the necessary communication network began to form itself in my mind. We must be able to talk to all columns, and to the base from which the supply aircraft came, and to the fighters or bombers that would be our artillery, and to Army. . . . How many mules to carry the sets? How to recharge batteries?

Burma . . . the language. We would have to rely on local intelligence. Interpreters. Couldn't wait for papers from enemy

corpses, or the results of prisoner interrogation, to be flown back
to us. A Japanese interpreter per column? My God, there weren't
that many in India. . . . Supply drops, the list of things we'd
need would be enormous. It would have to go in cipher. We'd be
forced to spend half a day, one day in four, sitting down in one
place merely to encipher and send off the messages. But our
success would depend on mobility and surprise. A way must be
found to standardize the drops so that a very short message would
suffice. . . .

What about the men? The Cameronians, also called the Scottish Rifles, were a regular battalion that had fought through the
first Burma campaign. "Damned good they were, too," Joe said.
"And they've still got a good many left from '41, officers and
men." They recruited most of their men from the streets of
Glasgow, and had the reputation of being one of the toughest
regiments in the British Army, in peacetime. They waged street
fights with secreted bayonets and broken bottles and, on at least
one occasion in Calcutta, with rifles and ball ammunition. They
carried razor blades in the peaks of their caps, with which to
wipe the grin off opposing faces by a careless backhand swipe from
the cap; and potatoes in their pockets, in which razor blades
were stuck. No one but their own officers could handle them, and
their touchy discipline vanished altogether for a week around the
great Scottish fiesta of Hogmanay, New Year's Eve.

The 4/9th Gurkha Rifles was a war-raised battalion. The 9th enlisted high caste Gurkhas—Thakurs and Chhettris—who were no-
ticeably taller and thinner than the "ordinary" Gurkha, but with
the same basic qualities.

I told Joe about Barbara. He said, "Christ. War seems so
damned simple sometimes." He had himself recently separated
from his wife. "Tell me when you need leave. Need it, mind, not
just want it. Now let's go to bed. Tomorrow—get cracking."

The brigade staff was complete, except for one, but so far, as
on my first arrival with 114, they were only faces and names. The
missing man was the brigade Intelligence officer.

Two days later a captain of the Burma Rifles entered my
office tent. His clothes were covered in mud and he had a rugged,
long-jawed face, lined, pale, and sweating profusely. He saluted
and said in a harsh, slightly nasal voice with the faintest touch

of London on the accent, "Good morning. I'm Hedley. Where's the manager?"

"The manager?"

"The Bara Sahib. The Big Cheese. The Boss."

"The brigadier is out," I said coldly. "I'm the brigade major. What do you want?"

My visitor divested himself of a rifle with fixed bayonet, a pack that must have weighed seventy pounds, a heavy haversack, equipment with full ammunition pouches and several grenades, a couple of huge knives, a dah, a kukri, a revolver, revolver ammunition, binoculars, compass, map case, a waterproof portfolio, and a large sack. His khaki shirt was black with sweat. "I'm the Intelligence officer of this crowd," he said. "The manager got me out of 63 Brigade. Here I am."

John Hedley, Eton and King's, by profession a merchant of the Bombay Burmah Trading Corporation, had reported for duty. Joe (I learned later) first came across him in the middle of a particularly gruesome debacle during the '41 retreat from Burma. Tramping along in command of the rear guard Joe saw an Englishman lying alone in the jungle beside the road, facing the rear, the Japanese. Joe stopped and asked him what the hell he thought he was doing. Without getting up the figure replied, "Captain Hedley, sir, Burma Rifles, attached to the [he named a notorious Indian regiment]. We were ordered to hold this line. Someone fired a shot in the jungle and the whole Blank Battalion of the Royal and Bright Yellow Blanks buggered off." Joe ordered Hedley to abandon his post, and rejoin his battalion. Hedley refused. When Joe had produced satisfactory proof that he was indeed a colonel and the commander of the rear guard, Hedley consented to obey, saluted, picked up his rifle and the one hundred pounds of kit without which he was never seen, and, striding along at his usual pace of six miles an hour, soon disappeared in the north.

I took my private chart of Brigade Headquarters Staff and wrote in: "B.I.O.—*Hedley.*" John's intelligence, determination, and unorthodox mind were to be of immense value to all of us.

Who else do we have? A staff captain, later to be replaced by a major—both regulars. Neither will come into action, but will be of vital service to us at the Air Base. . . . Briggs, the Signal officer: he is from H.M. Customs and Excise, and always wears

Civil Service socks. We are extraordinarily polite to him, thinking of postwar journeys through Dover or Southampton, until we discover that he is in the Excise Branch, and, worse, possesses a dour Yorkshire incorruptibility. . . . The Cipher officer, Rhodes James: he'd hardly left school when the war dragged him off the line that he was thinking of following—the Church; now, serious, but with a sense of humor, he plunges into the mysteries of the cipher books. . . . The brigade Orderly officer: an artilleryman and distinctly odd; he wears a huge opal ring on one finger, later shaves his head in order to look and think like a Gurkha, or perhaps a Burmese—he is not sure. A Wing Commander, R.A.F., who will direct the close-support aircraft . . . but what is this? He appears to be well over fifty, is covered with decorations for gallantry earned as an infantryman in the first war, but he has no wings. Between wars, he is a film producer, and he parades his four flight lieutenants every morning at five A.M., under monstrous packs, and drills them rigorously. The flight lieutenants are very modern types with few medals, but they do have pilot's wings, and they are on the edge of mutiny. One by one each of them tells me the old bugger doesn't know an undercart from a bomb sight, and must go. . . . Wish he were a Cameronian and young enough to command a column, though. . . . What can his films have been like?

More, and more . . . Karen officer of the Burma Rifles, complete with platoon of Karens. Large Anglo-Burman to assist Hedley. Small Japanese expert to assist the Anglo-Burman. A full colonel, Russian interpreter, to assist Joe . . . In the 9th Gurkhas there is a huge young lieutenant called Bill Travers (in another life he becomes a film star and takes a leading role in *Bhowani Junction*, which I have written).

In long evenings in the tent, long talks after the three-day exercises, while the monsoon rain bucketed down outside, we thrashed out the problems that arose as fast as others were solved. Gradually Joe's decisions took shape in training doctrine, in instructions, in the ever-growing files of War Establishments and War Equipment tables. We knew what we were going to do, and we were almost ready to do it.

Barbara wrote, "Hooray, hooray, I'm pregnant." I read the letter two or three times a day for a month.

The biggest single problem was food. Considering his total load, no man could carry more than five days' rations, and those had to be of a kind which he could eat without cooking, and which came in individual packs. And they had to provide the man with so many thousand calories per day. The best that India could give us was a soggy packet containing raisins, powdered milk, tea in a twist of paper, sugar, biscuits, and cans of corned beef. The biscuits had weevils in them even before they reached us; also the milk. The raisins had another kind of insect, and the Gurkhas were not keen on eating beef except in real emergency. The daily calorie intake was about fifteen hundred short of what it ought to be.

Orde Wingate had come out of Burma, and was called to England to report to the Prime Minister on his expedition. Churchill took him on to the inter-Allied conference at Quebec, August, 1943.

Wingate returned to India after feats of persuasion and conviction in Quebec which, even if he had done nothing else, would have caused his name to be spoken with awe wherever soldiers are gathered.

The roof fell in on us and our simple plans. When we picked ourselves up out of the wreckage we found that we were part of Special Force, a new and vast organization of Long Range Penetration troops, all of which soon came to be known as Chindits. A complete British Infantry Division was sucked into the Chindit maw; a West African Brigade followed. Each brigade grew from two, to three, to four battalions. Wingate became a major general. Equipment—mainly American—descended upon us in torrents . . . walkie-talkie radio sets, VHF radios, and, blessed above all, K rations. It was wonderful.

It was also awful. Joe was appalled. So was I. So were most professional soldiers concerned with waging the Burma campaign, the largest land campaign fought against the Japanese throughout the war. We were appalled because we believed that the new force was much too big.

As commander and staff of 111 Brigade we were more than content. We were getting more supplies than we had thought possible, better arms and equipment, and a Force Headquarters which would organize and run the Air Base better than we could have done it ourselves. Our distress arose from our underlying characters, as military technicians. Our view can be stated, briefly, as follows:

Operations by two brigades, acting in rotation behind the enemy lines, stood a good chance of containing—that is, occupying the attention of—Japanese forces considerably larger than those we put against them. But this containment would be wasted unless our main armies at the same time carried out important operations designed to strike at the enemy where our containment had weakened him.

Wingate's new Chindit force consisted not of four, but of twenty-four battalions of infantry. (It was supposed to have three more: the American 5307 Provisional Regiment, under Colonel Merrill, actually joined us for a few days before Stilwell grabbed it firmly into his own hands. It became better known as Merrill's Marauders.) Twenty-four battalions was the infantry strength of two and a half divisions, but we were not even as powerful as one standard division, where the infantry were supported by guns, tanks, and engineers. The number of aircraft that would be needed to supply and support us was enormous. If they were available to the Army commander they would greatly increase the mobility of his standard forces, and hence their power—for armies are like money; just as the total value of money is a function of its amount multiplied by the speed with which it circulates, so an army's power is a function of its mass multiplied by its mobility.

If Wavell had asked Joe, before Wingate returned from Quebec, for his views on the expansion of the Long Range Penetration, this is the substance of what he would have answered, and, indeed, of what Auchinleck, the new Commander in Chief in India, did answer when ordered to cable his views to Quebec. But the decision had been made and now Joe was one of Wingate's brigadiers. His job was to carry out his part of the operation to the best of his ability. It was not a new situation for a soldier, and never has been.

Joe said, "Well, if we're going to be part of Wingate's private army, let's relax and enjoy it. We're Chindits now and by God, we'd better all stick together, because the rest of the Army's going to be out for our blood."

He was right. We became, and remained, figures of controversy, now lit by the glare of an exotic fame as the elite of the jungle, now execrated as the spoiled darlings of a maniacal publicity seeker.

Work continued. Pill taking continued. We drank shark liver oil, cheaper and easier to extract than cod liver oil, just as healthful, and twice as foul-tasting. We took Mepacrine. Our faces turned a dark, unhealthy yellow, also our urine. Rumors floated about. Mepacrine made a man impotent. Caused his hair to fall out. And his teeth. But it kept down malaria, and a man out of action with malaria was a man the Japanese had removed from the battlefield without any exertion or risk to themselves. No soldier got his food until he had taken his Mepacrine, under the eye of an officer. A malaria rate above a certain figure meant the dismissal of the commander. The rate stayed low.

. . . On a steep, jungle-covered mountain, twelve hours out on a twenty-four-hour exercise, the voice of our U.S.A.F. liaison officer, Bill Lucas, rumbled angrily through the trees: "Hey, we passed Everest way back.". . .

We swam rivers and lakes, and slept among ruined temples in forgotten jungles. The veterinarians cut the vocal chords of our horses and mules, so that they could not bray.

We marched, rested, marched, returned to camp. A few days of paper work and preparation, and out again . . . These thin jungles through which we marched have always had a peculiarly disengaged atmosphere. This is the divide between major cultural areas extending up from the Pacific and Malaya on the one hand, down from Central Europe and the Asiatic steppe on the other. The hills are not high, nor particularly difficult to traverse, being of the reddish laterite rock, fissured here and there but generally not steep, interspersed with streams running in chasms, or through narrow valleys, the rocky beds empty for the larger part of the year. But for some reason the cultures coming down from the north stopped at the northern face of the hills, those coming up from the south at the southern face, leaving the hills themselves to be the refuge of the outcasts, of the failures, of the races and tribes and peoples who were successively driven out of the fertile plains. Here the aboriginal Gonds found their home; and here, thousands of years later, the ritual-murder system of thuggee reached its height; and here the roving freebooters, the Pin-

daris, who terrorized all Hindustan for fifty years, formed their
licentious bands; and here smoldered the last embers of the
Great Mutiny, marked now by individual graves of British en-
signs, killed in action against a forgotten rajah's ruined fort
nearby, where the still water lay green in the tank, and vines
climbed the broken wall, and each morning a tiger's pug marks
showed plain across the deserted courtyard—all these had been refugees from the history of their times; and all peculiarly Indian,
for the hills contained all their purpose, and they looked inward,
and did not know or care about any world outside these red
escarpments facing the dawn, and the rocky paths winding down
to the fords, and the tracks heavy with dust under the orgiastic
brilliance of the gold mohur and the flame-of-the-forest.

It was symbolic of India's near-awakening that we, who marched
now along these paths, saw in them only a road to the world
outside. Our gaze was directed eastward, toward Burma and beyond, to the rising sun.

The people of the forest, and of the small villages in the clearings hacked out of it, still lived a life which contained nothing
beyond what they saw. Much of India, particularly the cities and
large towns, seethed with political awareness—but not here. The
Congress' "Quit India" campaign was, in these parts, rather pre-
mature; the people of the Vindhya Hills seemed astonished to
learn that the British had even arrived.

In the course of a thousand miles walked through the country
between Jhansi and Jubbulpore I questioned several score villagers in different places as to what they knew about the political
situation in India, and the war. Most had heard of the war. Two
had heard of the Indian National Congress and three of Gandhi.
None had heard of Clive or Warren Hastings, or knew the name
of the viceroy, the commander in chief, or the provincial governor.

In one or two places particularly deep in the jungle a village
emptied at the sight of our leading troops—they had never seen
a soldier in their lives, most had never left the village; but they
always returned in a few minutes, when some grinning boy of a
rifleman had shouted into the forest after them, in dreadful
Hindi, to come back and not be such silly fools.

In one hamlet on the edge of the Bhanrer Ridge, looking out
across the plain toward Jubbulpore, Joe and I had the best meal

John Masters, 1942

John Masters, 1946

Willy Weallens

Joe Lentaigne

Pete Rees

Michael Roberts

Doc Whyte

Orde Wingate and Phil Cochran

Pete Rees and Bill Slim

Battle in Burma

Mandalay burning

Gurkha rifleman, Burma, 1945

of rice and dal we ever remembered. It was offered to us by a thin, vivid old man who looked like a retired Thug, and served by his women, one old and two young, all three very beautiful and self-possessed. They began to smile with delight when they realized that the vilely accented language in which we were talking to the old man was a version of their own, and the old lady kept chirruping for me to take more dal, and naked children gathered around, their mouths sticky with white berries, and I saw a young nubile girl's eyes droop with sheer, sudden love at the face and form of a handsome soldier striding by, rifle in hand.

We shouldered our packs. I began to dare to think it, to say it aloud—this time we're really going. There was a sense of urgency, of a fast onrushing fate, and we had so much to do, so much to learn, so much to prepare.

In Bombay Barbara, still a WAC sergeant, worked now for the R.A.F. as supervisor of a canteen. Her delicate ears were jealously guarded by the noncom in charge, Corporal Sidney Kidney, who fiercely reprimanded anyone using foul language in her presence. One day she asked the Indian manager the name of a certain dishwasher. The manager blushed, looked every way for help, and said he didn't know. Barbara insisted that he must know—what was his name? The manager, looking appealingly at Corporal Kidney for mercy, whispered, "Fukyeeruppa."

Then she worked for a spell with a Combined Operations School. Most of the other WACs there were Anglo-Indian girls, very young, incredibly small-boned, and quite ignorant of life outside their own environment. They had never met anything but reasonably modern water plumbing, and Barbara had to show them what the old-fashioned commode was; they thought it was a cupboard. Here she also met a sergeant-clerk who had been in 114 Brigade, and he told her, against all regulations, where I had now gone and what I was doing. She was a sensible girl though, and did not ask me for confirmation, which I could not have given her.

In 111 Brigade our admiration for Wingate increased when we learned that, at Quebec, he had obtained not only a private army but a private air force. Hitherto, our relations with our own Royal Air Force had been extremely frustrating. Whatever we asked them to do they declared to be difficult, impossible, or

against Air Force policy. Whatever they offered to do, we didn't
need. Now we were to have No. 1 Air Commando, U.S.A.A.C.
It consisted of a number of C-47s specially fitted with apparatus
to snatch gliders off the ground into the air; a lot of troop-carry-
ing Waco CG 4A gliders; a squadron of P-51 fighters; a squadron
of B-25 H bombers—the model with fourteen .50-caliber machine
guns, a 75-mm. cannon under the pilot's feet, plus a bomb load
of four thousand pounds; and many, many light planes, mostly
L-5s but with a proportion of L-1s. All these planes were marked
with five diagonal white stripes at the back end of the fuselage,
the mark of No. 1 Air Commando or, as we soon called them,
Cochran's Glamour Girls. (The British allusion was to C. B.
Cochran, a London impresario whose shows specialized in tooth-
some chorines. The American allusion was to the name of the
officer General Arnold had selected to lead the Commando—
Philip Cochran, the Flip Corkin of Milton Caniff's well-known
cartoon series.)

We were about to embark on final, week-long maneuvers. Before they began, Cochran spoke to a gathering of just about all
the officers in the force. He was short and square and young,
wore his cap on the back of his head, and did not appear to
be very tidily dressed. He began, with expansive good humor, to
tell us what he'd brought from America for us. We glanced surreptitiously at each other as he enlarged on the marvels of his
ships and his men. They would do anything. Any goddamn thing
we cared to ask for, they'd do it. . . . Would they let us control
the planes onto the target? (A major bone of contention between
us and the R.A.F.) "Why, sure . . . Hell, yes . . ." And much
more besides.

By the end the stolid British audience was frankly disbelieving.
Afterward we discussed the big-talking American among ourselves, and agreed that if he could do what he said he could he
wasn't an airman at all, he was the Angel Gabriel. But his manner,
with its evident desire to co-operate, had put us in a good humor,
and someone summed it up well by saying, "Look, even if nine-
tenths of what this chap says is bullshit, we'll still get twice what
the R.A.F. are giving us."

The maneuvers showed that the proportion of taurine dung
in Cochran's talk was very small. A mule leader got kicked "in

the family jewels," as Cochran breezily expressed it later; and his commander sent out an emergency call to the Light Plane Force to come and take him to hospital at once. The strip for an L-5 was supposed to be six hundred feet absolute minimum, but the only place available at the scene of the accident was a bumpy field no more than four hundred feet long. An L-5 went in, rescued the wretched man, and took off safely. The whole force had heard of it within five hours. The commanders' hopes and the soldiers' morale rose sky-high. Now, if we got hit in the middle of Burma we would not be left under a bush to die. Now we would not have to make the choice between destroying the morale of our men or saddling ourselves with wounded who would slow our movements so much as to invite disaster, and failure. Cochran risked a plane and an American pilot's life on that job. He gained, for his men, our immediate affection and respect.

At the end of the exercise, Wingate, who had barely recovered from a long and serious illness, left Joe to sum up the lessons learned. Joe had hardly begun with his reasoned analysis when Wingate changed his mind, took over himself, and gave us a pep talk. Those who wanted reason were depressed, those who wanted pep were pepped. I thought Wingate looked ill and fanatical, but very impressive, with his clean-shaven, handsome, urgent face, and on his chest the ribbon of the D.S.O., with two bars.

He came down to our brigade camp to inspect us. His visit coincided with the arrival of a small troupe of entertainers. I rather think the time was Hogmanay, but cannot be sure. At any rate, 111 Brigade was in a relaxed, holiday mood. Wingate had lunch in the brigade mess, and found himself sitting, not entirely by chance, between two of the most luxurious and metallic blondes of the entertaining troupe. Their giggling advances visibly embarrassed him, and then he came under attack from Lieutenant Bill Lucas, our liaison officer from the U.S. Air Force. Bill had decided that the general was full of horseshit, and now set about him with as little concern for his rank as Wingate himself ever showed when attacking others. Bill was soon on his feet, swinging round the tentpole opposite the general, and beginning to particularize his scorn for Wingate's mannerisms. Joe flashed me

an eye signal and I lured Bill out and to his tent. He collapsed
on his camp bed and glared moodily at me. "You're all the
same," he said. "Goddamn British. Worse than Goldwyn. U.S..
for chrissake."

My own head was firm on my shoulders, but a little muzzy.
"What?" I asked.

"U.S.," he repeated. "No goddamn good. I ought to punch
all of you in the nose. Un-Serviceable. U.S. No goddamn good,
for chrissake!"

At last I understood. Bill had been with us about two months.
All that time he had been brooding about our army's habit of
describing any article of equipment that had become useless as
U.S. That's what it sounded like, though in fact it was written
"u/s" and stood for "unserviceable." There was no time to explain. I could only apologize, and hurry off, for the general was
going to speak to the Cameronians.

When the seven hundred or so Jocks were gathered in front
of Wingate in a tight mass, the nearest some twenty feet from
him, he fixed one of them with his eye and said, "You're going
to die." He had a special rasping voice he used to impress
people with his ruthless personality, and he was using it now. The
rifleman addressed simpered nervously, but Wingate was now
staring at another man. "Many of you are going to die, or suffer
wounds, or near-starvation. All of you will meet hardship worse
than anything you have imagined."

This was an unorthodox way to speak to soldiers about to go
into action. Most generals indicate that a forthcoming operation
will much resemble a tennis tournament, and then when it is over
we shall be invited to have tea with the ladies. Wingate's approach was better, but he should not have used that voice on the
1st Battalion of the Cameronians. They were a very hard-bitten
lot, they all had hang-overs, and man to man they had already
beaten the Japanese. From Colonel Gillespie downward I could
sense an almost visible rising of the regimental *esprit de corps*
against the general. The regiment decided he was trying to
frighten them into bravery, and the real worth of Wingate's remarks—a message about sacrifice—was lost.

The day proceeded on its mountainous course. We climbed
slowly and painfully through the afternoon—more inspections,

more talks; passed the crest as the sun came over the yardarm, and gathered speed downhill, with no brakes. Joe and I, hurrying along a jungle path, met six Jock riflemen staggering the other way, arms linked in the dusty twilight. They recognized us. "Och, here's the bluidy brigadier. And the bluidy brigade major." They came to attention and flung us huge, ostentatious salutes. "Ye'll hae a drrink, wi' us, sorr!" They produced a bottle and we drank whisky from it. "Ye see, sorr, Ah'm goin' to die," their leader said seriously. "The general tol' me himsel'." They all burst out laughing and began to sing the Cameronians' own chanty, in which we joined:

> I belong to Glasgow, dear old Glasgow Town!
> What's the matter with Glasgow
> For it's going round and round?
> I'm only a poor little working chap
> As any one here can tell,
> But when I get a drop on a Saturday night—
> Why then Glasgow belongs to me!

We escaped with handshakings and back-slappings and cries of "Ye're a guid 'un, Joe!"

Darkness fell, we ate our dinner, and everyone began to move toward the cleared space where the troupe was going to give a show. Loud explosions in the Cameronians' lines rocked the night and a few minutes later a messenger reported to their colonel, who was with us, that two hand grenades had been detonated under the adjutant's camp bed. The adjutant escaped unharmed as he was not in the tent. The colonel said mildly, "That's going too far. Do we know who did it?"

"Yes, sir," said the M.P. He named a couple of soldiers.

"Put them in close arrest. Conduct prejudicial to good order and military discipline."

The entertainment began. General Wingate sat between Joe and Colonel Gillespie. It was a good show and the brassy blondes received the biggest ovation of their lives. It was fortunate that the Jocks were so drunk, I reflected, for they had been in the jungles, living a spartan life, for over six months. Even so, an almost visible aura of sexual longing wafted toward the curves of breast and thigh on the makeshift stage up there, clearly seen through the thin dresses under the glare and hiss of the pressure lamps.

And two soldiers stumbled forward from the edge of the audience and clambered up. The girls sang on. The two Jocks, both wearing heavy greatcoats, advanced upon them. Here it comes, I thought. What You Have Been Waiting For, What No One Has Yet Dared To Bring You, In Living Technicolor—Rape On Stage, As Thousands Cheer. General Wingate will not like this, I thought.

The M.P.s were after the two men by now. The men tried to dance with the girls. The girls edged farther over on the stage and kept singing gallantly. The M.P.s made a rush, one of the men danced away, and they both ran after him. The other soldier gave an enormous grin, opened his greatcoat, and from under it produced a large plucked goose. The M.P.s turned and made a rush at him. He danced with the goose, holding it by the neck and pirouetting prettily. The girls sang on. The audience was on its feet, whistling, cat-calling, shouting encouragement. I was laughing so hard that my belly hurt. The general wore a sickly smile. The M.P.s made a concerted rush at the goose boy. He stepped back and took a tremendous swing at them, with the goose. He missed and hit one of the blondes on her bottom. She fell down, picked herself up, and, with the other girl, clattered off stage, shrieking.

Their act was succeeded by a short ballet for policemen and soldiers, which was really much more professionally done. Colonel Gillespie, who knew his men, ordered a battalion drill parade for dawn the following morning.

111 Indian Infantry Brigade was ready for action. Soon afterward, in January, 1944, we set off for Assam by rail. My baby, our baby, was due in February. The brigade, commanded by Brigadier W. D. A. Lentaigne, D.S.O., consisted of Brigade Headquarters and four battalions, and each battalion of two columns, thus:

2nd Bn King's Own Royal Regiment (Lancaster)—41, 46 Cols.
1st Bn Cameronians (Scottish Rifles)—26, 90 Cols.
3rd Bn 4th Prince of Wales's Own Gurkha Rifles—30, 40 Cols.
4th Bn 9th Gurkha Rifles—49, 94 Cols.

13 Soon we are about to plunge into the jungle, into the close-quarter fog of an infantryman's war. To understand anything beyond the immediate limit of vision we must first ascend, as in a reconnoitering aircraft, and try to see the whole —the land, its peoples, the armies which tramped and fought across it; indeed, we must try and see into the minds of some of these men, what they were like, and what they were trying to do. It will be a longish flight, and since the thing that we are looking at, in all its aspects, is a major campaign in a major war, we cannot avoid a certain technicality. I do recommend taking the flight, but if you would rather proceed, uninformed, with the narrative, bypass this chapter and land on page 156.

First, the country: Burma.

A large salient of Burma sticks out eastward toward Siam. Another salient stretches southeastward along the shores of the Bay of Bengal toward Malaya. Excluding these two areas, which were beyond the scope of the 1944 operations, the rest of Burma is of a reasonably regular shape, somewhat like, say, an elongated left hand held up before the face, the back of the hand toward you. Two great rivers rise in the north—the Irrawaddy at the tip of the index finger and the Chindwin at the tip of the little finger— and flow south, join at the third knuckle, and continue south as one river, the Irrawaddy, to reach the sea near Rangoon. A railway runs due north from Rangoon, not along either river but by various subfeatures known collectively as the Railway Valley. At four hundred miles from Rangoon it reaches Mandalay, where it crosses the Irrawaddy; three hundred miles farther it ends at Myitkyina (pronounced Michina—it's simpler).

In all directions, Burma is protected by strong natural barriers. South and southwest is the sea. West—between Burma and India —lie range on range of mountains, deep and rapid rivers, and malarial forests, the whole so imposing an obstacle that not even a cart track linked the two countries by land, though Burma had been a part of the Indian Empire, ruled from Calcutta or Delhi, since 1882. Northward the land rises beyond the headwaters of the Chindwin and the Irrawaddy to ever higher mountains, at last to eternal snow and ice—the border with Tibet. To the east— more mountains, and three of the biggest rivers in Asia, the Salween, the Mekong, and the Yangtze Kiang, which there at one point all run south in deep, parallel gorges, each separated from the next by a severe range. This is the border with China. Southeast, toward Siam, it is the same.

The population of Burma, numbering about seventeen million, is divided into two categories—the Burmans and the rest. The Burmans, a small majority of the whole, live mainly in the river and railway valleys. They are a sophisticated, intelligent, hot-tempered people with beautiful women, a high state of civilization, and a long history, most of it spent in warfare against Siam, China, or both. Their religion is Buddhism of the Mahayana branch (the Greater Vehicle). They did not particularly like the British dominance that had been imposed on them in 1882, and many had helped the Japanese invaders in 1941.

"The rest" consist of four main peoples: the Shans in the east, the Chins in the west, the Kachins in the north, and the Karens in the south. The Karens are largely Christian, the others Animist, with pockets of Buddhism. Except the Karens, a highly civilized minority who can be compared with Armenians, Assyrians, or Jews, the others inhabit the jungles and mountains of the country. They are simpler people than the Burmans, they still have a tribal organization and a feudal pattern of life and they did welcome the British dominance, because it rescued them from the rule of the Burmans. The people who were to concern us were the Kachins in the north of the country, the most "backward," or most unspoiled, of all.

The Japanese invaded Burma in the cold weather of 1941–42, from south to north, sweeping the Allied forces before them up the railway and river valleys. At the end most of the Chinese retired into Yünnan Province, but some went with Stilwell into Assam, where the British and Indian forces also went.

By the beginning of 1944 the enemies faced each other on the general line of the Indian frontier, in three distinct areas. Outside the base of the little finger a Japanese corps faced India's 15 Corps in the Arakan. At the tip of the third finger the Japanese 15th Army faced our 4 Corps near the Imphal Plain. 4 and 15 Corps formed the 14th Army, under Lieutenant General William Slim. At the tip of the index finger one Japanese division, the crack 18th, faced Stilwell's Chinese, but in this area there had been little contact yet.

An earlier plan for 1944 having been scrapped when Chiang Kai-shek refused to co-operate, a new plan was evolved, and given the code name BLITZ. It consisted of four correlated operations. In the south 15 Corps was to make a limited advance down the Arakan coast. In the center 4 Corps, in contact with the Japanese about halfway between the Imphal Plain and the Chindwin River, was to advance to the Chindwin and be ready to exploit across it if a favorable opportunity arose. In the north Stilwell's Corps, consisting of five Chinese divisions plus Merrill's Marauders, was to advance to capture Myitkyina and Mogaung, with the intention of pushing the Ledo Road through to China as soon as possible. Wingate's Chindits were to dominate the area within forty miles of Indaw, a small town in north Burma, astride the Japanese lines of communication to their Stilwell front.

While our Supreme Command was making these plans, the Japanese were making theirs. The Tokyo government had told the commander in Burma, Kawabe, that there must be no bad news from him during 1944. Kawabe knew that bad news was only too likely unless he improved his situation. He saw that the Chindwin River, which was his main defense line on the central front, was too long and too vulnerable. He decided to advance and, from the Chindwin, to capture the Imphal Plateau, and Kohima.

There, the few approaches from India proper, through the mountains, could be more easily defended; the large rice crop of Assam would be available for his army; he could live and supply himself from our dumps and bases; he could upset our counteroffensive preparations by launching raids, guerrillas and spies of the Indian Traitor Army (formed from prisoners taken in Malaya) into Assam and eastern Bengal, where revolutionary cadres stood ready to co-operate with them; and since Stilwell's line of communication ran just below the Imphal Plateau and would be at his mercy, Stilwell would have to withdraw from the northern front.

All this was on the central front. But, as a deceptive measure, Kawabe decided to order an advance in the south, in Arakan, as though he meant to take Chittagong and Calcutta from that direction. This would take place in February, in sufficient strength so that we would think it was the Japanese main effort, and sufficiently before the true main effort so that we would have time to move reserves to the Arakan—three hundred miles from Imphal —and thus weaken ourselves where the real blow was to fall.

The tendency of these Japanese plans became suspected by our Intelligence. Plan BLITZ had to be resurveyed in the light of the probable Japanese intentions. The Allied field commander, Slim, appreciated that the center was the vital sector. If the Japanese attacked there it would be to our advantage to receive the attack in the best place for defense—the same Imphal-Kohima region which was the Japanese objective.

The Supreme Commander, Mountbatten, agreed to change half of Plan BLITZ. 4 Corps withdrew from its forward positions, retired to the Imphal Plain, and there prepared to receive the Japanese attack. By this maneuver Slim shortened his own lines of communication at the point of contact, while lengthening the Japanese. Slim's main bases, supply and ammunition depots, supporting airfields, etc., now lay very close at his back. The Japanese would be like divers at the end of a long lifeline which stretched for two hundred miles behind them through dense jungle and mountain and across a major river, the Chindwin.

Our 15 Corps, in the south, was ordered to hold its ground, without reinforcement; and also to be prepared, when the Japanese attack on it died down, to send reinforcements to Imphal.

No change was made in the roles of Stilwell or of the Chindits.

The effect of these decisions was to surrender the initiative to the Japanese, in the expectation that they would use it to destroy themselves. This is what happened, although, as Wellington said of Waterloo, it was a damned fine-run thing. It must be realized that the true roles of the two armies were the opposite of what they appeared to be. The Japanese were on the defensive; they attacked and attacked in order to secure a better defensive position from which to hold Burma. The Allies were on the offensive. They intended to force the road through to China and to retake Burma, and knew that the only way to do so was to destroy the Japanese Army; the simplest method to achieve this was to accept a defensive battle *à l'outrance* at Imphal.

The Japanese duly attacked, first in the Arakan. 15 Corps held them, though Colonel Tanahashi and the 55th Regiment made a bold and dangerous inroad into our rear areas. Here the Japanese suffered eight thousand casualties and we seven thousand.

On the northern front Stilwell started advancing in February, 1944.

On the central front the Japanese 15th Army crossed the Chindwin early in March and flung itself toward Imphal and Kohima. Our 4 Corps only just got back in time to be ready for them. The Chindits began to move into the battle. . . .

Who were the actors in this drama, what were they like?

The leading man was seven thousand miles away, and came no closer, but his personality projected itself sooner or later into every corner and every argument. Winston Churchill was a war leader, and a man, of a stature soaring above all of us. Admiration was far too small a word to express what every one of us felt about him—but idolatry was too strong a word. From Alanbrooke, Alexander, and Auchinleck down the ranks and the alphabet we were his loyal servants, but not his slaves. If the Prime Minister had an area of weakness, most of us would probably agree that it was India—past, present, and future. Of extraordinary humanity and understanding everywhere else, here he was biased, narrow, and reactionary. He had been in India as a subaltern in 1895 and formed opinions which forty-five years had not altered—though India had. To an Indian officer, that is, someone like myself, or to an officer of Indian race, Churchill was a dominant and superb figure; but on military matters he could be wrong, like the rest of us; on Indian matters he could be right, but he seldom was.

Our juvenile lead was Supremo, the handsome sailor. Lord Louis Mountbatten was popular, capable, and shrewd. He exuded confidence and charm, and his reputation as a fighting sailor, who had had numerous ships shot from under him, did him no harm either. He affected a somewhat overdone folksiness with us, but this was a revolt against the icy aloofness of World War I commanders (such as Haig, who, when advised that he should open up a bit, stopped by a nervous private in the trenches and said with forced geniality, "Well, my man, and where did you start this war?" The soldier stammered, "P-p-p-please, sir, I didn't start it").

General Sir George Giffard commanded all the land forces under Supremo, except Stilwell, who didn't like him and would not place himself under him.

Giffard's chief battlefield commander was Slim. Brilliant, bold, publicizing himself only to his troops and then only so that they should have confidence in him, he seldom made a mistake or missed an opportunity throughout the war; and when he did, he said so. Every fighting man in the 14th Army knew him by sight, and admired and trusted him—none more than I, for I had seen him coming back from the Pai-Tak Pass with the shell hole through his car, and I knew from the inside the determination and skill with which he conducted war.

Besides being a good soldier, Slim has since proved himself a good writer, and his book about the two Burma campaigns, *Defeat into Victory*, is in a class by itself among the generals' narratives. A few lines from the preface show why we respected him: "*Victory in Burma came not from the work of one man, or even of a few men, but from the sum of many men's efforts. We all, even those among us who may have seemed to fail, did our best. Luckily, that combined best proved good enough.*"

Stilwell was in a special category. He never wore less than three hats, and Supremo could only *order* him to do something when he was wearing the one labeled "Allied Corps Commander." As Commander of the U.S. China-Burma-India Theater he had a direct responsibility, and of course a right of appeal, to President Roosevelt; and as Chief of Staff to Chiang Kai-shek he could appeal to him. (On such occasions he probably did not call him The Peanut, as he usually did in his diary.)

Stilwell was an unmitigated disaster for inter-Allied relations. At this time the extent of his anti-British feelings was not generally known—certainly not to me; nor had his diary been published to show the consistent pattern of petty disparagement which bespeaks an inferiority complex of frightening dimensions. We thought of him simply as good old Vinegar Joe, and rather admired him for his unkempt appearance, salty language, and crotchety ways. He had an extraordinarily difficult task as President Roosevelt's military representative in China, where the war against the Japanese was regarded as a curtain-raiser to the struggle between Chiang Kai-shek and the Communists, each side trying to use the period to get itself into the best position for the all-out civil war that would follow defeat of the Japanese. Whether another man could have performed this task better than Stilwell, or more efficiently represented the interests of the United States, I am not qualified to say. In his dealings with America's other principal ally, though—Great Britain—he was animated chiefly by a desire to "burn up the Limeys." For a man who insisted that he was a simple infantryman he had strange blind spots about the normal reactions of fighting men. When Merrill's Marauders arrived at the Ledo Road front after a long march from Assam, Stilwell did not bother to go out on the road to watch them pass, though he was nearby. With Slim he got on comparatively well, and Slim liked him.

I don't think Stilwell liked our own commander, Wingate. Personal or petty reasons apart, Wingate had got supplies, men, aircraft, and arms from the U.S.A., when he himself had failed to do so. He distrusted the idea of Long Range Penetration operations; he loathed the British; he despised Indians and Gurkhas. This was the general with whom we were to co-operate.

There is Orde Wingate. . . . It is sixteen years, as I write, since he died and the reports have been coming in ever since, many still written with a passionate loyalty or a passionate dislike which brands everyone in the other camp as an unimaginative clod at the very least and, more usually, as a conniving traitor. In 1943 Matron McGeary, nursing Wingate back to life from typhoid, could write, "There were moments when it seemed as if he wanted to die. And I knew why. Those busybodies and mischief makers at G.H.Q. were trying to get at him again. They heard he was ill and they tried to ruin him while he was defenceless." This refers to the expressed doubts of people who thought that Wingate was wrong as honestly as Wingate thought he was right. And Matron McGeary was a superb and intelligent woman.

Even after the war, it went on. I was asked to subscribe to a memorial to "our Leader." I subscribed, but it was an unfortunate word to use at the end of a bloody war against *der Führer*. To me Wingate was one of the commanders in the chain that stretched from Mountbatten down to me; to others he was, and had always been, "our Leader." There is a difference.

In 1944 only his closest associates knew that two years earlier he had attempted to commit suicide, depressed by a feeling that his work in Abyssinia had not been properly appreciated. Nor did we know of his prewar brushes with military authority and civil policy in Palestine, where his ardent Zionism (he was not Jewish) had led him into acts that can be interpreted as treason, and had almost cost him his commission. I wish we had. It would have removed, much earlier, suspicions that his intenseness was a theatrical trick, not a genuine part of his nature.

We did know that, taxiing on an airfield with a staff lieutenant colonel after landing in a C-47, the door open, Wingate said abruptly, "Out!'"

The colonel said, "She'll be stopped soon, sir." Wingate kicked him out of the open door onto the runway, and jumped after him. This was in India weeks before the campaign began.

One can say that Wingate acted here like a determined man; or one can say something else. One can say that the incident showed a flaw in Wingate's character—lack of common sense to guide his demonic power.

We did not know that at Quebec Wingate had referred to us, the soldiers of India, as a "system of outdoor relief." If we had we would certainly have asked to draw our dole in less drafty places than Keren, Cassino, and Prome. But he did not need to state this attitude in words, for it was well understood after the 1943 expedition. He had had the 3/2nd Gurkhas in his brigade then, and his personal magnetism had not worked on them. Any experienced officer of Gurkhas could have told him that Gurkhas are not subject to mass suggestion but require careful training, familiar leadership, and love—and a great many did tell him; and were called obstructionists for their pains. The Gurkhas did not do well in the expedition. Wingate blamed them and their officers.

I believe that Wingate lacked humanity. He thought in great terms, and worked for great ends, among great men. For that huge majority which is less than great he had little sympathy. They were merely the muddlers and fools whom he must use to attain his ends. Churchill, too, has felt this but there has never been a moment when Churchill did not know that the only worth-while great end is the betterment of that majority, of those muddlers, fools, and weaklings.

For these reasons I am glad that none of us knew of Churchill's minute of July 24, 1943: "I consider Wingate should command the army against Burma. He is a man of genius and audacity and has rightly been discerned by all eyes as a figure quite above the ordinary level. The expression 'The Clive of Burma' has already gained currency."

The expression may have been heard in Westminster, but not in India, the scene of Clive's exploits. The appointment of Wingate to command the 14th Army would have led to a major disaster in the field. Apart from his imbalance he suffered from strategic astigmatism, caused by his penchant for and skill in guerrilla-type operations. Throughout his life he never seemed to grasp that against a brave and well-led enemy all war hinges on the ability to destroy the enemy's main armed forces in pitched battle—or, of course, to subvert his will to fight at all, a case not applicable in Burma. The reason for this stark fact is that sooner or later one side will attack something—a city, a port, a supply line, the army itself—which the other side *must* defend. Civilian leaders have always hated the idea and tried in a thousand ways to find a way round it. But—to take recent history alone—after needless expenditure of blood, time, and treasure they have always had to call on the Grants, Pershings, Fochs, Haigs, Montgomerys and Slims to do the job. None of these men necessarily did the job in the best possible way; they commanded their nations' armies because they had a single-minded grasp of the nature of the job itself. (Churchill's desire to attack Gallipoli was not in the category of fact-dodging; it was an attempt to fight the inevitable pitched battle under conditions, and in a place, advantageous to his side.) Wingate's unsoundness was shown in his proposal that the whole of 14th Army should be broken up into Long Range Penetration groups, presumably in the expectation that the Japanese would rush about Southeast Asia trying to mop them up, one by one. The Japanese, of course, would have done no such thing. They would have advanced, and seized the depots and air bases from which the groups were supplied. To have prevented them would have entailed a pitched battle. . . .

Wingate also possessed little reserve of force to draw upon when his plans went awry. This was shown on our D-Day when an unexpected obstacle left him unable to make, or even to recommend, a decision. His biographer, not an impartial recorder, tells of other such moments during the 1943 expedition. Twice Wingate tried to bluster Slim into changing an order, and twice climbed down when he found that Slim was not in the least afraid of him or of the specter of the Prime Minister which he conjured up in the way an angry small boy threatens to call his big brother. He had a persecution complex that was almost paranoid in its intensity.

I have given space to this negative side of Wingate because not enough has been said about it. He was no army commander and he was no Clive, in spite of their both having tried to commit suicide. He was not, on the other hand, a poseur or a publicity seeker. I and others who had thought so were idiots to imagine that he could have fooled men of the caliber of Churchill, Arnold, Alanbrooke, and Mountbatten.

His sense of mission, of his rightness, were genuine and deeply felt. He was a prophet of the Lord and those that stood against him were to be thrown down like the traitors they were. He was an original thinker on military matters. He was an excellent planner, an uneven commander in the field. To say that he aroused the offensive spirit on the Burma front is to insult every officer and soldier already there; but his 1943 expedition and the large scope of his plans for 1944 gave all of us the feeling that we were not neglected on the world stage, outshone by the greater glamour of Italy, the Pacific, and the obviously forthcoming D-Day invasion in Europe. The 14th Army, already labeled by its newspapermen as the Forgotten Army, waging a murderous campaign in difficult country and bad climate, could do with a Hero, someone beloved of the sulky, distant gods of Washington and London. Wingate was it.

Wingate, above all, is a study in the byways of the human spirit. At what point, and why, did he decide that he would enter the Hall of Fame by the back way?—for he was mentally and morally equipped to walk in at the front door. But he decided early that whatever the rest of his class and his associates did, he would say and do the opposite. If they believed in good manners, he would cultivate rudeness. If they loved the Arabs, he would love the Jews. If they dressed well, he would receive callers while lying naked on his camp bed, scrubbing his person with a toothbrush. He declared war, then. But why?

He lived in a state of war. He won an early campaign during his days at the Royal Military Academy. As a punishment for nonconformity he was sentenced to pass, naked, between two rows of cadets armed with wet and knotted handkerchiefs. They would flog him as he ran the gantlet. When all was ready Wingate, aged nineteen, appeared. He stopped at the first youth, looked him in the eye, said, "You first," and turned his back to receive the blow. The cadet struck him. But the next one did not, nor the next . . . nor anyone else, as Wingate went slowly down the lines, looking each of the young fools in the eye. Thus he established, very early, a moral ascendancy over the ruck, and a scorn for the weak and the foolish. Thus, later, he looked in the eye, scornfully, many who were neither weak nor foolish and had no intention of flicking his sensitivity with a wet handkerchief; nor of giving away all that they had of knowledge, experience, and opinion, and following him. Thus, by unflinching moral courage he attracted fanatical loyalty, unswerving distrust. Thus was established the world he lived in—his side and the enemy: there could be no neutrals. Thus he performed great feats—and they are great by any standards—in Palestine, Abyssinia, and Burma.

Before and during the war the Wingate Problem, as we may call it, was waged over the question—is he right or wrong, in this idea, that plan? Nearly everyone who writes or speaks about him even now, sixteen years later, is concerned with the same question. This has led to a fruitless and sometimes disingenuous controversy, endlessly renewed, with Wingate's blatant follies minimized on one side, and his acts of sheer genius denigrated on the other. He himself was compelled to believe that he was always right, to fight bitterly against anyone who questioned it, to accept no friends, only disciples—but we are not under the same compulsion.

Wingate was sometimes right and sometimes wrong. It really does not matter. What does matter is that he possessed one of the most unusual personalities of recent history. He had a driving will of tremendous force. His character was a blend of mysticism, anger, love, passion, and dark hatred, of overpowering confidence and deepest depression. He could make all kinds of men believe in him, and he could make all kinds of men distrust him. Why, why, why? Here is the true theme of Wingate's life. It is quite unnecessary, if trying to prove Napoleon's greatness, to show that he was always right, generous, kind, and humble. He wasn't, but he was a phenomenon. So was Wingate.

The tragedy of Wingate lies not in his early death but in the unknown and unknowable quality of what he might have achieved if he had loved instead of despising the generality of his fellow humans.

Between us and Wingate stood his staff. While we were in training, General Willcox, the commander of India's Central Army, had said to me, "Wingate's coming back from Quebec soon—and bringing most of his term at the Shop [the Royal Military Academy] with him." The quip was made without malice —Willcox did a great deal for Wingate and the Chindits—and I took it in the same spirit. What made us in 111 Brigade quail was the prospect of being handled through a bunch of converts who had come out from England imbued with Churchill's (and Wingate's) conviction that India was a hotbed of obstructionism. Such people, I knew from experience, were not only ignorant of the Indian administrative setup, but determined not to learn anything about it. We would be the sufferers.

There was Wingate's opinion of the Indian Army, of Gurkhas and their officers, already mentioned—and we had two Gurkha battalions, a Gurkha brigade major, and a Gurkha brigadier; whom Wingate had not chosen; who had considerably more battle experience than he; who was a brilliant graduate of the Staff College, which Wingate was not; who would not necessarily agree with Wingate all the time and would quite definitely not automatically enroll as a disciple; who had been thinking over the problems himself for months and reached his own solutions.

We expected a certain pressure to be exerted upon us, or even against us, through the staff. We were quite wrong. The staff duly arrived and set up shop. Derek Tulloch, the Brigadier General Staff, turned out to be the only R.M.A. intimate of Wingate's. We met no discrimination. There were some contretemps; once Joe sent me hot foot in the middle of the night from our camp to Gwalior, ninety miles, to have a certain order changed or bring him Tulloch's sweetbreads on a plate—and, if Tulloch persisted, he was going to follow himself and get Wingate's. But such occasions were few. Tulloch himself was approachable and sympathetic, and the chief A.Q. officer was Brigadier Neville Marks of the 3rd Gurkhas, who had been a D.S. while I was at Quetta. Between them they performed marvels. I do not recall that during the campaign any troops of 111 Brigade ever went short of anything, or were ever unclear as to their immediate task, whether or not they agreed with that task. This is a rare thing to be able to say about any staff and I would like to say it here about Wingate's. In view of the natural antipathy between troops and staff this good feeling is all the more remarkable when it is remembered that the nature of Chindit war cut out all personal contact between the two "sides."

Below the generals, below the staff . . . and above them all, were the soldiers. The theater, and this campaign, gathered to itself, like a whirlpool, men from the ends of the earth. There were English, Irish, Welsh, and Scots, and, in the R.A.F., Newfoundlanders, Australians, Canadians, New Zealanders, and South Africans. There were Chinese; there were tall, slender Negroes from East Africa, and darker, more heavily built Negroes from West Africa, with the tribal slits slashed deep into their cheeks— an infantry division of each. There were Chins, Kachins, Karens, and Burmans, mostly light brown, small-boned men in worn jungle green, doubly heroic because the Japanese held possession of their homes, often of their families, too; and, until about now, how could they be sure which side was going to win?

There were men from every state of the United States. They flew heavy bombers, they ran railroads, they drove titanic trucks at breakneck speeds through the narrow streets of primeval villages. In the back areas some behaved with a certain bombast, an air of "We'll put this mess straight, meanwhile everything in sight belongs to us, especially your women"—which was rather galling to people who had not found it easy to get the mess straight by themselves, and had fought so long alone; but most back-area soldiers behave unpleasantly, and the Americans were merely more noticeable, with their funny accents and funny clothes—and their extra money. But, the closer you got to the front, the more you found that the Americans, whether or not they saluted with great punctilio, meant business, and the closer became the ties between them and the rest of us.

Lastly, and in by far the greatest numbers, there were the men of the Indian Army, the largest volunteer army the world has ever known. There were men from every caste and race—Sikhs, Dogras, Pathans, Madrassis, Mahrattas, Rajputs, Assamese, Kumaonis, Punjabis, Garhwalis, Naga head-hunters—and from Nepal, the Gurkhas in all their tribes and subtribes, of Limbu and Rai, Thakur and Chhettri, Magar and Gurung. These men wore turbans, and steel helmets, and slouch hats, and berets, and tank helmets, and khaki shakos inherited from the eighteenth century. There were companies that averaged five feet one inch in height, and companies that averaged six feet three inches. There were men as purple black as the West Africans, and men as pale and wheat-gold of skin as a lightly sun-tanned blond. They worshiped God according to the rites of the Mahayana and Hinayana, of Sunni and of Shiah, of Rome and Canterbury and Geneva, of the Vedas and the sages and the Mahabharatas, of the ten Gurus, of the secret shrines of the jungle. There were vegetarians and meat-eaters and fish-eaters, and men who ate only rice, and men who ate only wheat; and men who had four wives, men who shared one wife with four brothers, and men who openly practiced sodomy. There were men who had never seen snow and men who seldom saw anything else. And Brahmins and Untouchables, both with rifle and Tommy gun.

No one who saw the 14th Army in action, above all, no one who saw its dead on the field of battle, the black and the white and the brown and the yellow lying together in their indistinguishable blood on the rich soil of Burma, can ever doubt that there is a brotherhood of man; or fail to cry, "What *is* Man, that he can give so much for war, so little for peace?"

Lastly, there was our common, single enemy—the Japanese. They are the bravest people I have ever met. In our armies, any of them, nearly every Japanese would have had a Congressional Medal or a Victoria Cross. It is the fashion to dismiss their courage as fanaticism but this only begs the question. They believed in something, and they were willing to die for it, for any smallest detail that would help to achieve it. What else is bravery? They pressed home their attacks when no other troops in the world would have done so, when all hope of success was gone; except that it never really is, for who can know what the enemy has suffered, what is his state of mind? The Japanese simply came on, using all their skill and rage, until they were stopped, by death. In defense they held their ground with a furious tenacity that never faltered. They had to be killed, company by company, squad by squad, man by man, to the last.

By 1944 many scores of thousands of Allied soldiers had fallen unwounded into enemy hands as prisoners, because our philosophy and our history have taught us to accept the idea of surrender. By 1944 the number of Japanese captured unwounded, in all theaters of war, probably did not total one hundred. On the Burma front it was about six.

For the rest, they wrote beautiful little poems in their diaries, and practiced bayonet work on their prisoners. Frugal and bestial, barbarous and brave, artistic and brutal, they were the *dushman* and we now set about, in all seriousness, the task of killing every one of them.

14 Late in January, 1944, 111 Brigade entered the Assam war zone. After detraining at the head of the Cachar Valley we marched at once across the mountain range separating us from the Imphal Plateau. The rivers ran south here, and our course was east, so each day we climbed up a long, steep bamboo-covered mountainside, on a track that would just take a jeep, and descended equally abruptly to the next valley, where a wide, cool river ran under huge trees and the fish rose in the evening. In the mornings the mist covered the mountains, and sometimes we climbed up through it, as an aircraft would, before the sun dispersed it and then we looked out across a vast pearly gray sea, as a pilot would, and the Gurkhas sang their cheerful *jaunris*. Every night we lit a huge campfire, and after dinner five or six of us gathered round the fire, and I read aloud from *Paradise Lost*, and we discussed the universe. Twice, climbing through the feathery bamboo toward the clouds we halted in awe at piles of dung in the road, monstrously big, like lumpy sacks thrown down; and twice heard the wild elephants grazing on the slope above us. After seven carefree days we descended to the Imphal Plain. My father had been here in 1904 as a very young subaltern. It was then almost the Ultima Thule of the peaceful life in India. The duck shooting on the Logtak Lake was the best in the world. Mahseer up to sixty pounds abounded in the Manipur

River. Thousands of square miles of mountains and jungles to
roam in, gun under arm and dog at heel.

In 1944 it was an advanced suburb of Armageddon. Beyond
the Logtak Lake—it was still there, reed-rimmed, silent, pale
blue—lay the border ridges, and beyond them, Burma.

Through February we waited near Imphal, feverishly studying
maps and intelligence reports, trying to find routes by which we
could infiltrate through the Japanese lines into Burma. It was
going to be damned hard; they were very thick on the ground,
and as agitated as a swarm of bees. One of our brigades, Fergus-
son's 16th, had already set out, starting from far to the north
near Ledo and marching south, roughly between the Stilwell and
the Imphal fronts, through country so appalling that the Japanese
had not thought to patrol or guard it in any strength. For the
others, who would have to travel through the main body of the
Japanese 15th Army, it looked as though we would have to buy
our tickets not with sweat but with blood.

Now Wingate showed his imaginative quality. He arranged for
the rest of his force to fly into Burma. Advanced groups would
land in gliders and hack airfields out of nothing. Powered planes
would follow. Ten thousand men and sixteen hundred mules were
involved. Calvert's 77 Brigade would go first, followed by Lentaigne's 111 and parts of Rickett's 81st West African.

So, we were going to fly. . . .

I hurried to my tent and opened my Staff College files. Airborne operations. Air loading tables . . . We were working like
demons. How many planes, how many gliders were we going to be
allotted, on each night? No one knew yet. What payload was
for our use—in a tow plane—in a nontow plane—in a glider?
This they told us. We had to apply the principles to the actuality.
Fighting units must go before administrative units, but remember more than two units can't fight without communication and
control; and that means a headquarters, or at least the tactical part
of it. Subunits must not be broken up, but must fly together,
and with all their arms and ammunition, and, if anything was
carried by mules, the mules had to go along too. Long conferences
with battalion commanders and adjutants succeeded hectic meetings with our own headquarters signalers, doctors, and other
specialists.

One detail we were spared: we didn't have to weigh anything or anybody. That had been done, down to ounces. Apart from heavy weapons, reserve ammunition, and radio sets we were going to carry everything on our backs. For seven months we had been waging a furious but indecisive battle in an attempt to give the soldier the means to fight and eat, and at the same time allow him to walk and run. The results were appalling to look at in cold blood, but represented the best compromise we could reach. The No. 1 of a Bren-gun team, when carrying the gun, and just after a supply drop had put five days' K rations in his pack, toted a load of 86 pounds. For a Gurkha with a total body weight of about 130 pounds, who was expected to run up and down mountains, this was a lot. The weights ranged down until the brigadier and a few technicians carried about 42 pounds.

And now—how, actually, do you get three large Missouri mules into a C-47, at night, to a tight schedule? How do you keep them there, so that they do not injure themselves and cannot kick their handlers or the sides of the plane? What do you do if one breaks loose in the air? Shoot him? The bullet will go on through the sides of the plane. From what angles is it safe to engage in gunplay inside a loaded aircraft?

We were going to land, from the air, in the center of North Burma. But where, exactly? The gliders would go first. They needed a strip of reasonably smooth ground, at least one hundred yards wide by four hundred yards long, not on or near any routes actively used by the Japanese. The strip had to be capable of expansion and improvement, quickly and with such equipment as the gliders could take, into an airfield eight hundred yards long, for use by C-47s. It had to be fairly close to the assigned area of operations.

One suitable place was already known. Some men of Wingate's 1943 expedition had been flown out of it six months earlier. Another was found nearby. These were given the code names of Broadway and Piccadilly, and designated as the main landing targets. A reserve field had to be found.

Searching the half-inch maps, Joe and I had already noticed a dotted line enclosing a rectangle of nothing in particular, inside the great bend of the Shweli. It looked as if it might be a clearing in the jungle. If so, it would suit in all respects but one:

it was on the wrong side of the Irrawaddy from the area of our operations. Wingate's staff had noticed the same place. It had to be looked at. So Colonel Jumbo Morris of the 9th Gurkhas and I went one morning to Imphal, and at Tulihal airfield boarded a B-25 of the Air Commando to make the reconnaissance. Standing under the wing with the pilot, we made sure that the latter understood exactly what it was that we wanted to see. Then we climbed up into the belly of the plane and the plane took off. The engines settled down to the familiar racket of the B-25, a very hard-edged sound with a distinct thrashing rhythm in it. We turned east across the Logtak Lake. The waist gunners stared out over the barrels of the .50-calibers, steadily chewing gum (so was I), baseball caps on the backs of their heads. We crossed the last ridge, and the land dropped sharply away below us toward the Chindwin.

It was tremendous country, not tall in the Himalayan sense, but big, the dark jungle rolling away beyond the horizons, seemingly without a break—then the sun caught a flash of water and I saw a silver river among the trees.

I stared down with all my mind concentrated. We were not flying very high, but it was quite impossible to see under the trees. Whole divisions might be encamped down there—actually, they were—but unless they made heavy smoke fires, I would see nothing. So—nor would the Zeros see us when, soon, we began to march and live under that dense roof. We would have to be careful crossing fields and rivers—the sandbanks showed up like neon signs—but otherwise, with our own air force so much in the ascendant over Burma, we could ignore the risk of being discovered from the air when on the move. This was good news, and vitally important news, too.

On in the B-25 . . . we passed over that freak of nature, and nature's rainfall, called the Dry Zone. The forests thinned and gave way to long strips of cultivation. Here was the railway. A message came through on the intercom for us to go forward. I clambered up on ammunition boxes, and slid on my stomach like a snake, through the narrow tunnel between the top of the bomb bay and the arched roof of the plane. Followed by Jumbo I slid headfirst into the forward compartment, behind the pilot. The engines made less racket here. The jungle began again, and

beyond it the broad ribbon of the Irrawaddy bisected the landscape. The large-scale map was ready in my hands and as we
crossed the river we flew onto the map, and I pinpointed the
exact place. The pilot pointed to his compass and I penciled
the course lightly in on the map. Twenty miles northeast there
should be a break in this vastness of forest.

Ten miles. I saw it quite clearly, ahead and to port. We were
flying at five thousand feet, and must neither go lower nor circle
the place, for we must not give away our interest in it. It remained in full view for about four minutes. No houses nearby.
No new roads. Couldn't tell about the surface for sure, but there
were no obvious pits or bumps, and no trees. No water visible. I
scribbled a note on the edge of the map. Very important. We'd
have to carry water in for men and mules, for at least two days.
That meant more weight on the planes. We'd allowed for it.

The clearing, nearly a thousand yards long by two hundred
wide, disappeared astern. Ten minutes later we came to the
Shweli River, and swung to port, the sun wheeling back and
around until it shone in on the pilot's side of the nose perspex.
We flew down the river, past its junction with the Irrawaddy, and
on, as though searching for river traffic. We saw none and headed
back for the railway. The bombardier, crouched in the nose,
settled himself more carefully in position. Unless we used up our
bombs on the river, the target was the railroad station of Kawlin.
(Every reconnaissance was "covered" by a bombing mission.)
The bombardier spoke in an unexcited voice to the pilot and the
plane wavered left, and steadied. The plane heaved, settled, and
at once swung sharply left as the pilot turned. The bombs marched
like black and brown mushrooms beside the track and just behind
the station.

The pilot said, "We'll give them a few rounds of artillery."

The bombardier scrambled back and loaded a 75-mm. shell
into the breech of the gun. The gun barrel passed under the
pilot's seat on the left. Jumbo and I looked at each other. It was
one thing to read, while on the ground, that our B-25s had a
75-mm. gun among their arsenal, quite another to hang on those
thrashing propellers, a mile in the sky, and see that these madmen
actually intended to let off that great field piece inside the flimsy
contraption. The fools! Had they never seen the recoil of a field

gun? . . . It was too late, for our nose pointed sharply down, and we headed straight for the station. Some old boxcars stood on a siding outside the shell of the station building. The plane leaped violently as the pilot fired—and again—and again. The shells burst some way from the target. A terrible racket broke out as the copilot opened up with the forward .50-caliber machine guns. We were low now, swinging up and around, and the waist gunners poured streams of tracer into the station. Around again . . . *boom*, the lurch and jump, the cataract of machine-gun fire.

The wings leveled slowly and the pilot shouted in my ear, "Got to leave some ammunition in case Zeros jump us on the way home." Jumbo and I scrambled quickly back to the waist, where we asked the gunners to show us how to work their guns. They showed us, and then hinted with a grin that we might as well look after them ourselves if we were so goddamn keen. We weren't keen, we were frightened. We sat tensely searching the skies, while the B-25 roared westward. At last we recrossed the Chindwin. The trees grew larger and more distinct. They climbed toward us in menacing heaves, then sank back, but in a minute rose again, lurching drunkenly up to grab us. I stiffened at the handles of the guns, and glanced at the gunners, who were talking about food. The last trees brushed by a few feet below the wings and slipped down. Imphal lay forty miles ahead under towering cloud.

At headquarters we reported that the jungle clearing would suit very well as a landing point, apart from the serious drawback of its being on the east side of the Irrawaddy. Force gave it the code name Chowringhee, after the main street of Calcutta.

Two or three times I had to fly to Hailakandi to confer with Cochran, Allison and others of the Air Commando about the details of our fly-in, about the light planes, about the tactical support we must receive from their fighters and bombers. Once, on an occasion when Paulette Goddard was entertaining the Air Commando, I stayed overnight. I noticed with amusement that the American airmen, whose free and easy discipline was a cause of much huff-puffing among our Blimps, behaved a great deal more quietly than the Cameronians had. After the show some of us held a long session in a pilot's quarter, with his pals. A fattish, balding flight officer was introduced as Coogan. "Not *the*

Coogan!" I exclaimed idiotically; but he was, and I felt doubly delighted to meet him—because I had loved those old movies with Charlie Chaplin, and because he and I were born on the same date, October 26, 1914. Later we played The Game, and Coogan performed a feat which convinced me that his early acting success was no fluke. He had to act out "The Theory of Relativity." He got the message across in two seconds flat, by altering his face to look like Einstein, complete with the well-known aura of white hair; Coogan, as I have said, was almost bald. We also got a good deal of inside dope about Chaplin and Betty Grable, but I don't think he had his heart in those reminiscences; his comrades had made them into a stock turn which he was expected to put on.

We came up to the start line. Wingate's Operation Instruction reached us, and I worked twenty-four hours at a stretch to prepare ours. (If any reader wants to know something of what was involved, the order is reproduced as an Appendix to this book.) Across the hills at Hailakandi, the last precurtain crisis leaped upon 77 Brigade. A final air photographic sortie showed Piccadilly covered with tree trunks, laid out at regular intervals over the whole area where the gliders were to land. The Intelligence officer jumped into a jeep and drove like fury, with the wet prints, to the edge of the runway. There all the responsible figures were gathered, watching the preparations—Slim, Wingate, Cochran, Calvert. One hour to take-off.

Had the Japanese got word of the operation, in so much detail that they knew the exact landing spots? Wingate thought so, and insisted that the Chinese had betrayed us. Or had the Japanese merely foreseen the possibility of airborne operations and decided to block off some of the more obvious landing places? Or was it a pure accident? What decision to take—cancel altogether? Postpone for a few days until the situation could be clarified? Carry on, using Broadway and Chowringhee only? It was here that Wingate's fiber again showed its lack of tensile strength. He became highly emotional, said the operation would now be murder, and at last, when Slim had calmed him down, said that the responsibility was Slim's, and Slim must make the decision. Slim did

so, ordering the operation to go on. Troops destined for Piccadilly would be diverted to Broadway and Chowringhee.

Mike Calvert and his men had not paused in their preparations. At dusk the lead planes took off down the runway, each
towing two gliders, both the tow planes and the gliders loaded to
capacity.

Over the mountains to the east, Joe and I were drinking with
the officers of the 3rd Battalion of the regiment to which we both
belonged, the 4th Gurkhas. There was a lot of rum and a lot of
noise, and the moon one day short of full. I had an eye on my
watch, and though the orderlies kept pouring rum into my glass
it had little effect, nor could the *jaunri* dances wholly distract my
attention.

"It's nearly time," I muttered to Joe.

He went outside, and we all followed him. The singing stopped
and we waited. The trees were widely scattered in the camp, and
very tall. For two or three minutes we heard nothing, and no one
spoke.

"Here they come."

We heard the distant, growing throb of the C-47s—a full, round
sound, soft-edged and with a slow pulse. We had heard it many
times before, but this night we first *heard* it, to know it from any
other sound, forever. The black wings swept across the moon,
and at the roots of the wings I saw the red glow of the motors.
For a long time they passed, eastward. 77 Brigade was on its way.

The telephone started ringing and we went up to the office.
New plans, caused by the blocking of Piccadilly. We were going
to Chowringhee. All right. Our orders would have to be rewritten. Then the Brigadier, General Staff of 4 Corps came on. Some
administrative change, sending us earlier to Tulihal airfield than
we had planned, or was necessary; removal of trucks that had been
promised.

Joe's face darkened. "Get me the Corps Commander," he
snapped. A pause, while the brigadier at the other end obviously
hinted that the Corps Commander was a busy man, and unavail-
able. "I don't care a damn what he's doing," Joe shouted. "Get
him, or I'm coming into Imphal." A longer wait, while the tips
of Joe's ears glowed a deep purple. He had an Irish temper as

famous as his energy and good humor, but he usually kept it under rigid control.

The Corps Commander, Lieutenant General Scoones, came on. Joe raised his voice still more and fairly bellowed into the phone. "I'm not going to have my brigade buggered about, I don't care what your bloody staff said or what they do. You're not going to take away those trucks and we'll go to Tulihal on the date already planned. It's a bloody disgrace and I won't put up with it. Do you understand?" And on, in the same vein, for some minutes. General Scoones, not a man noted for his forbearing charm, must have had a depth of understanding few of us credited him with, for he kept calm and polite, and never thereafter mentioned Joe's insubordination; but Joe got what he wanted.

Of the sixty-one gliders that set out for Broadway that night, only thirty-five reached it. Tow ropes broke, aircraft engines overheated, fuel ran out. The gliders crash-landed all over Burma, causing the Japanese great confusion. Of those that did reach Broadway, some crashed into the trees. As one of the missing gliders contained the ground control organization there was no way of controlling the other landings. Twenty-three men were killed and scores injured—but only by these battle accidents. No one had betrayed the plan. There were no Japanese. (The teak logs of Piccadilly had been dragged out there to dry in the course of ordinary Burmese logging operations.)

Three nights later, on the evening of March 8, 1944, I dressed myself for battle—nailed boots, two pairs of thick woolen socks knitted for me by Barbara, underpants, green cotton trousers held down at the boot by short puttees, vest, khaki flannel shirt worn outside my trousers, silk panic map of Burma around my neck, carbine over my shoulder; web equipment containing a water bottle, carbine ammunition, compass; binoculars slung around my neck, the strap shortened so that they hung high on my chest; Gurkha hat with the big IV badge of my regiment. On my left hip a haversack containing maps, code books, pencils, message pads, carbon papers, first field dressing, two condoms (watch, compass, and matches would be wrapped in these when we had to swim a river). On my right hip a kukri in its leather case, that in a green cotton cover. On my back a big pack, containing five days' K rations, or fifteen packets; a green light wool blanket cut in half (half a blanket a man), a ground sheet, two spare pairs of wool socks, toothbrush, toothpaste, Mepacrine tablets, razor, soap, a small hand towel dyed khaki, *Paradise Lost*, a pair of nail scissors, iodine pencil, sneakers, a U.S. field jacket.

I felt strong and alert. The long months of learning, of training and working toward an end, were over. It was two and a half years since I had been in action. Whether Wingate was right or wrong in his grand scheme no longer mattered. I felt grateful to him, and respectful, for it was he who had brought me to the edge of Tulihal airfield, in the dusk, to send me out on a great enterprise. Stilwell, Slim, Giffard, Supremo, also faded from reality. They lived, and performed their roles, but the focus had fined down to the men immediately surrounding me—the Gurkhas of the Defense Platoon, standing in groups according to their plane loads. Briggs, Macpherson, Baines, Rhodes-James, Jennings, Smith, Saw Lader the Karen. Joe, his glasses gleaming, his hat on the front of his head. The two men closest to me, John Hedley and Doc Whyte.

I had had no word from Barbara for many weeks. Our move, the secrecy, the battle—it could be explained, but no explanation soothed my worry. I had heard nothing.

An officer who would stay behind was shaking my hand. "Thanks," I said. "Same to you." But he was saying something, not just a "good luck." I had to bring my mind back from a distant place, and listen. "It's for you. The telegram," he said, giving it to me.

I moved a little apart and opened the telegram, which had taken three weeks to reach me. Barbara had given birth to a girl. Mother and child were well. All her love, always.

After a time walking by myself among the ranked aircraft and the waiting men, seeing nothing, I told Desmond Whyte. He wrung my hand and grinned his warm grin. "You old bugger!"

"Not that, surely," I said. He pulled a small medical bottle from his haversack and we drank a toast.

"Aircraft B-19—load!" the Planing Master said. At the head of my plane complement, I walked forward.

Book Three **ACTION, EAST**

15 It was dark now. The aircraft, C-47s from the R.A.F. and the U.S.A.F., stood in the center of Tulihal airfield, in several ranks, back to back. Planes had already begun to take off, two at a time. There were no gliders. I marched my plane load to the check point, and gave my plane number to the guide waiting there, shouting to make myself heard above the roar of engines. The guide led off between the tails of the aircraft. The engines blew up dust in great whirls so that I bowed my head and jammed my hand on top of my head to keep my hat on. Half an hour earlier all mules for this night's flight were reported loaded, so as I climbed the ramp I was expecting to see what I did see, the stern ends of three large mules jammed tight across the forward half of the cabin, their noses close against the forward bulkhead and the door leading to the cockpit. Two mule leaders and our Transport *havildar* stood in the narrow space forward of the mules, soothing them as they fidgeted and nervously tossed their heads. A strong bamboo pole, anchored to ring bolts in the body of the aircraft, stretched across the cabin forward of the mules, and their heads were tied fast to this pole. Thinner poles ran down between them, anchored to an extra-thick breech pole which ran tight under their quarters, pushing them forward and giving them no room to maneuver or kick. Their saddles and loads lay stacked on the metal floor which now, before take-off on a C-47, was sharply tilted down from front to rear. The mules only kept their footing because of the straw spread under them.

I counted my men and shut the main door of the aircraft. So far everything, including how to close the door of a C-47, had been practiced and rehearsed. Now began the unrehearsed, and unrehearsable.

The flight lieutenant in command of the aircraft stood in the forward doorway, and stared interrogatively at me between the twitching ears of the center mule. I raised my thumb, he raised his. That door shut with a clang. The lights went out. The engines started up.

The engines changed pitch and the plane throbbed wildly. Airfield lights and the lighted cabins of other aircraft and the blue flare from engine exhausts passed slowly by, shining fitfully through our windows onto a dark, damp face, a rifle barrel, a rolling eye. The mules threw up their heads and tried to kick, long ears back and huge teeth gleaming. The pilot opened his throttles. The plane surged forward and I felt myself being pushed down and back. The mules bucked and fought and I heard one of the bamboo poles break. The *havildar* readied his carbine. Faster, faster, the tail began to rise and the floor to level off. Five of us jumped up and pushed forward against the mules' sterns. The airfield lights sank and disappeared, and a steady moonlight illuminated the cabin. I was staring down the muzzle of *Havildar* Shivjang's loaded carbine.

Slowly the mules calmed as we steadied on course and the bellow of the engines cut back to the throb of cruising speed. The pilot poked his head round the door and Shivjang turned, the carbine up. The pilot withdrew his head and the door slammed. It was the breech pole that had cracked and I kept three men there, in turns throughout the flight, pushing forward against the mules. Those orders given, I unfolded the small-scale map tucked into the outer flap of my haversack and looked out of the window. There was the Chindwin. We ought to cross it directly over Thaungdut. If so, out of the right-hand windows, I should see the horseshoe curve near Sittaung, and a smaller river coming in on the left bank.

It was so. I checked the pilot's course all the way. This plane load, at least, was going to know exactly where it was, in case

Operations of III Brigade, Burma, 1944

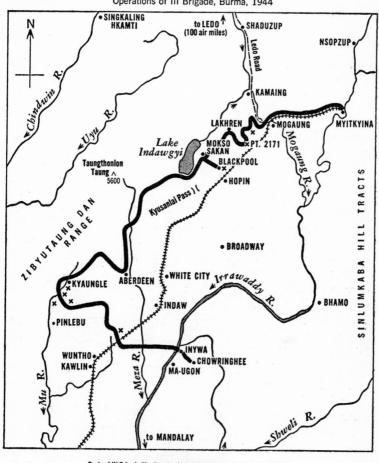

of a forced landing. It is much worse for Brigade Majors than for ordinary mortals to shoot up their own troops, or ask the Japanese for a cup of tea, both of which had happened among the gliders that never reached Broadway.

After an hour the plane's nose dipped and the mules slid forward. Now they were pressing against the forward bulkhead, and the three unhappy muleteers. But any further displacement would only send them into the pilot's compartment, to look over his shoulder, and perhaps offer him advice in his task. They would not slide back on us, so I withdrew the rear guard and prepared for the landing. We crossed the Irrawaddy five miles north of Tigyaing. The moon shone bright on the silver river, over a mile wide there between dark, featureless jungle.

The pilot switched on his landing lights and a moment later I saw Chowringhee. It was very different now from that silent clearing which I had flown over in a bright midday two weeks earlier. Down there, under the port wing, lights glittered in a long rectangle, more brilliant in the surrounding blackness than the great Calcutta street after which it had been named. Two cones of brighter light advanced slowly at the far end, turning. Other cones shone outward into the jungle, or diagonally athwart the strip—C-47s, taxiing to the dispersal points, standing, unloading. A plane passed directly below us, its swept-back wings black against the lights, and pale points of fire shimmering from the exhausts. Another plane circled above us, in silhouette against the sky, and another above that. I saw a bright cone of light rushing toward the strip . . . she was down . . . now us.

The pilot eased the throttles, we heaved and lifted as the undercarriage came down, heaved again for the flaps, nose down, down, and I was staring down the long beam of our own landing lights, as far forward as I could see, pressed against a window. Trees flashed by, pale green, closer, faster, now racing earth, long-streaked and blurred. Bump, gently bump again, and the tail began to sag. Three men jumped to the sterns of the mules. We taxied to a stop, I wrenched open the door.

Two Gurkhas ran up. What plane? I gave the number. Four more Gurkhas came, hurrying with the long planks down which the mules would be unloaded. But by then I had jumped down to the soil of Burma, 150 miles behind the Japanese lines.

Guides led us off the strip, away from the lights and the growling engines, into the edge of the jungle. There, sitting under a tree, I found Joe. All was going well, no accidents, though one plane, turning too quickly on the ground, had chopped a section off the tail of another already parked. Colonel Allison, U.S.A.F., in charge of the flying operations, was using the cockpit of a C-47 as his control tower. One plane landed and one took off every three minutes. Each plane was allowed twenty-four minutes on the ground. Overhead our aircraft cruised like shoals of winking, luminous fish and their multiple drone filled the air.

I checked the brigade H.Q. defenses, examined the slit trenches, read the latest messages from Force and 77 Brigade, and ate my first K ration in Burma. It still tasted wonderful. Swarms of large red ants scurried hither and thither across the ground, but they did not bother us, and I wrapped myself up in the green half-blanket and lay down. The red ants crawled patiently over the new obstacles, my face and neck, and I went to sleep.

For one more night the fly-in continued. We sent out patrols to search for water and, for the rest, waited, dispersed in the jungles round Chowringhee, ready to defend the airfield in case the Japanese came. Through the hot, dry hours we scanned the sky and listened for the sound of strange engines; but the Japanese did not come.

Near dawn on the third morning it was done. Brigade Headquarters and Columns 30, 40, 49 and 94 had all landed. Allison climbed down from his control C-47, with two other Air Commando officers, and walked over to the only other powered aircraft left on the strip—the R.A.F. plane with the piece cut off its tail, which had been abandoned. I went near and heard one of them guess that the thing would fly, probably. Allison nodded. They both looked at the third man. He said, "Hell, I'll take her out." He climbed up into the cockpit, started her up and flew her off. As she climbed away in a wide turn, followed by Allison's plane, I wondered how many minutes after she landed at Hailakandi she would be wearing the U.S.A.F. star and the diagonal white stripes to show that she belonged, and had always belonged, to No. 1 Air Commando.

The sound of the engines faded. Now we split up. Jumbo Morris and his two columns of the 4/9th Gurkhas headed east, for they were to operate in the extreme northeast of Burma, near the Yunnan frontier. The rest of us headed west in battle formation, the flank scouts on the right moving along a jungle path that led to the Irrawaddy at Inywa. Our first task was simply to get to the rendezvous point where 111 Brigade would concentrate, for the Cameronians and the King's Own had landed at Broadway. Today was March 10, and we were due at the rendezvous, about 130 march-miles away, on March 24; but in between flowed the great river.

An hour after setting out, in full daylight, we heard the hum of aircraft. They were not C-47s, or B-25s, or P-51s. Here at the edge of the dry zone we were in *indaing* jungle, small teak trees scattered two or three to the acre among other trees, also small, the whole thin and seeming to give no shade and no cover. Here and there stood the gaunt, gray-white skeletons of trees that had been girdled and killed for felling. The flat ground was covered, first, with a powdery compost of decayed leaves from the past and, above that, with the huge, curled leaves only recently fallen. So loudly did the leaves crackle and crunch under our boots that for a moment, as the sound of the aircraft increased, I believed the pilots must have heard us.

Up and down the column hands signaled the Air Alert. We stopped moving. The Bren gunners stood ready, their guns propped on the shoulders of the Numbers 2 of each gun. The mules stood unconcerned. My heart sank. Christ, what stinking luck, to be caught by Zeros in such a place, at the very start.

Nine Zeros passed directly overhead at about five thousand feet. The low sun shone on the red circle of Japan under their wings. I waited. Deir-es-Zor again; they would turn and come down at us out of the rising sun. . . . Nine times six made fifty-four. Fifty-four machine guns. Well, we could shoot too, and there were men here from the same Nepalese mountains, and the same regiment, that had bred Deva and Ghanbahadur, the Young Rolands of the Turkish frontier.

The Zeros peeled off and dived, out of sight. The ripping roar of machine guns came thin to us, then the crash, crash and double crash and echoing crash, crash, crash of bombs. It went on for five furious minutes but by then Joe and I were laughing together, and every face down the column was grinning into the earth under its nose. On the first night of the fly-in gliders had come, bringing bulldozers to improve the strip. Three or four, having suffered minor mishaps on landing, had been abandoned on the field. The Japanese were now giving these derelicts hell. Columns of oily black smoke rose to the east—we had left some gasoline cans in the gliders—and the Zeros, in formation again, passed over us on their way back to base. We continued our march.

We marched with 30 Column ahead, followed by Brigade H.Q., 40 Column in the rear. We expected every moment to meet a Japanese patrol, but there was nothing—no enemy, no birds, no animals, nothing except the trees sliding slowly back toward us, the air shimmering in the still, breathless heat, the sweat blackening our shirts and the long roar, like a subway train, of the teak leaves under our boots.

I began to hear a shrill throb inside my head and thought, Damned funny, must be a reaction of tiredness—but I wasn't tired—or a negative sound created inside the eardrum to counteract the positive of the crunching leaves, as when a blue flash exploded before one's eyes creates afterward a yellow spot. I marched on. The sound grew louder and more piercing. I glanced out of the corner of my eye at Joe. It was just crazily possible that it was an objective not a subjective experience. Joe looked at me as strangely. After a time he said, "Do you hear anything?" I nodded, and looked round. All the men were staring at each other, or at us. By now the sound was piercing loud and Joe gave the signal to halt. The crunching roar of the leaves stopped and we stood still, listening. The jet plane had not yet been heard but that is how, now, I would describe it—a loud shrilling note, almost steady, very high in the scale. We turned our heads this way and that, but its direction could not be placed. It came from everywhere. Every man's hand tightened on his weapon, though we could see for hundreds of yards through the shadeless, flat forest.

Captain Saw Lader of the Burma Rifle platoon came toward us with a grin and said something. John Hedley roared out a short laugh and said, "Cicadas."

Cicadas. Of course. But—well, none of *us* had heard anything like it. Rather shamefacedly we marched on. Slowly the throbbing shrillness faded.

We harbored early on the banks of the Thayetchaung, but it contained no water. Joe at once began to discuss the crossing of the Irrawaddy. We had made a basic plan, from a study of maps and air photographs, before leaving Imphal. Now we had to review it and put it into practice.

Joe intended to cross about two miles south of Inywa. We must therefore seize Inywa, and another village, Ma-ugon, two miles south of the selected crossing place. Intelligence reported small Japanese posts on the far bank, ten miles up and down stream. We must prevent those posts communicating with each other, and from receiving messages from patrols on the river bank itself. The map showed a telephone line running down that far bank; we must try and have it destroyed, and the two posts themselves should be attacked from the air.

The Japanese had long since removed all small boats from the river, so gliders were to land assault boats, complete with outboard motors, and experts to work them, near the point of our crossing. We must select the landing strip, and light fires there a few minutes before the gliders were due. Later, other planes would return to snatch off the empty gliders and return them to India. All this we had planned as carefully as possible in terms of D-day and H-hour. Now we must confirm that D-day would be tomorrow, March 11, and H-hour would be 2000 hours (8:00 P.M. on the military twenty-four-hour clock). As to the glider landing strip . . . we couldn't confirm it until we got there. Allowing the aircraft two hours to take off and fly here, we must send them the final signal by 1800 hours. By then we must be in possession of the near bank where we intended to cross, and also of Inywa and Ma-ugon. It would be most unwise to launch aircraft to a spot about which we knew nothing from direct personal observation. Major Sujimoto might be sitting on it with forty unfriendly Nips.

One by one, we filled in the details. Joe's short sentences rapped on. I made notes and pencil lines on my map.

Joe sat back, closed his eyes, and took a nap. I began to prepare messages for Force H.Q. and Air Base. The signal office runners came to me with signals from Broadway, a hundred miles to the north. The King's Own were in. The Cameronians were already ten miles out, on their way to the rendezvous. Then I prepared a short confirmation of what Joe would say, so that commanders would have the important points in writing. All this while the soldiers had been digging defensive positions and slit trenches. Joe gave the orders.

Time to eat. Joe allowed no fires this day, for we could take absolutely no risk of being discovered. Immediately after eating —dusk, and stand-to. Every man equipped and prepared himself for action and went to his alarm post. The mortars waited in position ready to fire, the machine guns were sited to enfilade the path on our northern flank, and to cover the open jungle in crisscross patterns, particularly to east and west—west, where the unknown enemy lay, east, where our path could be followed through the jungle by the wide belt of crushed teak leaves.

Half an hour after dark Joe ordered stand down. The sentries stayed at their posts. The rest took off their equipment, laid it under their heads, and went to sleep. Signal and cipher men kept at work for another two hours, sending and receiving messages. As soon as Briggs reported that my last message, a summary of our plans for the morrow, was in transmission, I too slept.

Next day, late in the morning, we marched. By then no one had drunk for over thirty hours, but all the water bottles were still full. The mules moved listlessly and the men looked a little drawn. We all had glue in our throats and it hurt to swallow.

We reached the edge of the jungle. Two miles of fields, tall reed grass, sandbanks, and bamboo clumps separated us from the Irrawaddy. We went on. Now and then we saw the silver water, but it was the farther bank that held our attention—a uniform cliff line about forty feet high, then a short flat ledge perhaps four hundred yards deep, and then the rolling jungled hills of the Gangaw Range.

A brief burst of firing from the north warned us that the fighting patrol sent to Inywa was in action. Soon afterward we reached the river, among sand dunes and short grass. Robbie and Chesty, our R.A.F. flight lieutenants, hurried off to inspect the sand bar selected for the glider strip, and soon returned, reporting that the strip was as advertised—reasonably smooth sand, unoccupied.

The signalers unloaded the sets and erected the antennae. I gave Briggs the message that lay ready in my map case, already enciphered. It was 1730 hours.

Again the soldiers began to dig. Others went up and down the river bank collecting driftwood for the signal fires. Others went out on reconnoitering patrols. Others snatched a hurried meal. Joe took Frank Turner and the column transport officers down to the water's edge to work out our biggest problem—how to get our 240 animals to swim a river a mile wide, from a sandbank toward a cliff.

The gliders came in the early dark, first the accustomed drone of C-47 engines, then the sight of the planes, each towing a single glider, high and black above us. The fires burned bright on the sand, and the first tow rope snapped loose. The drone faded as the C-47 turned for base. The glider swept inexorably down. At last the *whoooosh* passed low, directly above our heads.

"They're too high," Robbie muttered. "They'll overshoot." He bent again over the radio set and spoke urgently to the pilots of the other tow planes. Joe asked, "What's the matter?"

Robbie said, "There must be a wind the other way a little way up."

Before the pilots could make the proper corrections another two gliders had landed, all three touching down nearly a thousand yards beyond the fires. There was plenty of safe sand and no trees in that direction, but this was a minor disaster. Instead of getting the assault boats within a few yards of the crossing place, we had to drag them over half a mile.

The unloading parties ran off in the starlight to reach the gliders. Slowly and painfully in the hot night the men and mules dragged and carried the heavy boats toward us, and the outboard motors, and the ropes, and life jackets, and gasoline and oil. The fighting patrols had long since reported Inywa and Maugon in our hands. At Inywa they had driven away some Burman armed police.

About two o'clock the Air Commando C-47s returned to snatch the empty gliders off the sandbank. I went down to watch.

First the crews helped two sick Gurkhas into the first glider. They were not very ill but Joe had decided to send them out as a demonstration of the speed of our evacuation system. Then we manhandled the glider into position. It carried with it two long poles, each armed with a blue electric light on top—self-contained and battery-operated. A third blue light shone above the pilot's cockpit. Under the pilot's direction we first stuck the poles into the sand about two hundred feet in front of the glider and fifty feet apart. Then we took the glider tow rope, which was of double length, and fastened one end firmly to the tow hook in the nose of the glider. Thence we led the rope to the first pole, over the top, stretched it to the top of the second pole, and thence back to the tow hook, again fastening it firmly.

The snatch plane arrived overhead, flashing its recognition signal. Robbie talked to it and confirmed that we were ready. The glider pilot waited, the three blue lights burning, brakes off and controls set for take-off. The C-47 lowered under its tail a long steel boom carrying a hook with a self-operating catch. With engines throttled back, flaps full down, propellers set in full pitch, the C-47 came growling up the sandbank at about thirty feet. He groaned over . . . the trailing hook missed the taut glider rope between the poles by a few feet.

Round again. And again. The third time the hook caught in the rope, snatched it off the tops of the poles, a moment later flew taut, direct to the tow hook of the glider. The sudden jerk was taken up by the natural elasticity of the nylon, then the strain came onto the powered plane. The pilot rammed his throttles fully forward and lifted his nose. The sudden roaring growl of anguish from the engines filled the sky. The glider—jerked from zero to eighty miles an hour during the stretch of the rope, perhaps a second and a half—rose in the air. The C-47 and the silent glider swept up into the darkness.

I repeated the incantation that Mountbatten had made when he first saw this remarkable feat. "Jesus Christ All Bloody Mighty," I muttered and went back to headquarters. Robbie began to get the next glider into position.

Several of the outboard motors would not start. Now moonlight shone over the river and on the sand, and on the dark knots of men struggling with boats and motors. Progress was slow, but just before dawn Mike Dibben of the 3/4th Gurkhas, with two platoons, climbed into assault boats and chugged out into the river, each powered boat towing two others. We waited, machine gunners ready with their thumbs on the double buttons, mortar men ready with bomb in hand and sights set. Above the low cliff opposite, we saw no sign of movement, heard no sound. Mike's men reached midstream. We heard aircraft coming up from the south. In a flash they were over us. They wore the diagonal stripes—three P-51 fighters come to cut the telephone line on the far bank and to guard us against air attack.

They dived from low altitude and bombs thundered, raising huge gouts of earth. "They're going to need some luck," Joe muttered. "A single telephone line's a tricky target." They were releasing their bombs from less than a hundred feet up and the volcanoes of earth and smoke rose higher than their tails behind them as they flashed on northward. I shook my head in admiration. The telephone line ran on poles twelve or fifteen feet high over there. Through binoculars we could just see it in one or two places where the light caught it, running among the trees and across small clearings. The boats puttered slowly on.

Upriver the Mustangs banked and came back. They leaned down toward the earth, and sank lower as they came, the sound of their engines echoing forcefully from the Gangaw Hills. Lower . . . The bomb blast would blow off their tails at that height! I wanted to scream, It doesn't matter, you've done enough, go home! The lead plane swooped and banked sharply. His lower wing tip ripped momentarily across an open space in the jungle, perhaps three feet above the ground. Then he climbed up and away in a spiral turn under full power. The second plane swerved inland and then banked steeply out toward us, coming straight at us out of the land in a tight turn, wing tip brushing the ground. This time the light flashed for an instant on the length of telephone wire trailing from his wing. The third followed. A moment later all three of them were flying in lazy, watchful patterns high above us. Now it was Joe's turn to repeat Supremo's incantation.

Mike Dibben's men landed, climbed the steep little cliff, and disappeared into the scattered trees. Fifteen minutes later a red Very light floated up into the morning sky. Soon Mike came up on the walkie-talkie. "No enemy in the position, and no signs of them. Nor in Thagaya or Hlebo. Telephone wire hanging around in festoons at the edge of the jungle." Yes, he had taken up covering positions. The crossing could begin.

Joe nodded at 30 Column Commander, and the main crossing began. 30 Column was part of the 4th Prince of Wales's Own Gurkha Rifles, the regiment to which both Joe and I belonged. The date was auspicious, being close to our Regimental Day. But, as I have said, some of the outboard motors would not start, and the mules had never heard of the Regimental Day, or they were Japanese agents in disguise. They refused to swim the river.

Mike MacGillicuddy—a MacGillicuddy of the Reeks and descendant of Irish kings, slight, sandy-haired, reckless—mounted a horse, bareback, and led a group of fifteen animals into the water, a few ridden by good swimmers, the others on their own. A powered assault boat hovered downstream, ready to pick up men in trouble. Mike's horse reached the deep water and began to swim. We had practiced this successfully a score of times in the rivers and lakes of Central India. Here, where it mattered, some mules swam a few strokes after Mike, then turned downstream with the current and soon heaved out once more onto dry land, on our side, fifty yards from their starting point. The rest didn't even begin.

Mike swore, turned his horse, and returned. He tried again, and again, and again. At the fifth or sixth attempt with Mike riding the best mule we had—Maggy, a ponderous lady from Missouri whose normal load was one of the big radio sets, and an assault boat forcibly towing two other mules by their headropes, twenty animals made the crossing. Mike returned at once for another trip. Meanwhile Frank Turner had got a batch started—but they turned back almost from midstream. We sweated and swore, and became very tired.

The hours passed, much too fast. We got most of the men of 30 Column over, and Joe sent me across to check the positions on the far bank. All down the east bank there were mules, saddles, stores, damaged boats, ropes, radio sets, struggling men.

I got into the boat and we started off slowly, men leaning far out over the gunwales with their two inches of freeboard, dragging mutinous mules. The water grew deeper and suddenly the mules were swimming. I saw Mike MacGillicuddy twenty feet off the port quarter, riding Maggy again. So he had swum her back, because the other animals seemed to trust her, and now she was swimming the Irrawaddy for the third time. Close astern our two mules rode high in the water, their great hoofs flailing just behind the flimsy craft, their mouths set in a wide snarl, showing all their rows of huge yellow teeth. If we stopped they would try to come inboard. They would trample us under and then eat us. They looked like dragons, water dragons. . . . I was glad to step ashore. I found all in order, and an hour later returned to the east bank. It was near noon and very hot.

Joe began to eat a K ration, and talk over the problem. By now the crossing should have been completed, but less than one-fifth of the animals were over. At the same rate we would have two-fifths on the far side by dusk. At night, in our experience, mules and horses would not make long water crossings at all. Our operations had been in full view, all day, for four or five miles in both directions. It was reasonable to assume that by now the Japanese must know what we were doing, and where. They would probably not have strong enough forces within reach actually to prevent us crossing if we continued our efforts all next day, but they would certainly inflict casualties and, worst of all, could tail us and harass us before we had even got near our area of operations. The rest of the men we could get over before dusk—but a mass of men would be useless without their heavy weapons, their reserves of ammunition, demolition sets, explosives, medical stores, picks, shovels and, above all, radio sets. All these needed mules.

It was an unpleasant decision. Joe made it at about one o'clock. He ordered the crossing to stop at three P.M. 40 Column would not cross at all, but would head back eastward to join Morrisforce (49 and 94 Columns) in their operations in the Sinlumkaba Hill Tracts. Those columns were already two days' march east of Chowringhee, and 40 Column would have a hard job catching up with them.

Brigade Headquarters and the rest of 30 Column would cross. We would be short of mules, but would have to make do. In a trance of weariness, I wrote out a message for Force H.Q., and gave it to the cipher office.

A little after that I crossed the Irrawaddy once more. Mike MacGillicuddy was in the water again, for his tenth crossing. His fair hair shone in the sun and his loud, high-pitched voice, yelling in execrable Gurkhali, rang out over the water.

On the far bank, we wrecked the assault boats and their motors, and sank them. My pack weighed a ton and I could hardly stand. None of us had slept for thirty-six hours. Across the river we saw nothing. 40 Column had disappeared into the sand dunes.

Joe nodded and I raised my right hand two or three times, palm up. Every man staggered to his feet. I gave a slight forward sweep of the hand. We began to march north, the river on our right, the Gangaw Hills on our left. After dusk we harbored, a mile in from the river and a quarter of a mile off the path, in dense jungle. Rhodes-James and I crouched under a bush, blankets draped over it and a flashlight shining, and worked for an hour to prepare our first QQ—the message calling for a supply drop; the place—map reference 7772, nineteen marching miles from our present position; the time—2200 hours, March 14, two nights hence.

16 We were like a man trying to make a hidden-ball play from end to end of a football field thickly planted with trees. The distant rendezvous was the goal line, the opposing team those Japanese who crossed and recrossed the area on their own occasions, knowing we were somewhere about, but not knowing where we were going and, as yet, no more ready to come and look for us than we were to go and look for them. We were strong enough to force past any single group we might run into, but then they'd call the rest of their team, and our object was not to get involved in a free-for-all struggle in midfield but simply to reach that goal line.

It was a beautiful stadium. . . . At night, the second night after crossing the Irrawaddy, I awoke about three o'clock, gently pulled up out of sleep, without cause. I listened first, but there was no sound at all. I could not hear the men around me breathing, nor the mules in the lines, nor any sound of the wild earth. We lay in the rough circle of our harbor high on the slopes of the Gangaw Range, among *kanyin* trees two hundred feet tall. The boles swept up straight and clear for a full hundred feet to the first branch; then, high above, spread out into giant canopies topped by red or white flowers. Since the *kanyins* overshadowed and pushed out the teak and most of the lesser trees, I could see a long way down the slope, where the shapeless masses in the deep shadow were men and animals. After a time I knew why I had awoken. It was night in Burma. The quality of the night, of the silence, was different from anything I had known, and it was that which had touched my senses and called me out of sleep. The moon, a little past full, hung a deep orange color among the high leaf canopies. In the long aisles of our cathedral a pale gray-violet mist seemed to move slowly up the slope, in absolute silence. The edges of the trees round the moon had an unreal quality as though they were not leaves and boughs but the brush work of a painter, using some technique not yet explored before this, for I was watching the painting grow and change under his hand as the night advanced.

Before dawn we stood to arms as usual. There was no color now, everything pearled and pale and sheened in the morning. A hand signal passed round: *Stand down.* I walked forward from the perimeter with Jagbir, my orderly, to eat my breakfast out there, only a few yards beyond the sentries but a world away from the bustle at the center of the harbor and the shrill, soft, ceaseless cheeping of the radio sets.

The note of a tenor bell rang full and true out of the thinning mist below. I sprang up and ran back to the sentries. They had heard it and waited intently. Again the bell sounded. The Japanese used the calls of birds to signal to each other . . . but this was no bird. A third time the single bell tolled.

The words of a poem came into my head, and I spoke a word to the sentries. They relaxed, and I walked forward again.

> As the dawn was breaking the Sambhur belled—
> Once, twice, and again!
> And a doe leaped up, and a doe leaped up
> From the pond in the wood where the wild deer sup.
> This I, scouting alone, beheld,
> Once, twice, and again![1]

It was not the first time that Kipling's miraculous gift of description had helped me to recognize the new and the unexpected. I had heard the belling of a sambar stag, the great red deer of India and Burma.

A supply drop: I describe the one at Map Reference 7772, but

[1] "The Hunting Song of the Seeonee Pack" from *The Jungle Book* by Rudyard Kipling. Reprinted by permission of Doubleday & Company, Inc., Macmillan & Co. Ltd., the Macmillan Company of Canada Ltd., and Mrs. George Bambridge.

it was never very different. . . . When we reached the drop zone
we found no enemy, but the trees stood between 70 and 120 feet,
with some individual giants considerably taller, and the hills to
the north looked closer and steeper than the map showed them.
I told Chesty Jennings to report within fifteen minutes whether the
DZ was safe for the supply-dropping aircraft. They would be loading now, at air base, but would not take off until about 8:30 p.m.

Chesty returned. (As tail gunner of a Catalina, he had been the
man who first spotted the *Bismarck* after she had disappeared.)
The DZ was not good, but it would do, provided he could warn
the pilots to shorten their drop runs and turn sharp left—south—
as soon as they had passed over the last fire. I told Joe and he
ordered that the supply drop should take place. Chesty sent the
warning message to air base at once.

A quarter of a mile down the trail ahead, and as far behind,
platoons dug in to ambush Japanese interference with the drop.
A large party began to collect wood and stack it in the spots
marked by Robbie for the fires. In the center of the area a
platoon lay to arms ready to counterattack any enemy infiltration.
Listening patrols went out half a mile to the flanks.

About the danger of air attack we could do nothing. We must
light the L-shaped row of fires that marked the DZ as soon as we
had identified the C-47s above us. From that instant the C-47s,
passing regularly and low across the fires would be sitting ducks
for any Zeros who were lurking in the night sky. The same fires
would pinpoint our own position to enemy bombers. The men
in their trenches might not suffer too heavily in a bombing raid,
but the mules would fare badly indeed. Now the muleteers took
special care to picket and shackle them, so that even if they
panicked they could not break free and gallop away.

Five men stood by each fire, to keep it going. Each aircraft
would unload two or three tons of supplies in half a dozen low
runs over the drop zone, and we might get three aircraft. The
parachuted loads, as we knew from training experience, might
land anywhere in the drop zone and up to quarter of a mile off
it if the wind or a bad approach caused the pilot to be off his
correct course and altitude at the moment of the drop. Finally,
to save parachute material, only "fragile" loads were dropped
by this means. The supply crew in the plane pushed the rest

out of the door to fall free among us—boots, socks, clothes, fodder for the animals. We had to collect everything, where it lay or hung, in the dark, without delay.

A few minutes after ten o'clock we heard the soft throb of C-47 engines. Soon they passed directly over us, rather high. Joe, standing by a fire said, "*Ag laga!*" The *havildar* struck a match. In a moment the dry wood burst into flame. Six columns of yellow fire writhed up, throwing the tree trunks and the faces of the men into strong relief, and turning Joe's spectacles into shimmering orange pools. The sound of engines had gone and, with the loud crackling of the nearest fire, I did not hear it again until the lead plane came in on its first run.

High branches crackled. A square box burst through and hung suspended by its parachute, swaying violently, ten feet above the ground. More parachutes floated down, scarlet and yellow in the glare of the fires. The engines throbbed closer, farther. Groups of men, each always carrying his rifle or carbine but otherwise without equipment, ran into the jungle. Others trudged toward us with cartons of K rations, small padded boxes of medical supplies, Mepacrine tablets. Parachutes blossomed among the stars and in the tall trees like exotic night flowers.

Sweating, excited Gurkhas hurled huge logs onto the fires until the flames towered up thirty feet. Joe bawled, "Jack, tell those bloody fools to stop it! They'll set light to the planes in a minute." *Boom crash, crash,* a broken teak bough sailed past my head and after it two big sacks. The sacks bounced five feet on impact, burst, and showered us with khaki shirts. A sharper explosion— and another—another, coming quickly. Joe's head went up like an old pointer's.

"Grenades!" he snapped. The *havildar* at the nearest fire doubled up with laughing. "Bamboo!" he yelled, pointing, and we saw a young soldier hurl another great section of bamboo onto the fire. Joe shouted, "*Dumshi ko dhanda!*" The *havildar* leaped at the rifleman and gave him a tremendous clip over the ear. The boy went sprawling, choked with laughter. Brueghel, I thought, Brueghel, set to the music of war and the tempo of flame. Fires raged like dragons, men ran and scurried and pushed and pulled and dragged and climbed and chopped.

I went back into the jungle, checked the counterattack platoon,

walked down the trail, checked the eastern ambush platoon, returned, and lit a cigarette.

The last plane reported that it had completed unloading and
was heading for home. Chesty passed them our thanks and the
dropping part of the supply drop was over. The supplying part
now began. Frank Baines, the Orderly Officer, estimated that 30
per cent of the drop had fallen out of the DZ. Although he had
men detailed to "mark" stray loads, he didn't think we would
find more than half of them in darkness. Of the 70 per cent
that had fallen in the DZ about a third were at the tops of trees,
or swaying rhythmically from lower limbs by their parachutes,
but still forty or fifty feet up. Since the beginning of the drop
parties had been out climbing trees, attempting to lasso loads or,
in a few cases, chopping down the trees themselves. Now the fire
parties went to help.

The dump of supplies at the ration point grew fast, and Baines
and the column quartermasters began issuing. One by one platoons came, drew their supplies, and returned to their positions.
Joe ordered the march to continue at two A.M. We would march
for about half an hour, in order to get away from the DZ, conceal
our tracks, and harbor again, this time to sleep. Any supplies
that could not be gathered in by 1:50 A.M. must be abandoned.

At five to two the eastward ambush platoon reported in. At
two we marched. Parachutes hung on many trees but we had gathered in about three-quarters of the drop, including almost all the
K rations. Heavily loaded again, we trudged westward for a time
through the darkness, then carried out another operation we had
rehearsed many times, the concealment of our tracks.

A column of several hundred men and several score mules,
forced by the country to move in Indian file, leaves a very obvious trail on any ground except dry grass. A Japanese patrol, coming across such a trail, had only to follow it to come at last upon
the tail of the column. To counter this we had developed a battle
drill of lateral movement. At a signal every man, except the leading platoon, halted and turned right (or left). At the next signal the whole force moved into the jungle, now in line, so that
no man trod in another's footsteps. Every man moved carefully,
trying not to disturb the leaves and undergrowth. After two or
three hundred paces, going very slowly, each man turned again

to face the original front, and the march continued. The leading platoon continued for half a mile on the original track, making as much trace as possible, then returned, formed line, and joined the rest.

Before dusk each day, and at each long midday halt, we went into harbor. We had practiced and practiced this until we could do it in any terrain, in total darkness, at great speed. Sometimes we were heading for a particular place chosen off the map, sometimes we had to select the best available near where we were at the time. In any case, Joe gave the signal to halt and said, "Harbor." Pointing to a tree—any tree—he said, "Brigade Headquarters. Orders at 1800." If we had had more than one column with us he would have allotted sectors of the perimeter at this time. Sometimes he would also tell me what special defense arrangements were to be made, but usually he just went straight to the Brigade Tree, his orderly at his heels, took off his equipment, and leaned back to rest, have a look at the map, and think. When he said, "Orders at 1800" he meant that he would give orders for the night and the following day. But before then there were the harboring orders to give out; these I usually gave on his behalf. 30 Column commander, with his staff and orderlies, was already on his way in. Meanwhile I took some compass bearings. Knowing that the axis of the morrow's advance would be about due west, i.e., 270 degree magnetic, I was ready when the column commander arrived. I said, "There's the Brigade Tree. Axis of advance 270. Brigade Headquarters radius 70 yards, perimeter radius 150 yards. Fires until 1800 hours. Brigadier's orders at 1800 hours. Any questions?" There were seldom any questions and the column staff tramped off, compasses in hand, measuring their paces.

My own subordinates, the commanders of every department of Brigade Headquarters, now gathered round me. In ordering "Brigade Headquarters radius 70 yards," I had notified the column commander that all the ground for 70 yards round the tree belonged to us. The ground beyond that, for the next 80 yards, belonged to him. He must occupy and be responsible for the defense of all ground between 70 and 150 yards from the tree. The axis of advance was useful information in case we had to form up and continue our move at night.

The whole harbor looked like a round cheese. Now I had to suballot the inner part of the cheese, seventy yards in radius, which was the quota of Brigade Headquarters, among all its various components. Unless the ground presented peculiar difficulties this too was a drill, for we always sent the same subunit to the same quadrant of the cheese.

Within a quarter of an hour everyone was settled in. Then the brigadier called John Hedley and set off to inspect the perimeter and set the defenses. At the same time I checked the defense of headquarters. I made sure that the air sentries were at their posts, that a local reserve stood ready under arms, with ground sentries in position. Then I began on the other sections. . . .

I look at Briggs's signalers. Two are dozing against a tree and the rest, under Briggs, already have the big radio set in operation. The signal lieutenant is working out the compass bearing of Force H.Q., two hundred miles away, in order to align the antennae which are strung between trees, in the right direction. I ask Briggs whether he is yet in contact with Force, and he shakes his head briefly. The signal mules are offloaded and tethered, saddles still on but girths loosened. Good. When they have cooled off they will be unsaddled for the night.

Ciphers. I hand Rhodes-James a message giving the map reference of our harbor, some information picked up from a villager, and otherwise NTR, nothing to report. Rhodes-James settles down with the cipher books.

Transport . . . Frank Turner bustles around giving advice and help. The few animals directly under his command—the rest are under the sections whose loads they carry—are in good order. One saddle gall, one girth gall among the rest. He begins to reprimand the muleteers, but I take him aside and tell him to blast the officers in command, not the mule men themselves.

Defense platoon again. I check the sentries and the relief roster. Baines looks weird, his shaven head shining and his huge ring gleaming. He'll frighten the Nips out of their wits. I send him to 30 Column, with the task of showing the commander of its reserve platoon exactly where we are, and to note exactly where they are, so that we can help each other in case of need.

Burma Rifles. All as happy as sandboys. Naturally, this is their country. Saw Lader looks as though he has just stepped out of a bandbox. Macpherson is staring at the teak trees, but not with war in mind. In peacetime it was his job to cut and extract these trees for the mighty Bombay Burmah Trading Corporation.

R.A.F. . . . They are trying to get through to air base on their radio set. Chesty asks for permission to run the small motor that recharges their batteries. O.K., until 1800 hours. Tell the Signals too, please. Should have thought of that myself.

I come upon a brisk argument going on between a *jemadar* of 30 Column and the *jemadar* of our defense platoon over the ownership of a particularly succulent-looking tree. One side claims it stands sixty-nine yards from the Brigade Tree, the other seventy-one yards. I award it to 30 Column on principle—always favor troops over headquarters—but first give both *jemadars* a small rocket for not settling the matter amicably.

Food . . . K rations were like love. There's not much use explaining: you know what you know. Or perhaps sex, ancient Hindu sex, would be a better simile. Certainly the regular, straightforward methods of taking them soon became unappetizing to us, and already we were carrying out experiments as complicated, in their field, as the recommendations of the Kama Sutra or the contorted copulations of the Black Temple at Puri. (I have seen a soldier mix the whole contents of his breakfast packet into his mess tin, and cook the lot together—coffee, powdered milk, fruit bar, compressed ham and egg; he left out the gum and the toilet paper.)

It was not the food that refreshed and renewed us as much as the occasion. You collected a few sticks of dry wood, tore off a piece of the wax-impregnated wrapping, and set light to it. That started your fire. Each squad or section had its own fire, sometimes every pair of men. Soon a hundred little flames grew like potted geraniums under the boughs, you lay beside your own with a Roman sense of luxury. Best of all, you had a defeated enemy to gloat over, for the monstrous pack, its front black and impregnated with your sweat, squatted there against the tree, off your back at last, and could not move or even ask for food, but just had to sit and be jeered at while you ate. (This was the psychology of the punishment used by Tim Brennan in the Cameronians. Instead of the floggings and abandonments in the jungle which we had devised as the only punishments available to us, he used to make the criminal sit beside the company sergeant major and watch the latter brew coffee and cook his meal.)

We wrote letters. We wrote them on message forms, in pencil, wrote the name and address on the back, and handed them to the censor officer, who made sure they said nothing the enemy would like to know. Whenever we got a light plane the mail followed the route of the wounded and sick—in an L-5 from us to the nearest stronghold, in a C-47 from there to air base. There our rear headquarters put each letter into an envelope, addressed it, and mailed it.

We received letters, in the supply drops. I got one at 7772, which had come far faster than the telegram. My daughter weighed seven and a half pounds at birth and looked beautiful. Barbara was already out of hospital. She had reached it only just in time and labor was so quick that the doctor's only function had been to say hello to the baby. Bombay was getting pretty awful. It used to be a comparatively clean city but now there were bugs everywhere, bedbugs. They lived in chairs, sofas, and wooden toilet seats, and knew whether a lady was sitting down for a short or a long stay. The ladies caught them by simulating the latter, then suddenly leaping up and pouncing. Every few weeks all beds had to be taken into the yard, soaked in kerosene and set fire to, to burn the bugs out of the cracks. Liz and Mike had got lice in their hair, which had to be washed in kerosene. The baby was well, a darling, lively, lovely.

Bugger, bugger, blast, and hell. I understood much better the private soldiers' habitual, senseless swearing, and the endless repetition of a single word, at first meaningless in the context and then, by sheer repetition, becoming a long and subtle statement of feeling.

Once we came across bamboo in flower, acres and acres of the white blossom in dense jungle. It only happens every thirteenth year. Thirteen was Barbara's lucky number, and she was born on the thirteenth.

Once we had a night alarm. Lights approached our harbor through the trees, the sentries whispered the stand-to, everyone awoke, picked up rifle or carbine and knelt, waiting. We'd had several long, very hard days and Joe was not recovering as quickly as the younger men. He ordered the mules saddled and when I began to protest that it was not necessary yet, he cut me off curtly. The lights came closer and a Burma Rifleman challenged, in Burmese. No answer. The sentry fired a Bren-gun burst and the lights disappeared, also the people. Nothing more. Joe ordered an immediate move. The Burma Rifles went outside the perimeter and found a couple of baskets of dried fish. Most people moved about at night then, for fear of our aircraft. John Hedley came to me with a sad, worried look on his face. Silently he handed me a message in Joe's writing. It reported that we had contacted strong Japanese patrols. John said, "It's to be sent off at once, before we move." I knelt, my pack beside me, thinking. I took the message and put it in my pocket, and said, "All right. I've got it."

When we harbored again, in the morning, I gave the message to Joe and said, "I don't think we ought to send that, sir." If he had insisted on sending the message I intended to feign sick, fly out of Burma, and tell Wingate that he must come in himself and judge whether Joe was physically fit for the job. At this point I do not think I need to stress the agony of mind I was in, but this was a time when my responsibility to victory, and to the men, far outweighed any other consideration.

Joe said, "Thanks . . . By God, I was tired, Jack." He had passed the crisis. He never became so tired again, nor showed any imbalance; but the truth is that no one over thirty-five ought to have been sent into Burma as a marching Chindit.

Once, when we were preparing to cross a road heavily used by the Japanese, we saw a monk. We had formed up in the jungle, out of sight of the road, and our ambush platoons were on their way out, left and right, to block the road while we crossed. A tall, middle-aged man suddenly materialized, walking down an invisible path, diagonally across our front toward the motor road. His shaven head glowed and the strong light seemed to pour out from his orange robe, upward through the barred dust and out through the trees to the sky. We saw him and he saw us. A dozen men held him in their sights, waiting for an order. Joe, beside me, watched him with a frown. "Those buggers were always spies, in '41," he said.

"If you want him caught, we'd better start now," I said.

He waited. Now we could only let him go, or kill him. He was too far to catch with any certainty. Joe said, "Oh, well, this isn't '41, is it? Let him go."

We were ordered to prepare a glider strip and protect the

landing of a small detachment, called Bladet, which was going to
carry out railroad demolitions farther south. The map showed a
likely spot near Shwemaunggan, on the bank of the Meza River,
and there we went. Our patrols reported no Japanese in the nearby
villages. Robbie and Chesty looked at the bare fields near the
river and reported them suitable for a glider strip. Joe set headquarters in a patch of forest and bamboo on the river bank and
we began to prepare the strip, by leveling the low earth bunds, or
partitions, which separated the paddies.

Deep in the night Bladet came, and we lit the fires. The first
glider touched down in the mathematical center of the strip, at
perfect speed and with a beautiful, slow, gentle caress, but his
direction was at right angles to the correct one. He raced off
across the unleveled paddy in a long-drawn rending and crashing.
We hardly had time to wonder what had happened to the poor
devils inside when the second glider came in. This one also landed
in the exact center of the strip, and going the right way; but when
he reached the end he was still doing forty miles an hour. Again
the horrible splintering and the pistol-shot crack of boughs as
the wide-winged beast plunged into the thickets at the end of
the strip, where Joe and I waited. The third came, landing better
but still too far up, so that he reached the end of the strip at
20 mph. At this speed, just at the end of the runway, his wheels
vanished, he slid onto his belly, hit a giant clump of bamboos
and upended on his nose.

A dozen of us slashed and struggled through the bamboo to
reach the second glider, which had quite disappeared. After five
minutes we found it, on its back, a twisted mass of wreckage.
We hacked through the fuselage. A British private climbed out,
said "Fuck," without emphasis, and turned to help us. One by
one five other soldiers and an officer followed, each making the
same comment. Finally we dragged out two mules. Being devocal-
ized, they could not say anything, but one of them tried to bite
me in the arm, and I don't blame him.

We neared the brigade rendezvous. The maps were confusing
and sometimes, when we met Burmans in the forest, we asked for
information. Macpherson, Saw Lader, Smith, or Hedley did the
interrogation. I do not speak Burmese, but I can set out what was
said, for I heard it a hundred times during the campaign: "Oo

*galay ba wa galay? Kalay galay ma shee bu. Ma thee bu. Ya malay?
Ooo. Nga galay, pa kalay thet galay. Ywathitkon ooo malay? Ma
thee bu. Ma shee bu. Ooo."* It was impossible not to be impressed
when John turned to the brigadier after each of these exactly
similar colloquies and told him, in his usual loud definite voice
that the man had said, "The nearest village is that way. There
are ten Japanese in Ywathitgale and a hundred in Napi-gon. There
is no water in the Yindaik Chaung"—or something totally different.

On March 21 we crossed the railway, and that night radioed to
our other columns the firm date and exact position of the rendezvous—March 24, within the bend of the Ngane Chaung at map
reference 477730. We moved slowly forward on the twenty-
second, only a short distance, and our engineers went to reconnoiter the railway bridge over the same Ngane Chaung, which
we intended to blow up. On March 23 we took a supply drop.

The King's Own and the Cameronians arrived at the rendezvous after their long march from Broadway. Joe did not permit
beards in training, but on entering Burma had allowed them at
battalion commanders' discretion. The King's Own wore them,
the Cameronians did not, nor did British officers of the two
Gurkha battalions. Gurkhas can't grow them until old. Now a
Gurkha messenger came, from 30 Column's northern outpost,
that a *gora paltan* (pale-face battalion) was coming, with beards.
Soon Tommy Thompson, the colonel of the King's Own, came
striding through the trees followed by Major Heap, his second-
in-command. Again the message from the Gurkha outpost—another *gora paltan*, without beards. Bill Henning and Tim Brennan
arrived.

We talked over our adventures. The Cameronians had run into
the enemy on the upper Meza and killed a score, suffering three
or four casualties themselves. The King's Own had slipped through
without contact. The 111th Indian Infantry Brigade was concentrated and ready for its first task, the destruction of Japanese
rail and road communications in this area.

The next morning a column went off and blew up the railroad
bridge over the Ngane Chaung. Joe completed plans for our first
major series of ambushes, demolitions, and assaults. We took another supply drop so that the columns could go out fully rationed.

I was very hungry and the K ration supper had tasted like boiled paper. Sixteen days in Burma at three packets a day made, let's see, forty-eight packets. Suppose the campaign lasted another eighty days, that would make . . .

"Sir. Brigade Major, sir . . . Would you like a tomato?"

I sat up with a start. Smith, our Anglo-Burman Intelligence officer, knelt beside me. He was a big man, grinning, and held out a handful of small tomatoes in his big palm. "I've got a little cooked rice, too," he said.

He gave me some rice and two tomatoes. I settled back against the tree and ate them, wondering whether I ought to. No one else had any.

A little later, full and calm, I prepared for bed. . . . Take off my boots and the two heavy pairs of woolen socks, place the socks inside the boots, and the boots, laces pulled wide, beside my pack. Settle the pack so that the soft things—the extra shirt, the other pairs of socks (every time I see them I think of Barbara)— are on top; make sure it is properly fastened. Spread out the fighting equipment on my right side. Flashlight and message pad to hand, in their haversack, carbine between my thighs, muzzle down, magazine full, breech empty, safety catch on. Loosen belt and top fly buttons. Place hat on top of boots to keep them and the socks dry. Slip chin strap underneath boots to keep the hat from blowing away.

A signal office messenger came softly toward me, bent over. "Messages from Force, sir."

I pulled out the flashlight and read the first message. "General Wingate killed in an air crash. Lentaigne to fly out immediately to assume command of Force."

The second message changed the task of 111 Brigade. The great Japanese assault on Imphal was in full swing, and we were to operate against their lines of communications in an area around Pinlebu, about forty-five miles northwest of where we then were.

I put on my boots and took the messages to the new commander of the Chindits, who lay asleep twenty feet from me, under a tall tree.

17 When he had read the two messages, Joe ordered the cancellation of the operations due for the morning, then said nothing more but turned over and, apparently, went back to sleep. I passed the orders to the columns and, myself, tried to sleep.

It was not easy. Wingate's death did not seem entirely real, but then neither had Wingate. He had come to represent an attitude rather than a man, or even an idea, and the attitude would still live, perhaps even intensify itself, though no longer under the encouragement of the man himself.

I awoke early, my mind much occupied with the new task. As we flew into Burma eastward, we had passed over the Japanese 15th Army hurrying to attack Imphal and Kohima. Our new orders obviously meant a switch from the northern, Stilwell front to the central, Slim front. In theory it implied no other change, since the actual task—to harass an enemy line of communication—was the same in both cases. But the new brigadier, whoever he was, would be working under Joe Lentaigne. Wingate's tactical doctrine, as it emerged after Quebec, had seemed to us—to Joe and myself, among others—to lay too much stress on attacking Japanese prepared positions, a task for which Chindits, without artillery or tanks, were in our opinion unsuited. The thing could sometimes be done, obviously, but always with losses disproportionately greater than the rewards gained.

Now the brigade would have an opportunity to work on a theory which I held to be the core of Chindit war, that is, to force the enemy to attack us, on ground and at times of our choosing, under circumstances which enabled us to disengage at will—in order to engage elsewhere.

Pinlebu, for example, was an important staging point and probably a local headquarters of the Japanese L. of C. We *could* attack and capture it. Under Wingate's new theories, we should. I estimated we would lose three hundred men in the process, and cause one thousand units of damage—let the unit be what you wish—in the form of casualties inflicted, stores and vehicles destroyed, communications interrupted.

Or, under my theory, we could ambush the supply road with one column. The column would destroy the first Japanese party to come along, probably a truck convoy. The Japanese would then need something between six and twenty-four hours to launch an attack on the ambush. If the ambush had successfully concealed its strength, the Japanese might attack with insufficient force, and suffer a heavy repulse. If the attack were very strong, our column could withdraw into the jungle after forcing the enemy to deploy, begin the attack, and suffer casualties. But meanwhile two more columns would be resting and taking a supply drop, and the remaining two getting ready for the next ambush. When the first ambush withdrew, a second would get into position, five or twenty-five miles away. The whole process could be repeated almost endlessly, and with variations. We could make the enemy come out with a whole battalion, to find that we had only ten men in the position . . . who vanished. The next time we would put the entire brigade in, and could annihilate any force they had available to attack. By this means, never attacking but always forcing them to attack us, I thought we would suffer perhaps one hundred casualties in a month, and inflict two thousand units of damage.

I took out the map and began to study the area to which we must now go. This was going to be really good, really worth while. . . .

Joe's orderly came up. *"Brigadier sahib salaam bhanchha."*

When I reached him, "Any ideas on where we can make a light plane strip?" he asked.

I pointed to a white area on the map, nine miles north. It was probably paddy, and the absence of contour lines showed that it was reasonably flat. Joe nodded. "That's where I thought. About an hour after first light tomorrow . . . I've got to appoint a new brigadier. Any ideas?"

I had thought about the matter, although it had always seemed more likely that Wingate would relieve Joe and put in a more malleable commander of his own party. (Wingate thought that the whole Chindit force was his to dispose of, like a piece of real estate; three different officers later told Slim that Wingate had promised they would inherit its command from him.)

To Joe I said that in my opinion two of the battalion commanders (lieutenant colonels) and one of the column majors were fit to command the brigade. At air base we had a full colonel, and a good one, but I personally doubted whether he had sufficient Chindit training to be able to take the reins at once, in action, and with full confidence, as he had only recently come to us. Every other brigade in the Force similarly had a full colonel as second-in-command. Some were not fit for the role. Of those that were, I thought that Claud Rome of 77 Brigade would probably best suit us, with our classical outlook and training.

Joe said nothing, nodding occasionally, and at the end ordered the march to begin in one hour. I sent off the request for light planes and we marched—26, 90, and 30 Columns with Brigade Headquarters, 41 and 46 Columns to follow a day later on a parallel route.

At the long midday halt Joe handed me a message for dispatch. Brigade majors, like all chiefs of staff, hate their masters to do anything on their own. I quailed, wondering what disastrous solecisms, such as using incorrect abbreviations, he had committed.

The message, addressed to Force H.Q. and all columns, appointed Lieutenant Colonel Morris, 4/9 Gurkha Rifles, to command of 111 Brigade, with the temporary rank of brigadier. Morris, 140 miles away east of the Irrawaddy, already in command of the three columns operating entirely independently of us in the Sinlumkaba Hill Tracts, was to stay with his force. That part of the 111 Brigade west of the Irrawaddy would be commanded by Major J. Masters.

Joe was speaking while I stared dumbly at the message. He said,

"Seniority didn't matter a damn to Wingate and it doesn't matter a damn to me—not for its own sake anyway. And what you don't know is that you were going to get a battalion, as a result of Michael Roberts' reports on you, when I asked for you as my B.M. That would have made you senior to all the present C.O.s. But I'm giving you the job because I think you can do it better than anyone else. Don't let the brigade down."

Command! Command of this brigade, command of troops I knew and respected, whom I had helped to train, in operations which I was completely confident I could control. The two lieutenant colonels who had apparently been passed over would be puzzled and perhaps hurt, and since Jumbo Morris had got the red hat I would have no actual rank with which to assert authority. I did not think I would need it. I had served the brigade, and all its men, as loyally as I knew how, and I trusted them to serve me.

The knowledge that I would command again, for the first time since commanding a company before the war, fell like dew on my head and face, ran like cool water over my tired (and stinking) feet. Civilians are apt to think that this hunger for command is a psychological disease in a professional officer; that he craves it to serve his ambition, or to feel power, to have many men at his beck and call. It may be so sometimes. To me, command was the function toward which an officer directed his life. It was the sole reason and justification for his existence.

Staff work, even of the most complex kind, can be learned by civilians, for only a quick and accurate mind and a retentive memory are needed. A commander can do with less of these attributes, but he must add a quality easy to recognize but hard to define—a strength of character, a determination with no obstinacy in it, something that inspires but does not arouse febrile excitement. He needs wisdom rather than cleverness, thoughtfulness rather than mental dexterity.

The higher he stands, the more he needs, too, another quality which cannot be taught by any quick means but is either there, by a stroke of genetic chance, or, more usually, is deposited cell by cell on the subconscious during long years of study and practice. It is this quality which tells a commander, instantly and without cerebration, whether a plan is inherently sound or unsound.

It is this that enables him to receive the advice of specialists and experts, and reach the proper decision though the specialists conflict; and, on other occasions, to overrule them even when they speak with one voice.

I had spent ten years aiming at the attainment of that quality. I knew I had something of it, but by no means all. My power of command, until I gained experience, would be a patchy thing and it was the men in the ranks and the young subalterns who would suffer from my mistakes. The wonderful thing about soldiers, though, is that they know you have to learn the same way they do, and will permit any man a fair and just time to prove himself, provided he does his best. After that they will take almost anything, do almost anything, for a competent commander who combines pride in himself and in them with a humble recognition of his privilege in commanding them. The pride I had and, I believed, the competence. The humility I felt deeply, standing there, tears very close, the message in my hand.

I said, "Yes, sir."

Joe said, "Think over those new orders, and tell me tonight how you intend to carry them out."

"Yes, sir," I said.

If I was going to march along with my mind elsewhere, thinking of tomorrow and tomorrow and tomorrow, someone else must think of today. I would need a brigade major. I sent for Major Geoffrey Birt, the senior engineer officer, and told him to hand over his duties to his captain and assume the post of brigade major, effective immediately. We smiled suddenly at each other; it was just twelve years since I had been head of the Beresford dormitory at Wellington and he the senior fag, responsible for collecting and distributing all the boys' mail.

We settled into the rhythm of the march.

18 In the early light a heavy ground mist lay over the paddy. Joe and I stood at the edge of the jungle, smoking, and watching the two hundred men at work on leveling the paddy bunds. Close by, Doc Whyte squatted beside two men, a Gurkha and a Jock, who involuntarily moaned and twitched in high malarial fever. It was nearly time and when the sappers reported that four trees which stood across the end of the strip were ready for blowing, I ordered them to go ahead. They set off the charges —packets of plastic explosive tied to an instantaneous fuse around the girth of the tree a few feet up. Three of the trees started vertically in the air, shattered at the waist, and fell. The fourth cracked but did not fall. The light planes came, two L-1s.

The engineers worked frantically to set a new charge on the last tree, and Chesty fired off a red Very light to warn the pilots to stand clear, but they swung round and came in downwind, where the jungle, a hundred feet tall, reached the very end of the strip. They floated on, sinking, their motors purring. Suddenly the lead plane dipped his right wing sharply and he was among the treetops. Level again, then left wing down . . . he came on between the trees, spilling air by violent sideslips, branches and leaves brushing his wings and wheels. He burst into the open, sinking fast, but still fifty feet up, the second plane weaving like a drunken moth among the trees behind. Down, down, and we were all pressing our feet down against the earth, willing him down, but he floated on and on. He touched down thirty feet short of the unblown tree, rolled, and stopped, with five feet to spare.

The second plane landed a little sooner, turned slightly, and rolled to a stop. The pilots climbed out. They were both smoking cigars. Down the strip we were all cheering and clapping. Joe went out, shook the lead pilot's hand, and cried, "That was the best landing I've ever seen!"

"Thanks, General," the sergeant said.

Joe recovered himself, "But why the hell didn't you wait till we'd blown down the other tree there?"

The sergeant shook his head in mournful acknowledgment of his fault. "Hell, we could make it."

Joe and I shook hands and wished each other luck. Five minutes later, as the wheels of the L-1 left the ground and my hand came down from the salute, I assumed command. During the night I had removed the crowns from my shoulders. For a major, they were correct. In this job, they would be inappropriate. I had no rank, therefore. I was, simply, the commander; and that was how I signed myself and thought of myself from then to the end of the campaign.

We marched north and west. The sun had risen and soon we passed Burmans working in a field below the path as we climbed into low hills. They turned as they heard the sound of our boots, and stared at us, first in fear and then in wonder. One very pretty girl smiled at me, and shyly waved. She wore the largest straw hat I have ever seen, the brim nearly five feet in diameter, made of weather-darkened plaited bamboo strips, with a dropped outer brim six inches deep, and a small domed crown in the middle. It was a wonderful hat, a superb hat, and she would certainly sell me the hat for a few annas, or a piece of parachute cloth. Mac-Arthur wore a hat with gold lace all round it, Monty wore a beret with an unauthorized quantity of badges. I would outdo all of them. . . . I waved to the girl. She waved back. I marched on, and have never forgotten her.

Across the smoky blue Kanbat Range, which we were now climbing, lay the area of our operations. It was a broad valley, sixteen miles wide and, for my purposes, nearly forty miles long, entirely covered in jungle except for half a dozen villages and the small areas of cultivation around them. The farther limit of the valley was clearly defined by the precipitous Zibyutaung Dan Range. The motor road ran up the middle of the valley from south to north and then, at Kyaungle, turned west and crossed the Zibyutaung Dan toward the Chindwin and Assam.

This was our new "field," but we weren't going to make a hidden-ball sneak this time. We were going to drive the Japanese out of the area, make it impossible for him to use it in any way, by the methods I had planned—ambush after ambush, up and down the whole valley.

We marched fast and far for three days, reached the foot of the valley, and began. . . . Now I was like a quarterback, choosing the play, trying to keep my headquarters in one place as long as possible so that the columns could always get in touch with me and I with them, watching how their movements and battles made patterns on the map and trying to use them to deceive the enemy, staggering the supply drops so that at least one column was always ready to go several days without one, and hence was available for suddenly presented opportunities.

The football metaphor is not as foolish as it usually is in the description of battle, for the men went at the work with an almost boyish *élan*. It was not my appointment which caused this heightening of morale, but the knowledge that we were now getting down to business, and in a role they knew exactly how to handle.

This time presents itself to my memory in a series of vignettes. Another part of my mind tries to place the events chronologically, and form them into the proper military sequence of an ordered, co-ordinated plan. . . .

Everyone needed a supply drop. I sent 30 Column southwest to attack the Japanese post which air intelligence reported at Naungkan and keep it occupied, without getting themselves pinned down, while we took the supplies. Three successive nights the aircraft came. You could see the parachutes on the trees for miles. 30 Column reported contact. A probing attack. Shot up trucks on the road. After moonset, a counterattack from the enemy. One killed, one wounded, two missing. The column came back for supplies, its work done. I'd have to clear a light plane strip for the wounded man, somewhere the far side of the road. Meantime he must go strapped on horseback.

Tommy's 41 Column moved off to set its first ambush, ran into the Japanese just before crossing the road. I heard the stammering roar of automatics and the crash of grenades in the middle of the night, dulled by distance. Four killed, four wounded; but they thrust the enemy aside, killing half a dozen, and went on with very slight delay. Good. A Chindit column that could meet the enemy unexpectedly in the night, kill them, and continue its march without losing cohesion, could do anything. (Imagine dense thick jungle, black night, men in Indian file, each hearing but hardly seeing the man in front and the man behind, the column a quarter of a mile long from front to rear; the creak of mule harness, clink of metal on metal. Right beside you, the explosions, the brief flashes of fire, the man in front jerking back, falling, knocking you down, something hot and wet pouring over your head, a voice you recognize, calling, cut off to a meaningless wail of agony. The mules jerking, tugging, one broken loose from its leader, perhaps he's dead, crashing away through the trees. Roar of Bren guns from close, very close, the bullets seeming to come straight at you.)

I moved, with 30 Column and Brigade Headquarters. About four o'clock in the afternoon we reached the Manyu Chaung. It was small, but lined by a wide belt of open paddy. When a third of the force had crossed, a third was on the paddy, and the rest still in the southern jungle, I heard the drone of many engines. Twelve Zeros drifted overhead, coming from the south, not very high. They were obviously patrolling the road. I stopped, and looked back. My heart leaped with delight, and pride. Every man and mule had stopped dead where he was. Not one face was turned up to see what the enemy aircraft, which could slaughter most of them in a single run, were doing. The Zeros droned on, and disappeared.

Crossing the road: About a quarter of a mile before reaching it, the ridge we were following turned sharply left, directly toward it. I was walking with my battle-command group a few yards behind a company of Gurkhas. As I reached this sharp turn in the ridge I glanced up, and saw, straight ahead of me, a hundred feet distant, four soldiers. Down the slope beyond them I thought I saw huts in the trees. I stopped. There *were* huts somewhere round here, Tommy had reported; and probably occupied by Japanese; but the huts should have been at least half a mile to the north of our present position. It was an interesting problem in map reading, certainly.

I realized that the four soldiers were Japanese. They were staring at me. I moved behind a tree, called the nearest officer, Baines, pointed out the Japanese, and told him to kill them. When he had done that he was to keep the huts under observation until the rear of the force got well past the spot. Baines, too, stared at the Japanese. "My God, so they are," he said. The Japanese kept staring. "Get going!" I snapped. The Brigade Defense Platoon ran down the ridge, firing. Two Japanese ran away, two were killed. They were all armed. Ten minutes later, we crossed the road, unmolested.

This incident, at an unmarked place on a vague map, still baffles me. What were those Japanese doing there, staring at us as we marched by? Why had no one in front of me seen them? It was inexplicable; as inexplicable as the conduct of the defense platoon *jemadar*, whom I noticed leaving the platoon when it went cheerfully to attack. That evening I reduced him to the ranks, and sent him back to India at the first opportunity.

Tommy Thompson and the King's Own laid their ambush and caught a small convoy the first night. Our P.I.A.T.s (antitank projectors) set the leading truck on fire, and the machine guns completed the slaughter at close range. Forty-eight enemy killed, two or three of our own men wounded. The next night Tommy withdrew and moved west, then north.

The Cameronians took position five miles farther north, and drew successive attacks by a platoon, a company, and a weak battalion. The enemy company attacked across open paddy fields, without supporting fire, against dug-in machine guns and suffered accordingly. By the end of the second day, over two hundred enemy casualties, about half dead; five of our own. (During that company attack, when most of his comrades lay dead or wounded in the paddy, one Japanese continued the charge alone. He arrived finally at the muzzle of a Cameronian machine gun, which cut him to pieces. His bayonet was not fixed and his rifle was not loaded.)

April 11—the Japanese buzzing like angry bees all up and down the valley: 30 Column ran into the enemy while reconnoitering for an ambush. Mike MacGillicuddy left his mules, seized a Bren gun, climbed a tree fifty yards from the enemy—in broad daylight, and the tree had no leaves—and stayed up there, directing the fire of his men, in a very loud voice, until a Japanese flanking party began to put accurate bursts into his tree. He killed a few with the Bren, then came down, swearing. (Mike got an M.C. for that. I congratulated him, but he would only talk about the death of a rifleman. When he climbed the tree, two Gurkhas of a Bren-gun team ran out to a flank, where they could see the enemy and obey Mike's fire orders. The No. 1 was seventeen years old—I knew him. His No. 2 lay on his left side, beside him, head toward the enemy, a loaded magazine in his hand ready to whip onto the gun the moment the No. 1 said, "*Change!*" The No. 1 started firing, and a Japanese machine gun engaged them at close range. The No. 1 got the first burst through his face and neck, which killed him instantly. But he did not die where he lay, behind the gun. He rolled over to the right, away from the gun, his left hand coming up in death to tap his No. 2 on the shoulder in the signal that means *Take over*. The No. 2 did not have to push the corpse away from the gun. It was already clear. When Mike finished telling me, I was again near tears, for I remembered the brown, beaten earth of the football field at Bakloh, our regiment's home, and twenty pairs of young men like Dambahadur lying there, practicing this drill, the crests of the Himalayas shimmering white in the north, and basketball games in the afternoon.)

Barbara was well and the baby was well, though all were suffering a little from the close, damp heat of Bombay. She was hoping to go to Kashmir soon, with her own three children, her sister's small boy, the English nurse and *her* small boy. Gossip and love and little items of news; apart from that—NTR. For me, the usual ache, and suddenly felt misery of separation; then the self-reprimand—some of these men around me had not seen their wives or sweethearts since 1939—five years; then find something to do, and do it.

There was plenty to do that night, at the supply drop where I got the letter. Desmond Whyte came to me and said, "Death from flying fruit, sir . . . It's Captain Hanley of the King's Own, and he's not dead yet, but he's pretty bad. Cracked skull."

Death from flying fruit was our generic term for injuries caused by dropped supplies. Desmond and I had coined it when wondering what we should write in an injury report on a man killed by a sack of pineapples, and how inglorious it would look among the g.s.w.s. (G.s.w., meaning gunshot wound, was the usual notation of a battle casualty—g.s.w. chest, g.s.w. head, multiple g.s.w.)

We must get Hanley out at once. Only the day before we'd cleared a strip three miles back, in a stretch of paddy, and sent out casualties from all five columns. Now I was moving north, with the King's Own. The Cameronians were back on the road and the Gurkhas just coming away from it. Since I believed we had drawn most of the Japanese garrisons onto the road now, I intended to attack their dumps and staging center at Kyaungle; but I could afford a few hours' delay.

Desmond and the King's Own doctor took Hanley, a group of stretcher bearers, and a small escort, and set off at once, in the night, to go back to the strip. We asked for a light plane as soon after dawn as possible. I went to sleep.

About eight A.M. Desmond returned with all his original party —plus two U.S.A.F. lieutenants. The Air Commando had sent two planes. One cracked up on landing; the other, with the unconscious Hanley on board, cracked up on take-off, slamming Hanley, headfirst, against the forward wall of the cabin. The pilot climbed out of the wreckage as Desmond and the others ran up, and said, "Aw, shit, I ought to be shot." This immediately became a favorite expression in the brigade . . . but meanwhile, I could wait no longer, and gave Desmond an hour to devise some means of carrying Hanley. Then we would march.

Soon Desmond asked for Maggy. Briggs protested halfheartedly, for Maggy carried the most important radio set in the force; but I said yes, and a medical orderly led her away. The doctors cut two bamboos about twelve feet long, and fastened the thick ends one on each side to Maggy's saddle. The flexible thin ends trailed astern. Across these they fastened two short, strong pieces of bamboo, one just above Maggy's tail and another six feet lower down. These held the two poles thirty inches apart. In this rectangle they fastened two doubled blankets, laid Hanley in them, and tied him in with another blanket.

We marched. Maggy's leader led her, a medical orderly walked at Hanley's head to protect him from whipping boughs and to warn when Maggy lifted her tail, and two men walked behind, holding cords attached to the thin ends of the poles, so that they could guide the whole around corners and up and down steep slopes. Maggy carried and towed Hanley for five days, and a distance of about fifty miles. She never kicked, bucked, slipped— even on the worst ground—and she never lifted her tail while Hanley was under it. I will swear that she knew what she was doing and although I am not unduly fond of any animals except cats, more than once I found myself, at night, hugging Maggy round the neck, stroking her and whispering into her ear what a good, brave, and clever girl she was . . . beautiful, too, I would add, remembering her sex. She snickered coyly.

Hanley remained unconscious the whole time. The doctors fed him every two hours, day and night, with a mixture of water, sugar and brandy, passed by a tube down his throat. They emptied his bladder two or three times a day by passing up a catheter, an operation which must be carried out under rigidly antiseptic conditions: they did it with dirt-stained hands, in dusty jungle, among the blowing mules and the sweating men, for we came across little water at this time.

We crossed the main road six miles west of Kyaungle, where it ran toward the Zibyutaung Dan. Stops were out to right and left, but they must have been fast asleep, for just as I was about to cross the road a battered old Chevy chugged down it, containing a middle-aged Japanese officer. I have seldom seen such a strange expression on a man's face, as he realized he was driving through the middle of a large enemy force. He did not dive to the floor, but sat up and looked straight ahead, as though we had committed a grave social *faux pas* by being there. When he was past I recovered myself and banged off a shot after him with my carbine, soon followed by a few rifles and a Bren gun, but he got clean away. When I stopped laughing I gave the column commander a fearful rocket for the negligence of his men, but everyone was laughing and I really welcomed the incident as a proof of the brigade's morale. We had established that we belonged here, and the sight of Japanese carried no alarm, even when unexpected. That too was just as well, for Maggy's carrying harness collapsed right in the middle of the road—the only time it did. The orderly just saved Hanley from falling, but for five minutes there they all were, in the middle of the road, trying to put it together again.

I moved east, joined now by 30 Column, and sent out orders for a pincer attack on Kyaungle and its conjoined hamlets. The Cameronians were to attack first, from the south, astride the road. I gave them a definite limit, and told them to press hard toward it, capturing it if that could be done without heavy casualties but in no case to go beyond it, because the real purpose of their attack was to hold the attention of the Japanese while the King's Own made the true attack, from the north. This attack Tommy would press home to its objectives, regardless of casualties; and the Cameronians would be there to kill any Japanese who fled before the King's Own. (Even the Japanese sometimes ran, if their orders were unclear, or when thrown into confusion and made uncertain of what they should do.)

Now secrecy of movement became more than ever essential. The Japanese at Kyaungle must be kept facing south, toward the Cameronians who were coming up the road at them without any great efforts at concealment. I, with the King's Own and the Gurkhas, swung stealthily northeast, then southeast through heavy jungle, then due south.

On the last afternoon of our silent approach we heard firing from the south. As soon as we harbored, a mile in from the edge of the paddy surrounding Kyaungle, messages came from the Cameronians. They had attacked, met little opposition, killed a score of Japanese, and reached their limit line. The Japanese still held the northern part of the village group. Tommy and I went forward and, lying concealed at the edge of the jungle, planned the support for his attack. . . . Bombers we wanted; mortars of course. During the evening and the night we fixed it all.

The next morning, just after first light, the King's Own moved off in battle formation through the jungle, marching on a compass bearing for Kyaungle. I followed with my command group, and 30 Column, in reserve, followed me; but at every check and halt it faced the rear, in case some wily Japanese were trying to do to me what I was trying to do to them.

Just before the limit of the jungle we stopped. Men crept and crawled forward, manhandling the mortars and machine guns and their ammunition. The assault companies lay in their lines, ready. At H minus twenty minutes the mortars began a systematic bombardment of the forward edge of the enemy positions. We had asked for the bombers to come at H minus ten.

H minus ten came, but no bombers. The mortars kept firing, but we could not carry much ammunition, and something had to be kept for the unexpected or for the usual Japanese counter-attack. A few shots, a few bursts of automatic fire crackled over us. The mortars battered the huts at the edge of the village and inside it two or three houses began to burn. H hour . . . H plus ten: still no bombers.

We could wait no longer, or Tommy's men would get no covering fire at all as they crossed those two hundred yards of open paddy. We tried to get the bombers on the radio, but couldn't. The mortars changed to smoke and the King's Own attacked. We were in overwhelming superiority, as I intended. This was our first formal attack and both for the benefit of the Japanese and of my own men I wanted it known that when 111 Brigade attacked, it was not much use trying to resist.

The King's Own disappeared at a steady parade ground pace into the smoke. Automatics stammered and grenades exploded, and the enemy fled without causing more than three or four casualties. To the south the Cameronians killed a dozen more Japanese. Tommy sent up his success signal and reported on the walkie-talkie.

The bombers came. Chesty and Robbie swore and cursed into the radio, but the B-25s made their runs and dropped their bombs right in the middle of the King's Own in Kyaungle—the target they had been given. Fountains of earth rose in the village, whole buildings vanished. Grimly I repeated what I had said to myself at Raqqa after the Blenheims attacked us; and told Desmond to get an emergency casualty team ready.

The bombers flew away, and I went into the village. Tommy

reported that as far as he knew, they had caused no casualties at all. The men had found shelter in the Japanese trenches.

Leaving a small garrison in the village, we withdrew slightly, cleared a strip, sent out the U.S.A.F. light plane pilots and our casualties (including Hanley: he survived), got a heavy supply drop which replenished the ammunition we had used, and made ready for the next phase. I had a plan. It was . . .

An urgent message came from Force. The R.A.F. said that they had totally destroyed the road over the Zibyutaung Dan some fifteen miles west of Kyaungle. But ground sources of information—villagers, agents, etc.—obstinately reported that Japanese vehicles were still using it. . . . "Send a patrol to find out." I called John Hedley, told him to collect a few men from headquarters, and make the reconnaissance. Where and when he would find us again, God may have known but I didn't. He'd find us around somewhere. Ask the Japanese. Smiling delightedly at the prospect of a hard and dangerous mission, John strode off.

My plan . . . The few enemy who had escaped from Kyaungle would take news that they had been attacked by a considerable force. The Japanese would collect a considerable force—probably by denuding Pinlebu, twenty-five miles south—to come and deal with us. I intended to leave 30 Column in Kyaungle, with orders to look like a considerable force—and move the other two battalions, by forced march through the jungles, to Pinlebu. When we got there, I would attack it.

I gave the orders. . . . Within the hour an urgent message came from Force. "111 Brigade will march to Aberdeen at once, and there concentrate for further operations, probably the establishment of a permanent block farther north."

Aberdeen was the stronghold, hidden in dense jungle on the Meza River about thirty miles east, which 16 Brigade had established some weeks earlier. A permanent block was the kind of thing which Calvert's 77 Brigade had put down north of Indaw. They had come out of the jungle, seized some low hill features overlooking the railway and road, and dug in. The Japanese had attacked it furiously, and were still doing so, but had so far failed to dislodge 77 Brigade.

I did not like the orders at all. First, our operations here were affecting, in a small way, the vital Imphal battle. The Japanese, who had carried their supplies with them when they headed for Imphal would not *now* miss the stores we had burned in Kyaungle (two hundred truck tires, two thousand gallons of gasoline, tons of clothing, thirty tons of rice)—but they would miss them like hell when Slim advanced and they had to fall back on these dumps.

Secondly, I thought that permanent blocks were a waste of the Chindits' greatest asset, jungle mobility. Fighting in our own way we had destroyed nearly 200 tons of stores and 20 vehicles, and inflicted 430 casualties, suffering only 40 ourselves, a proportion of 10 to 1 in our favor; and this in two weeks.

Then I had misgivings about trying to repeat, closer to the front line, what Calvert was doing so successfully in a rear area. Had I been more experienced, or had I held the rank of my status, I would have sent Joe a signal asking for these orders to be reconsidered; and I ought to have done so, but I didn't, and it would not have made any difference, because the hand that pulled us away was not that of Joe, but of Slim, acceding to Stilwell.

But no doubts must show in my manner, so I told the column commanders that we were going to have a chance to outdo 77 Brigade, and sent out orders for the march to Aberdeen.

On the second evening we harbored by a lovely stream east of Mansi. The hills rose steadily to the east in the clear, still air. To the north the massive bulk of Taungthonlon Taung, 5,600 feet above sea level, blocked the horizon.

John Hedley, pale and sweat-stained as always, swung into camp with huge strides at the head of six of the most exhausted-looking men I have ever seen. He was carrying three of their rifles as well as his own. I offered him a tot of rum but he refused— he had sworn not to take a drink until he was back in Mandalay, having driven out the Japanese who, in 1941, had driven out him and his family. Taking off the pack, the equipment, the rifles (it was all exactly like his first arrival at Ghatera), he gave his report.

The country across which he had traveled was *perfectly bloody*. Gorges, cliffs, mountains, and dense forest, much of it spiny bamboo, whose spines, sharp as needles and hard as steel, are three to ten inches long. The second evening he took up position beside the disputed road, and saw trucks moving cautiously and wide-spaced along it. The R.A.F. were wrong, and his job was done. But that was not enough for J. D. H. Hedley. In the middle of the night he walked along the road with his orderly, felt the surface and noted what it was made of, what damage had been done by bombing, where and how it had been repaired, and what signs he saw of damage to trucks. During this walk he found a truck stopped, the driver asleep in the cab. Having shot the man dead, John catalogued the contents of the truck, and only then set out to rejoin us.

With John back I felt good and warm and happy again. The brigade and I had established an extraordinary rapport, and all but the Gurkhas of 30 Column were here under my hand. I felt a certainty that the Japanese were nowhere near, and that if they were, they—not we—were the frightened ones, the hunted.

I called the column commanders, told them to push their protective platoons a quarter of a mile farther out in all directions, and to relieve them at midnight. Meanwhile, fires were to be lit—not smokeless, concealed cooking fires, but bonfires—as many as they could cut wood for. I had called for a double rum ration after the Kyaungle battles. Now I wished to hear talking, singing, and shouting, and the damned brigade could get as stinking drunk as the ration allowed. We had instilled silence, as second nature, for so long that Major Heap asked me cautiously whether I meant, really, they could make a noise. He looked at me as though he thought the strain of command had unhinged me. I waved my hand expansively and said I meant exactly what I said. What's more, it wasn't a suggestion, it was an order. *Light bonfires, drink, and sing!*

I settled down to some rum with Doc Whyte, Geoffrey Birt, and Briggs. Slowly the noise up and down the stream grew as the British soldiers began to speak in normal tones, then to shout, then to wander round the camp in groups yelling raucous songs and pretending to be drunk, which—alas—the rum ration could not really stretch to. Later I walked about myself, and four hundred men must have tried to give me their precious rum ration, and during the night I awoke once or twice and heard many of them still at it, and the tall fires made the jungle a wonderland of dancing light and glowing shadows.

The next morning the march continued in absolute silence, but even my three pannikins of cold water, each containing a table-spoonful of salt to ward off thirst and heatstroke, tasted good. I doubt if anyone has ever taken a more confident and cheerful brigade toward battle. This was our forty-fifth day behind the enemy lines in Burma.

19 Just before we reached the Meza River we came upon a riot of wild red roses near a burned hut. I plucked half a dozen and put them in my hat because it was April 23, St. George's Day. Here, at the Aberdeen stronghold, my new orders were confirmed and explained.

The Chindits were to move north, all of us. In essence, Stilwell felt that we were not helping him as much, by our operations around Indaw, as our numbers warranted. He had insisted that we come more directly into his battle. Since the Chindit Force and the Air Commando had been planned at Quebec specifically to help Stilwell, and Stilwell was not a big enough man to see that his fate was actually being settled on the central Assam front, he had his way.

111 Brigade was to lead northward, its task to establish a block somewhere north of Hopin, in the railway valley. 14 Brigade was to come north as soon as it could, and support me. 77 Brigade was to capture Mogaung, the West Africans to hold the White City (the original block) until I was in position, then abandon it and come north. 16 Brigade, exhausted by their long march and their unsuccessful attempts to capture Indaw, were to fly out of Burma.

(The sixth Chindit brigade, 23, never entered Burma. Slim kept it, and used it on his left flank against the main Japanese offensive.)

Before continuing the march I flew twenty miles in an L-5 to have a look at the White City, for I needed to see how various defensive theories had worked out in practice. The place became visible almost as soon as we had gained height from Aberdeen, for hundreds of parachutes hung in and around it—they had given it its name. Scores of Japanese corpses, phosphorescent-black with decay, sprawled on the barbed wire. Quicklime had been scattered everywhere and portable flamethrowers (Lifebuoys) used in an effort to dispose of the bodies, but the sickly sweet smell hung in the air, and stayed for hours afterward in my own sweaty shirt and trousers. Most of the trees were shattered and bare of leaves. The Japanese had attacked every night in the same way—artillery bombardment at five P.M. followed by heavy and repeated attacks all night, and every night on the same sector of the perimeter. During the day they withdrew two or three hundred yards or more. After a long and careful examination of all the defensive and administrative arrangements I flew back to Aberdeen in a thoughtful mood.

The next morning we set out. I sent the brigade by two separated but roughly parallel routes through the Kachin Hills. Brigade headquarters marched with the left-hand columns, of the King's Own and the 3/4th Gurkhas.

The track led up the valley of the Meza, which soon narrowed. After an hour it crossed the Meza to the opposite bank. Ten minutes later, as the forest-covered hills closed in, it crossed back. Five minutes later it recrossed.

"Are you sure this is the right track?" I asked John Hedley crossly.

"Yes, sir," he growled. "Look, there it is, crossing again." He pointed upstream. Groaning, we settled our packs on our backs, hunched forward and began to slog upstream. The Meza averaged two feet deep at the crossings, and perhaps ninety feet wide, though some of the early fords were wider and some of the later, when the hills towered up close on either side and the river ran in a deep gorge, were less, but the water deeper and faster. The Meza is one of the most beautiful small rivers I have seen in my travels about this beautiful world; but after we had forded it forty-five times that first day, and spent at least one of our precious ten-minute halts standing in it, bent forward, cursing steadily, no place a mile back or a mile forward where we could sit down (except for a few stalwart fellows who sat in the river), looking like a long column of overloaded herons—I had had my fill of its beauty. Nor could I help looking up at the cliffs, and wondering what orders I would give if the Japanese ambushed us here. . . .

That night we found a point where the path deigned to use dry land for three hundred successive yards, on a six-foot shelf on the left bank. We all jammed ourselves onto that, a thousand men and scores of animals, placed outposts in forked trees up and down stream and went to sleep. But not before 41 Column's Karen platoon disappeared upriver, warning us to take no notice of bangs and booms, and came back at dusk with about a hundred fish.

The next day we forded the Meza twenty times more, in a deep canyon with the black trees meeting overhead to shut out the sky (but it was wonderfully cool), and then, at last, we left it and climbed slowly into sunlight.

We marched across rolling hills, not so dense with jungle as those to the south. Near the end of the day we came to a Kachin shrine. The Kachins, the people of these hills, are animists by religion and outside every village, to guard it and its inhabitants from evil spirits, they build these shrines. This one, like most we saw later, was a bamboo platform set on top of four stilts about five feet high, the tops of the legs splayed out to form funnels. A few dried and withered flowers and a fresh hibiscus blossom lay on the platform, and the bleached skull of a buffalo was tied to one of the stilt legs.

We came to the village which the shrine guarded, Kaungra. The Kachins, like most other outlying peoples of India and Burma, were strongly pro-British. In the Wingate expedition of 1943, as in the retreat of 1941–42, the Kachins freely gave shelter to our wounded soldiers. In some cases they had hidden men from the Japanese for over two years. In 1942, and again in 1943, the British forces went back to India, leaving the Kachins at the mercy of the Japanese, but the Japanese have no mercy. Now we were in Burma again, and again we could do with help—

guides, scouts, topographical information. If Slim lost the Imphal battle, we would once more leave these people in the lurch. But I thought Slim and the 14th Army would win, and accepted a glass of Kachin home-brewed beer, *tsaku*, with a good conscience. Glass, did I say? It was a two-foot section of giant bamboo, six inches in diameter, the top cut on a slant for ease of drinking. A few yards away John Hedley, having exhausted his two or three words of Chingpaw, talked to the headman in Burmese. (*"Ywathit gale? Ba gale? Ka-maw ma shee bu?"*) We were among friends, not soldiers, just ordinary people. Why, there was a pretty girl, though rather dirty, looking at us from behind a hut, and a fat baby crawling toward my feet. It was a lovely evening.

Full of *tsaku*—we paid for it—we all slept well. Next day we marched on north. The going was very hard and the men visibly more tired than they had been two weeks earlier. Daytime temperatures, through all our time in Burma, had been ninety or ninety-five. Now it was about one hundred.

At the noon halt a light plane came over us where we rested beside the wide Namsang River, and dropped packets of air photographs for me. These showed the area north of Hopin, where I was to establish my block.

We climbed out of the Namsang Valley. This was physically the worst day's march yet, by reason of the bamboo jungle. It was not particularly dense, though the lead platoon had to be relieved every half-hour as they became exhausted from cutting a path wide enough to take the mule loads. But the ground was smooth and steep, and thin, fallen bamboo branches, all smooth, lay in sheaves straight up and down the slope, never across it. You put a foot down and began to transfer weight to it. It slid back on the bamboo stems, which might have been greased and specially placed there for the purpose. You made a net upward gain of three inches. Now the other foot—another three inches. You slid back five inches. . . . Time and again I clung to a bamboo, head bowed and sweat dripping, shaking with exhaustion and helpless anger, no breath to swear at the trees, no strength to shake them, cut them down, jump on them, burn them.

Two days of this, then we crawled over the top, to harbor in low scrub. The land sloped gently away to the north. The great Lake Indawgyi, fourteen miles long and five miles wide, the largest in Burma, lay in the sunset, and low clouds hung over the hills separating it from the railway valley. All the land round the lake was flat and open, scattered with villages, marshy streams, and reed grass. It would take us a long day to cross it. I decided we would cross in battle formation, a battalion and a half strong, with flank guards to right and left, and gave orders accordingly. A supply drop was on its way and I handed all arrangements to Tommy Thompson, telling him and the Brigade Major that I was not to be disturbed except in emergency. Then I withdrew for a final study of the map and the air photographs. I must think about the site of the block.

After an hour or two I made my choice—a hill feature near a stream junction not far from the village of Namkwin. North and south of that place I noted other possible sites, but they had disadvantages which convinced me that I should only go and look at them if my first choice was, on actual inspection, not reasonably good. It would not be perfect, of course—nothing ever is—and I would have to make a quick decision because the best is the enemy of the good, and it might take me a week to inspect other sites. Long before then the concentration of my brigade in the jungles west of the railway valley must have attracted Japanese attention. Attention I did not want for at least forty-eight hours, because I felt that this block, being close to the northern battle front, was liable to run into difficulties not met with at White City.

The site was about twenty miles south of Mogaung, where the Kamaing and Myitkyina roads forked. The Japanese were holding Myitkyina and fighting Stilwell above Kamaing. Mogaung must, then, be a focal point in their plans. If so, they must have hospitals, ammunition dumps, truck parks, rest areas, and the like south of Mogaung—i.e., in the area of the block. As soon as 14 Brigade joined me this would be an advantage, for they could create havoc among such lightly defended installations. Until then, the effect was opposite. Establishing an all-round permanent defensive fortress and building an airfield in enemy territory is not easy at the best of times. If we chose the area of a Japanese dump to do it we would have a hard time indeed, for every Japanese soldier can fight, and fight well. In brief, I believed that my block would not be in the enemy lines of communication proper, but in an area under control of his forward commanders. His reactions would be faster and more violent. My own movements must, consequently, be fast and decisive.

I returned to the map. A path led over the forested hills from a place called Mokso Sakan, at the edge of the lake reeds, to my chosen site at Namkwin. I would concentrate the brigade at Mokso Sakan, stock up with supplies, then cross the hills and get into position as fast as possible.

Next morning we crossed the Indawgyi Plain. In a tiny village the King's Own killed a couple of Japanese, who seemed to be sleeping there in such odd circumstances that I wondered whether they were deserters. At the midday halt most of us swam in the lake, in relays. Floating naked on my back a hundred yards from shore, lazily watching the white clouds sail across the sky, I blessed our Air Force; and made a mental note that our sort of war would be quite impossible without the near-monopoly of the air which they had established.

On, through marshes and swamps and tall reed beds, past a village on stilts, at noon on the second day to the five deserted bamboo shelters which was Mokso Sakan. Next day the Cameronians arrived, we took a heavy supply drop, and were ready. Leaving 30 Column—except their pioneers, whom I took with me— to hold Mokso, the summit at Nawku, and the path between, I set off on May 5 with the two British battalions.

It was a stinking day, very hot, and the initial climb to Nawku both long and steep. The map demanded not only skill at map reading but a sixth or seventh sense to tell me which of those vaguely sketched contours was the one we were struggling along, and which did not exist. In my mind I had set the day's objective as the village of Pumkrawng, clearly marked about halfway down a long eastward running ridge which eventually sank into the Namkwin stream some five crow-flight miles from the railway valley. We trudged on, keeping as high as possible on the spine of the ridge to avoid taking the wrong ridge and also to avoid going up and down, up and down across the sweep of the country.

The problem of finding Pumkrawng was caused by the custom of *taung-ya* cultivation, used by the Kachins and many other hill peoples. When the soil round a village becomes exhausted the villagers move to another site, one or fifteen miles away, burn twenty acres of jungle, plant their crops, build a new village, and call it by the same name as the one they have just left. Ten years later, the soil again exhausted, they move again. The Pumkrawng we were headed for might be occupied, abuilding, or long buried in secondary jungle.

At dark, men and mules swaying from exhaustion and thirst, I could have sworn we were exactly on the site of a clump of houses shown a mile up the ridge above Pumkrawng—but there was nothing, nothing at all, no water, a steep dry slope running far down to the right, dense scrub, tall jungle, otherwise nothing. I cursed the Kachins, and Burma, and *taung-ya*, and John Hedley, but we could go no farther. We harbored where we stood, without water. Only the enormous quantities we had drunk with salt before leaving Mokso saved many of us from heatstroke.

As I lay down to sleep, I thought that for the first time in my life I was lost, and had also lost a brigade headquarters and two battalions of infantry. We were not lost in any SOS sense, because we had only to turn down the hill to reach water and then follow it to come eventually to Namkwin—but what a damned tinker's way to move soldiers!

In a foul temper I ordered the continuation of the march the next morning. Since I was lost I acted on the assumption that I was not, and made no change in direction. After we had gone a hundred paces John Hedley cried, "Wait, sir!" He darted into the jungle, heading for a clump of just visible plantains. My spirits rose. Plantains, the ancestor of the banana, usually mean human habitation. John reappeared dragging a balk of squared timber. "House beam!" he bellowed triumphantly. We had, after all, been very close to the clump of houses above Pumkrawng.

We marched down the ridge, passing Pumkrawng itself (overgrown), Pumkrawng II, Pumkrawng III (both vanished under jungle) and, unmarked on the map, near the stream, the only genuine article, Pumkrawng IV. We harbored along the stream two miles from my chosen site for the block. Again I withdrew to think.

First thing next morning I must go and look at the place. I must not attract attention. That meant a small party. Myself; my chief R.A.F. officer—to O.K. the airfield site; a Burma Rifle officer—to interpret if I ran into Burmans; a small escort. Six or eight men in all. I must take no papers, no marked maps, no notes. Must remember, in series, what to look for—fields of fire; observation; protection against artillery; against bombing; water; the airfield. F-O-A-B-W-A—FOABWA. I could remember that. And then, of course, I must appreciate it as a whole, and strike a balance, Yes or No, for the *F* might be good, the *W* bad.

I called the column commanders and we shared a bottle of rum, Thompson, Heap, Henning, Brennan, and I. Together we studied the map and the photographs, and I told them of my reconnaissance plan for the morrow. If I failed to return by dawn the day after, they must make no effort to find me. Tommy would assume command of the brigade and carry out our task. I advised him that if I disappeared he would probably do best to move the brigade right up to the position that night, inspect it personally the following dawn, and, if it were at all possible, occupy it. Tommy agreed, but I knew I was really just wasting breath. The moment I vanished the responsibility would be his, and no post-mortem instructions from me could release him from that load.

Just before first light the next day I left the harbor, with Flight Lieutenant Jennings, Major Macpherson, and three Gurkha Riflemen. As the light strengthened we climbed out of the shallow valley, crossing a patch of very heavy going which had once held a village, probably Pumkrawng Minus One. We struggled through dense thorn underbrush, lantana, prickly bamboo, and weed and crops run wild. We were very glad to get into the jungle again on top. After rest, and now over an hour from harbor, we moved along the hill toward the railway valley. From this ridge, in places between the great trees, I could see the hump shape of the ridge between the Namyang and Namkwin Chaungs where I intended to place the block. The Gurkhas wore tattered, dirty uniforms. Chesty, Mac, and I wore boots, a length of filthy checked green cotton material wound round our waists in the fashion of the Burmese *longgyi*, and shirts, hats, and light equipment.

We went carefully down the end of the ridge and entered the Namkwin Chaung, here running full between low cliffs. We walked a quarter of a mile down the bed, in the water, and then climbed out into the actual complex of ridges of my chosen site.

FOABWA. Or was it FAUBWA? No, that was some kind of Shan potentate. FOABWA. I began my inspection.

The flanking hills stood too close to the north; but the water was excellent, plenty of it, good, and defiladed from all directions. The total perimeter length was about right; but reverse slopes, for protection against artillery fire, were only just adequate. I searched the valley and the neighboring hills through binoculars. Observation, good; fields of fire, fair in most directions. The aerial photographs had shown nothing better than this, and inspection confirmed it. We could hold this place for a good time against any attack and, when 14 Brigade arrived within the next week or so, what a bastion! Supported by guns in here—for artillery would be flown in to me as soon as I had a C-47 field—we could really chew up any enemy within five miles, north or south.

As for getting into position, there was the railway, in plain view, and the village of Namkwin, probably occupied by a few Japanese clerks and supply personnel. Nothing else; but of course they had to move at night, for fear of our air forces; and they would learn soon enough that we were coming in, and react quickly; but not, I thought, in enough strength to prevent us making the block secure.

Now for the last, the vital question—the airfield.

We slipped down to the forward foot of the hills, and crouched in low scrub at the edge of the paddy. Some Burmans were working in a field between us and Namkwin railroad station; no one else in sight. Chesty Jennings adjusted a cloth round his head and stuck his carbine down his leg under his *longgyi*. The paddy fields lay under the hot morning sun, with tall *kaing* grass at the far edge, and some trees beyond. I inspected Chesty. He didn't look at all like a Burman really, although marching for days with no shirt, his magnificent torso bared, had given him about the right color. He'd have to do. Mac and the Gurkhas prepared to give instant covering fire. Chesty and I walked out onto the paddy, and continued down the middle of it as though going somewhere, but not in a hurry. After four hundred yards we came to a steep drop of five feet; beyond, the paddy continued. I stayed at the drop, crouched as though smoking, my carbine ready. Chesty strolled on. I counted his paces. Another four hundred yards to the end of the flat, cleared land. Eight hundred yards in all.

Chesty reached the end, drifted into the scrub, and came back around the edge of the fields. When he joined me, sweating richly, he muttered, "Couldn't I do with a beer! . . . It's all right if we can get the hump flattened."

"Can we?" I asked.

Christ, I should have brought an engineer officer. And Uncle Tom Cobleigh and all. What the hell was I a commander for if I couldn't make that kind of estimate? I looked at the fields. Two nights with bulldozers, and two hundred men. Good enough. We rejoined Mac and the Gurkhas. Mac was sweating. I was soaked.

"Flying approach all right?"

"Good enough."

Now I must make the final decision. I had a long, close look at the block site from down below there. . . . It stood up too high. Go high on the face and the perimeter will be short, men jammed tight into the sheltered areas behind. Come low on the face and the perimeter will be long, more troops exposed to direct shell fire. Compromise. . . . The airfield: I will dominate it, from the block; but can't possibly protect it except by the operations of the floater brigade when it comes. Trying to defend it, statically, will be a sheer waste of time and men. The same will apply to any other airfield. I made up my mind.

"We'll put the block here," I said, and we returned fast to the brigade harbor.

By early afternoon I had made a sketch of the position, and worked out sector allotments. I explained these briefly to the column commanders and, about two hours before dusk, led the brigade back to the site. As the light failed we were marching up the bed of the Namkwin Chaung, first the brigade defense platoon and Burma Rifles under Macpherson, then myself and a small command group, then the two battalions, with main Brigade Headquarters sandwiched between them. As I reached the spine of the block site, a single, long burst of light automatic fire roared in the Namkwin Chaung below, or among the dark hills beyond. Dreadful surmises flashed through my mind. We had been seen reconnoitering this morning! An entire Japanese regiment lay concealed under our feet, ready to spring the ambush! . . . The steady advance continued. No one ever did find out who fired that burst, or why; but it was a Japanese, because the fire was the extra-quick light crackle of his gun, not our Brens.

An hour after dark the tail of the brigade entered the block. Now, barring more serious disturbance, we had the night to dig ourselves in.

No one slept that night. Sweating, weary, we dug our trenches, we stacked our ammunition, we worked, in hundreds, to level the paddy bunds for the gliders, which I had already requested for the following night. The gliders would bring bulldozers, wire, mortar ammunition, and extra tools. On the hill, in a northward facing re-entrant, Brigade Headquarters dug in. Briggs set up his radios, and established communication with Mokso Sakan, Air Base, and Force Headquarters. 111 Brigade's block was in position: code name—Blackpool.

20 The Blackpool hill looked something like a sharp-spined animal, say a boar, lying with head down, fore-arms and legs extended sideways, and short tail outstretched. There were other minor features and cross ridges, but that is the general outline. The area between outstretched members constituted defilade (shelter) from enemy fire, from three directions in each case. The Namkwin curved in round the animal's left forefoot and then on past its nose. Our water point was sheltered just inside that forefoot. The airstrip extended along the animal's right side, the near edge about one hundred yards away from the tips of right forefoot and right hind leg. The tail joined another hill feature, which was not part of the block. To left and straight ahead were tangled hills, split by streams and gorges and folds, all heavily forested.

To every part of the position I gave a code name. I might have used the animal simile, calling the points Neck, Right Fore, and so on; but all my men were cricket players and I named the positions as on a cricket field—Cover Point, Midwicket, Deep, etc. I wondered whether these names might displease Mr. Church-ill if he ever came to hear about them. He fulminated, rightly, about soldiers who lost their lives in operations called Lollipop; if they were to die, let them die in Crusade and Armageddon. But Tommy, who knew British troops better than I did, assured me that the small, familiar names gave comfort and familiarity to the foreign field, so they stuck. . . .

While the battalions filed into the block I gave orders for the evacuation of the animals. At the White City I had seen the effects of shellfire on the beasts, which could not be adequately protected. Nor did I have room for them in Blackpool. I kept only twenty-five, for emergency, to go out with patrols, and to help carry stores up from the strip. The rest I sent back, under Macpherson, over the hills to the Mokso Sakan base.

At first light I went round the perimeter with the battalion commanders and arranged the junction points, exact siting of reserves and headquarters, mortar defensive fire and SOS tasks, and the usual other details. The rest of the day I spent between the paddy fields, which would become the airstrip, and the block itself. I had pushed strong detachments across the paddy into the dense thickets the other side, and toward Namkwin village. The mortars began to range on their defensive tasks. On the strip, under the merciless sun, two hundred men worked stripped to the waist, with rifles slung. Now, certainly, the Japanese knew we had arrived.

One by one the paddy bunds disappeared, and early in the afternoon Chesty Jennings told me that gliders could land on the northern half. If they landed too far down they would have a roller-coaster ascent up the five-foot bank, on which we had not made much impression, to the southern half of our split-level field.

The gliders must have been waiting, ready for take-off. The first arrived in the twilight. Our mortars put down smoke bombs in front of Namkwin—they could not quite reach it—while the glider circled out over the valley. I heard the stutter and pop of small-arms fire from Namkwin, and our Vickers machine guns began firing slowly at it. The glider came on in a long, graceful approach. He picked up his line, steadied, came on. Quarter of a mile short and two or three hundred feet up, his tail flicked and he dived vertically into the ground just the other side of the Namkwin Chaung. The heavy crash reverberated across the fields and echoed back from the block. Beside me Chesty spoke urgently to the pilot of the second tow plane, even then circling high above us. "Bring him in from the hills, right-hand turn!" Chesty said. They heard and obeyed. The second glider turned over the hills, and came in faster. He landed safely, followed soon by four more. (I sent out a patrol to the crashed glider. The three men in it were dead, but none appeared to have been hit by bullets. Chesty thought that the glider had stalled. I don't know, but I shall not forget the sudden lurch in my own stomach, and the bitten-off cry I gave as the tail went up and the nose straight down.)

The tired soldiers pushed the gliders to the edge of the strip and unloaded them. Within half an hour two small bulldozers and a grader began work, and Chesty had taken over one of the gliders as control tower for the field, and began to put down the strip lights. Working parties, some with mules, began the long slow carry of wire, ammunition, and tools up into the block.

All night and all next day work continued at a frenzied pace— inside the block, digging and wiring and laying of cable, ranging mortars, cutting of fields of fire—on the paddy, the tremendous task of making the five-foot bank into a slope which a loaded C-47 could take at 50 or 60 mph in the middle of its landing run.

About four o'clock in the afternoon I went down to the strip to make the final decision. Was it ready? We walked up and down the hump. "It's not good," Chesty said, "but it ought to do." He looked at me, "How urgent is it that they should come in tonight?"

"Very urgent," I said.

The Japanese had used tanks against the White City, and I wanted field guns in, quickly. Nor had we so far received anything like enough wire, mortar ammunition, or medical supplies. Even as I spoke a shell, coming from the north, sighed lazily over the block and burst on the hills behind us. It was soon followed by another, which fell short. "Desultory shelling," an innocent might have said; but it was ranging. The Japanese were preparing to attack.

I told Chesty not to conceal the state of the strip but to make it quite clear to the air forces that I expected them to make the attempt that night.

That night they came. The lead plane circled over the valley, a dark triangle in a dark sky. Chesty pulled the switch that lit the thinly spaced rim of lights round the field. A few rifle shots went off from Namkwin out there in the valley and the droning sound of the motors came closer. Chesty talked quietly to the pilot. His headlights stabbed out above the northern jungle.

"You're high," Chesty said sharply. "Put her down."

The pilot put her down, she hit just short of the step in the middle, bounced high over it, landed out of control, swung sharply left and roared off the runway into the bushes, making a long, loud noise. After a short interval flames rose. By their light I saw men jumping out of the door, and the silhouetted black figures of Cameronians, who were on close guard that side, running to help. A few seconds later the flames went out.

Chesty called down the second plane. This one landed well, rose twenty feet into the air as she went over the hump, bounced, and taxied to a halt off the runway at the far end, where control officers and unloading parties waited.

The third plane landed smoothly, but did not stop in time. The last paddy bund ripped off its undercarriage and it slid on its nose into the bushes. The fourth landed safely. I heard rifle fire from somewhere in the block behind me; it would have to wait.

By now I had another brigade major, "Baron" Henfry, late of the Indian Cavalry, retired to Kenya, returned to battle. Geoffrey Birt, whom I urgently needed as an engineer officer, had returned to his own job. At this moment he was at the far end of the strip with a squad of sappers, waiting to unload explosives and other engineer stores from the planes. He went to examine the third plane, the one that had lost its undercarriage.

It lay dark and deserted, doors open. He stooped to have a look under the wing. From immediately behind him someone threw a grenade. Geoffrey saw it by the strip lights, and dived flat. The grenade exploded under the wing of the plane a few feet from him. The plane caught fire. A patrol of Cameronians rushed into the scrub, Tommy guns crackling. The fifth plane came into land. But the burning C-47 lay across the wire that linked the field lights, and all the lights went out.

The plane now landing opened up its engines with a great roar and climbed away. The crew of plane No. 4, who had just opened the doors, saw No. 3 burst into flames, heard the grenade, the clatter of Tommy guns. They felt something must be amiss, and I don't blame them. Their doors slammed shut, the engines groaned, and the plane tore off down the strip in the dark. Be-

fore it reached high speed its wing caught the only other undamaged plane, No. 2. It slewed and skidded to a halt. That made
two C-47s written off and two damaged as the price of the night's
work. I could think of nothing but Beatty's remark at Jutland—
"I don't know what's the matter with our bloody ships today.
Steer two points closer to the enemy."

Chesty said, "The strip's not that bad. They're jittery."

"Can you get the lights fixed?"

"In half an hour. But there are only two more to come in for
tonight and I think we'd better send them back. By tomorrow
they'll know what asses they've made of themselves, and they'll
do it right."

I didn't agree with Chesty's harsh judgment on his fellow airmen. It was a difficult strip and no pilot can feel encouraged,
when lumbering in low over enemy territory in a C-47 to see the
plane ahead of him burst into flames on landing. He can't know
that there are no casualties or, if he does, guarantee that the same
will apply to his own plane. But neither we nor 14th Army could
afford to lose any more C-47s, and, after confirming that the
planes already down contained some stores that I regarded as
vital, I told Chesty the rest of the flight could go home.

A messenger arrived, panting: "The enemy are attacking the
Deep, sir. Seems like probing, Colonel Thompson says." The
Deep was the tip of the boar's nose, the extreme north point of
the block. I climbed back into Blackpool, joined Tommy, and
listened to a desultory battle going on down the ridge below. The
shooting, never very strong, died down about one o'clock in the
morning, and I returned to my headquarters.

Unless I were a bloody fool or, far worse to think about, unless
the Japanese had changed their tactical doctrine, the night's attack
was designed to locate our strong points and machine-gun posts
in the Deep sector. That, in turn, meant that the Japanese would
make a serious assault on the same sector the following night. The
Japanese had not learned much, though, because Tommy knew
his stuff perfectly well and only Bren guns and rifles, and mortars
from the central keep, had fired. The queens of the battlefield,
the machine guns, had kept quiet.

Before I got to sleep John Hedley limped in, his knee heavily
bandaged. I had sent him out, with a small reconnoitering patrol,

to find what use the enemy were making of the road and railway. He had found out (during four hours of darkness the enemy had used neither), but he had run into a similar Japanese patrol, killed some of them, and got a grenade splinter in the knee. Doc Whyte came and said, "He'll have to go out." I swore, and John pleaded; but he had to go.

The next morning the Japanese began harassing fire with 105-mm. guns from up the valley, the guns they had ranged in the previous afternoon. I had a lump of homogenized ham and egg halfway to my mouth when I heard the distant *boom boom* in the north. I dived, map in one hand and egg in the other, for the slit trench behind me. Baron Henfry was as quick; Pat Boyle (the new Intelligence officer) a shade slower. The shells whistled with a sudden rising shriek and burst ten feet away, one behind and one in front of the trench.

I returned to my study of the map, and my breakfast. The Baron said, "I think Pat's been hit, sir." (The Baron, a wise, amusing, and extraordinarily brave man, was some fifteen years older than I and so always very punctilious to pay me all the due forms of respect.) I looked down and saw that Pat, crouched in the bottom of the trench between the Baron and me, seemed to be unconscious. Actually, a shell splinter had creased his skull, temporarily paralyzing him but not depriving him of his senses. He has recorded as the most pungent memory of his life those moments when he lay in the bottom of the trench, with more shells bursting far and near, unable to speak or move, and hearing the Baron's remark and my reply, "Oh. Is he dead?" And then the Baron: "I think so."

Until then Pat had been pretty sure he was alive, but now he had doubts. It wasn't until the Baron's saturnine face approached his that he managed to roll his eyes. Even now, he says, he can feel the welling up of joy as he heard the Baron's surprised, "No, he's alive."

Before the shelling ended we suffered several casualties in the area immediately around my headquarters, including the artillery major who had arrived only ten hours earlier, in one of the C-47s, to command the troop of field guns that would soon follow. A shell splinter in the spine killed him instantly.

After a couple of hours the shelling stopped. I had not liked it. I remembered Willy outside Deir-es-Zor—"Wait till you've really been shelled." There would be worse to come. Meanwhile, now that I knew where the Japanese had put their artillery—in the north—I could at least move headquarters and the main dressing station from their northward facing re-entrant to a more sheltered spot. This I did at once. My new command post lay high up behind the boar's left armpit.

Like a flywheel, a noisy flywheel worked by a rackety motor, the battle gathered momentum.

An hour before dusk shelling began again, on the Deep and on the sectors supporting it to left and right. After dark the assaults began with screams and yells and the Very lights shining on bared teeth, pot helmets, long bayonets—then sudden darkness and the clatter of bullets. An hour later the C-47s came. They made their last turn exactly over the spot where I calculated the Japanese officer directing the attacks would have his command post. I did not go down to the strip that night but alternated between my own and Tommy's command post, the latter on the crest of the ridge overlooking the sectors being attacked. By two o'clock the attacks faded, having lasted seven hours, almost continuously.

I got a little sleep and at daylight went down to the strip. Work was going slowly as the men's exhaustion grew on them. The guns had come in, with the gunners, and the dozers were moving them into position. Tons of stores and ammunition had come, but there were not enough men, with the battle going on and reserve companies standing to their alarm posts, to do the carrying. Everyone had been up most of the night, and now we had to carry the stores up from the strip, put down more wire, dig some positions deeper, repair others, bury the dead, patrol the jungles, protect the airstrip. I decided to remove all three-inch mortars from the battalions' control and use them as a single battery, so that I could bring the fire of all eight of them down on any sector with no delay. That meant more cable laying, more ranging. The field guns, no sooner in position, began to range on Namkwin. I sent an urgent message for sound-ranging and flash-spotting equipment so that we could find and engage the enemy artillery. The monsoon was building, the sky was seldom clear, and our fighters had not come over as frequently as earlier. Partly this was due to the demands of Stilwell, in action north of Kamaing, and to the great Imphal battle, then reaching its climax. The result was the same—the enemy artillery grew increasingly bold, and used plenty of ammunition. They were probably sited close to ammunition dumps. They were certainly not short of shells.

We buried our dead, treated our wounded. Shelling continued. Baron Henfry chose the heaviest shelling to stroll around, thumbstick in hand, talking to the soldiers.

Tommy reported that during the night assaults some Japanese had dug in ten to twenty yards from his wire, with snipers up trees, who could look almost directly into his forward weapon pits. Over a part of his sector no one could move without being shot at. I crept up with him to the ridge crest to look. Enemy field guns began firing on some of the rear positions. King's Own snipers lurked among shattered trees, Bren guns ready, watching the tattered forest below. Single shots rang out, Bren guns stammered, leaves whispered, boughs cracked. "Got him!" Another shot.

We crept back. The forward company would have a very unpleasant day, but would suffer few casualties as long as they sat low and tight. The snipers in the trees dominated them, but from higher up the ridge we dominated the snipers. All the same it was an unpleasant development and I ought to have foreseen it. At the White City the Japanese had withdrawn a considerable distance during the day. At that distance our mortars and—above all—our aircraft could get at them. They had learned the lesson, and now were leaning up against our wire, so close that to attack them with aircraft would be very dangerous to us.

Tommy arranged to relieve his forward troops with a reserve company after dark. Meanwhile two platoons, heavily supported, went out by the Water Point and attempted to clear the Deep sector, sweeping right-handed around the block, their right on our wire.

The attempt failed, the force losing several killed, including its leader, a really brave and excellent young officer. It was a bad moment for me, rather different from the permanent knowledge that war is a bloody business, because I had emphasized to Tommy that this was an important job and he had better send his best man. He had agreed. Those words are the aching refrain of command. They beat without cease in the mind and over the heart: *Send your best man. . . .*

That evening, with more planes coming in and the monsoon liable to break any day, I knew I had to do something drastic to complete our defensive preparations. I had to have the absolute maximum possible number of men carrying up stores from the field. Eight mortars, going fast, use up sixteen hundred pounds of ammunition in a minute, and there were hundreds of Bren guns, rifles, and Tommy guns also eating it up, besides grenades; and food; and now the field guns. The Japanese had, so far, concentrated on the Deep, and they had left detachments there to harass us during the hours of daylight. Surely they would continue attacking that sector?

I decided to take the risk. I ordered the whole of the perimeter, except the Deep, to be stripped down to one section per platoon front, with no battalion reserves. The Deep, and a brigade reserve of one rifle company, I kept at full strength.

The Japanese continued their attacks—on the Deep. The actions for the next five nights defy description or reasonable analysis. At the northeast corner of the block, around the Deep, a furious battle raged from dusk till an hour or two before dawn, fought at ten yards' range with Brens, grenades, rifles, Tommy guns, two-inch and three-inch mortars and some machine guns. Three hundred yards to the left of the attacking Japanese, and in full view of them, C-47s landed with glaring headlights on the by now brilliantly lighted strip. From the hills behind, and from anywhere in the valley, they could see the aircraft being unloaded, our casualties carried into them, hundreds of men walking up and down between the strip and the block. Between the strip and the attacking Japanese I had no troops at all, though the area was thoroughly covered by machine gun and mortar emergency tasks; and the far side of the strip was only thinly protected. From my usual nightly position near the ridge top, or with the reserve company, I listened to the roar of battle from ahead and the roar of aircraft from the right. The Japanese never came anywhere but at the same place, the Deep, and head on.

The weight of this frenzied offensive fell on His Majesty's 4th

Regiment of Foot, the King's Own Royal Regiment, who fought back with grim ardor. The long battle reached three crises. The climate caused the first.

Before entering the block I had thought of burning the jungles around it, partly to remove cover which the enemy could use (our own cover would, I knew, soon be removed by their shell fire), partly to ensure that the Japanese could not set fire to it at a moment opportune to them. I decided against it because a fire, once started, is not easy to control. But, on the fourth day of the Deep battle we saw movement on the ridge to the west of the block, about one thousand yards away. The ridge overlooked both the Namyung and Namkwin Chaungs, and also gave a fair view of the reverse slopes of the Deep position. We began to mortar it. After ten minues I saw smoke rising and thickening over there. The jungle scrub had caught fire. The Japanese put it out, while we mortared them some more. Almost immediately, on the other side of the block, enemy shells or mortars set fire to the dense lantana scrub in front of the positions held by the Cameronians to protect the field guns. (This was roughly around the boar's right forefoot.)

I did not think the Japanese had done this on purpose, any more than we had in the other direction. The dryness of the air, and of the foliage, had reached their hot weather peak, and the jungle was like tinder. The heat was close, stifling, and very severe; it, more than the enemy, had caused the failure of patrols I had sent out to pinpoint and call down air strikes against the enemy artillery positions. But I had to treat this fire as part of an attack plan. I called an immediate stand-to and ordered the mortars to begin a heavy shelling with smoke bombs on and beyond the forward edge of the new fire. Smoke bombs have a fair incendiary action and I wanted to set fire to the rearward lantana, where the Japanese would be forming up if they intended to attack. Henning held a company ready to counterattack. The field guns, already half-hidden in drifting smoke, swung round to fire muzzle-burst over the positions we might have to vacate if the fire came on. Crouched on top of the ridge, looking in both directions, praying that the Japanese would not now start their daily harassing fire, Henning and I passed a taut twenty minutes.

I did not notice that the sky had darkened over. As the flames took full hold of the lantana, it began to rain.

Trembling, I returned to my headquarters and lit a cigarette. Every wonderful drop falling on my burning face and arms was like a gift from God; but every drop sparkled with new problems. The monsoon had broken. The weapon pits, in which men must lie and fight and try to rest, would fill with water. I could not now rely on the airfield, and that would delay our evacuation of casualties. One of the reasons why morale remained high was that the wounded received such prompt attention. Some badly wounded men had been on their way to hospital, in an aircraft, ten minutes after being hit. Worse, I would not be able to re-plenish ammunition, for we were using a great deal of it. Why the Japanese had been such incredible fools as not to shell the field and make it unusable, I did not know. Now the rains would do it for them. . . . And where in the name of God were the floater brigades? The White City had been evacuated thirteen days earlier, and 14 Brigade was supposed to come straight up here. My brigade had marched 140 route miles in fourteen days to establish this block. Surely those bloody nitwits could cover 120 route miles in thirteen days? Where the *hell* were they? Where were the West Africans?

I gave myself up to despair and anger. The enemy guns ought to have been silenced two days ago. The opportunities being missed! What use were field guns to me? They were here, inside my bastion, to support the floater brigades as they rampaged up and across the valley. The floater brigades weren't here. My men were being worked and fought into the ground while twenty bloody battalions, forty flaming columns of Chindit bullshit, sat on their arses and drank tea and wondered how we were get-ting on.

But soft, we are observed. A strange officer is coming to report to me. I learn that he is Major Douglas de Hochepied Larpent of the 5th Fusiliers. God knows how he got here. He just wants to fight.

(Douglas reports: *The officer in charge of the unloading party told us we must doss down on the edge of the strip and report to the Brigadier in the morning. I tried to get some sleep at the foot of a large tree. There were others sleeping nearby but I seemed to be the only one at all concerned at the prospect of being hit. It struck me as odd. At about the same time I became aware of a highly unpleasant smell which I was then too green to recognize. In the morning I found I had been sleeping in the mortuary. I was not a little relieved to get up and with the other new arrivals set out to find the Brigadier's Command Post and report to him. As we were soon to realize the situation was far from healthy but my chief impression of Jack was of his complete confidence. He seemed to be on top of the world, thoroughly enjoying himself and ready to cope with anything. . . .)*

. . . Command doth make actors of us all. Or as one might say, liars. But I recovered myself. We were holding the enemy, and would hold him. The floaters *must* arrive soon.

The second crisis came when the close-quarter fighting at the Deep reached the limit of human tolerance. I decided I must force the Japanese farther away, at any cost. First, we removed the secondary charges from the three-inch mortars and fired them with primaries only. The bombs, fired from the middle of the block, arched high and fell five or ten yards from our forward positions. Next, I called for a heavy air strike, and told the air force to use 250-pound bombs. I expected to kill twenty of my own men if they bombed accurately, forty if they didn't.

Six fighter-bombers came. Chesty, standing with a radio in a trench above the Deep, brought them down on successive east-west runs across the foot of the sector, their target being the outer limit of our wire. They raced down from the sky, one behind the other, the great bombs slipped loose and whistled, shining, down. All my mortars opened rapid fire, all the machine guns opened rapid fire. The hill quaked and heaved, the noise beat in huge waves against my eardrums, steel splinters whined and droned over the hill and far out across the valley, trees crashed and fell, raw white wounds gaping, all the leaves vanished and hung in the boiling smoke and dirt. The aircraft dived lower, firing their multiple .50-caliber machine guns. For long moments the monstrous tearing roar filled earth and sky and being.

When they flew away, no one moved for a long time, and no one fired. We went down to remove and replace our casualties. There were none.

One enemy sniper lived, and fired a few shots during the rest of the day, and the usual attack followed that night, but the following day no Japanese were within two hundred yards of our wire. I bombed them again, this time with B-25s.

The enemy began to use his heavy mortar. Its shell weighed sixty pounds (the shell of our heaviest, the three-inch, weighed ten pounds), and when it landed on a weapon pit it saved the need for burying parties. Every day Tommy and his padre moved about across the Deep sector, under sniping, speaking to the men in the trenches, pausing here and there to pick up a handful of yellow-stained earth and sprinkle it over the torn "grave," and say a short prayer.

The rain now fell steadily. The Deep sector looked like Passchendaele—blasted trees, feet and twisted hands sticking up out of the earth, bloody shirts, ammunition clips, holes half-full of water, each containing two pale, huge-eyed men, trying to keep their rifles out of the mud, and over all the heavy, sweet stench of death, from our own bodies and entrails lying unknown in the shattered ground, from Japanese corpses on the wire, or fastened, dead and rotting, in the trees. At night the rain hissed down in total darkness, the trees ran with water and, beyond the devastation, the jungle dripped and crackled.

A Japanese light machine gun chatters hysterically, and bullets clack and clap overhead. Two Very lights float up, burst in brilliant whiteness. *Click, click, click—boom, crash, boom,* three mortar bombs burst in red-yellow flashes on the wire.

The third crisis came on May 17. On that day our Lightnings (P-38s) patrolled the valley for several hours, searching for the guns which had done us so much damage. They did not find them. Toward evening the P-38s left and I went down to the water point, as I usually did, to wash, shave, and brush up for the night's battle. While I was shaving, the enemy began to shell the block with 105s and 155s. Twelve guns or more were firing. Soap all over my face, I looked across at the ridge to the west, where the enemy had once put a mortar, and saw movement there. Mortar bombs from the ridge whistled into the block. The shelling grew more urgent and I walked quickly up to my command post—I tried never to run.

The shelling concentrated on the Deep and became a violent,

continuous drumfire. My stomach felt empty and I was ready to vomit. I should have relieved the King's Own. This was more than human flesh could stand. Nothing to do now though. The attack would come in immediately after the bombardment.

The shelling increased again. For ten minutes an absolute fury fell on the Deep.

Major Heap, the second-in-command of the King's Own, tumbled in, his face streaked and bloody and working with extreme strain. "We've had it, sir," he said. "They're destroying all the posts, direct hits all the time . . . all machine guns knocked out, crews killed . . . I don't think we can hold them if . . . the men are . . ."

I didn't wait to hear what the men were. I knew. They were dead, wounded, or stunned.

I took the telephone and called Tim Brennan, commanding 26 Column of the Cameronians, and told him to bring his whole column to the ridge crest at once, with all weapons and ammunition, manhandled, ready to take over the Deep. "Yes, sir," he said pleasantly. I had time to call Henning and order him to spread out to occupy Brennan's positions as well as his own, before going quickly, my breath short, to the hill crest.

The shelling stopped as I reached it. Tim arrived. Johnny Boden, the mortar officer, arrived. *Now, now, the Japanese must come.* I told Boden to stand by with smoke and H.E. to cover the Cameronians. 26 Column arrived, at the double. Still no assault. Tim ran down the forward slope, his men behind him. I waited, crouched on the ridge top. Ordered Boden to open up with his mortars. The enemy must have this blasted slope covered by machine guns. I knew they had. They didn't fire. It was twilight, but down the slope in the smoke, I could clearly see Cameronians jumping into the waterlogged trenches, King's Own struggling out and up toward me. The Cameronian machine guns arrived, men bent double under the ninety-pound loads of barrel and tripod. Bombs burst, smoke rose in dense white clouds. I told the officer to move the machine guns again, after full dark, if he could. "Of course, sir," he said impatiently.

The men of the King's Own passed by, very slowly, to be gathered by Heap into reserve. They staggered, many were wounded, others carried wounded men, their eyes wandered, their mouths drooped open. I wanted to cry, but dared not, could only mutter, "Well done, well done," as they passed.

The minutes crawled, each one a gift more precious than the first rain. I sent wire down, and ammunition, and took two machine guns from Henning's 90 Column, and put them in trenches on the crest, ready to sweep the whole slope. Full darkness came, with rain. An hour had passed, a whole hour since the enemy bombardment ended. In our own attacks we reckoned a thirty-second delay as fatal.

With a crash of machine guns and mortars the battle began. All night the Cameronians and the Japanese 53rd Division fought it out. Our machine guns ripped them from the new positions. Twice the Japanese forced into the barbed wire with Bangalore torpedoes, and the blasting rain of the mortars wiped them out. At four A.M., when they launched their final assault to recover their bodies, we had defeated them.

The next morning, as the rain fell more heavily, our patrols found the enemy had gone altogether. They had left the Deep sector and the hills across the Namkwin. They had abandoned the mortar post on the westward ridge. They had all gone. The forest was full of blood and flesh, and mass graves, and bodies fallen into stream beds, and bomb craters, and thousands of cartridge cases.

I have no means of knowing how many casualties we inflicted during this first phase of the Blackpool battle, except a postwar Intelligence interrogation, when a Japanese officer said, "Fifty-three Division had little fighting against the Chindits except on one occasion only, when one regiment was annihilated near Hopin." This was us. A guess would be eight hundred to a thousand casualties. We suffered nearly two hundred, mostly in the King's Own.

We were now in sole ownership of the block, and all terrain for at least a mile around. I began to send urgent messages: 14 Brigade *must* get a move on; 77 Brigade now moving northward the other side of the railway valley, should come across to us. Obviously the Japanese would attack us again, and so give us a wonderful opportunity to sandwich the attackers between the block and another brigade. A decisive victory lay to hand. . . . But the rain continued to fall, and movement would soon be difficult. The battle must be fought before that happened. Then *we* would be in possession, and the Japanese line of communication totally cut, for the valley here was much narrower than at the White City, and he would have no chance of slipping even small parties past us.

If the floater brigades did not come, on the other hand, our situation would be precarious. And one particular sound I listened for above all others, for when I heard it the jig would be up—unless the floater brigades had arrived.

Meanwhile my two battalions were out on their feet, having marched hard for fourteen days, and worked and fought like maniacs for ten more, without cease. I should be surprised to learn that anyone averaged as much as five hours' sleep a day. My own figure was closer to three.

Two battalions, which had been holding the Broadway stronghold, did manage to cross the valley, and came under my command—the 2nd Battalion the King's Regiment (Liverpool) under Lieutenant Colonel Scott, and the 3rd Battalion 9th Gurkha Rifles, under Lieutenant Colonel Alec Harper. The King's did not arrive in top condition. One of their two columns ran into the enemy in the valley at night, and turned back. Mike Calvert sent them out again, but that column's morale was shaken when it finally arrived, and both were tired. The appearance of Blackpool, and the smell hanging over it, and the thin, determined ghosts who met them, cannot have reassured them. I sent the King's out at once—for they were less tired than my original two battalions—on a battalion sweep of the hills to the north, again in an effort to locate and destroy the enemy artillery. The attempt failed. The 3/9th Gurkhas I put onto the perimeter, withdrawing all the King's Own into reserve. The rain had not yet put the strip out of commission and a large daylight fly-in of C-47s, under fighter cover, evacuated all our casualties.

We heard that Merrill's Marauders had taken Myitkyina. This was most cheering news, and the brigade burst into a collective smile of joy and appreciation. (*"Will this burn up the limeys!"* Stilwell wrote in his diary.) But Myitkyina was seventy miles away and the key bastion of Mogaung, between it and us, had not yet been taken. Even if the American-Chinese advance started southward from Myitkyina immediately, no one could reach us for at least two weeks. In that time enemy pressure would build up relentlessly against me. By God, those floater brigades had *got* to come, at once.

I learned that Myitkyina itself had not fallen—only the airfield. Joe Lentaigne ordered me to meet him at Shaduzup on the Ledo Road, a hundred miles due north of Blackpool, and report to General Stilwell. I handed over command to Tommy and flew out in an L-5. After an hour or so I saw the great ribbon of the Ledo Road, looking like a trench cut through the dense forest, and landed near Stilwell's headquarters.

Joe Lentaigne met me and took me to the hut allotted to him. He was in good shape and full of his usual energy, but not very happy about the relations between Stilwell, himself, and the Chindits. Old Vinegar Joe, he thought, was basically rather a volatile chap. When things were going well for him, he didn't hate everyone; when they weren't, he did. Joe saw trouble ahead.

Then he took me in to meet the general. Stilwell wasn't hating everybody that day—the Marauders' successful march to Myitkyina was the reason—but otherwise he looked just as the press photographs showed him. He asked me if I was stopping all traffic in the railway valley. I said I had stopped all traffic on the main road and railway, by shelling and by what patrols I could find, but that some enemy were certainly sidling past on the farther side, near the Namyin Chaung, and would continue to do so until the floater brigades arrived.

I asked him when Myitkyina would fall and, I think, suggested that he fly the Marauders at once from the Myitkyina strip onto my own at Blackpool, where they could take over the block and release me to attack; or, perhaps, themselves go against Mogaung. (I know that this plan was in my mind at the time, but I cannot remember whether I put it to Stilwell, or only to Joe in our private talks.) Stilwell answered my question about Myitkyina by saying, "Soon."

That was all. Joe and I saluted and went out. In his hut again we talked some more. I told him I thought the Marauders were the key to future relations between Joe Stilwell and ourselves. They were fighting infantry, they had killed a lot of Japanese, they could march, and I was certain we would get on well with each other. (*"Stilwell's staff!"* Joe burst out. *"He's difficult enough, but they're impossible. There's one chap who keeps whispering in Stilwell's ear that the Chindits do nothing but march away from the enemy and drink tea, by Jove, eh, what?"*) I told him that in my bad moments I shared the man's opinion, about some at least of my fellow Chindits. Joe said sharply, "Fourteen Brigade's doing its best, Jack," and I apologized. We got back to the Marauders. Stilwell was flying large numbers of Chinese into Myitkyina to capture the town itself—all we owned so far was the airstrip; couldn't the Marauders be flown to Blackpool? I would willingly put myself under their commander. Joe didn't believe Stilwell would consider it, but he'd think it over.

(It was all a waste of breath. Stilwell and his devoted staff had destroyed Galahad [code name for the Marauders] by treating them like dirt, by running them into the ground, and by breaking every promise he made them. *"I had him in my rifle sights,"* an American soldier said. *"No one woulda known it wasn't a Jap that got the son-of-a-bitch."* Merrill had suffered a heart attack. The men's morale had faded with their last physical reserves of strength. Within a week of this meeting between myself and Stilwell, the Marauder's Colonel Hunter met Stilwell outside Myitkyina and handed him a document detailing the charges against Stilwell and his staff. Two days later Hunter declared that the Marauders were no longer fit for action and must be relieved. Stilwell left Hunter in front of Myitkyina with the troops who replaced the Marauders [Galahad II], then relieved him and sent him back to the U.S.A.—by ship, by special order; so that he could not reach Washington ahead of Stilwell's own whitewashing. Stilwell and his stuffed baboons (a Marauder's phrase), having disposed of their American infantry, their best fighting force, turned their attention to us. *"Galahad is shot,"* Stilwell had noted in his diary, with understandable triumph. His next target was not hard to guess.)

Neither Joe Lentaigne nor I knew anything of this, thank God, when I returned that evening to Blackpool.

There was a letter from Barbara. She was well, my baby was well. They'd be off to Kashmir soon. Oh, yes, there'd been a terrific explosion in the middle of April, when an ammunition ship blew up in Bombay Harbor and set off other ships, and large pieces of human body sailed through windows a mile from the docks.

Damn it, I thought irritably, this is too much. But I had many men under me who had lost wives and mothers in the German bombings of 1940 and 1941. Fold the letter carefully away, write a reply on a message pad. Fold that whole world away, and passion and love, so that they couldn't be hurt; yet of course they were there, in what I felt whenever I saw a man, any man, reading a letter; for we were all human.

Three more peaceful days followed. We patrolled, and worked hard to repair the damage and prepare for more assaults. On May 22 enemy forces began to push forward from the southeast. Four artillery pieces, from the same direction, shelled the airfield. Two light planes and a C-47, which were on it, took off immediately. The third phase of the Blackpool battle began.

I sent the Cameronians out toward the enemy, to delay his advance. I debated long and anxiously whether I should send out another battalion to lie in wait on the hill feature to the south (adjoining our boar's tail), where they would be on the flank of the Japanese advance—if it continued in the direction it seemed to be taking. I decided against it, and I think I was wrong. The grim, set-teeth, bulldog struggle to hold the Deep had had its effect on me, and I was incapable of repeating the stroke (bold to the point of rashness) which had stripped the defenses of Blackpool to concentrate on the vital area. I should have done it again, trusting to my knowledge of the Japanese in battle, but there was a purposeful and professional air about this new assault which I did not like. He was pushing in my patrols and outposts; he was shelling the field; he was not coming on like a mad dog, and I did not think I could trust him to do the obvious.

I held everyone, except the slowly retreating, overpowered Cameronians, inside the block. But, oh, God, let 14 Brigade come! The greatest opportunity of the entire Chindit campaign lay there, then, before my eyes. I sent out signals which passed from urgency to frenzy. Hurry, hurry, kill yourselves, but come!

Late in the afternoon C-47s came for a daylight supply drop, escorted by P-38s. From down the valley, behind the advancing

Japanese, above the intermittent pop and crackle of small-arms fire, I heard the one sound I had been expecting, and fearing, the sharp double crack of heavy antiaircraft guns. Puffs of yellow-black smoke appeared behind one of the C-47s. They turned for home. The P-38s searched and dived, but the A.A. guns did not fire again.

With a heavy heart I sent a Most Immediate signal to Joe asking for permission to abandon the block at my discretion. The direction of the new Japanese attack would prevent night supply drops on the airfield, and, with the A.A. guns, only night drops were now possible. Night drops on the block, or on the jungle to the west, could never keep us supplied with ammunition in heavy battle. It would take too many men, too long, to find and bring in the boxes.

The prospects were grim. Had my orders been more flexible I would have moved the brigade out of the block there and then, withdrawn a short distance into the jungle, and hung about there, ready to emerge and establish a new block when 14 Brigade and the West Africans appeared. But I had no discretion, and when my request reached Joe Lentaigne he had to take it to Stilwell.

It could not have come at a worse moment, for the attacks on Myitkyina had failed, the Marauders had reported their condition, and Stilwell's misanthropy was at its strongest. He told Joe Lentaigne we were a bunch of lily-livered Limey popinjays. Joe replied hotly. Every minute of argument, accusation, and counter-accusation at Shaduzup cost my men more lives, saw the expenditure of more irreplaceable ammunition, and locked us more closely into an action which could only have one end, and from which, minute by minute, it became more difficult for me to extricate my brigade if permission eventually were granted.

I was near despair, but apparently maintained a front of un-broken optimism. (I find this hard to credit, but there are witnesses. Douglas Larpent and Desmond Whyte noticed it and wondered whether recent strain had unhinged me. The Cameronians' padre went in a kind of horrified awe to Tim Brennan and told him he'd heard me telling Johnny Boden to "drop a few bombs over the wire," with no more feeling than if I'd been asking him to lob a couple of tennis balls.) But I was not commanding a bunch of children, or starry-eyed hero worshipers. Our work had been so successful because every man knew what I was doing and why, which means that he understood tactics. All officers and men understood the situation as well as I, and the superb courage which had fought the enemy to a standstill while we had an attainable purpose now lost some of its fire. The only battle my brigade really wanted to fight at that moment was against 14 Brigade and I told all battalion commanders to see that such bitter talk stopped at once. None of us could know the circumstances of the other brigades, and we must, in the old Rifle phrase, "Look to our front."

The battle marched slowly on. Slowly the enemy forced the Cameronians back. Our field gunners fired over open sights at large masses of Japanese advancing beyond the shell-pitted airstrip. The enemy shelling set fire to the wrecked aircraft and abandoned gliders. Our Bofors light antiaircraft guns depressed their barrels and joined in.

Night fell. Shelling caused slight casualties, except that a direct hit killed many wounded men in the main dressing station. Probing attacks reached the perimeter along most of the eastern face. The enemy held the airfield. We were using ammunition at a tremendous rate. We had to.

In the morning the enemy withdrew a little from our wire and ten Zeros bombed us. The bursting bombs and the tearing roar of machine guns sounded like the end of the world, but they didn't kill many of us and the soldiers treated the raid as a half-hour of relaxation, for during it the shelling and mortaring stopped. Soon afterward they began again. The Japanese were now using, in addition to battalion guns, regimental guns, 105- and 155-mm. guns, all types of mortar, including the six-inch coal scuttle, and, of course, all types of rifle, machine gun, and grenade.

I had called for a supply drop of ammunition, particularly grenades and mortar bombs. The C-47s came in the afternoon, through rainy skies and scattered cloud. I believe they were originally escorted by P-38s, which were drawn off by Zeros. All our planes were of the Royal Air Force. It was not night, but they came, in from the west, low, twisting and turning over the steaming, forested mountains. At the last they straightened and flew on a level, straight course. The boxes and crates dropped from the open doors, the parachutes opened. Hundreds of enemy rifles and machine guns blazed up at them through the irregular, drifting smoke of our mortar bombs. Then, clear as a knell, I heard from across the valley, the sharp coughing *bom-bom-bom* of heavy antiaircraft guns. Directly over me the port engine vanished from a C-47's wing; he swung down, the other engine frantically roaring. On, a wing whirled away, he hung, fell, turning like a maple seed. Another came on among the hills, only fifty feet above the jungle, twisting frantically, another crossed his bows, they were over, the loads shooting out, swinging, drifting, but oh, Christ, the waste of love and life, for some fell among the Japanese, and some we could never reach, and what we did would only last a few hours. The crashed plane burned opposite the Deep, with tall orange flames and black, black smoke. I ground my teeth, and waited, and watched. My infantry were dying, too.

The Royal Air Force never did anything more gallant. I believe only four out of eight aircraft returned to base. We received, and gathered, half of one aircraft load of ammunition.

Tim Brennan brought Sergeant Donald to my command post to tell me about a successful counterattack by which he had cleared the Japanese off a small feature outside the airstrip entrance. Sergeant Donald (who got a Distinguished Conduct Medal for this action) had been wounded and as I held out a cigarette to him I saw that he was shaking violently in reaction from the close-quarter bayonet and grenade fight. He took the cigarette and said, "Thank you, sir—" and then, strongly and in a broader Scots—"Ma han's trrembling, but Ah'm no' a wee bit frightened, sirr!" Once again, I nearly burst into tears. It wasn't the responsibility, or the battle that created the strain, it was the love and pride.

The night of May 23–24 passed in some confusion. Shells kept cutting the telephone lines and I felt, at moments, that I did not have full control over my own forces. Before dawn an enormous bombardment began and in the earliest light, under incessant rain, I learned that the Japanese had got inside the perimeter, overrunning a post held by the 3/9th Gurkhas. How it had happened, no one knew. Alec Harper at once began to try to regain the position.

The telephone buzzed. It was Henning. He began to say something but after a few words the connection was suddenly changed and a young frantic voice shouted, "They're all round! I can see them! They're in everywhere, I can't hold—"

I interrupted him. "This is the brigade commander. Who's speaking?" It was that uncomfortable facility for sounding calm when I am not, for the young officer's voice changed as though by a miracle—actually, by a tremendous effort of self-control. He gave me his name and post, reported that the Japanese had broken through in such and such places, and asked for orders. I told him to prevent the enemy from moving about, and to keep his head (keep his head, by God!). He said, "Yes, sir. Thank you, sir."

The battle spread all over the eastern half of the block. Desmond Whyte reported forty-five helpless casualties in the M.D.S., all space full, and more coming. Minutes later two direct shell hits solved some of those problems with murderous thoroughness.

The 3/9th Gurkhas could not dislodge the Japanese from the hillock they occupied. From it they swept the whole of the east side with light machine guns and mortars. We blasted them with mortar bombs and at the same time tried to clear other Japanese out of the forward areas around the field gun and Bofors pits, whence the young officer had spoken to me. We failed. I ordered all troops to withdraw from that sector, the guns to be spiked and abandoned. The men withdrew, suffering few losses under smoke and high-explosive cover from mortars and machine guns.

I saw, in the middle of the block, a line of men moving very slowly across a slope fifty yards from me. They looked like Japanese and I raised my carbine. The men trudged on in the drifting mist and rain and, just in time, I saw that they were my own men. But everyone moved like that, in a kind of cosmic slow motion. The Cameronians and gunners coming out of the forward eastern sector moved like sleepwalkers, so did the Japanese wandering about among them. A Cameronian lieutenant fell head-first into a weapon pit and two Japanese soldiers five yards away leaned weakly on their rifles and laughed, slowly, while the officer struggled to his feet, slowly, and trudged up the slope. The shells fell slowly and burst with long, slow detonations, and the men collapsed slowly to the ground, blood flowing in gentle gouts into the mud.

Johnny Boden reported that he was almost out of mortar ammunition. I went to the ridge crest, the center of the block. When I was fifty feet away a coal-scuttle bomb burst on a big tree there, and killed fourteen artillerymen, just arrived and coming into reserve under Douglas Larpent. The artillery lieutenant, closest to the blast, totally vanished.

I ordered Thompson and Scott, the commanders of the King's Own and the King's respectively, to attack the Japanese-held hillock in the southeast corner of the block, meanwhile trying to group the remnants of the gunners and the somewhat disorganized Gurkhas into a new reserve. The whole eastern half of the block blazed with fire and confused movement. One more Japanese breakthrough would cut us in two.

The supporting fire for the big counterattack failed and the attack failed, in spite of Tommy Thompson's personal heroism. When he came back, a severe wound in his shoulder, near the neck, I turned away from them all and lit a cigarette.

A signal giving me discretion to leave the block was probably on its way. After what happened to the C-47s yesterday any other order was lunacy, unless the floater brigades were at this very minute preparing to attack the enemy in the rear. And they weren't. But no signal had come yet. Bombs burst round me, bullets clacked by. I was therefore bound by the original orders to hold the position to the last man and the last round. The last bullet was not quite shot. After another hour of this, it would be. The last man . . . I had plenty of men left, far too many to see killed upholding my honor and military reputation. In any case they could only court-martial me, and I would be happy to have that chance to tell what we had done. Above all, my military knowledge told me that, unless Slim and Stilwell had gone mad, the discretionary order *must* be on its way.

I decided to withdraw from the block while we still had enough ammunition to use it in the difficult task of breaking contact. This is never easy to do in daylight, between forces as large as those engaged here. And we had, at a guess, about ninety men who could not walk unaided, and another thirty or forty who could not walk at all. The mechanics of the task I knew. I had learned them on the North West Frontier. The commander thins out the forces in actual contact and, with the men so obtained, sets up a series of covering positions, one behind the other and any suitable distance apart, depending on the ground. Finally the screen in contact breaks and runs for it, covered by fire from the first layback, as the successive positions are called. When they are well clear, Layback No. 1 withdraws, covered by Layback No. 2; and so on, leapfrogging continuously. It sounds easy but it can only be carried out by troops in full control of themselves. Once you turn your backs to the enemy, strong psychological pressures urge you to keep moving, faster and faster.

I gave the orders: Henning to establish the first and strongest layback astride the water point; Harper the second and third; withdrawal along the Namkwin Chaung to the *chaung* and track junction at 227105, about four miles away; Scott and some of his battalion to go there direct and prepare the area for defense; next day, if possible, further withdrawal up the track to Pumkrawng. I sent two last radio messages, one to Force telling them that I intended to withdraw from Blackpool immediately, and by what route, the other to 30 Column at Mokso Sakan, ordering them to march at once to meet us, bringing all horses, mules, rations, and ammunition. A hundred other details I should have settled—how the wounded were to go, who was to control them, covering fire between laybacks, action in case of meeting opposition from behind—but there was no time. I had to rely on the discipline and training of my brigade.

But one matter I must decide personally—the use of the animals remaining in the block. Having suffered surprisingly little at first, shells and bombs had killed many these last two days. Only three or four horses and perhaps ten mules were fit to move. It did not take me long to decide that two radio sets and a charging engine, together with the cipher chest, must have absolute priority. I think I ordered that the remaining mules should carry Vickers machine guns and ammunition, the horses severely wounded men. All animals were to be loaded to the limit of their strength. These decisions, and the hard circumstances, meant that men must carry picks and shovels, grenades, some two-inch mortars and ammunition, many wounded, and anything else necessary for our survival, in addition to their personal weapons and what rations they had left.

The orders given, men began to drift back past me almost at once—Scott and some of the King's; I went down with them, found our own barbed wire blocking the stream. Henning and I shot it away, strand by strand, with our carbines. Back up to my command post. Henning and 90 Column moving fast to the water point.

Battered, sleepwalking soldiers passed, here two fit men, here two more supporting a third with a shattered foot, then a man with a head wound, then half a dozen unwounded, each with rifle and pick or shovel. Some wore shirts and trousers, some wore one or the other, some neither. Many men had no packs, for theirs had been buried or destroyed by shellfire. Now came a group, with an officer, struggling under a three-inch mortar. These, I had specifically ordered, could be abandoned, for the barrel and base plate constituted very heavy loads, and the bombs weighed ten pounds each, but this mortar platoon was determined to hold on to at least one of its weapons, and I did not try to interfere. It rained, it stopped raining. For ten days none of us had felt any awareness of rain, or knew whether we were wet or dry, except as it affected our job, made the rifle slippery in the hand, caused the Bren-gun barrel to hiss and steam.

Men trudged on in a thickening stream down the muddy, slippery path past my command post. Shells and mortar bombs continued to burst all round. From the eastern ridge the thinning lines of our forward troops increased their fire. A soldier of the King's Own limped by, looked up at me and said, "We did our best, didn't we, sir?" I could not stop to think, to accuse myself of being unworthy of him and his like, I could only face the problems as they came, give answers, and try to keep awake.

A Cameronian lay near the ridge top, near death from many wounds. "Give me a Bren," he whispered to his lieutenant. "Leave me. I'll take a dozen wi' me."

I went to the mule lines and saw Maggy quietly eating bamboo, a red gash in her belly and her entrails hanging out of it. She seemed to be in no pain and I hugged her neck, then Briggs shot her for me. Henning reported 90 Column in position astride the water point. I looked through my binoculars at the westward ridge, which the Japanese had occupied during the first battles. If they held it now we would have a bad time, as it dominated the Namkwin for at least a mile. Mortaring from it we would have to grit our teeth and bear as we trudged past. No, I could cover it with machine guns, for a time at least. I sent a man back with a message to Alec Harper, to be sure to put strong protection on that flank of his layback.

The men passed and passed, walking, limping, hopping, supporting others, carrying them. Tim Brennan reported that he thought he could break contact when I ordered. The Japanese were not pressing their advantage, and at the moment seemed to be under shell fire from their own artillery.

A doctor spoke to me. "Will you come with me, sir?" I followed him down the path. It was clear of moving men. The whole block was clear, except for a part of 26 Column. A little way down the path we came to forty or fifty ragged men, many slightly wounded, who had carried stretchers and improvised blanket litters from the main dressing station as far as this. Here they had set down their burdens, and now waited, huddled in the streaming bamboo, above and below the path. I noticed at once that none of them looked at me as I stopped among them with the doctor.

The stretchers lay in the path itself, and in each stretcher lay a soldier of 111 Brigade. The first man was quite naked and a shell had removed the entire contents of his stomach. Between his chest and pelvis there was a bloody hollow, behind it his spine. Another had no legs and no hips, his trunk ending just below the waist. A third had no left arm, shoulder, or breast, all torn away in one piece. A fourth had no face and whitish liquid was trickling out of his head into the mud. A fifth seemed to have been torn in pieces by a mad giant, and his lips bubbled gently.

Nineteen men lay there. A few were conscious. At least, their eyes moved, but without light in them.

The doctor said, "I've got another thirty on ahead, who can be saved, if we can carry them." The rain clattered so loud on the bamboo that I could hardly hear what he said. "These men have no chance. They're full of morphia. Most of them have bullet and splinter wounds beside what you can see. Not one chance at all, sir, I give you my word of honor. Look, this man's died already, and that one. None can last another two hours, at the outside."

Very well. I have two thousand lives in my hand, besides these. One small mistake, one little moment of hesitation and I will kill five times these nineteen.

I said aloud, "Very well. I don't want them to see any Japanese." I was trying to smile down into the flat white face below me, that had no belly, but there was no sign of recognition, or hearing, or feeling. Shells and bombs burst on the slope above and bullets clattered and whined overhead.

"Do you think I want to do it?" the doctor cried in helpless anger. "We've been fighting to save that man for twenty-four hours and then just now, in the M.D.S., he was hit in the same place." His voice changed. "We can't spare any more morphia."

"Give it to those whose eyes are open," I said. "Get the stretcher bearers on at once. Five minutes."

He nodded and I went back up to the ridge, for the last time. One by one, carbine shots exploded curtly behind me. I put my hands over my ears but nothing could shut out the sound.

I found Titch Hurst of the Cameronians on the ridge, and Douglas Larpent, the latter commanding the rear party. I said, "Retire in five minutes. I shall be with the first layback at the water point."

We looked across the shallow valley where the forward sections were engaging the Japanese with a sharp fire. The fire strengthened, under Douglas' orders. I walked down the path, looking, but the bodies had been well hidden in the bamboo and the path was quite empty. I muttered, "I'm sorry," and "Forgive me," and hurried on, and reached the water point. There, with Henning, I waited.

Soon 26 Column started coming down, some running, some walking. Up ahead I could see that the slow trail of the severely wounded had already passed the second layback. I waited, growing very tired, with Henning, until the last of 26 Column was upon us. Now was the most dangerous moment. We stared up the path, waiting for the Japanese to come on. But they did not come, and at about noon, fifty minutes after giving the first order, after seventeen days, having been defeated, I left the Blackpool block in the rain.

21 The Japanese had not reoccupied the westward ridge, and they made no attempt to follow us up, except with a few mortar bombs at the very beginning. Layback by layback, ordering each to retire as I passed, I plodded slowly up the Namkwin Chaung. Extreme fatigue assailed me, for I had slept three hours in three days. Twice in a hundred yards I sank down and from a great distance heard my orderly and Douglas and the men of my escort preparing to lift and carry me, but each time I got up. The sight of the wounded supporting the wounded, of men carrying others on their backs, gave me the strength.

A mile out of Blackpool I ordered the laybacks to be replaced by a moving rear guard of the 3/9th Gurkhas, with whom I marched. Ahead, I knew nothing, but had heard no firing. My feet crawled and staggered, my mind raced. . . . If the forward troops met strong opposition before the rendezvous, I would swing the brigade left up that ridge, there in the rain. . . . If the enemy came down the upper Namkwin, I would block off that flank until dark, and then . . . If they pressed from behind I would restart the laybacks, and then . . . Tall green jungle, purple shadowed, stretched endlessly ahead, cut by the pale cleft of the river. The rain poured down and the stream was now over two feet deep. This rain might cause a flash flood in the night. Must get the brigade sufficiently far up the Pumkrawng track to be safe from that, and then . . .

At the rendezvous I found Scotty had put the brigade into a makeshift harbor, the *chaung* covered by our two machine guns, and outposts in position. The rain had turned the ground into a heaving ocean of mud under the trees. The Japanese could no more move fast in it than we could. No radio communication yet. I told the signals to keep at it all night. No panic or despair. Everyone too tired for that. Rather the opposite, a small lightening of atmosphere. Not hard to see the reason: no shells, no bombs, no automatics, and we were alive to record the fact. A somewhat ignoble joy, in soldiers, to feel after a defeat. But we were not supermen, nor Japanese, and we could feel ourselves living, eyes recording, slow throb-throb of pulse, and we knew we stood a good chance of being alive when dawn came, something none of us had known for a considerable time. We would fight again.

The wounded . . . scores unable to march, got this far somehow, Doc Whyte and the other doctors looking after them. One or two died in the *chaung*, but the rest are here, mud-colored, half-naked, their eyes alive with the same awareness the rest of us feel. Tommy Thompson's wound smelling a little of rot, but Desmond optimistic that gangrene can be prevented. Sulfa drugs. Give him my blanket. Big gesture, a blanket for a bullet two inches from the jugular.

30 Column ought to have reached Nawku, on the summit, by now. Our rate tomorrow will be less than half a mile an hour. What are those Staff College figures on the rate of collapse of walking wounded as shock takes effect? Something like 80 per cent unable to walk after twenty-four hours. Owing to oversight, have not got my Staff Officer's Notebook with me. *Careless*, in red ink. Will have to provide more ambulances at the appropriate distance from the front. Ambulances, yes, that was the word. I see the stretchers on the Blackpool path but soon they vanish.

We may not meet 30 Column tomorrow, as mud will also slow them. Thank God I saved most of the animals by keeping them at Mokso Sakan. They can carry the wounded to the lake, once we meet 30 Column. After that, two or three heavy supply drops and we'll have new mortars and machine guns, we'll replace all that we have lost, then we shall be ready again. Not until these men have had a rest, though.

Why am I worrying? The first signal will order me out for court-martial. Sorry, Joe, can't help it. They must have a rest.

It is night, has been for some time, and raining. A heavily built sergeant, his eyes dim behind the thick lenses of his spectacles, comes to me where I sit with my back against a tree. "Sir, take my blanket."

No, no, can't take a sergeant's blanket. Not done. What difference does it make anyway, lying in four inches of mud, under continuous rain? The rain feels chilly though. Perhaps I'm tired. Tommy's got gangrene and why didn't I lead that last counter-attack and get gangrene instead? Didn't know it was the last. No excuse. Mike Calvert would have, and led all the ones before, too. "We did our best, sir." Balls. *You* did. There is no such thing as a bad soldier, only a bad officer.

I am lying under half a sodden green lightweight blanket, on my side, facing the sergeant of ciphers. What am I doing here? How did I get here? The sergeant is speaking, nose three inches from mine. "I think, sir, that this campaign is a disgrace." Stiffen in anger. "What did you say?"

"Oh, no, sir! I mean, why we're here. To save the profits of the oil companies."

My head clears slightly as I listen. The oil companies insisted on the reconquest of Burma and bribed Churchill, Eden, and Attlee to commit troops to the job. That's why he and I are lying under a wet blanket at map reference 227105, in the monsoon rain among our wounded. Follow several thousand well-chosen words in support of this thesis.

My blood is up. I have heard the extreme anticapitalist position stated often enough, and I've never been fond of businessmen, pompous asses most of them—and ignorant, God!—but this is beyond reason. I launch into a lecture on strategy, *Weltpolitik*, and grand tactics. I explain the thirteen reasons—including oil, of course, but as a comparatively minor factor—which render imperative the reconquest. There, that ought to fix him.

The sergeant refutes me point by point, gives me a cigarette, extracts a match from his condom, and lights my cigarette. I

concede a point for a cigarette, but rerefute the rest of his refuta-
tions. The sergeant, I learn, was a member of the Communist
party in England before being called up, but not for very long.
They threw him out on account of his extreme views. Damned
good cipher sergeant though. It is two o'clock in the morning
and Briggs clumps toward us through the mud, muttering softly,
"Brigadier? Brigadier, sir?" He is mortified to find me in bed with
his cipher sergeant. Such an occurrence is but rare in the Civil
Service.

Communication established. The signal in Briggs's hand was
sent about twenty-four hours ago. From Force: permission to
abandon the Blackpool block. I am in danger of hysterical laughter. Send a message back, acknowledging theirs, giving position
and intention. And then sleep, soundly, until first light.

The next days did not pass. They stood still, but they contained the idea of motion, like a frieze of stumbling figures. We
moved, men clasping the belt of the man in front. Legs lifting
from the mud, sliding back, moving upward again. A man clasping another round the neck, his legs trailing, the khaki bandage
soaked with rain and blood and foul with mud where he had
fallen a hundred times. Stretcher bearers in teams, others carrying the rifles of the bearers. Horses, with two and three wounded
on them, all hang-headed, exhausted.

From the front I watched the whole column pass, then with
febrile energy made my way back to the front, pushed and pulled
by three Gurkhas. My rare orders were carried out at once, willingly, but at the pace of the dead.

All unwounded men were on half-rations, so that the wounded
would not go short.

We met men coming down, not first the Gurkhas of 30
Column, but, ahead of them, huge black Africans—the 6th Battalion of the Nigeria Regiment. Their colonel, Gordon Upjohn,
met me with a cigarette and a tot of rum, and told me he had
been urgently ordered by Force to meet us, take command of the
"scattered remnants" and re-establish control. My temper broke.
We stopped for the night and I wrote out a bitter signal to Joe
saying 111 Brigade was together, under my full command and
control, and expecting further orders. If he wished to relieve me
of command would he please say so instead of insulting my

brigade. Then I sent a second signal, of which Douglas Larpent still has the original: "Have approx one hundred and fifty casualties for evacuation. Send flying boats Lake Indawgyi. Masters."

I turned on Gordon Upjohn, who had been at Sandhurst with me. I was sarcastic and rude, taking out on him all my anger against his own brigade and 14, who had not come in time to Blackpool, and, of course, my anger against myself. Gordon treated me with patient courtesy, and soon I apologized. We agreed that his battalion would improve the track ahead, back to Mokso Sakan, while we struggled along at our best pace behind, aided by 30 Column. He formally placed himself under my command until further orders could sort out the situation.

Four days after leaving Blackpool we reached Mokso. Here, raised a few feet above the level of the marshes surrounding Lake Indawgyi, we lay down in the mud and slept. Chesty and Robbie went down to the lake, found a Burmese canoe and, with bits of wood anchored to stones, and parachute cloth tied to the wood, laid out a landing course for the Sunderlands. The big flying boats, taken from antisubmarine patrol in the Indian Ocean, came and went through dangerous monsoon weather, carrying out with them our battle casualties and the great number of men in whom shock, fatigue, and starvation had brought out sickness. The American pilots of the Light Plane Force came, hour after hour, day after day, to the little patch of swamp we had made into a strip, and shuttled back through the heaving skies to Shaduzup. Six hundred men went out in all. Tommy Thompson they took to Shaduzup, where Joe Lentaigne went to him in hospital and asked him what he could do for him. Tommy said he only wanted one thing in the world—a clean white handkerchief. Joe gave him his own.

The three padres, one Church of England, one Presbyterian, one Roman Catholic, came to my shelter and asked permission to hold a service of thanksgiving. I refused curtly. We had been defeated. Seeing the men of God so upset, I said then that they could hold a service of intercession, or prayer for the fallen, or whatever they liked to call it, as long as it was neither too goddamned gloomy nor too goddamned cheerful.

The next day I stood at the back of a dense circle of men

grouped around some ammunition boxes, on which the padres
stood. Listening to the service with half an ear, kneeling in the
mud when the others did, I examined the men. Before entering
Burma Joe and I had decided that ninety days would be about
the limit of a Chindit force's endurance. These men had been
in about eighty now. They could do perhaps one operation more,
provided it did not call for too violent and sustained an effort and
provided, above all, it resulted in a clear-cut victory. Anything
else might result in the permanent blunting of a fine instrument.
This was the soldier thinking, in terms of the war. The man,
Jack Masters, wished to God we could all go home and to bed
with our wives and girls, though it would be some time before
any man here wanted more than womblike security and com-
forted sleep from any woman.

The senior padre gave the sermon. The hand of God had been
with us, enabling us to disengage from the block in such conditions. We had been defeated, but not in spirit. Each man had
done his best, and each man could give thanks for the preservation
of his own life, knowing he had done his duty. We must, also,
realize our debt to the brigadier for his leadership which had
. . . I glowered at the man and he changed the subject.

At the end he asked me to say a few words. I climbed onto
the boxes and looked at the men, over a thousand of them from
three British battalions. A little distance off, at the four points
of the compass, pairs of sentries knelt, facing outward in a peculiarly formalized position of alert. I knew what they were, because, among the congregation, was the 1st Battalion of the
Cameronians. The Cameronians, as a regiment, are descended
from the Scottish Covenanters, Lowland Presbyterians whose meetings were in the seventeenth century proscribed by the government and the official Church. The Covenanters continued to hold
their meetings, of prayer and defiance, on the moorlands and in
lonely sheep pastures—but always with sentries out. Ever since,
the Cameronians never go to church, anywhere, without putting
sentries outside the place of worship. Here they were, at Mokso
Sakan, beside the great Lake Indawgyi, eight thousand miles and
three hundred years from the original meetings of the Covenant.
What was I to say to them?

The hand of God? Causing death and mutilation, taking sides

in violence? Not the Christian God, surely. Let each man believe
what he wished. I only wanted to thank them for their courage
and discipline, and to remind them that those qualities were not
to be cast away, for neither the campaign nor the war was over. I
said a few stumbling words in that sense, and climbed down,
amid a scattering of handclaps and cheers. It didn't sound like
much of an ovation, but those men were still half-asleep where
they stood and I had to hurry away before I broke down.

Letter from Barbara. They are well. I wrote to her, but what
could I tell her except that I was alive?

I prepared and sent off a formal appreciation of our situation
to Joe. He was engaged in a prolonged and bitter fight with
Stilwell at this time, but he should have come and seen us at
Mokso. So should Stilwell. It would have done much for my
men's self-respect, and the generals could have seen the brigade
for themselves and made up their own minds about the truth or
otherwise of my opinions. In my appreciation I told Joe that the
brigade, especially the British battalions, was near the end of its
tether. Gurkhas take a long time to get accustomed to new ideas
and so far they had not done as well. Now they were ready; with
them something more could be achieved; with the British battalions, very little.

Once again I was wasting my energy. The battles between Joe
and Stilwell were about my brigade and the Chindits as a whole.
Stilwell said that we had needlessly abandoned Blackpool, that
none of us was doing anything, that Jumbo Morris' force, across
the Irrawaddy from Myitkyina, was doing less than nothing. The
Marauders were going fine and meeting the enemy, he said—why
weren't we? While he was saying this he knew that the Marauders
had in fact folded. Mountbatten sent Slim up to negotiate the
Lentaigne-Stilwell impasse. Slim pointed out that it was a little
unfair to accuse Jumbo Morris, with 1,500 men, of failing to do
what Stilwell himself could not do with 30,000. (By now Stilwell
had 30,000 Chinese attacking Myitkyina, held by 3,500 Japanese.
They were getting nowhere and this was the real reason for the
accusations of cowardice and incompetence which eddied back
and forth like poison gas.)

Slim persuaded Stilwell to give us a chance to reorganize, and
to keep us in operation until the fall of Myitkyina, which was

now expected at the end of June. This was an unhappy decision, because Myitkyina did not fall, and Stilwell's frustrated rage grew with every day. He was in no way responsible for the fall of Blackpool, except to the extent that he might have ordered its establishment so far north in the first place; the responsibility for that failure belongs to me and other Chindits, including Joe Lentaigne. But, from here on, Stilwell's is the guiding hand.

While we waited for orders, as though to underline the message of my appreciation the brigade began to suffer a fearful falling off in general health. The malarial rate remained comparatively low, though double what it had been. What horrified me, as the days passed, was the absolute lack of reserve strength in the men's bodies. Beginning about June 1, a man with a cut finger would probably show anemia; then the cut would go bad; then his whole body would droop, and in a day or two, he would die. Men died from a cold, from a chill, from the exertion of a patrol to the nearest village four miles away. Mild malaria cases became helpless, men with jungle sores or dysentery collapsed. Certainly a few of these men were taking the easy way out, but Desmond Whyte was a fighting doctor and, when I called all the medicos together for a conference, he and the others assured me that a high proportion of the British troops, officers and men, were in fact on the threshold of death from exhaustion, undernourishment, exposure, and strain. It needed only a small push to send such men over.

Orders came. Three brigades—111, 14, and the West Africans —were to move north and operate against the Japanese west of Mogaung. The only other Chindit brigade in the field—77—was already locked in a bloody battle to take Mogaung itself.

On June 9 and 10 I started my brigade northward, five and a half battalions and half a dozen elephants which our Burma Rifles had collected, complete with their *oozies* (mahouts). On the right, parallel to our line of march, stretched the mountains separating the railway from the lake. On our left lay the marshy basin of Lake Indawgyi, filled to overflowing by the influx of a thousand streams from three sides. We marched along the path that marked the precise division between the mountains and the marsh. Unlike the mountains, it was flat, and unlike the swamp, the average depth of mud or water on it was only six inches.

It offered no place to sleep so we harbored the first night a few feet up in the foothills, under the endless rain, having covered eight miles. We lay down, soaking wet, in the muddy pools under the trees, and went to sleep.

The chief fauna of the district were large, vicious, striped mosquitoes, biting flies, eye flies, and leeches. Our short puttees, tied tightly round the join of boot and trouser, kept out most of the leeches, but a halt seldom passed without an oozing of blood through the boot eyelets telling us that some particularly determined beast had found its way in. Hair-fine when they passed through the eyelet holes, they fed on our blood, and when we had taken off puttee, boot, and sock it was a bloated, squashy, red monster the size of our little finger to which we applied the end of a lighted cigarette. One of the sights of the march, a comic spectacle which we all awaited with grim fascination, was to watch the legions closing in as soon as we halted. From far and near, in front, behind, left, right, they arched toward us, along the ground, along the boughs of the trees, smelling blood.

On the fourth day I heard automatic fire from my advanced guard a couple of miles ahead. Soon, among giant trees, we came to two or three collapsed huts about the size of outhouses. In and near them we found several emaciated Japanese, some in advanced decay, who had apparently died from natural causes, and three or four recently shot to death. A glance at the map showed that the place where this engagement took place had a name— Lakhren. Two tracks crossed there, the one we were using and another that went up eastward into the hills. Harboring for the night, I reported our position and the facts of the "battle."

Next day we turned into the mountains and that night Briggs came to me almost hysterical with laughter, bringing a transcript of a BBC broadcast his radio had just picked up. Troops of the 3rd Indian Division (the cover name for the Chindits) had captured the important communication center of Lakhren. The news spread through the brigade and the next day everyone was laughing. It was a high point of the campaign. Long after the war ex-members of 111 Brigade, meeting in the street, would urge one another to remember the railways, the roads, the night clubs, of teeming Lakhren, and with what effort we had captured it. A poor joke, but as anyone who has been there will know, wretched conditions have the same effect on bad jokes that starvation has on bad food.

That was the last laugh of the campaign, and we had it on June 14. The succeeding days dissolve into a meaningless blur of cloud and rain, of fog and mist, clay-colored faces, dying eyes. I remember the names of villages—Padigahtawng, Ngusharawng, Hkamutyang, Labang, half a dozen others, all the same—bamboo shelters, low cloud, the throb of C-47s above the cloud, looking for us.

I was ordered to take Point 2171, a high point on the crest line of the mountains, and from there push down onto the Japanese lines of communication in the railway valley below to the east. 14 Brigade, which was also moving northward several days' march behind us, would join us in the latter phase. On the way to Point 2171 the 3/9th Gurkhas drove about fifty Japanese off a small feature above the valley, with half a dozen casualties. Then, in the utter weariness of the time, someone left the hillock and the Japanese came back, and reoccupied it. But the nearest company commander grabbed the nearest platoon, attacked, and swept them off again, just like that. It was a rare thing to hear in those days, and I sent for the officer. He was a young man of perhaps twenty or twenty-one, handsome, shy but self-possessed, with a good smile. Sir Galahad, I thought. Soldiers come in all shapes and sizes, and I have no preference. Some of the men who perform these acts are lechers and some are thieves, some are sodomites and some are saints. Saints also run away, and so do lechers. I remember thinking what a wonderful young man this particular one was. The memory stuck.

Three days later we came to the assault on Point 2171. The operations, lasting from about June 20 to July 5, were as hard on the soldiers as anything in my experience.

The battle began when my advanced guard ran into the enemy on a mountain shelf about a mile from the crest line and a thousand feet lower. Myself still moving along the *chaung* bed, I heard firing from ahead and began to hurry forward. I met mules and muleteers and a few riflemen coming back, not running but walking fast. I stopped a young Gurkha and asked him why he was retreating. "Someone" had given the order. Oh, that "someone" who takes concrete shape in the imagination of overwrought men and gives concrete, disastrous orders! A lieutenant came, and I grabbed him by the belt buckle and ordered him to collect all retreating men into a layback, facing the enemy. When they stopped coming back, which they would very shortly do, he was to continue the advance. If one single man moved farther back than the position where we now stood, I would have him, the lieutenant, shot before dusk.

I hurried on, reflecting how easy it is to be brave when a little experience has taught you that there is nothing to be afraid of. It would not be so pleasant up with the advanced guard. . . . As I thought, the senseless rearward movement had so far involved very few men and I soon reached the plateau. The leading troops had driven the enemy off. I saw a dead Gurkha, two wounded. A pair of Japanese lay on the grass of the open, untreed alp, their helmets full of brains and their packs full of postcards—beautiful Japanese-style paintings, Fujiyama, misty trees, naked whores holding their hairy sexual clefts apart, wide smiles in all directions—the usual stuff. (Later I sent some of the impersonal ones to Barbara, but though she aired them and dried them and even washed them she had to burn them in the end because they smelled of death. I couldn't understand why. We had killed those men only a few minutes before.)

The mountain swept steeply on to the crest line, covered in the densest jungle we had yet encountered.

We must push on as fast as we could, not allowing the Japanese to recover from their surprise. And this grassy shelf I must hold for supply drops, main headquarters, dressing stations and the like. Leaving Scott of the King's to organize all this, I sent the 3/4th Gurkhas at the ridge. Near the foot, at the edge of the trees, they ran into the enemy. Heavy firing.

Bugger! The Japanese were withdrawing up the ridge in good rear-guard fashion, and at about a company strength. We would not seize Point 2171 without a battle.

The firing strengthened. Our leading men reached a point about two hundred yards up the narrow footpath that followed the spine of the ridge. At the foot, where the ridge began with a sharp curve to the right, I looked down and saw a steep re-entrant leading up to the place where I stood with Ray Hulme and his battalion headquarters. I pointed out to Ray that the lay of the land would funnel any counterattack into that re-entrant. Ray brought up two machine guns as fast as the weary mules could trot. The tripods slammed down in the mud, the gunners rocked the barrels into the mounts, pushed through the holding pins, jerked in the belts, cocked the guns—and the Japanese came, preceded by a shower of grenades and a heavy clatter of rifle and automatic fire. The machine guns annihilated them at twenty and thirty yards. Ray sent down a platoon to mop up, and they reported fourteen corpses. They brought back the enemy platoon leader's map—a neat little sketch in blue and red pencil, showing where we were, where he had been, what he was to do, and how he was to do it. The sketch had been made, the plan put into effect, and defeated, all within ten minutes. I had a wretched feeling that I was fighting myself. The Japanese commander's mind seemed to work in exactly the way mine did, but rather more efficiently.

The 3/4th continued attacking. The ridge was steep and steep-sided, falling away into deep troughs, the whole densely covered with jungle, tall trees, and thick scrub. It kept raining, and the path up the ridge spine was deep in heavy, reddish mud. The Japanese held the path, one behind the other. The recent Japanese counterattack, a short left hook, had come downhill. To outflank the enemy on the path by similar maneuvers the 3/4th had to go uphill—cutting their way. To put twenty men onto the path by this means, a hundred yards ahead of the position held by our leading section, took forty-five minutes. Even then it failed unless the men on the path also got up and charged at the critical moment. Charge? No one could move more than one slow foot at a time, sliding back, trying again, holding onto a tree with one arm, firing his weapon one-handed with the other.

Our mortars went into action, blasting the ridge and the path, but they had to be careful with ammunition for we could not get more until a supply drop came. Enemy machine-gun fire swept the path, and their mortar bombs boomed and crashed about our support platoons, and in the jungle where the flank attackers crawled and stumbled through the mud and the ferns and the great trees, and on Ray Hulme's headquarters, and on me.

The momentum of our attack died away in the fading strength

of the men doing the job. Japanese reinforcements must have come down from the crest, for their firing increased. For a while nothing moved.

A *havildar* passed me at the head of his platoon. I recognized him—Mohbat Sing. He had been a young signaler in the 2nd Battalion in the frontier campaigns of 1936–37, when I was a lieutenant and signal officer. More than once I had sworn at him for his unkempt ways and skill at avoiding work. Now his eyes were dull red and he exhorted his platoon in a gasped-out monologue of Gurkhali oaths and endearments: "Come on, you porcupines' pricks. It's all right. Move, move, kids! We're nearly there. O pubic hairs, keep at it. You, you—" his head turned as he saw me—"*Salaam, sahib!* Of course we can do it! . . . The Gurkhas are coming! Third-Fourth, *Third-Fourth!*" He broke into a shambling run, followed by all his platoon. How they did it, I do not know. They passed from my view up the path. The firing increased suddenly, grew to a mad clatter . . . at first nearly all Japanese; then even; then nearly all ours, the heavy roar of our grenades and the powerful, grunting stammer of the Bren guns. Wounded men came down the path, a corpse sprawled in it right at the limit of my vision as I lay behind a tree peering forward. Ray came to me. "They made two hundred yards," he said. "I'm passing another platoon through."

More firing, again Japanese. Advance held up. What else, on a one-man front against a determined enemy? Only about a third of the way up the ridge, and now late afternoon. I passed the 3/9th Gurkhas through the 3/4th. Found Mohbat Sing and promoted him to *jemadar* on the spot for gallantry in the field. The 3/9th pushing hard, suffering casualties, not getting anywhere.

This won't do. Tell Alec to keep pressure all night, in case the Japanese pull out, which I think very unlikely. Follow them hard if they do. Remind him to guard his flanks. "Yes, sir," wearily. I'm giving too many orders. Back to the plateau. On the way pass a mortar of the 3/4th, firing. As I arrive a bomb wheezes out of the muzzle and falls on the wet bamboo five feet in front. Hurl myself to the ground, as do mortar crew. Count ten. Nothing happens. Look up slowly, the bomb lies, a dull metal fish in the rain. Pick up bomb, knees absolutely shaking and body turned to water by terror, and throw it over steep drop, frantically flattening myself into the mud. Cowering, hoping. No explosion. Click, *bang!* The mortar is back in action.

On down the path. Japanese field guns, small but loud, in action from far end of grassy shelf, shelling headquarters, and of course the main dressing station and Doc Whyte. Move the M.D.S. to reverse slope—didn't know which it would be till now, just like Blackpool. Baines's orderly, Lalbahadur, hit. Left side of chest stripped, exposing lung. Right wrist smashed. Send a company of the King's at the enemy guns. Firing, not much damage either side. Guns continue to fire, two or three of them, they are not doing much damage though, nothing after Blackpool.

Must think. The ridge up which we have been struggling is not the only way to the crest line. To the right, south, the next ridge is a long way off. To the left, north, taking off just short of the enemy gun positions, is another. Can't see in the mist and cloud and dusk but it appears to reach crest very close to Point 2171. No path up it. I will launch a strong assault up that. They must move up unseen and unheard, then rush the crest. At the same time the troops on the path must attack. It'll take the flanking force hours to get up that ridge. Very easy to lose the way. Easier still to find the difficulties too great, fail to press on, fail to press home the final attack. Must send the best man.

Call battalion commanders, explain the plan, and order Harper to carry it out. I will hold the King's in close reserve, ready to consolidate summit when taken. Harper must send his *best man* on the flank attack. He looks at me. We are thinking the same thing, and of the same man. The young Galahad of a few days ago. Captain Jim Blaker. All right.

H-hour, support, ammunition, medical, intercommunication. Any questions? All right.

Night, mild shelling. Bloody awful being shelled at midnight, slung up like a pig in a jungle hammock three feet above the ground. Oh, yes, I got a jungle hammock somewhere along the line, I and about twenty others, bloody well intend to hang on to it, too, so that I can sleep sometimes, and think. Bedraggled, sodden soldiers all round, without hammocks, but my name is not Philip Sidney. Shelling. Better think in the waterlogged hole immediately below the hammock, dug by my orderly. *Bang bang.*

No casualties. No sleep either. Mild dysentery for some days now. Take half a pound of sulfaguanidine tablets. Revert to thinking. Firing up on the ridge. Near me, a man howling like a train in the American night. Sweating, send Douglas Larpent to *stop it!* He finds young Gurkha in hole, shrieking his head off, glassy-eyed. Sends for *subadar major* and doctor and punches Gurkha hard in jaw. Old Douglas is British Army, doesn't know you can't knock a Gurk out that way. The boy looks at him, howls, runs away, everyone chases—*bang bang bang* of enemy artillery—can't catch him. (Next day he returns, starts barking, eating equipment, Doc Whyte keeps him under sedation a long, long time.) Back to thinking. Not long to dawn.

The flank attack slipped off. I saw it start and told Blaker to make bloody sure he was on the right ridge and that he got to the top. Then tried to smile. Blaker really did smile, saw it in the radio light.

The Gurkhas file past in the darkness. They must get to the foot of their ridge, near the enemy guns, behind the King's flank guard, before light so that the Japanese out there can't see them.

Silence . . . *pop pop pop* up the main ridge. Breakfast. Struggle up the path to Alec's forward battalion headquarters. The Gurkhas showing their quality now, pressing doggedly, a steady slow trickle of casualties. One small advance. Another. Short right hook, held up. Try again. *Must* make the enemy think this is still our only route of advance. The harmless little deception costing blood and mucus every minute. A naik of the 3/9th carried past with right thigh shattered, bone sticking out through rotting trousers. Wonder whether he'll live? Well done, well done, *amaldar-ji!*

At noon, main advance about three hundred yards from the crest line. Walkie-talkie comes through. Blaker ready, very close. Ready to go. Order strong mortar fire on the crest. Machine guns the same, when they can see. The men on the path gather strength and will, scrape the heavy mud off their boots. Tremendous firing, to the left and above.

Blaker going in, *now*. On the path the 3/9th Gurkhas, in single file, surge forward. To the crest, followed by the King's. Frantic firing. Running shapes in pot helmets and untidy puttees.

Japanese corpses among trees, and wounded. We have taken
Point 2171.

Now quick, dig in. They will return.

(It took Jim Blaker an hour and a half to reach the foot of
his ridge. Nearly five hours to climb up it. This for a mile and
a half without opposition. Near the top he saw that the crest and
the northern flank of Point 2171 were strongly defended by automatics, woodpecker machine guns, and mortars. After sending
his message to me and waiting for the covering bombardment,
Jim ordered the charge. His leading men came under machine
guns firing straight down the ridge. They dived into the dense
jungle, tried to crawl on up on hands and knees. Men fell, the
advance stopped. Jim went forward alone then, firing his carbine,
calling, "Come on, C Company!" Seven machine-gun bullets
through the stomach. He sank down, against a tree, turned his
head. "Come on, C Company, I'm going to die. Take the position." The Gurkhas swept on and up. Bayonets. *Ayo Gurkhali,*
the Gurkhas have come! That night I wrote out the citation for
Blaker's Victoria Cross, which was immediately awarded, post-
humously; but we pushed his body and the bodies of his comrades over the edge of the steep, far down into the tangled
jungle. No one had time or strength to bury them, the bravest
of the brave. Three months later a Graves Registration Unit
found them, bamboos six feet tall growing among and through
them.)

Consolidation. All the men sleepwalking. Mules struggling up
with wire just received in a supply drop down on the plateau.
Ammunition needed. A Japanese counterattack, heavy and well
supported. Destroy it. Again. Same. We are supposed to push on
down toward the valley. The King's do so. Meet more Japanese,
are stopped. Where the hell are they coming from? Sapper *havildar* runs into position, hands at throat, blood pouring out. Was
setting booby traps, a grenade went off. David Wallace, sapper
captain, kneels beside the writhing, dying body, weeping tears of
love and rage.

No supply drops possible on 2171. Same old problem—carrying
ammunition and stores up to the battle. Men and animals fewer,
and moving like snails. It takes all our effort to hold 2171, and
keep the wire clear. Not going to have the Japanese leaning on

us this time. No air support, weather too bad. Twice a day I visit 2171, stay an hour or more. Takes me an hour and a half to reach the top, with a dozen long rests. For Christ's sake get here, 14 Brigade, another opportunity going fast. We are falling against each other, the Japanese and 111, spent, drugged, crazed fighters at the end of the 125th round, bare knuckles, pawing at each other, falling down.

No other brigade comes. It is hard to believe that anyone else can be as tired as we.

Orders. Pull out, move to the region of Ndaogahtawng, co-operate on the flank of a Chinese attack. We struggle down and away. This was the worst time, of the multiply wounded men, and the diseased men. Foot rot, sores, carbuncles, boils, septic teeth, malaria, dysentery, meningitis, pneumonia, typhus, typhoid, every kind of gunshot wound.

One night we harbored beside a stream, and in the morning the mist slowly lifted, the sun rose, and it was the most peaceful sight I had ever seen, great trees leaning over the purling stream, wide and shallow among the mountains. Firing ahead. My leading battalion engaged with . . . the Black Watch, of 14 Brigade. No casualties.

Orders. Stilwell's Chinese, fighting southward from Shaduzup, had passed Kamaing and were now almost level with us. I was to seize this, assault that, in co-operation with their attacks. I began—driving men, like foundered beasts, up mountains, through dense lantana scrub. The attacks going in at a snail's pace; held; counterattack, pick up casualties, try again. Where were the Chinese who were supposed to be co-operating in this attack from positions at 393425, 488410, and 410400? Well, actually they weren't within miles of those places. They'd only said they were there to please Stilwell.

My men dragged themselves back up the hill, dying now from foot rot, I mean dying, dead. A patrol of the Cameronians, all the "fit" men from two rifle companies, went out sixty-three strong. The next day four were able to move.

From Force H.Q. the chief doctor sent Doc Whyte a kindly message telling him that foot trouble was inevitable unless the men kept their feet dry and wore dry socks at all times. I found Desmond, naked except for a *longgyi* and boots—the shirts were rotting on our backs—drafting a reasonable reply. I tore the message from him and wrote one myself, personal from Commander: "ONE kindly arrange for rain to stop falling TWO please turn mud into dry land THREE please terminate war so that we can build huts and stay in them FOUR am confident cases of footrot will then materially decrease." The chief doctor wanted to court-martial Desmond for that, although the message was from me, but, fortunately for him, thought better of it.

The C-47s found us often enough so that we did not actually starve, and their courage and skill in doing so, in that weather and those mountains, is beyond praise. Our casualties, mainly sick now as compared to the earlier overwhelming preponderance of battle casualties, piled up on our hands, because we could not spare men or mules to escort them to roadhead.

Death from flying fruit, really—two men killed by canned peaches at a supply drop. A Gurkha hit by a mortar bomb burst during the battle for Point 2171; splinters of metal enter the back of the right side, severing liver, ribs, and lower part of the lung; splinters removed, tissue sewn over; lower part of right leg fractured at the same time—this set and put up in a plaster of Paris splint. Doc Whyte straps the rifleman into a pony casualty saddle and he is still with us, days later, still alive . . . but now dullness on auscultation with the stethoscope indicates pneumonia, right side; and, although he is receiving Mepacrine, malaria becomes manifest within the vessels of the brain. The natural functions of the body cease to act, he is kept alive by the administration of a mixture of sugar, water, and brandy, through a tube passed from the nose into the stomach, at halt periods. (They were trying to keep the leeches from entering him, with the other hand; and the rain with the other; and wiping off mud splashes with the other; and emptying his bladder by catheter with the other.) In torrential monsoon rain the pony slipped, and fell thirty feet on top of the rifleman, breaking his back. He died two hours later. That was the only time I saw Desmond Whyte show despair or even fatigue. That, and one more time, when he and I and Alec Harper and a medical orderly sat up all night with the saline drip beside a private of the King's: meningitis, pleurisy, bacillary dysentery. He lasted forty-eight hours. Desmond Whyte, half-naked, soft-voiced with the Ulster brogue, kept at his work day and night, as he already had for a hundred days and a hundred nights.

He asks, one day, if he can have another mule. What the hell for? To stew, to make broth for the wounded and the sick. O.K. We have some wounded mules. Shoot one. I write out another Victoria Cross citation; this time for the man who, above all others, has kept the brigade going—Desmond Whyte. It is supported by my four battalion commanders—but Desmond has not dashed out and rescued one wounded man under fire, he has only saved two hundred, over a hundred days, calm and efficient and cheerful while shells blast the bodies to pieces under his hands. The Cross is refused and he gets a Distinguished Service Order instead. This is not good enough.

My top secret personal-to-Lentaigne protests became stronger. I insisted that my brigade have a medical examination immediately, and that all men not fit for action be evacuated at once. (The Marauders had made the same request, before they reached the end of the rope. Request refused, on Stilwell's orders.) My request, too, was refused, on Stilwell's orders. I signaled asking to be relieved of command of the brigade as we were being given tasks we could not carry out in our physical condition. The morale was still there but failing fast as the men became convinced that Stilwell meant to murder us. We had had a dietary deficiency of about eight hundred calories a day for 110 days. The average weight loss per man was between thirty and forty pounds. With all this the brigade had had less than a dozen psychiatric cases and the discipline remained fantastically good. . . .

Get an idea a column commander miles away is not doing his best. How can *I* know? Remove him from command by signal. Furious remonstrances from him, copy to Force. Good. Insist on my order being carried out forthwith repeat forthwith. Is done. Why doesn't someone have the guts to fire me? Because they know I'm right and anyone they put in my place will say the same.

The 3/4th Gurkhas reach an objective, look for the Chinese. The Chinese are not there. Mike MacGillicuddy, tireless, indomitable, shot dead through the throat, leading two companies through the lantana to find the Chinese. *Send your best man.*

Firing machine guns knee height into dense jungle, whence shots. God knows where, except it was by a lovely stream and we found two rotting Japanese in the bushes. The thunder of the battle for Mogaung has ended at last. Mike Calvert has taken it. Sorry, the Chinese have taken it. They come across the Mogaung River the last day and clear out half an acre at the northwest corner of the town, and Stilwell announces to the world that his Chinese have taken Mogaung. Casualties in the battle for Mogaung: 77 Brigade—800; the Chinese—30. Calvert has not lost his sense of humor though he is so angry he can hardly see straight. He signals to Stilwell that as the Chinese have taken Mogaung 77 Brigade will proceed to take Umbrage. The stuffed baboons try to find Umbrage on the map.

Rain. I lose the 6th Nigerian Regiment, who rejoin their own brigade under their own brigadier for an attack on Sahmaw. Good luck, Gordon. You did bloody well by us. Indian Army pride just as high and foolish as British Army pride, when it looks down the nose, and your West Africans fought well. I can't find Ricketts, their brigadier, but his brigade major is a little offhand when I strongly advise limited objectives, tight control, continuous small bites. His look tells me I am tired, have lost the offensive spirit. They charge off, and fail. They do it later though, much later, by limited objectives, tight control. . . .

In the continuous attempt to keep balance, to retain the power to think, to try to carry out orders which I know cannot be carried out, to keep my men from despair, my minds works like a machine that is about to seize up. It creaks, and catches, and races. Will not start or stop at command, but goes on its own volition, fastened to a narrow track, the battle, the columns, Stilwell . . . so many men fit to fight, so many sick and dying; so many days' food in hand, so much ammunition; the Japanese positions, the mud, the rate of movement possible compared with the distance. Only soldiers and battle, this battle, existed.

Some Kachins shocked me back into feeling. Four villagers from Ngusharawng came to my headquarters—the headman and three more, one with his hands bound behind his back, all wizened and starved. An Intelligence officer and two men of the Burma Rifles led them. I stared at them. Civilians, by God. Now what? Had they got any food for us?

"This man betrayed us to the Japanese, because we helped your soldiers a week ago [provided guides for the Cameronians]. The

Japanese came, crucified my wife and bayoneted my eldest son and five others whom they caught in the village. We escaped."

Terrible. But what the hell has it got to do with me?

"The government," the old man said, and waited.

The government was back. Me. They could not themselves kill a murderer. That was against the law. So it was. Rule of law, first principle of British justice.

I held a court-martial. It took about half an hour. The Intelligence officer had seen the bodies. The accused said he hadn't told the Japanese. The others said he had. Why should they bring him to me if they were trying to work off a private grudge? A knife in the back, in the jungle, and no one would ever have known.

Guilty. Under no circumstances could we afford to let anyone in Burma help the Japanese now, and get away with it. I sentenced him to death. The Intelligence officer took him away with two Burma Riflemen. I tried to write a message, listening, until two shots exploded very close down the hill and the Burma Riflemen came back.

On July 17, after a particularly bitter series of signals, my demands for a medical examination of my brigade were granted.

At nameless spots in the jungle, over the next three days, every man in the brigade was examined by medical boards consisting of two or three doctors. The strength of my four and a half battalions then totaled about 2,200 men. Those adjudged fit for any kind of action, in any theater of operations, numbered 118, being 7 British officers, a score of British soldiers, and 90 Gurkhas. I ordered Desmond to amend the figure to 119, since he had not included me, and whatever my faults as a commander I knew one thing for sure—I was going to be the last man of my brigade out of Burma. They could say anything else, but they were never going to say I left them.

Without waiting for further instructions I ordered all the unfit to move out to the road in their battalion formations, and march toward Kamaing, where Force H.Q. staff would take over. This road, only about ten miles away to the north, had recently been cleared by the Chinese. With bitter sarcasm I asked for orders for the remaining "fit" men.

I must say that Joe Stilwell had me beautifully there. He sent me orders. 111 Company, as I had called it in my message, was to go and guard a Chinese battery of medium artillery in position at the P in PAHOK, 492368.

I sent Doc Whyte out, though he claimed he was fit, marched my 117 men to the P in PAHOK, and introduced myself to the Chinese major and his puzzled but friendly American liaison officer. They said, really, they did not need guarding very much, since the Japanese were now in full retreat and an entire new British division, the 36th, had arrived and was even then passing through. (They certainly were. I saw a battalion commander pass, followed by his batman carrying his umbrella and his shooting stick. They fought well, though.) I wasn't going to let the Chinese get away with that nonsense. When a major of Chinese artillery gets a brigade commander of the Regular Indian Army assigned to protect him, he's damned well going to be protected. I reconnoitered the position, dug trenches, organized alarm posts and counterattack forces, and practiced stand-to alarms involving all the gunners as well as my own men. They begged me to go away, but we dug deeper holes.

Ten days later someone got tired of this farce—I think the American liaison officer's despairing signals were at last read—and 111 Company was permitted to leave Burma. I handed over the defense plan to the now hysterical major, marched my men ten miles into Mogaung, had my teeth fixed by an excellent U.S. Army dentist, who seemed delighted to have a customer, and entrained for Myitkyina. The train was five flatcars pulled by a tiny Diesel. It was August 1, 1944, the day Stilwell was promoted to full general, two days before Myitkyina at last fell. Sometime that night, having watched the last of my men board planes, I scrambled into a C-47 and, not knowing or caring where it was going, fell asleep.

22 Very near now. I could see the sprawling wooden house—a residential hotel—across the wide stretch of rolling grass, everything fresh in the clear air. The hill pony walked steadily on and I straightened in the saddle. Desmond Whyte rode on my right and Douglas Larpent on my left.

Another, smaller pony came careering toward us, a girl of about seven bouncing wildly in the saddle, shouting with laughter, urging the animal to a faster canter. A Kashmiri boy ran fast, grinning, a little distance behind. I recognized the child as Liz, Barbara's eldest daughter, and called to her.

She did not recognize me, though, until she came close. Then she cried, "Uncle Jack!" She hauled her pony's head round and galloped away across the grass toward the distant building.

When we reached it Barbara was on the steps, Liz and Mike beside her. The sun had tanned her and the mountain air put color in her cheeks. She looked well, and very lovely. I slid slowly down from the saddle and went forward. She held out the baby in her arms and I took her. My daughter, six months old, looked seriously at me for a moment, then laughed. She was perfectly formed, beautiful, happy, secure. I hugged her tight, but could not release any emotion. After Blackpool and 2171 and the succeeding sixty days, I have never been able to. I gave her to Douglas. He had children of his own back in England, whom he had not seen for four years.

I did not want to go inside. It was better out there on the lawn. The deodars and pines began just behind the house, rising to the thirteen-thousand-foot peak of Apharwat. Across the shelf, over the rolling green of the alp, I saw far snow, electric in the sparkling atmosphere. Gulmarg, the best hill station in India, is set high above the Vale of Kashmir, at nine thousand feet above sea level. The air passed like champagne into my lungs, and I laughed and smiled foolishly while my friends made cooing faces at my baby, and Barbara held my hand, and the older children stared up at us. I was again drugged, stupefied beyond the limit of emotion. We went into the house slowly, all of us. It was important that Barbara should know and love these men, for they were parts of me and I of them.

That midnight I awoke suddenly, alert, taut. "What is it? Speak up!" That was my voice. She held me fast. "It's nothing, nothing, darling. No one's here but us." I sank back. She was crying, trying not to let me notice. What else had I said? There was no need for her to cry now. It was all over, and I could sleep peacefully. Sleep, then! That's an order.

When we went to the club, the three of us would take her, Desmond, Douglas, and myself. Desmond and I had the blue and red ribbon of the Distinguished Service Order on our chests, and Barbara could be proud of us, but I wished I could wear some kind of a mark on mine to show that it belonged to me only as a personification of the brigade, of the dead and maimed and sick who had obeyed me. "I sent . . . ," "I ordered . . . ," "We cleared . . . ," "We took . . ." Oh, I was there, I heard the bullets, and the steel splinters whined over me too, but think what it was like for the individual man who *was* ordered, who *went*, who *cleared*, who *took*, the man for whom there was nothing between his body and the black bore of the machine gun.

There was no escape. I had to learn, to think back, to work out what I did wrong, what I did right, for I would lead again, and again, until the war was won. So, in the high nights the situations unrolled again, again I worried over the next order, which I had given fifty days ago. Again I studied the faces of men, the faces of the terrain.

"It's all right. Go to sleep, darling. . . ."

In the mornings, laughing, we played golf. I had never held a

club in my hand, and the first day I did nine holes in 121, counting every stroke, including a score of total misses. The next day
I did eighteen holes in 121. A marked improvement.

At the club we had sherry and lamb eggs, invented by the
secretary, Major Lamb (Ret.). When he heard my name he came
to us at our table and said, "Was your father in the 16th
Rajputs?" He was. "Your mother used to sing here, in the
twenties. One of the finest voices I've ever heard." Thanks. The
past enveloped you in Gulmarg, a different past according to your
background and temperament. The Moguls and their pale hands
beside the Shalimar for some, at some time; for me, my father
and mother and the last days of the Indian Empire in its glory;
and my great-uncle, riding up in the seventies, a young blood
of the Central India Horse.

I did not feel well. Food tasted nauseous and I vomited. I had
lost only fifteen pounds during the campaign. What was the
matter with me now? Jaundice. The local doctor ordered me to
bed, no liquor, no eggs, mushed food, rest. I fretted and fumed
and worried. To hell with doctors. There was only one in the
world I really trusted. Doc Whyte came, said, "Jaundice." And
the treatment? He shrugged. "Eat anything you like. Drink anything you want to. You won't want to, until you're better."
I had a large Scotch and soda and began to recover rapidly. Jim
Blaker and Mike MacGillicuddy and Tommy Thompson and the
Gurkha naik came less often in the night, showing their wounds.

We walked and rode miles along the bridle paths. At the
hotel there never seemed to be less than six children clutching
my knee or hand, yelling to be taken for a ride, to be told about
the battle, *bang bang bang*. I loved them and the plump innocence of them, but it was an oversudden transposition from
Point 2171, and I barked orders at them, and they were very
respectful but took little notice. I relaxed a little more.

The letters, thank God, were all done. I had written them in
Dehra Dun, after handing over to Jumbo Morris, the real brigadier. I wrote a personal letter to the next of kin of every officer
killed under my command. The battalion commanders also wrote
to the next of kin of every soldier. It had meant long conferences
to find the exact circumstances of each death, for some had occurred far from me, known only by a name in a signal. Then

came the composition of the letters, imagining that I was the mother or wife who would read them; trying to avoid the clichés of the form: "He died gallantly, doing his duty" . . . "Leading his men" . . . "Example to all of us." But too many of those deaths *were* clichés. They were doing their duty. They did set an example. (But how to tell a mother that her son has been blown into nothing at all before your eyes, has totally vanished?)

Walking, riding, lying down, I relived the campaign, for I thought that until I achieved some sort of order in my own mind, I could not rest. I was wrong. I soon learned to rest, with many doubts unresolved, for only time could solve them and then only partially. But now sixteen years have passed and perhaps this is the place to look back with the same far, high view that we used before entering Burma.

The course of the campaign confirmed that the original expansion of the Chindits was a mistake. War demands return for value, and after a certain point we could not give that return by our special tactics. The high command therefore called upon us to join in the normal battle. For this we were not properly armed. It would have been better to confine the Chindit force to three brigades at the most, and to keep in being the standard infantry division which was broken up to increase us.

Whatever the size of the force, it should have been used against the Japanese lines of communication to the central front, the decisive one. But since our role, worked out at Quebec, was to help Stilwell, this would probably not have been permitted without serious disagreement and accusations of bad faith between the Allies. Contrary to an idea that seems to have been spread by some overzealous partisans of Wingate, the original object—to help Stilwell—was never changed. Wingate himself started an aberration from it when he sent 14 and 111 Brigades west, and Lentaigne for a short time compounded the muddle. During this time no one knew quite what the Force as a whole was supposed to be achieving. Then Stilwell restored unity by insisting that we all come north.

Fierce controversy has raged, also, over Lentaigne's failure to carry out Wingate's master plan—the capture of Indaw and the making of it into a secure base, garrisoned by a standard infantry division. This was Wingate's plan, certainly, but it was not that of his superiors. His orders were merely to dominate the area around Indaw and he had been told long before we went into Burma that under no foreseeable circumstances would he get any more troops to garrison it even if he did capture it. His insistence on the attempt—16 Brigade tried two or three times, sometimes aided by 14—must be read as an attempt to force Slim to change his strategic thinking by presenting him with a dramatic *fait accompli* of a kind which would particularly appeal to the Prime Minister and might lead, if Slim remained obstinate, to his replacement by Wingate himself. Some Chindits whose opinions I respect—Calvert among others—are convinced that Wingate was right, and that a division in Indaw, acting as a bastion for six Chindit brigades, would have achieved more than the same division could on the Imphal front. I do not agree, for reasons given earlier.

The outstanding mistake of the Chindit campaign was the failure of anyone not marching in the field to realize the strain of Chindit war. Slim and others have emphasized the folly of telling soldiers that they are only going to be in Burma for eighty or ninety or a hundred days and will then be relieved; and, indeed, it is dangerous, for no one can tell what any future situation will be like. But the fact is that we who had trained and prepared for this form of war calculated professionally, before we went in, that after ninety days we would be worn out. So it happened, but still we were not believed. The difference between our war and normal war was simply extraordinary—the absence of supply lines, the knowledge that if you are sick or wounded your future is incalculable, looking always in all directions, always undernourished, always extremely vulnerable to certain types of enemy action—the cumulative effect bears down on even the hardiest. We were certainly no feebler than the men of standard divisions —though we were not, as has been rumored, hand-picked—but whereas with a normal formation I felt that it could go on forever, with reinforcements and occasional rest periods out of the line, with the Chindits I knew there was a definite time limit.

The effect was dual: senior commanders thought they could use us like ordinary troops and objected to giving us the special treatment which we in fact needed. And, if we got what we needed, they found we were even more expensive in manpower than figures indicated, for we needed two brigades to keep one permanently in the field.

The over-all generalship was good. The Arakan disasters of 1942–43, achieved by awfully decent chaps, and as needless as anything in British history—which is saying a lot—were forgotten in the bloody but decisive victory of Imphal. Stilwell, in his sphere, showed the Chinese that they too could beat the Japanese. Everyone made mistakes: Slim didn't get his forces back to Imphal soon enough, Stilwell overestimated his capacities at Myitkyina. The only senior man who never made a mistake, as far as I know, and worked real miracles, was Brigadier General Olds of the U.S.A.F., commanding all the transport aircraft in the theater, both R.A.F. and U.S.A.F. The feats he and his pilots did in supplying China over the Hump, in getting food and ammunition to divisions and brigades cut off by the Japanese, in ferrying reinforcements hundreds of miles at a moment's notice, in keeping the Chindits operating in their scattered groups all over North Burma—all this in the worst of the monsoon—this was the one faultless operation of the campaign.

We Chindits had done well, though. We did not do all that we were called upon to do, but I don't know anyone who did, except Olds and his staff and his pilots.

This book is not the place to review tactics and individual battles, more than they have already been described in the previous chapters. We were all very young—I was twenty-nine and the other brigadiers not much older—and we made mistakes. I must emphasize, though, that this is a personal narrative and when I wrote of my bitterness against the brigades that did not come to Blackpool I was trying to record what it felt like to be in my position, there and then. Whether the brigades could have come, whether any different orders or courses of action anywhere along the line by me or by them, would have brought us together at Blackpool, it is not now worth trying to find out, except for a military historian.

The only evil—as opposed to tragic—occurrence of the campaign was the long struggle of Stilwell and his staff to pin a charge of shirking onto the Chindits. There was no bitterness at all between the fighting men of any nationality. It came from above and in the main it came from Stilwell's headquarters, though some of our own brass, never having been near an American formation in battle, and not apparently having heard of Tarawa, did a good deal of monocle-type sneering from a safe distance. But Stilwell was rather different, and unlike any other American I have met before or since, in that he worked at fomenting this bitterness. He had a favorite staff officer he used to send on missions, solely to tell Chindits they were yellow. Since the man seemed to relish his task, he was not popular. Calvert took to standing with him on the fixed lines of Japanese machine guns, hoping. An officer of my own regiment, after the campaign, hearing that the man was in a certain hill-station club, went with a pistol to kill him. His standing was as high among the Marauders. Charlton Ogburn, Jr., the author of that excellent book, *The Marauders*, wrote to me about him: "I had not realized that his qualities had transcended national boundaries to such an extent. With us, too, his name was certainly one to conjure with, in a manner of speaking. Indeed, feeling was so intense that I did not know how to handle him in the book." No more do I.

As to the substance of the accusations: Here are the figures for battle casualties, killed, wounded, and missing, during the campaign. They do *not* include sick. The Marauders—481; 111 Brigade—about 700; 77 Brigade—1,578. These figures do not represent an accurate accounting of the work done. I believe the Marauders got more value for their blood than we did. But they do not, either, represent grounds for accusing anyone, American, British, Gurkha, or West African, of avoiding battle.

And what had happened to me? I had learned something about minor tactics, a lot about the handling of a brigade. These would help me, in the future, to make fewer mistakes and save lives. Far more important than any such lessons learned was the expansion of my capacity as a human being. It has always seemed to me that there must be some quality which defines humanity, which, in essence, *is* humanity. We know what this quality is when we talk of race horses, or pigs or bulls; the racier race horse is faster and has more stamina and better looks; the piggier pig has more usable meat, the bullier bull begets better, milk-giving calves. The quality of being more or less of a human being cannot be defined by any existing word. Lincoln and Schweitzer are, in my opinion, men about as large as men come, but we are very far from communicating our idea of their size if we define them as human, humane, humanistic, or possessing humanity—still farther if we say "superhuman."

Hard though it is now to explain, and almost impossible then— I was merely groping after the shadow of the idea—I knew that something of this had happened to me. The man who rode up the mountain to Gulmarg to see his child for the first time was not kinder, braver, less lecherous, more humane, more modest, less selfish than the one who had climbed into the C-47 and set out for Chowringhee; but he was bigger, and I, his puzzled guardian, knew he was. The growth was not due to any virtue in me but to the humanness of others touching me—Barbara so far away, the soldiers so close. In an odd and special way I felt that I had physically absorbed something of all men and all women.

In Gulmarg I swam slowly up, through the smoky memories, through the doubts and the fears, to a certain peace. When I had almost regained my normal weight, after a month, and the battle raging on in Burma, it was time to go back.

I rejoined 111 Brigade, now in the capacity of a lieutenant colonel, commander of the 3/4th Gurkhas, to which I had officially succeeded in June when Ian Monteith was killed opposite Myitkyina. We trained, deep in the Central Provinces, for three months of the cold weather, readying ourselves for the next Chindit operation. I was not looking forward to it with any enthusiasm, because my battalion had been chosen as the spearhead, to go in by glider, and I did not approve of gliders. Barbara found a bungalow nearby for herself and the children, and we spent a few scattered days together.

Then, in January of 1945, all senior Chindit officers were called to Lalitpur airfield. There Mountbatten told us that because of our expensive way with manpower, the Chindits were to be broken up and the battalions dispersed among normal formations. Five days later what I knew would happen did happen. Staff-trained colonels were rare and becoming rarer. I got a telegram posting me as General Staff Officer, Grade 1, to the 19th Indian Infantry Division, then part of 33 Corps, in Burma. To report at once by fastest means.

I was subjected, too young, to the most moving ceremony of a regular officer's life, the relinquishment of command of his battalion. Nothing could assuage my melancholy as I walked slowly out of the camp, *Subadar Major* Debsing beside me and the battalion lining the dusty path in the twilight, flowers strewn in the dust, every *havildar* and *jemadar* coming forward with a garland to hang round my neck, then their two hands pressing mine, and the pipes playing a slow march behind me. What had I done for them, to deserve this? Nothing. But I had existed, and loved them, and worn the badges, and done my best. The *subadar major* helped me into the truck and the pipes were playing in a circle round it, and slowly I left the camp, men running alongside now, throwing flowers and the pipe music fading.

If the bloody war went on long enough I'd probably be a major general before I was thirty-three; and what exactly did that matter to me, personally, compared with this, hearing the pipes die, my head bowed under the weight of the garlands round my neck? I was ambitious, but there was something terribly important here. *It isn't worth it.* That phrase whispered itself over and over.

The truck bumped out onto the main road and headed south. *It isn't worth it.*

What isn't worth it? The top of the tree. What *is* it, though, that the top of the tree isn't worth? Loss of this feeling, loss of permanent close contact with people, as people. That's all very well, but you can't avoid duty, and say, "I want to command a battalion for the rest of my life." True; but you can record the sense of values you now have, and hold onto them very hard; put them into storage, live by them, even out of the army, even in your family life, from time to time making sure that they are still accurate by checking back to what you feel this night.

I told the driver to stop, and changed places with him. I needed something to occupy my mind. We were winning the war, and someday it would come to an end. What would then happen to the Indian Empire, the Indian Army, the 4th Prince of Wales's Own Gurkha Rifles, and Jack Masters, God alone knew. But I knew that happiness, in the long run, would depend on a true and firm retention of what I now felt.

I put my foot down and rammed the truck fast through the night and the jungle, to Saugor and the railway.

23 Waiting for a plane in Calcutta, a general hailed me. "Where are you going, Jack?"

"G-1 of 19 Div, sir."

"H'm. You'll be back in a month. Shall I reserve a room for you at the Bengal Club?"

I asked what he implied. He told me that the commander of the 19th was Pete Rees. He'd fired thirteen G-1s in a year. I had met Pete Rees eight years before, on the North West Frontier, when he was a major and I a lieutenant. He had the reputation, then, of being a ruthless fire-eater. Apparently he had not changed. Thoughtfully I boarded the plane.

At Kalewa the R.A.F. had put up a huge sign—IT'S SAFER BY ROAD. But I flew on to Shwebo and reported to Corps Headquarters. The Corps Commander, Monty Stopford, gave me a cordial handshake and invited me to have a few private words with his Brigadier General Staff. I was beginning to have a curious itchy feeling round my neck, as though it were encircled by a rough surface, possibly hempen.

The B.G.S. said, "Your general's a superb soldier, but we're having difficulty finding out what he's doing. And he doesn't always pay the strict attention to orders that the Corps Commander would wish for. General Pete sometimes seems to think 19 Division must win the war singlehanded. You'll see that the situation improves, I'm sure. . . ."

The itchy feeling vanished, replaced by a distinct choking sensa-
tion. The B.G.S.'s parting "Good luck" sounded sardonic, if not
actually diabolical.

I got a jeep and went on east, and came at last to the bank
of the Irrawaddy, one hundred miles south of the place where
I had crossed it, going in the opposite direction, eleven months
earlier. There seemed to be a good many troops about, and
boats and DUKWs were busily crossing and recrossing the flood,
here about a mile and a half wide. On the far side I heard
desultory shelling.

A senior artillery officer came up to me and asked me who I
was and where I was going. I told him. His anxious expression
deepened. "See if you can do something," he cried. "He's over
the other side, with the leading infantry section, as usual. Or
perhaps he's decided to keep closer touch with the rest of his
division today. In that case he'll be just behind the leading
platoon. . . . Do you see that sandbank?" He pointed an accusing forefinger.

I saw a low, rather small sandbank on the far side of the river.
The artilleryman's voice trembled. "Do you see all those men
and vehicles crowded onto it? Those are *the guns!* The entire
divisional artillery, no more than four hundred yards from the
front, and the enemy liable to counterattack at any moment. He
insisted they cross over. The C.R.A. [Commander of the division's Royal Artillery, a brigadier] protested. I was there! The
C.R.A. said, 'Sir, I must remind you that I'm responsible for the
artillery of the division.' And do you know what *he* said? He
said, 'Mac, *I'm* responsible for the whole division, including the
artillery!' God, I hope you can do something to control him."
He inspected me more carefully, and ended despondently, "But
I don't expect so."

The condemned man smoked a last cigarette with calm and
dignity, and boarded a DUKW. It did not take me long to find
the general, for he was five feet two inches high, was wearing a
Gurkha hat with a gold general's badge on the front, and a huge
red silk scarf. His divisional pennant, a scarlet flag bearing the
gold device of a hand thrusting a dagger, fluttered from the top
of the radio mast of his jeep. The whole setup would have
been instantly recognizable at a mile on a foggy day. The enemy

were about two hundred yards away.

I introduced myself to Major General T. W. Rees, C.I.E., D.S.O., M.C., late Rajputana Rifles, Indian Army; forty-eight years of age, clean-shaven; always wore a small, kind smile; spoke softly, never swore, never drank, did not smoke. He had won his D.S.O. and M.C. as a young man in the First War, by enormous personal gallantry.

He welcomed me pleasantly; and then told me, his eyes steady on mine but his voice never altering its polite tone, that he had wished to promote his G-2 (Ops.) to be G-1 in place of the last incumbent, and had been foolish enough to tell the man he could expect the appointment. But G.H.Q. had overruled him, and posted me. He did not hold it against me, but I had better be aware of the situation.

That was all it needed. Might as well be hanged for a sheep as a lamb. I found the G-2, who was close by, took him aside and told him that I had not asked for this appointment but now that I had got it, I intended to run the General Staff my way, and expected his co-operation. Privately I decided to wait a bit and, if the situation warranted it, to force a showdown which would enable the general to fire whichever one of us he then chose. Relations between a commander and his staff, and within the staff, must be so close that no ill will can be tolerated.

I will not here attempt to go into any detail about the situation, but the reader must know that at this time Slim was driving south, down the center of Burma, with two corps, 33 and 4. Of these, our 33rd was aimed at Mandalay. 19 Division had just forced the Irrawaddy crossing and was now on the east bank, the same side as Mandalay, and about forty miles north of the city. The other two divisions of the corps were advancing south, on the west bank, intending to cross almost opposite Mandalay itself, while we drew the defending Japanese north to attack our bridgehead. But all 33 Corps's operations were designed to draw in as many Japanese troops as possible, for Slim was secretly launching 4 Corps, including an armored brigade of tanks, at the real core of the Japanese position in Burma—Meiktila, 120 miles south of Mandalay.

The country was fairly flat, heavily cultivated, interspersed with irrigation canals, small sluggish streams and many villages embowered in palms, each with its pagoda. Isolated hills, densely jungled and thick with bamboo, rose here and there out of the cultivation. The weather was ideal now, but would soon become very hot and sticky.

For myself, I felt fit and surprisingly healthy. I had not really recovered the weight or the reserves of stamina lost in the Chindit campaign, but a return to action had summoned up nervous energy to replace them. The state of the division also helped. It had only been in action four months, all of triumphant advance and successful attack under General Pete's dashing leadership. It was on a regular supply line and the men looked fit and full of fire, very different from the gallant, ragged, dead-beat scarecrows my Chindits had become when I left Burma. The division consisted of three brigades—62, 64, and 98, each of one British, one Indian, and one Gurkha battalion, plus the usual reconnaissance, defense, and machine-gun battalions, artillery, engineers, signals, and services. The 4th Battalion of my own regiment was in 98 Brigade.

We continued our southward pressure and I settled into my job. I found that the G-2 (Ops.) had the headquarters well organized both for battle and movement. This meant that I could concentrate on my real task to be the confidant and alter ego of the general. For the first week I spent nearly all my time with him.

It was a racking experience. One day, after we had been sniped for an hour or so while standing near a forward platoon position, I asked him with heavy sarcasm whether we shouldn't paint his jeep red too, so that it would show up better where it was parked a few yards behind us. Pete thought it an excellent idea. I only prevented him having it done by pointing out that the fire it would draw would cause casualties to the signal and escort sections who had to follow him wherever he went. Pete was inordinately brave anyway, but his insistence on going as far forward, and as conspicuously as possible, was based on memories, and books, about the First War. So much was written, after that holocaust, about generals sending the troops into hopeless battle while they themselves stayed in the rear and, eventually, toddled home to die in bed, so much bitterness generated against the Brass Hat, that young regular officers of that era—who became the generals of 1939–45—were usually to be found a good deal

farther forward than was strictly necessary. But what they lost in
control they gained in the morale and confidence of their troops.
Nothing raises morale better than a dead general. Pete did his
best.

When I had established some kind of a personal relationship
with him I began to inquire, cautiously, into his tactical doctrine.
Why, for instance, had he pushed the divisional artillery onto a
sandbank the far side of a wide river, and so close to the forward
troops that the guns could not give defensive fire to those troops
if they were attacked? Pete said, "The Japanese weren't going to
attack—not in force. *I* was. By moving the guns up early I didn't
have to hold up the advance while I got them across the river."

H'm. Very risky. Not according to the textbook. But, damn it,
he'd been right. The Japanese had not counterattacked. Tactics
is fine—but rightness is all. General Pete kept on doing dreadful
things, and being right.

The work load became very heavy at main H.Q. and I took
to spending more time there, driving forward every day, usually
in the afternoon, to visit Pete for three or four hours, and returning with him in the evening. Those rides out to find him
became a regular Aunt Sally show, with me cast as the Sally. The
enemy had many guns in the hills to the east, and my jeep always
raised a high dust trail. Every afternoon some damned Nip
sniped me with a 155-mm. gun, a very large weapon, but it was
a pallid inconvenience compared with the pleasure, and value, of
my hours with Pete. Wherever he went, from far away the
soldiers saw him coming. By the time we arrived there were
always smiling faces to greet us, and usually a brew of tea. He
was a Welshman, and besides Welsh spoke Urdu, Marathi,
Pashto, Burmese, and Tamil. Now he asked me to teach him
Gurkhali, and soon he knew enough to cause a look of startled
pleasure to cross many a stolid Gurung face.

One afternoon, when driving out to find him, I met him coming back with what looked like a small hornless deer tied across
the hood of the jeep, further held down by a Gurkha soldier. I
was rather shocked to see that his trophy was a Japanese lieutenant. I have an unalterable conviction that it is quite enough to
kill and wound people, without submitting them to barbarism

and indignity. Pete saw my expression, stopped his jeep, and said, "It's all right, Jack. The poor fellow's very badly wounded, and this is the quickest way of getting him back to hospital. He has to be up there on the bonnet so that we can keep his leg straight in the splint."

I became very fond of Pete, for his military aggressiveness was combined with a rare personal gentleness and unfailing good manners. He began to trust me, too, though still paying too much attention to detail for me to feel that he was getting all he could and should out of a G-1.

Pete became restive. We were supposed to be drawing the enemy north from Mandalay. If the Japanese really were in strength opposite us, an attack would commit them to battle here, not at Mandalay. If they were not—well, privately, Pete had an idea that the division which captured Mandalay would be wearing a dagger on its sleeves, whatever the corps plan might say. Pete decided he was going to break out of the Singu bridge-head—but how?

Our two leading brigades were some miles south of Singu, in contact with the enemy. The motor road to Mandalay ran five or ten miles inland from the river bank. Cart tracks and village paths could be strung together to make another route closer to the river. One night he called me to his quarters, the stone platform outside a small pagoda on the bank of the Irrawaddy. We set a small lamp on a folding table, and I brought a bottle of whisky. Pete opened a huge cake, one of those which his wife made for him every two weeks and sent out to him from England. He also opened a jar of hard candy, and his orderly brought a big pot of tea. We were ready for a military conference.

He began to talk. He thought it would be best to throw the main weight of the division down the motor road. It was more heavily defended, but it would make for easier movement. I disagreed. I thought that we should force down the river line; we would meet fewer Japanese, and if we moved fast enough we could cut off their main forces on the road, instead of pushing them back on themselves and so enabling the same people to fight time and again. At midnight Pete accepted my view.

We began to thrash out the details. The level of whisky in my bottle grew lower, the orderly had made half a dozen pots of tea, and we'd eaten most of the cake. Every hour or two a prospecting Zero flew over and we blew out the light and sat in companionable darkness, watching the faint starlight reflected in the Irrawaddy. The Zero droned away and we got down to it again. . . . Surprise? Maintenance of the momentum of the at- tack? Artillery support for two forces, which would be some miles apart after the first two days, if the plan went right?

By three A.M. I knew exactly what the general wanted to do, and how he intended to do it. I was also rather soused so, when Pete bade me good night, I routed out all the G Staff and clerks and dictated the operation order for the battle, and its appendices, and took the first copy to Pete at dawn. He looked at me with almost exactly the same quizzical expression Michael Roberts had worn two and a half years earlier—and said almost exactly the same words. I suggested he recommend the G-2 (Ops.) for a decoration, as he was a thoroughly competent and loyal officer. It was an oddly emotional moment. Pete beamed and I, as usual, felt like crying. This was the time, I am sure, when Pete decided to give me a brigade in the division as soon as he could manage it, though I didn't hear about it until much later. Exalted and exhausted, I went to bed.

The problem to which the operation order gave General Pete's solution was of almost textbook clarity. The Irrawaddy marked our right (west) flank with great precision, and also pro- tected it, since British forces held the far bank all the way down to nearly opposite Mandalay. Ten miles to the left (east) the mountains began. Down this corridor between river and moun- tains ran the two passable routes: the motor road on the left, the cart tracks on the right.

Pete had decided to put our main effort down the right road. Our first task, therefore, was to make the enemy think it was coming down the left road. The enemy commander would think nothing of the kind unless the attack that *did* come down the left road was of the strength he would associate with the full effort of an infantry division, such as he knew was facing him. (We knew he knew, because we had recently captured some of his marked maps, found on corpses.) So the attack down the left road must be fully supported by artillery and tanks, and must employ at least a brigade. It must be pressed home to an extent that would force the enemy to move his reserves to that flank, thus leaving the right road comparatively unguarded.

But, once our main attack was launched, down the right road, it too must be fully supported. To do this we must place the guns in a position where, without moving, they could fire on the enemy positions on both roads. And they must be well forward, to extend their reach. And they must not hint, by their positioning, which way they later intended to move. The same applied to the reserve brigade, and to the bulk of the tanks.

Pete intended to keep the whole division close in hand during the early stages, when we expected to have a hard time breaking the Japanese defenses. If, after all, we found that the right road was harder to crack, he could switch the main weight to the left by a single order. For a time he meant to keep all three brigades in mutual supporting distance of each other, though he might have to slow some of them down to achieve this. This also meant that in the beginning there would be no large gaps through which the Japanese could counterattack our gun areas or communications.

The preparations went forward fast—stacking of ammunition by the guns, bringing forward reserve fuel for the tanks, last-minute maintenance of all vehicles, a hundred other matters. I performed cold-bloodedly one of my most important duties—estimating the number of casualties, so that the Medical Staff could make the necessary preparations. (As a comment on what training and experience can mean, I will note here that my estimate was right within 3 per cent. I believe the figures were 400 estimated against 390 suffered.)

We were very nearly ready. . . . A worried cavalry colonel arrived, carrying a copy of our operation order. He was the second-in-command of a tank brigade, the parent formation of the Indian tank squadron which was allotted to us—thirteen Sherman tanks in all. His brigadier had sent him to protest against the way Pete proposed to use the tanks. We called for Alastair Mac-Kenzie, the young squadron commander who would actually have to do the job, and settled down for a discussion beside the battered pagoda. I detected a certain hardness at the corners of Pete's mouth, and thought the cavalryman was in for a rough passage.

In the plains of central Burma, still many miles ahead, tanks could be used "properly," i.e., making full use of their characteristics. In our immediately forthcoming battle they could not, since the topography often limited them to a one-tank front. Even so, we could advance a great deal faster with them than without them, with many fewer casualties over all, though obviously some of those fewer casualties were going to be suffered in the tanks instead of solely by the infantry and the mine-clearing engineers. Alastair MacKenzie was another Mike MacGillicuddy, whom he quite resembled—a shock of flaxen hair, thin face, sharp nose, quixotic gallantry. He had agreed that the going would be tough for his squadron, but certainly they could and would do what was asked of them.

The cavalry colonel now insisted that they could not. Pete listened patiently, but when the colonel would not yield Pete asked him politely whether, in that case, he thought the cavalry should be excused from this war as it was too dangerous. The wretched colonel flushed violently and reiterated that it wasn't "tank country." Pete said, "It isn't infantry country either, but unfortunately the wicked Japanese have chosen to fight in it." The colonel said, "Sir, I'm responsible. . . ."

I slipped away, beckoning Alastair to follow. As the necessary witness I had recently been present when Pete fired an infantry brigadier for allowing difficulties to dominate him, instead of vice versa. This was going to be worse.

Barbara was still in Saugor. Her husband had taken Liz and Mike and sent them to England. She had only our daughter now, and needed me more than ever before or, perhaps, since. Joe Lentaigne was visiting the brigades of the disbanded Chindit force he had commanded, saying good-by to each of them before they were split and scattered all over the East. Going out to 111 Brigade he took Barbara with him, for I had commanded the brigade and the 3/4th were still in it. Joe got very drunk that night, as did nearly everyone else, and poured out all his own domestic troubles to Barbara. She has always had a remarkable

*faculty of easing other people's woe. When they started back
to Saugor at two A.M., she in the front seat of the truck with Joe,
they saw two full moons shining in the bushes near the road.
Investigation of this strange phenomenon proved the moons
to be the bare behinds of two Burma Rifle officers, as sadly overturned by the occasion as the rest, but rather more obviously.*

Before dawn on D-day the artillery opened the bombardment.
The left brigade advanced and at once became heavily engaged.
The right brigade slowed down, though unopposed, as the lead
tank had become bogged in a muddy canal. Pete and I hurried
to the spot and he ordered three three-ton trucks to be manhandled into the canal and overturned. The remaining tanks
crossed over the wreckage. The engineer major at the spot lost a
sizable area of skin from Pete's tongue for not thinking of the
solution himself.

By midmorning it was clear that the battle was working out
exactly as Pete had planned. He decided that there was no chance
of an enemy counterattack; they had their hands full with the
left brigade. He let slip the main attack. The rest of the division
plunged straight ahead for Mandalay, with orders to go hell for
leather, the leading troops to contain and by-pass small enemy
pockets, leaving them for following troops to wipe out.

We rumbled down the cattle tracks in the heavy dust, past
stands of jungle where the crackle of small-arms fire showed that
we had caught some Japanese. The tank treads clanked through
villages blazing in huge yellow and scarlet conflagrations, palm
and bamboo exploding like artillery, gray-green tanks squatting
in the paddy round the back, ready to machine-gun any Japanese
who tried to escape that way before our advancing infantry. We
passed the twenty-five-pounder gun-hows of the artillery, bound-
ing and roaring in a score of clearings, hurling their shells far
ahead into yet another village. Tanks again, the troop that had
cleared the village back there, rumbling on, twenty Gurkhas
clinging to the superstructures. Infantry, trudging along the sides
of the road, plastered with dust and sweat—we were not a motorized division and most of the infantry had to march, when they
could not clamber onto tanks and trucks and gun quads. The
mules of the mountain artillery, the screw guns, pounding down

the road, trotting out into the paddy when the road was blocked, never a change of step, and the jingling of the harness and the creak of the leather. Japanese sprawled in the road and under the burning houses, their chests blown in, some by tank shells, some by suicide, for they often died clasping a grenade to their own bodies and rushing out at the assaulting infantry. The light hung sullen and dark over all, smoke rose in vast writhing pillars from a dozen burning villages, and spread and joined to make a gloomy roof above us. Every village held some Japanese, every Japanese fought to the death, but they were becoming less and less organized.

Far behind, the left brigade began to feel the Japanese resistance on the motor road softening as the enemy learned— very late, his communications slashed to ribbons—that he would soon be cut off from Mandalay. That brigade had been fighting day and night for three days. At divisional headquarters, far ahead on the right, the radio crackled. The brigade commander back there wanted to speak to the general. Pete came and I picked up another set of earphones. They used a sort of code which was secure enough for operations already in progress. The brigadier reported his position, said he had temporarily lost contact with the enemy in the dark, and was now going into harbor for the night. He would continue the advance at first light.

"Well done," Pete said. "You are doing marvels. Press on at once, keep pressing on. Over."

The brigadier's strained voice came up. "The men are exhausted, out on their feet. Half the vehicles need maintenance and repair. We'll push on at first light, sir. Over."

Pete's gentle voice said, as though the other had not spoken, "You've done very well indeed. Keep up the pressure. Over."

The brigadier could not keep the nervous exasperation from his voice. The general did not seem to be able to understand the simplest sentence. He repeated what he had last said, with emphasis.

Pete's voice was a shade harder. "I said, keep up the pressure. *Do not harbor or stop at all.* Keep advancing, all night. Every day we stop to rest and collect ourselves now means a week's more fighting later on. Over."

"Yes, sir. But . . . I don't think we can do it. Over."

"You can do it!" Then, in a tense and suddenly very sharp voice, "*Who's winning this war?* . . . Out!"

The radio was silent. I took off the earphones and looked at the small, tired man sitting hunched beside me. He said, "We've all got to be driven sometimes, Jack. He's cursing me and thinks I don't know what it's like there. But I do. I also know what it'll be like for them tomorrow, and next week, and the week after, if they don't conquer themselves now."

We passed Madaya, over halfway to Mandalay. That night a cipher office check (message carrier) handed me a message. I glanced at it, then at the battle map, swore, and went to Pete. I said, "There's a message here that I don't think you'll want to see, sir. It's from Corps. I can lose it."

Pete smiled. "You'd better give it to me. Thank you all the same, though."

I handed it to him. Corps had ordered all its three divisions to hold back one brigade no more than twenty miles from Shwebo, to be ready at hand in case of a Japanese counterattack.

Pete said, "Come along to my tent." Recognizing the symptoms, I went first to my own bivouac and got my whisky. In Pete's tent, beside a table, the hurricane lantern burning between us, Pete said, "What am I going to do about this? It's absolute nonsense."

I agreed. Shwebo was on the other side of the Irrawaddy, twenty miles west of the river. To obey the order we'd have to pull a brigade out of the advance and send it back to Singu. Shwebo was certainly vital, since it contained the airfields which were receiving our supplies, but . . .

Pete said, "The way to defend Shwebo is to keep attacking as hard as we can, so that the Japs don't have troops to spare, or time to think of sending them back there."

Obviously, but I wondered why Pete was so upset, why he needed so badly to talk to me. He said, "You know I've lost one division already from saying what I think."

I didn't know. He gave me the details, munching angrily on a slice of cake. It was in the Western Desert in 1942, at the time of Rommel's big advance. Pete, commanding the 10th Indian Division—the division which contained Willy Weallens and the 2/4th Gurkhas—had not approved of his corps commander's

plan, and had told him so. The corps commander replied that if
he had no confidence in the plan he could hardly carry it out
effectively, and summarily relieved him of command of the
division. Pete had been right, as usual, for when the Germans
attacked the dispositions were proved to be unsound.

Pete said, "Should I have kept my mouth shut? It was a bad
plan, but it was my division, and I knew it, and I could have
fought it better than anyone else. Perhaps if I had been there, it
would have held. . . ."

The message from Corps lay on the table. I thought of the
time, last year, when I had so strongly felt that my brigade
should continue to operate in the Pinlebu area, on the tactics
it knew best. I said Pete must do what he thought was right, regardless of the consequences. They could only try to relieve
him of command again, and I did not think Slim would accept
that.

Pete nodded slowly. He said he would take no action on the
order. If anyone was going to destroy the momentum of this
attack, it was not going to be Pete Rees. He would fly back the
next day and protest personally to the corps commander. He sat,
thinking. He would have to go back twenty miles by jeep to the
nearest airstrip, then by light plane to Shwebo. He would be away
at least six hours. I asked which brigadier was to command the
division during that time, as he would have to be called in from
his brigade, and be given time to make his own arrangements.

Pete said with a twinkle, "No brigadier, Jack. They've all got
their hands full. You are. You can reach me on the radio if you
have to."

The next morning, after he drove off, I drew a deep but somewhat grumbling breath and took Tactical Headquarters forward. Commanders always resent staff officers and vent on them
the helpless anger they are often bound to feel at their superior's
orders. If any of the brigadiers chose to protest that what they
were being told to do was impossible, I would be in a nasty spot
indeed. So would they when Pete came back, but that was another story.

Those six hours were the summit and culmination of my military life. Knowing Pete's mind so intimately, I did not have to

hesitate when faced by the few moments demanding positive decision. The leading brigade met opposition at such and such a point; I told the brigadier to attack as soon as he could, and passed the next brigade round him. Twice the C.R.A. came with artillery problems, but I had only to forecast my next moves, and leave the detailed solutions to him. Once a brigadier came, but it was Jumbo Morris of 62, who had wanted me to get back 111 Brigade soon after the Chindit campaign, he already having been given this "normal" brigade in 19 Division—and he cheerfully agreed with my order and went off and did it. Twice the dialed face of the radio tempted me in moments of petty crisis. I had only to pick up the microphone and ask for Daddy, and all would be well. The familiar gentle voice would tell me I was doing well, solve the problem, and I would be covered. I managed not to do it, telling myself furiously that if I couldn't command a division for a few hours, after all I had seen and done, I'd better go back to being a brigade major.

In the afternoon Pete returned, having won his fight with Corps, and the sight of his face, beaming with pleasure at what we had achieved in his absence, was enough reward. The experience itself made me understand even more fully Lee's saying that it is fortunate war is so terrible, otherwise men would love it too much. The 19th Indian Infantry Division numbered about 1,000 officers, 14,000 men, and 180 guns, besides its trucks and tanks. This whole mass of strength and skill and courage, of flesh and steel, reacted like a sword in the hand. But it was Pete who had made and tempered it, and I handed it back to him with pride that he had allowed me to wield it, but also with humility, for I knew I had much strength of character to develop before I could forge and handle such a weapon in my own right.

The rapport between us became almost psychic. Some forty miles to the southeast of us now, up in the tangled mountains, lay the city of Maymyo, astride the Japanese-held road to Yünnan and China. Pete said, during one of our nightly discussions, that we ought to be able to seize Maymyo if we detached a brigade for the job. I said sternly that it would be all wrong to detach a brigade—concentration of force, maintenance of the objective . . . the strategical clichés reeled off my tongue with great au-

thority. Pete said glumly that a brigade *could* capture Maymyo,
it *ought* to capture Maymyo, and it *would* capture Maymyo . . .
only he didn't see how it could get there.

"You would really send a brigade if it could get there?" I asked.
He nodded. "Or a part of one."

"It can get there easily," I cried. "We moved through much
worse country than this in the Chindits. Look at these tracks!
Give me two battalions and a mountain battery, sir, and I'll do it."

He was smiling with delight. "Oh, no," he said, "you're staying
with me. But I'll send Jumbo and 62 Brigade. He was a Chindit."
And off they went.

The lion-like bulk of Mandalay Hill climbed over the southern
horizon. Rising nearly a thousand feet above the plain, the spine
of it is covered from end to end by temples, linked by a covered
stairway. Under the temples lie cellars and dwellings and storage
rooms. The Japanese held the whole complex, in strength, and
from it their artillery observers directed a heavy gunfire onto our
leading troops.

Pete and I spent an unpleasant hour under its western slope
on two successive days. Every movement, particularly of vehicles,
drew prompt and accurate fire from 105s and 155s. On our first
visit a shell made a direct hit on a jeep twenty feet from us. After
picking ourselves up we ran forward to help the man lying there
beside the burning wreckage, but he was dead, incredibly shrunk
so that I thought it must be a child; but it was a mangled mess of
adult humanity, an Indian sepoy, red flesh thrown anyhow into
torn green trousers. A dozen more shells were on their way and we
left him.

We could make no further advance until we took Mandalay
Hill. The general allotted the task to 98 Brigade, and they to the
Royal Berkshires. But the 4th Battalion of the 4th Gurkhas was in
that brigade, and its commanding officer came forward to protest. Hamish Mackay, very quiet and shy-seeming, in reality full
of fire and a fey humor, pointed out that he knew the area well,
having been seconded to the Burma Rifles from 1937 to 1942.
Hamish thought he could take the hill with his battalion, that
night, using little-known paths of approach. The orders were
changed, and Hamish given his head.

On the night of March 10–11 (again, our Regimental Day),

the battalion went up to the assault, led by *Subadar* Damarsing and *Jemadar* Aiman. All night they fought up the steep, up the long stairway and along the flanks of the ridge. At dawn they took the summit. An hour later Pete and I stood on the highest point of Mandalay Hill, looking down into the city and into the palace of the ancient kings of Burma. Once they had been spacious and beautiful, with avenues of shady trees; now three and a half years of war had battered them, and columns of dust rose in the streets where our shells fell, and half the houses had no roofs, and to the south acres of corrugated iron, which had once been a warehouse or factory, glittered dully in the early sun. The Irrawaddy ran wide and yellow on our right and immediately below us the old splendor still lived in the brilliant white of the pagodas climbing down the ridge toward the moat and the wall of the fortress.

24 We stood, so to speak, on top of Mandalay. We also stood, at much closer range, on top of a good many Japanese. The temples, cellars, and mysterious chambers covering Mandalay Hill were made of reinforced concrete. The 4th Gurkhas had taken the summit, and no Japanese was alive and visible; but scores of them were alive, invisible, in the subterranean chambers.

A gruesome campaign of extermination began, among the temples of one of the most sacred places of the Buddhist faith. Sikh machine gunners sat all day on the flat roofs, their guns aimed down the hill on either side of the covered stairway. Every now and then a Japanese put out his head and fired a quick upward shot. A Sikh got a bullet through the brain five yards from me. Our engineers brought up beehive charges, blew holes through the concrete, poured in gasoline, and fired a Very light down the holes. Sullen explosions rocked the buildings and Japanese rolled out into the open, on fire, but firing. Our machine gunners pressed their thumb pieces. The Japanese fell, burning. We blew in huge steel doors with PIATs (bazookas), rolled in kegs of gasoline or oil, and set them on fire with tracer bullets. Our infantry fought into the tunnels behind a hail of grenades, and licking sheets of fire from the flamethrowers. Grimly, under the stench of burning bodies and the growing pall of decay, past the equally repellent

Buddhist statuary (showing famine, pestilence, men eaten alive by vultures), the battalions fought their way down the ridge to the southern foot—to face the moat and the thirty-foot-thick walls of Fort Dufferin.

Pete brought up the medium artillery, and the 5.5s hurled their sixty-pound shells at the wall, over open sights, from four hundred yards. The shells made no impression. He called in the air force. P-47s tried skip-bombing, B-24s dropped thousand-pound bombs, some inside the fort and some outside—among our troops.

We found a municipal employee who knew where the sewers led out of the fort, and prepared an assault party. All the while the infantry fought in the brick and stone rubble of the burning city, among corpses of children and dead dogs and the universal sheets of corrugated iron. The night the sewer assault was to go in, the Japanese withdrew from Mandalay. Next morning coal-black Madrassi sappers blew in the main gate, and Pete walked in, surrounded by a cheering, yelling mob of a dozen races. Just as Pete—but not his superiors—had planned, the Dagger Division had taken Mandalay. At the same time Jumbo Morris took Maymyo.

But I was not there. A few days earlier Supremo descended upon us, bringing the corps commander with him. Pete took the august sight-seers to the top of Mandalay Hill, and I trailed along a few paces astern. While we were up there an orderly arrived from headquarters with signals and mail. I glanced through the signals—nothing of importance; but one of the letters was from Barbara. Her divorce had just been made final.

I looked out over the smoking city. The sounds of battle came up clear and ugly to the summit. Barbara . . . did she exist? Did any woman or child really exist, except frightened, staring brown ones, and dead ones? What was this "marriage" that people talked about, and committed? We were still here, and they there, and would be forever. After nearly three years it seemed impossible, and it was, for I was here, and she there.

Pete asked me why I was looking so moonstruck. I told him —he knew of my private affairs. He said, "Go and get married." I began to protest that it could wait, that I would ask to go when we had a lull in the campaign. "We're going to have one now,"

he said. "The big battle will be at Meiktila, and we won't be in it.
Go at once. Be back in ten days." My heart jumped. The impossible, the unattainable, had been put within my grasp.

I began to run. I asked the corps commander if I could borrow
his light plane to get to Shwebo. General Stopford generously
agreed at once. General Pete patted me on the back with a wide
smile, and I ran down the hill as fast as I could go. . . . I don't
know whether any International Olympic authority recognizes a
free-for-all record between the summit of Mandalay Hill and No.
14 Bungalow, Haig Road, Saugor, C.P., India; but if they do, I
hold it. . . . Run down the sacred stairway, jeep two miles to
Main Headquarters, grab up valise, get the A.Q. to make out
travel warrant, shout to the G-2 (Ops.) that he is the G-1 for
the next ten days, jeep to the light plane strip. Forty-minute
flight to Shwebo, hurry to control tower, where I find the crew
of a U.S.A.F. C-46 being briefed for the return flight, empty, to
Chittagong. Twenty minutes later I am dozing in the back of
the plane, alone with my thoughts. Reach Chittagong about
three P.M. No plane continuing westward until nearly six; then
another U.S.A.F. C-46 and we take off into darkening weather.
An alarming flight, me sharing the metal tomb with one huge
piece of machinery—a dynamo or generator. We fly in and out
of thunderheads, and leap and shy and buck like a young stag,
the monstrous cargo creaks and heaves at its ropes, leans over me
where I lie on my spread valise. Tropical rainstorms hiss at us,
the clouds disappear in the night, to be replaced by lightning
bolts, which strike the wet shining wings and dance along them in
blue and white fire, all the while the engines drone, the plane
jumps, the roped monster inside growls and groans.

Barrackpore. Converted B-24 going to Allahabad at three A.M.,
but no place on it. Wait. Someone fails to turn up, and I am
on, with Wee Georgie Wood and a troupe of entertainers.

Allahabad, borrow a truck for furious ride into the city, just
catch the Calcutta Mail, on its way through from Calcutta to
Bombay. Late in the afternoon it deposits me at the junction of
Katni. Miles and miles of nothing, including trains to Saugor.
Hop freight, sleep in boxcar, arrive Saugor four A.M., the bungalow at four-thirty. Forty hours from the smell of death to the smell
of a drowsy, startled woman, having used my feet, three jeeps,

four aircraft, two trains, and a horse-drawn tonga. I felt that I had, at least a little, repaid Barbara for her efforts in coming to the Kagan, through the floods, in 1942.

That afternoon I went down with some mysterious fever, but four days later the deputy commissioner married us. All the battalion commanders of 111 Brigade (still waiting disbandment in the jungle) came down to share our happiness. Our daughter, too, not realizing the unorthodoxy of her position, enjoyed the occasion. She was already becoming highly female, though just over a year old, and there was much coy giggling and many sultry looks as she was passed around and hugged among a score of colonels and majors. Ayah, after her second glass of champagne, burst into tears and announced that I would return safely from the war and become a great *bara sahib*, and Barbara would have ten more children. Barbara burst into tears. She looked beautiful, and her hair was in a bit of a mess again.

It was hard to go back, but I had to, and the accomplishment of our marriage took a heavy load off my night thoughts. Three days later I rejoined Pete and the division, still in Mandalay.

The strange interlude of peace continued a day or two longer, and one night a troupe of Burmese dancers put on a *pwe* for us in the palace grounds. The clown clowned, the incredibly delicate and fine-boned girls, so tightly sheathed in silver and gold dresses that it seemed impossible they could move, writhed and gesticulated to the whine of *saing waing* and the rattle of bamboo clappers, their faces white as death under the masks of rice powder.

Then we hurried through our last preparations and set out on the next phase of the campaign. There was a great sense of purpose in the air. Slim had transformed the forgotten 14th Army into a vivid extension of his own personality. We were still forgotten in terms of the whole war—I don't know whether we were still lower, on the general priority list, than the Caribbean, but we certainly weren't very far up it. Whatever we needed and did not have we had to make for ourselves. The planners were still determined that Burma should fall by a sea and air landing launched from India, but Slim meant to destroy the Japanese in Burma and still reach Rangoon ahead of the airborne landings. The monsoon was four weeks away, and Rangoon 350 miles.

During March and early April, 4 Corps fought the decisive battles at Meiktila and Pyawbwe, destroying the core of the Japanese forces in Burma. During these battles our infantry, accompanying tanks in assault, frequently found Japanese soldiers sitting in small foxholes, a 250-pound aerial bomb clasped between their legs and a stone ready in the hand to strike the detonator when a tank passed over. The Japanese seemed doped, for they made no attempt to defend themselves, or strike the bomb, when our men looked down on them. They only peered up, seemed to say to themselves, "A man! I'm waiting for a tank," and again bow their heads, in which position they were shot.

Burma still contained thousands of enemy, but they were retreating ahead of us, fighting tenaciously all the while as only Japanese can, and trudging along side paths and tracks through the jungles while Slim launched his spearhead straight down the main road toward Rangoon. Pete and I were there one sunny morning on the outskirts of Meiktila, our jeep parked well off the road, when Bill Slim personally let slip the final advance. I had not seen him close to since Persia, three and a half years earlier, but he said, "How's it going, Jack? Pete driving you mad?" And then I stood back, wishing I had a camera, as Slim, 4 Corps Commander (Frank Messervy), and three divisional commanders watched the leading division crash past the start point. The dust thickened under the trees lining the road until the column was motoring into a thunderous yellow tunnel, first the tanks, infantry all over them, then trucks filled with men, then more tanks, going fast, nose to tail, guns, more trucks, more guns—British, Sikhs, Gurkhas, Madrassis, Pathans, Americans—young men of the American Field Service, the most popular and admired group in the Army. All these men knew their commanders and as the vehicles crashed past most of the soldiers were on their feet, cheering and yelling. The Gurkhas, of course, went by sitting stiffly to attention, whole truckloads bouncing four feet in the air without change of expression. . . . The romance of war—but only a fool would grudge us the excitement and the sense of glory, for no one on that plain had wanted the war, and all of us had known enough horror to last several lifetimes. (The 17th Indian Infantry Division had been in continuous contact with the enemy from January, 1942, till now—three years and three months.)

This was the old Indian Army going down to the attack, for the last time in history, exactly two hundred and fifty years after the Honourable East India Company had enlisted its first ten sepoys on the Coromandel Coast. These men were not all Indians or Gurkhas, for every Indian division contained British elements, often up to a quarter of its total strength and a third of its fighting units. Once, this arrangement had been made so that the stubborn and phlegmatic British soldier could steady his volatile Indian comrades in times of stress. This was no longer so. Now British and Indian and Gurkha were mixed by happenstance, and of each race some fought well, some not so well, depending on age-old principles of leadership and morale which have nothing to do with color or creed. I have personally seen to it that British troops were placed to support Indians whose morale was low; and I have placed Indian troops to support British for the same reason.

This moment, of the launching of the assault, held a particular meaning for General Slim, for the Japanese had defeated him here in 1941. It held as vital a meaning for me and my life, and represented an even greater triumph. I and my forefathers, and hundreds like us, had worked for generations in India. Certainly we had been masters, and imperialists, but we had not been afraid to die with these men and we had always loved them and their country, usually with an intense, blind passion which could ignore all theoretical considerations of right and wrong. Once we had obviously been their superiors in many qualities beside fighting ability, and we had dominated them, but the domination had seemed almost immaterial to the heart of the matter, which was love and understanding, or loyalty to each other, or faith in each other's intentions, or whatever you like to call an almost mystical sense of dependence.

Now, as the tanks burst away down the road to Rangoon and the torrent of guns and radios and trucks and machine guns swirled and roared past in one direction, south, past the bloated Japanese corpses, past the ruins of the empire the Japanese had tried to build here, it took possession of the empire *we* had built, and in its towering, writhing dust clouds India traced the shape of her own future. Twenty races, a dozen religions, a score of languages passed in those trucks and tanks. When my great-great-grandfather first went to India there had been as many

nations; now there was one—India; and he and I and a few thousand others, over two and a half centuries, sometimes with in-
tent, sometimes unwittingly, sometimes in miraculous sympathy,
sometimes in brutal folly, had made it. Whether we ought to
have gone to India in the first place is a moral problem of meaning only to England, because it is quite certain that if we had
not taken over, France or Russia would have. Nor can we know
what they would have made of the ramshackle subcontinent they
would have found. I only know that I saw, beside the road outside
Pyawbwe, what *we* had made.

The Nehrus and the Gandhis and the Crippses talked in the
high chambers of London and New Delhi; and certainly someone had to. But India stood at last independent, proud, and incredibly generous to us, on these final battlefields in the Burmese
plain. It was all summed up in the voice of an Indian colonel of
artillery. The Indian Army had not been allowed to possess any
field artillery from the time of the Mutiny (1857) until just before the Second World War. Now the Indian, bending close to
an English colonel over a map, straightened and said with a
smile, "O.K., George. Thanks. I've got it. We'll take over all tasks
at 1800. What about a beer?"

My India went on down the road to Rangoon. Pete and I
turned back. 19 Division's job was to guard the left flank of
the advance, driving the Japanese back along two roads that
led into the main north-south axis from the east, one coming
in at Meiktila itself and the other at Toungoo, some one hundred
and fifty miles south and therefore, of course, not yet in our
hands. We could expect the Japanese to hold obstinately to both
roads, with the double object of threatening the flank of our
main advance, and of maintaining strong points to which their
disorganized forces all over Burma could rally.

Pete detached 64 Brigade to deal with the first road, and the
rest of us set off south, trying to keep up with the motorized
divisions ahead of us. It was a hard task. The leading tanks of the
7th Light Cavalry, Indian Army, moved so fast that they often
came upon Japanese rear guards marching along the road, and
hardly bothered to do more than machine-gun them as they
passed. In Pyinmana a Japanese traffic policeman was still on duty
when the tanks rolled in, and the colonel of the regiment ran

straight over him. The gasoline supply stretched and thinned, and caused more delay than the enemy. Slim put everyone on half-rations, so that available airlift could be used for gasoline and ammunition. We, far behind, loaded all our vehicles well past the limit, as on our drive to Mandalay. We allowed no vehicle to pass us, going forward, without stopping it and cramming as many men onto it as we could. 19 Division went south like a herd of buffalo, the supply and maintenance services howling for us to stop. Pete said, "Keep moving. There'll be plenty of time for maintenance in Rangoon."

In all the rush three sex-starved Madrassi drivers of the Service Corps found time to rape a Burmese woman. It was the only such case in the division, that I knew of, throughout the campaign, and one of only about a dozen in the whole army, over a year. The three men found the woman and her husband beside a stream. Threatening to shoot the man, they drove him away, and then raped the woman in turn. She complained and the men were arrested. Her complaint was a rather touching one: she had at first been terrified, expecting death . . . and then, just when she was beginning to enjoy it—no more men. (They got fifteen years apiece.)

In the early part of the race we received a peculiar Intelligence report from Force 136. This was a Fifth Column organization which operated in the jungle, using Kachins and Karens and friendly Burmese of all kinds, partly to gather information and partly to prepare the hill tribes for a rising against the Japanese when the time was ripe. Their reports, usually sent by a British officer with a high degree of training and intelligence, could be trusted implicitly according to the reliability stated in them. If the officer had himself seen something, he would grade his report A. If one of his men had seen it, or brought the information, it would always be graded lower, no matter how reliable the man usually was, because he had not had the training always to understand just what he saw.

This particular report was graded Reliability A, and when Pete had finished reading it, his eyebrows rising incredulously, he passed it back to me. It said that on such and such a night, between 2323 hours and 0346 hours the following westward enemy troop movements had been observed at map reference so-and-so (this turned out to be a spot on a main road some distance to the east): 4 captured jeeps, 5 captured British trucks of 1941 vintage, 43 Japanese trucks, 8 Burmese buses, commandeered. These vehicles had contained: of engineers—23 privates, 4 corporals, 2 sergeants, 1 captain (probably Captain Shimeyoki Masatsu); of artillery—78 gunners, 23 corporals, 9 sergeants, 4 lieutenants, 1 captain, 1 major (probably Major Banzai Hideiki), together with two 105-mm. guns in tow and three 75-mm. regimental guns inside the trucks; of infantry—367 privates . . . and so on, and on.

It was the most detailed Intelligence report I had ever seen. It was ludicrously detailed, in fact. Not even the Japanese could have given information as accurate as this, in the present state of their communications. I was just about to agree with Pete that we had better regard the report as the product of an overstrained imagination, when a memory struck me. There *was* one man in the world capable of getting this information. I remembered John Hedley's report on the reconnaissance to the Zibyutaung Dan. I could see his face peering into the back of enemy trucks, counting, lifting up the canvas, opening the sacks, tasting the contents. . . . After his evacuation, wounded, from Blackpool, had not John gone to Force 136? This must be his work.

I checked. It was. (He got a D.S.O. for this and other, similar exploits.)

At Toungoo, hard on the heels of the leading divisions, we stopped. From here the second road led due eastward across the Sittang River to the Mawchi tin mines, a ferry over the Salween and, eventually, to Chiengmai in northern Siam. The Japanese held it in some strength. In fact, when we arrived, they were counterattacking into Toungoo and our first task was to drive them out again.

We—but I have called this a personal narrative; why do I use the impersonal and collective "we"? I must, because the "I" had disappeared, except in a personal relation with Pete and one or two others, and become a brain and an emotion connected to every unit, every man of the division. Seldom myself in physical danger—shelling of divisional headquarters morning and evening until we had pushed the Japanese out of artillery range; stray gunfire on the roads that I traveled; a few bullets passing overhead as I talked to battalion and company commanders—yet I knew of every danger and obstacle, and in my mind faced all of them.

The Mawchi Road wound and climbed east through dense hanging jungle. Our infantry began to slug remorselessly along it, day after day. How can that leading man be protected, enabled to move faster, kill more Japanese? A squadron of tanks fights with them, a week at a time, for no tank crews can stand the strain longer than that. The road bends every hundred yards, and round every corner is an antitank gun, or sometimes a 155, protected by machine guns, bunkers, men. Can the leading company by-pass them? How long will it take? A thousand yards a day is good going, and thirty casualties a day—day in, day out. How can we cut that figure down, move faster, save blood, save time?

The Japanese bunkers are heavily roofed with logs, steel bars, and corrugated iron. It takes a direct hit from bomb or shell to destroy them, but the shells burst on the trees, 150 feet high, far short of the target. We must use aircraft, really close. The Chindits, having no artillery, had learned a great deal about air support. I give lectures. I run demonstrations. The infantry need mortars. Can't we get some of the heavy American 4.2-inch pattern? Orange flashes from the tank guns throw sudden light into the shadowed, dark jungle, and the rain gleams on the gun barrels.

There is a burned-out armored car, ours, soon after the road crosses the new Sittang bridge. It lies at the edge of a crater, made by an aircraft bomb that was used as a mine. For several days there is a lump of meat inside, about ten inches cube, with a big bone in it, all heavily charred: the driver.

We are suffering too many casualties in the engineers, who have to advance with the leading infantry to clear the road of mines so that the tanks can go forward—but the tanks need to be closer still in that country. Every tank squadron suffers a casualty on the last day of its seven on the Mawchi Road. Each loses one or two tanks earlier, brewed up by direct hits, tracks blown off by a mine, some men wounded but no one killed. But on the last day they always get hit, tank burned, and the crew burned inside it, or machine-gunned as they come out of the turret and front hatch.

What's this message? What's this got to do with the division?

. . . The other "I" came to life, weary and bitter. It was from His Excellency the Commander in Chief in India, professional head of the Indian Army. He wanted to know why Lieutenant Colonel J. Masters, D.S.O., 4 G.R., having been involved in a divorce case, should not be called upon to resign his commission, *vide* such and such an Army Instruction. I wrote out a two-page reply, pointing out that neither His Excellency nor anyone else but the people directly concerned knew all the background of the matter, which was hardly likely to appear in a divorce suit. Furthermore, it was, with respect, none of his business, whatever the Army Instruction said. If, in view of this, H.E. wished to call upon me to resign my commission I would be delighted to do so, and would happily remove from my shoulders the rank badges I had earned serving an organization whose purpose I seemed to have misunderstood: I had thought it was to fight; I regretted my error.

It was quite a letter. It had to go up through channels, though, the first step being General Pete. He read it, nodded once or twice, and said, "That's wonderful." The next morning still weary but the bitterness gone—after all, I had known what I was running into, and had acted deliberately—I was preparing to go up the road when Pete sent for me. He said, "I think it would be better to send this. If you agree, sign it." He had personally typed a one-line reply, as from me, in which I stated that I had nothing to say. Below the space for my signature he had written: "Lt. Col. Masters is doing excellent work. I do not think he should be called upon to resign his commission," and signed it. Thankfully, I too signed. Pete said, "I don't think we'll hear any more of that." I went away, thinking how nearly I had broken one of my own rules, made years ago—"Never explain, never complain."

Back to the road . . . How to rescue casualties without suffering more? The American Field Service are bloody marvels. They seem to be, in equal proportions, pansies, Quakers, conscientious objectors, and altruistic young men; but damned nearly all heroes. They have jeeps with double-tiered steel-bed structures on them so that each can take two or three casualties at a time. See a tank burning in the road. Two more, fifty yards back, firing their 75-mm. guns into the jungle. Men lying in the road, machine-gun bullets ripping the leaves, thudding into the earth, turbans and steel helmets flattened in the ditch, an overturned Japanese gun, half a dozen Japanese corpses strewn round it, one over the barrel, shells whining and bursting among the trees.

Put put put, the Field Service motor forward, past the firing tanks, stop by the burning tank, the young Americans jump out, lift the wounded, stack them, turn the jeep, back, forward, back, and away, the way they had come. Perhaps the Japanese did not fire—sometimes—at them because they wore red crosses. Not often though. They were killed, and wounded, jeeps blown up on mines, destroyed by shell fire, burned to death, the same as the rest of us, and they never fired back, for they were unarmed.

Another six furlongs today. Talk with Pete again, late, about the possibility of finishing the Japanese on the Mawchi Road with a single big battle instead of a perpetual little one. Can't we put a brigade far behind them, cut them off? Air supply needed. No aircraft to spare. (Alastair Mackenzie gone, killed by a Japanese sniper, his head and body out of the turret as usual, seeing what he was doing.)

Another tank squadron, of the Gordon Highlanders, come and gone on the Mawchi Road; got away with it after seven days, no killed. They pulled back three miles and harbored for the night. Cleaned up. A machine gun in the turret of one tank, gun fully depressed for inspection, had a round in the breech. Slowly cooked off from the heat of the gun, fired, killed the gunner, standing directly in front of it.

Slim and Messervy (we are now under 4 Corps) visit Toungoo. I sit in the background, listening, as the three generals talk about these operations, and the next, and the next. . . . This is the day that brings home most deeply the peculiarly privileged position luck has given me, being of this age and this training at this time. The generals know me. From the talk I understand what is happening far beyond the circle of the room, the jungles, the corpses on the Mawchi Road, the warm rain (the monsoon has broken; we have taken Rangoon), and why. We drink mugs of steaming sweet tea. Then Slim goes on his way, Pete and I take Frank Messervy to see the Mawchi Road for himself.

I slip away from the official convoy after a time, and find the 4/4th. Soon I am having a mug of tea, not quite so hot this time, with half a dozen riflemen of C Company. Where is the *subadar* who led the assault on Mandalay Hill. *"Kasto-chha*, subadar sahib? *Remember the time the mule kicked you outside Mamirogha in '37? You were transport* havildar *then." "Surely, sahib—but it was '38. We did not go to Mamirogha in '37."* . . . Some shells bursting not far off; get into a hole in the ground and continue the conversation. The riflemen, too, know me. From the talk I understand also what is happening here, what men feel and think in these jungles where plans become blood, and the corpses on the Mawchi Road.

After thirty days we had pushed the Japanese back twenty-one miles from Toungoo. The rains had broken long since, washing away in their steady downpours any last Japanese chance to stage a counteroffensive. The enemy on the Mawchi Road broke into full retreat, heading for Siam. They would have a hard time getting there, and by the time they did, we might be ahead of them, having gone by sea and air. Meanwhile the Burma campaign, the longest of the war, had reached the last scene of the last act.

The 14th Army held a line right down Burma from north to south. Twenty thousand Japanese were cut off west of this line, in the Pegu Yomas, a low but densely forested and extremely unhealthy chain of foothills. Their only hope was to cut through our lines and escape eastward into Siam. To do this they had first to emerge from the Yomas, on the few tracks. Then they had to cross several miles of open rice paddy, all now under water. Here, too, irrigation channels and streams would force them to use the paths, which ran on raised bunds above the flood water. Finally, they must cross the Sittang River, also in full flood and about as wide as the Hudson at Albany or the Thames at London Bridge. At all these points we made ready to destroy them.

Barbara had moved from Saugor to the Himalayan foothill station of Ranikhet. The hospital there was full of Indian tank soldiers, some from the Mawchi Road, being treated by skin grafts for their burns. Up the hill there was a U.S. rest camp, and all the grass widows and abandoned wives were instructed to attend the American dances, so that the men should have partners.

19 Division's sector of the line on which we waited for the Japanese was thirty miles long. Pete and I drove up and down

it, making dispositions as though for a rabbit shoot. We were ready to give mercy, but no one felt pity. This was the pay-off of three bitter years. By fighting far back at Imphal, Slim had offered the Japanese the chance to overextend themselves. With typical optimism and logistical rashness, they had taken the challenge, and lost. Since then Slim had systematically divided them into smaller and smaller groups, destroyed their supplies and communications, and broken their fighting strength in a hundred battles, ranging from set pieces like Meiktila and Mandalay to scores of small but relentless engagements. Between March, 1944, and now—June, 1945—more than fifty thousand of them had died. Now those remaining had no chance, and we knew it and they knew it.

Machine guns covered each path out of the Yomas and each track between the flooded fields. Infantry and barbed wire protected the machine guns, all dug in on the only ground above water level. Behind, field guns stood ready to rain high-explosive shells on every approach. Behind the guns, more infantry waited. We had removed all the boats from the Sittang, and no one but a strong man and a good swimmer could cross its hurrying yellow flood. Tanks, like steel fortresses, stood at road junctions and in villages; others patrolled the road. Fighters and bombers waited on the few all-weather airfields. Ahead, patrols and scouts and informers in the Yomas observed each trail, telling us long in advance how many enemy were coming, and by which paths. They were grim messages, from any point of view beyond the immediate necessities of the war. "Twenty-three enemy at 657892, moving east. Seven armed, rifles. One nurse. Four men one nurse died yesterday, starvation." Seventeen here, five there, a hundred somewhere else, all without food, many unarmed, most diseased.

They came on, and out of the sheltering Yomas. The machine guns got them, the Brens and rifles got them, the tanks got them, the guns got them. They drowned by hundreds in the Sittang, and their corpses floated in the fields and among the reeds. In July, 1945, we of the 14th Army killed and captured 11,500 Japanese for a loss of 96 killed.

The Burma campaign had the shape and pattern of epic drama. The first scene of the first act had shown the defeat of Slim and the 17th Indian Infantry Division at this very place,

on the banks of the Sittang, early in 1942; the second scene, their
long, disastrous retreat to India, eight hundred miles away. The
second act had covered a year and a half of close, grim fighting
in the jungle-covered mountains along the Burma-India border.
The third act—the Chindits, Imphal, Meiktila, and the rushing
advance back south over those same eight hundred miles. And
now, almost as an *envoi*, this calm, efficient slaughter in the paddy
fields, Slim still leading, the 17th Indian Infantry Division still
in its place, in contact.

It was over. No time to rest, though. What next? Malaya
probably, and after that a quick leapfrog to Siam. Or perhaps direct at Japan. I was becoming tired again, and found difficulty in
concentrating, more in getting enough sleep. It was the Chindit
campaign, catching up with me once more. I told Pete that I
thought, if I didn't have a break soon, I would make a serious
mistake and cause loss of life. It was not physical rest I dreamed
of. I needed respite from buzzing telephones and chirruping radios,
from situation maps carried complete in my head, from messages
and orders half-drafted in my mind, figures crawling around and
among them, plans between. To escape from this mental rat
race I needed physical exercise, to walk far on high, open mountains, to lie down exhausted in the legs and spent in the wind, to
sleep, knocked out by simple bodily fatigue.

Pete told me to go away for two months, as soon as he could
get a replacement for me. At the end of my leave, he said, he
would bring me back to the division in one capacity or another.
I went to bed wondering, hoping, for there was only one capacity,
other than G-1, in which I could return—as a brigade commander.

For the three years since leaving the Staff College—and the
two years before going there, for that matter—I had served with
field formations. I knew I would now have no difficulty at all, if
I asked, in getting an appointment in the rear, somewhere where
Barbara and I could live together, where I would have a little
time to enjoy my wife and daughter. I also knew that I could
not ask; and that I would be miserable, although I loved my wife
and yearned for her company, if I were given such a job. Barbara
had married a professional fighting man and while the war lasted,
I must fight. I longed for the leave—and I prayed that after it
I would return to 19 Division.

The new G-1 came and I began to hand over. But before I left, Pete himself was suddenly called away to England to make speeches about the Far East, particularly in Wales. The capture of Mandalay had made him a popular hero in the British press. The Green Gremlin they called him, and loved his being Welsh and very small and very brave. I saw him off, feeling sad and tired, and returned to headquarters to complete my own preparations.

The night before I was due to go, Charles Coulter, the officiating divisional commander, called me into his room. He showed me a signal that had just arrived. It asked whether I was available and willing for command of a parachute brigade. Brigadier Coulter was looking at me with silent sympathy. I sat a long time, holding the message but not seeing it. This was generous of the Auk. Appointments such as this would be approved by the Commander in Chief in India and it was only a few weeks since he had written asking why I should not be called upon to resign my commission. I felt the straight pull of pride and ambition.

I remembered the Kagan. Had I not learned something there, something about permanent values? And reinforced those lessons in the loving melancholy of walking at night through my battalion, the pipes playing?

The parachute brigade would be in action very soon, probably at the invasion of Malaya, which I guessed would be set for September, about six weeks away. I must not choose rest and comfort, and expect others, who had not been given such a choice, to follow me. But had I not, before this offer came, made up my mind that for duty's sake I must have a rest? If I was too tired to be G-1 of a division, how could I be strong enough to command a parachute brigade, in action? Finally, there was the chance of a brigade here in 19 Division, under Pete Rees, when I was fit and well.

I told Charles Coulter that I felt I must have leave, if given any choice. If ordered to take the parachute brigade, I would of course do so. He leaped up and poured out two double whiskies, his craggy, pleasant face breaking into a wide smile. "Pete'll be glad," he said. I suddenly realized that Pete would be glad. I had got off the DUKW at Singu, in February, determined to *show* him. Now, I only felt an enormous and simple pleasure that he would be glad to see me again. This mattered, this above all, always. It had taken a long time, and I had waded through seas of blood to learn it, but I had got it now, once and for all. I was thirty years of age.

Two nights later, blacked out, the troopship *Devonshire* slipped down the Rangoon River, bound for Calcutta, carrying a thousand men time expired from the Eastern theaters, many sick and wounded, and myself. Along the deck of this same ship Willy Weallens had paced with his efficient, officious, impatient, and very raw adjutant on the way to Basra, four years and three months earlier.

25 Barbara and I walked slowly up the track toward Gwaldam, in the Garhwal Himalayas. The motor road ended nine miles behind us, the Forest Rest House lay one mile ahead. I was eager to see it, to smell again the seasoned wood and the subtle perfume of bound fifty-year-old copies of *Punch*.

The Burma campaign was over. It seemed almost indecent. Burma was a place to fight in, a country set aside for that purpose. It would be a waste of housing and good arable land to fight somewhere else. Both we and the Japanese knew Burma. We ought to invite their armies back into the country for the next round. . . .

Where was Barbara? Dropped yards back, bending over something beside the trail. I hurried back. "What . . . ?"

"Ground orchis," she said. "And look, peonies over there."

I examined them without curiosity. Women were different from men, thank God. Nothing exciting about these spots of white, but I had better show some appreciation.

The sweat poured off us, though it is an easy climb and a short stage. The Gwaldam Pass cut the skyline ahead, and the scent of the pines was sharp in my nostrils, just as I had dreamed. We were moving up a narrow valley. Suppose the enemy held the crest line. Not Japanese, but a German Mountain Division. Some of their men would be better alpinists than any Gurkha, but in the mass ours would be better, and faster. Use speed and mass then, in a place where they would only expect. . . . Damn it, the Germans too were out of it.

We breasted the ridge. The monsoon was in full swing but it was not raining at that moment. The sunlight filtered fitfully through heavy cloud masses sailing over from the southwest. The gigantic mass of Trisul, 23,360 feet high, its ice battlements surmounted by its trident peak, dominated the northern horizon. A plume of wind-driven snow stood out from the summit, like a pennant, twenty miles long. We came to the Rest House, flopped down on the lawn, lit cigarettes.

Ah, this was the life. Our daughter back in Ranikhet with ayah, both living in a friend's house. No one here but Barbara and me, and cool air, and weary legs.

I sat up. The man coming toward me wore a dhoti, thin two-tone shoes, purple socks held up by green suspenders, and a small, round velvet cap. He had an umbrella in one hand and a hurricane lantern in the other. It was Nain Singh, the foreman of the fourteen porters who were carrying our food, tents, and spare clothing. The bowed figures of the other porters trudged up behind him. One by one they sank to a sitting position, and bent back their necks. The load, which they carried on headbands, sank to the ground, and the men sat up. *"Phoo! Jhan tato chha!"* I agreed that it was very hot. They were Dhotials from extreme western Nepal, only fifty miles away, so they spoke Gurkhali, two had served in Gurkha regiments, and we understood each other.

I inspected and counted the loads: fourteen days' supply of the staples—rice, wheat flour, and lentils, items we expected to replenish en route; thirty-five days' of sugar, oil for the lamps, butter (in cans), canned beef. I wish Daljit could have been with us. He would have loved this. But Daljit was gone, missing, believed killed in action. When we came to a high, lonely place I would lay flowers on a stone for him.

Next day we descended to the valley of the Pindar; and climbed again, two long days; over a pass (prayer flags fluttering from a cairn of stones on the summit, and an old man with a gray beard, alone under a tree, who offered us milk from a brass jar); down the northern slope again, now the ice cliffs of Trisul leaning over us, and Barbara increasingly entranced by the flowers. I remonstrated with her, "We'll never get anywhere if we crawl, along at this pace."

"Where do you want to get to?"

Damned silly question. I fumed, because there was no simple answer. The Kuari Pass. Joshimath. Badrinath . . . anywhere up ahead, over the passes, beyond the mountains. Meanwhile she showed me acres of pink balsam. The pods exploded when we went near them, scattering seed far and wide, and we got to giggling. It was really a ridiculous thought, those foolish flowers waiting for a change in the air pressure and then, *bang*. "Suppose men acted the same way," Barbara said. We laughed so much, the two of us, describing the possibilities, that we couldn't move for five minutes.

Why can't the principle be adapted to an antipersonnel mine? Must remember, and make a note about it. . . .

There had been Rest Houses all the way so far, at ten- or twelve-mile intervals along the path, for the use of touring deputy commissioners, *tehsildars*, and forest officers. Now, near Kanol, we were going to use the tents for the first time. I chose the site, under the lee of a big slope, beside a swollen stream but twenty feet above it. It was raining, and the valley loud with noise of wind and water and thrashing trees, mist and cloud low overhead. The porters started a huge fire, and it hissed and crackled in the rain.

This was what I liked best of all—rain and cold, but shelter for us. I noticed Barbara looking glum.

"Are we going to sleep *here*?" she asked.

"Certainly. What's wrong with it? Wonderful spot."

She indicated the weeping mountain wall above, the thunderous torrent, the sodden tent. One of the porters was inside, arranging the blankets and ground sheets, his bare heels sticking out into the rain.

"I've never slept out in a tent before," Barbara said in a small voice.

I couldn't believe my ears. How was it possible for a human being to reach our age without . . . ?

"Never?" I asked incredulously.

"Never. And I'm frightened," she said firmly.

I felt much better. There's nothing like someone else's fear, as long as I know it to be groundless, to bring out the protective lion in me. The porter lit the lantern and the inside of the tent glowed like a little peak-roofed house of gold, all our own, and the blankets were warm and dry, and Nain Singh was crouched over the fire, one hand stirring a pot, the other holding up his umbrella. I showed Barbara how safe and cozy we were, and after hot food and a drink, and changing into dry clothes, she began to believe me. For added luck it poured with rain all night, thunder boomed in the mountains, lightning struck all round us, the stream rose five feet—and we remained dry, warm, and unhurt.

Next day we started up toward Trisul. We were not going to climb it, only go high on the grassy alps below the western face and find, if it existed, a mysterious lake we had heard about. A retired *subadar* of the Royal Garhwal Rifles was the headman of the nearest village and we could not pass until we had spent an hour and a half with him, drinking tea and eating small, sweet cakes. Now it was Barbara's turn to be impatient, for his talk was of long past battles and skirmishes, but nowadays the old gentleman seldom saw a British officer, and he had forty years of reminiscence to unburden himself of, so we stayed.

When we left he sent a grandnephew up with us to show us the way. The young man was about twenty. He wore the usual clothing of these hills—bare legs and feet; round his body a single large coarse home-woven blanket, worn rather like a short toga, tight-belted with many turns of a long rope, and held at the chest by a silver pin. In his right hand he carried a spindle, which he worked constantly as we climbed, feeding into it strands of gray and black wool from the toga fold above the belt. His face was Apollo-handsome, with a touch of the Mongolian, his hair long and shaggy. He climbed without any effort on the steep muddy path, in alternate mist and light rain, taking one stride to our three, the even rhythm of his breathing never altering, and talking the while.

"Naples is a good city," he said.

"Never been there," I said. I swallowed and stopped. "What did you say?"

"I liked Naples." He pulled aside the toga, baring his torso. A ridged white scar marked his flat belly near the navel. "A shell splinter through the stomach, below Cassino," he said, smiling. "Now I am on pension, for the rest of my life."

We climbed on. India was changing, the world changing. This was the same simple, honest man his fathers had been, the fathers we English had loved. The old *subadar* had fought from end to end of the North West Frontier. This young man had marched the Appian Way. I wondered whether there would be any place for me in the new India.

At the head of the first long slope, two thousand feet above the village, giants glided toward us in the mist. I stepped back, afraid, for they were huge, had no human or animal shape, and moved as though in a ritual dance, bending, rising, bending, gliding. . . .

The young ex-soldier glanced over his shoulder, saw my expression and smiled. "Women, sahib," he said, "picking pyrethrum."

We went on, and the ogres shrank in the mist, and indeed became women, wearing large sacks as cloaks, one side and one end cut open.

They stopped work and gathered round us. "What's this about a bomb?" a man with them asked. "A big bomb?"

Bombs! They had come to the right man with their inquiries. I told them the R.A.F. had bombs of *ten tons.* Dropped where we stood, one of these monsters would destroy everything from here to—there! My audience looked dissatisfied. The young soldier said, "A new bomb, sahib. There are no newspapers or radio here, but we have heard about a new bomb, much, much bigger."

"There is no bigger bomb," I said, nettled. What was the world coming to, that ten-ton bombs weren't big enough for hill peasants in the back of nowhere? I told them about artillery, pointing out a far, vague ridge and indicating that medium artillery in position here could drop shells—there, and there. The young man nodded, but no one else seemed interested and we climbed on, now no longer needing a guide.

Three days later I found the lake. It was a black tarn at about seventeen thousand feet, below Trisul. We climbed to it in mist, I and two of the porters. When we reached it, myself panting and suffering from a sharp altitude headache, I wished we had not. Concealed from all directions but above, the lake was littered with bones and skulls. They lay under the still black water, on the verge, in the scree slope; and there were broken baskets and the remains of leather sandals. Where had these people come from, why had they died here, how long ago? A bank of perpetual snow lay under the north face of a rock ledge nearby. The cold would preserve the relics for a long, long time, and there was a little flesh left, dry and sinewy, on the larger bones.

We hurried down the mountain, oppressed, and I asked the old *subadar* and other minor officials about the lake. No one knew. No one knows. The skulls had been there when the villages were settled a century earlier. The tarn does not lie on or near any path. That is all.

That night, I thought—there would be many such entombments all over Eastern Asia after this year and the next. In China, Siam, Burma, Malaya, Cambodia, in the Japanese mountains themselves, centuries hence, travelers like us would come upon bones, far from anywhere, all trace of clothing rotted away, where defeated, hopeless soldiers had found their way to die.

It was cold under the blanket, the chill seeped in from the mountains, I pressed close to my wife and held her tightly. *From the halls of Montezuma to the shores of Tripoli, we fight our country's battles. . . .* I had fought from Aleppo to Mandalay, from the Tigris to the Irrawaddy. In deserts and mountains, in jungles and villages and ancient cities. I had known the height of battle exhilaration, at Nyaungwun, in the thunder of the tanks on the road to Mandalay; the depth of exhausted misery, at the abandonment of Blackpool, in the final days above Ngusharawng. I remembered the debonair chivalry of our assault on Deir-es-Zor, and the precise execution of eleven thousand sick men only a month ago.

I had been at war, with intervals, since March, 1937. I had fallen in love, found out not exactly where I was going, but how I intended to go, and joined my body and spirit with a woman's, and fathered a child, and founded a family.

I had seen Willy Weallens walking down the road, the shells bursting round him, smiling encouragement. Michael Roberts, alert on the mountain, quick of voice—"There, we'll hold that." Joe Lentaigne, eyes agleam, riding a jeep like a bronco; grim and tired against Stilwell. At the Staff College, the harsh opening chords of the *Eroica* melting into the first theme, the faces soft in the dim light and the wind from Central Asia rattling the windows. Desmond Whyte, Douglas Larpent. Tim Brennan, his thick hair tousled, running down into the Deep at Blackpool in the dusk. Mohbat Sing going up to 2171. General Pete's suddenly hard voice, "Who's winning this war?" Bill Slim . . . something between the lines here, for he, too, had been at Aleppo, and at Mandalay. I wondered whether he and I were joined, unknown to him, but much in my consciousness, by an intangible cord, for where he went, I went, three or four levels down, twenty years younger. He was a Gurkha, like myself, and a star to steer my course by. Who knew—perhaps some younger man was setting his course by me?

Women came with the men. There was no distinction of atmosphere, no change from battlefield to boudoir. I saw the young British gunner who had lost both legs outside Toungoo and did not know it, sliding down into his morphia sleep, Pete kneeling, smiling, beside him; next to them a nurse at Habbaniyah, laughing, lying in the road, her thighs and breasts curving up as she lay, silhouetted against the hard flatness of the road. Tommy Thompson, the bullet's exit hole gaping at the base of his neck in the dark rain, and the long-legged girl at Karachi, kneeling beside me in the sand, laughing down at me. The Persian serving girl, suddenly presented, dark in the cradle of her thighs, warm slit, under a bright electric light, distant music around us; the broken men lying in the Blackpool path naked, revealing also their slashed flesh, but cold (both states integral to the human condition).

Mountains again, around us in the tent, and in the village below the old *subadar* asleep in his small house, dreaming of his own past, secure that for him the future was known, not only the end but the road to it. For us, what next?

The influence of the tarn and its skulls stayed with us. The perpetual rain and cloud had not oppressed us before, now it did. Three days later we came to a torrent which the rains had turned into a chute, almost a waterfall, it fell so steeply between its steep banks, six feet deep, twenty feet wide. The plank bridge had gone, and we made another, cutting down a pine with our kukris and laying it across the stream from rock to rock. Then we fastened a lifeline of rope, and began the crossing. Barbara and I passed

safely, and half the porters, each walking steadily along the tree,
bent under the heavy loads, lightly holding the line with one
hand. Then Maite, a young man, slipped. He grasped the line, but
his load swung him round by the head and jerked him backward
into the torrent. He was gone, vanished, before we realized he had
fallen. We hurled ourselves down the bank, some on one side
and some on the other. Birbal ran far down, seized a dead branch
and lay out on a rock. Maite appeared twice, turned over, vanished
again in the boiling chute, and reappeared under Birbal's hand.
Birbal grabbed him by the hair and held. Then we reached him
and dragged him out. He was unconscious and I began artificial
respiration at once. After two minutes he vomited water, groaned,
vomited again. Half an hour later he sat up, very pale and suffering from shock.

We carried him to the next village, Kaliaghat, and put him
in a cow byre, well wrapped in blankets, and made hot sweet
tea. Examining him as well as I could, I did not think he had
broken any bones, but feared he might have concussion or a
brain injury. During those fierce swirls under water he could have
been dashed against a rock sufficiently hard to crack his skull.
His temperature fluctuated seriously for a few hours, and he had
no control over his eyes and features, which twitched and worked,
and he suffered from shivering fits such as in malaria. But late
at night his temperature dropped and he fell asleep.

The next morning a strange golden light suffused the towering
cloud banks that marched perpetually over us from the southwest.
We stared wonderingly at it, and guessed that it must be the sun,
which we had not seen for many days. Later, yellow fire broke
through and long shafts, gold and gray and purple lined, struck
down on the vast landscape, on the lime-green water of the lake
in the gorge, on the white face of Nandakna at the head of the
valley, and beyond that, on Trisul. Maite was fully recovered,
though not strong.

The last obstinate links with the war, and the aura of the death
tarn, vanished. The moments of Maite's crisis had brought back,
too vividly, black hours of battle when I had stood beside the
dying, being responsible, and I had felt hounded by fate that here
in the Himalayas, beside my wife, wanting nothing but love,
having only love to give to her and the mountains and the people,
I should again bring death.

The sun disappeared again before evening, but now we had come to terms with the mountains and the rain. We went on, and the physical tiredness that I had sought came easily and refreshingly to me at the end of each day, with hunger that made a plate of lentil stew the fulfillment of a magician-granted wish. We decided where we would go, to the Valley of Flowers, that Bhyundarganga valley, explored by Frank Smythe a few years earlier, where grew the finest alpine flowers in the world. Five more days' march to reach it. We would replenish our supplies when we reached the pilgrims' route at Joshimath. For two days from there we would be going with the pilgrims, trudging up the valley to immerse themselves in the icy, sacred waters at the source of the Ganges near Badrinath.

Rain and cloud swung about and around us in a slow dance. Now they wrapped us in a close-woven net of pearls, so that we walked for hours on short grass seeing nothing but each other . . . then hearing faint the music of a wooden pipe, and coming suddenly upon a shepherd boy, the silver pin glittering at his chest, the music suddenly stopping, the sheep dog growling, restrained . . . the boy getting up with a smile.

Now the pearls dissolved. . . . We move high on the side of a valley, the earth falling away two thousand feet below, to rise again in streaming cliffs, and beyond, far snow.

Late one afternoon, nearing camp, we heard a leopard sawing in the pines below. Every day Himalayan pheasant rose from the stones in iridescent green and black and scarlet; six hurried, hard beats thrashing the air as they launched themselves, then silence as the great birds glided down the long slopes. Sheep passed us, going down toward India, flocks of two hundred, each guarded by three men, each sheep carrying two ten-pound bundles slung across its broad-fleeced back—salt and borax and jade from Tibet. Later, these same men would bring up tea and sugar and oil from India, on the backs of the sheep, and cross over the passes—the Niti, the Mana, the Kungri Bingri, the Bara Hoti—into Tibet. The sheep herders always stopped to have a cigarette with us, and always asked us about the big bomb. I told them they must not listen to idle gossip, or spread silly rumors, and returned to the list we were making of all the flowers that we had seen.

The path climbed past a waterfall where wild raspberries spread across the rock face, and I shot a pheasant. That night, in the tent at nine thousand feet, we ate roast pheasant, and raspberries and cream. Next morning the path climbed slowly in heart-breaking switchbacks, on and on and up into the fading cloud to the Kuari Pass. Halfway up, when the sweat streamed into my eyes, and my light pack, in which I always carried our midday meal, felt ready to break my back, Barbara cried, "Look, look! Beside your foot!"

Six inches from my right boot, a veined pattern of pale blue ice grew beside the path. It was one of the rarest and quite the most beautiful flower in the world, a Himalayan blue poppy. We watched it for ten minutes—watched, because the thrusting sun and the stir of wind across the mountain gave it life and movement, and we waited for it to rise up and dance away. Then the porters came, and, warning them not to tread on the flower, we went on up.

Heavy mist shrouded the pass, 12,400 feet above sea level, and we could see nothing of the immense view that should have spread out to the north, where Hathi Parbat and the further Kamet and Mana peaks rise like towers along the Tibetan frontier, beyond the trench of the Dhauli River. Marmots whistled at us from every stone, and we came upon two shepherds, with their flock, living in a stone shelter which they willingly shared with our porters. Their dogs were Tibetan sheep dogs, huge beasts of the chow family, their coats so thick and matted that even a leopard would have had a hard time sinking his fangs through them; and they wore collars made of solid steel, with triple rows of spikes, hand-beaten and sharpened, six inches long. The shepherds told us that these two dogs had killed a leopard down in the valley only a month earlier. The dogs eyed us coldly, slow growls rumbling in their deep chests, as ready to kill us as any leopard, if we had come to harm the sheep. When we patted them they looked very puzzled. One tried to wag his tail but he didn't really know how to, and almost threw himself over. Affection was something they had never known, or had forgotten. They were guardians. But they came back for more, and I pulled the thick coats and pushed the heavy heads this way and that in a flood of sympathy. I had something to tell them about our common lot, if I could only speak to be understood.

We went to bed early in the rain. It was unaccountably hot

in the tent and we both awoke in the middle of the night, listened for rain, and heard none. Pulling on socks and boots, we went out. Clouds filled the sky, not solidly as with a carpet, but in banks and formations, covering each other in depth from a few thousand feet above us to the utmost heights. In the north an oval of greenish light, hanging in the void level with our eyes, showed where the full moon had found a continuous gap and poured its light through. The wind blew, we threw the cigarettes away and made ready to return to the tent.

Barbara gripped my arm. The oval of moonlight moved with the clouds and seemed to be getting larger, brighter. Then fast, fast as the racing winds in the upper atmosphere, the wide shaft of light fell on a single mountain of ice. The mountain hung in the sky, without base or pillars, supported only by the darkness, so high above us that the back of my neck creaked. My skin shivered, the hairs crawled on my scalp and up the back of my neck, and our hands were clasped, hers and mine, so tightly that I heard the small bones creaking. The ice mountain shone more brightly, glittering, pendant, diamond-sharp, huge and far, for a long minute—and another. . . . The darkness climbed fast on its face and I closed my eyes. When I opened them it had gone, the wind whistled across the pass and the sheep dogs stood silent beside us, staring, as we had, into the northern night.

Two days later, the vision on the pass a part of our life, we entered Joshimath. The porters lagged far behind us and I did not know where the Rest House was. A white house on the right of the narrow street offered promise of someone who could tell me. We knocked and a servant came. I asked him my question and he said, "Wait," and ushered us into a large room furnished in European style.

A small, middle-aged man, dressed in white, entered and we rose. His skin was quite dark, his bones fine and small, and he was obviously from South India. I wondered what he was doing in these Himalayan gorges, so far from the palms of Coromandel. He answered our question about the Rest House, and offered us tea. We conversed in English, which he spoke excellently.

He always liked to meet British mountaineers, he said. I told him quickly that we were not mountaineers, just walkers. Ah . . . Mr. Smythe and Mr. Shipton were personal friends of his. He had

had the honor of greeting them and perhaps being of some assistance to them, once or twice, when he had been at Badrinath.
Did he know Badrinath, I asked. Indeed, yes, for twenty years he
had been the Holy *Rawal* (High Priest) of the temple there, one
of the most sacred in India. Now he was retired. He feared that
many of his English friends had died or suffered wounds in the
war. For their sakes, though the possibilities of the invention
filled him with foreboding for humanity, he was glad the fighting
was over.

"I beg your pardon?" I felt queer, numb, a sense of approaching
madness swirling in my brain. "The fighting . . . ?"

He looked at us keenly. "When did you leave Ranikhet?"

"August 6."

"Wait."

His Holiness left us. Barbara and I watched each other but
did not speak. He came back, carrying a newspaper, over two
weeks old. A black headline across the front page screamed:
"ATOMIC BOMB DROPPED ON JAPAN."

I felt a physical shock, as though a stranger met in the path,
a man with whom I had been passing the time, no more, had
shot me. The war is over, finished, the *Rawal* was saying.

There was a sense of insult that I, dedicated to war, a professional of professionals, should be one of the last people on
earth to hear about it. There was a sense of loss, not of regret
but of loss, as when a factory that has hammered and clanked outside your window for six years is suddenly, one morning, vanished.
For a moment I could only see what would be gone—the sense of
purpose, unselfishness, comradeship, sacrifice, courage. There was
no reason why these qualities should not be devoted to peace in
and between peoples, but they had not been after 1918, and I
did not believe they would be now.

I believed with instant conviction that there could be no more
war. No more tactics, no more strategy, only total destruction—
or peace. The training and experience of a lifetime had vanished
into the thin Himalayan air and I was happy.

I took my wife in my arms and kissed her. His Holiness said,
in Hindi, "May God bless you, in peace."

Envoi

(*August, 1960*)

Willy and Biddy Weallens live on an island off the coast of County Mayo, and win prizes with the linen they weave on their own looms.

Usman the Apeman, though a Mohammedan, chose India when partition split the old Indian Empire. He was killed, gallantly, early in the Kashmir fighting of 1947. Goff Hamilton, after Indian independence, transferred from the Guides to the British Army, and now commands the British infantry brigade in Berlin. His wife, Molly Kaye, is a successful artist and novelist.

Joe Lentaigne commanded the Indian Defence College for many years after Independence. When Mr. Nehru ordered that it was time for British officers to give up the honorary and honorable post of Colonels of Regiments, our serving officers of the 4th Gurkhas, by then all Indian, asked that an exception be made in Joe's case; and it was. Joe retired from India finally in 1956 and died of a heart attack a few months later, at the age of fifty-six.

Desmond Whyte, D.S.O., F.R.C.P., F.R.F.P.S., F.F.R., M.D., is a Senior Consultant Radiologist in Northern Ireland. John Hedley is a housemaster at Bromsgrove, a boys' boarding school in Worcestershire. Douglas Larpent, who has had heart trouble, is retired and works in a British Army records office in Germany; Tim Brennan is a partner in one of the underwriting groups which make up Lloyds of London; Mohbat Sing has just retired on pension, having served his time as *Subadar Major* of the 3rd Battalion of the Regiment; Tommy Thompson is a bank manager in Bristol and Bill Henning a farmer in Kenya.

Two of the men mentioned in this book have been before the criminal courts, one for a heterosexual and one for a homosexual offense. In the war both fought a great fight, and risked their lives time and again while most of the people now socially ostracizing them were comfortably abed. I am proud of their friendship.

Michael Roberts works in the British Cabinet Offices, with other retired officers, writing the official history of the war.

Hamish Mackay, full colonel, twice wounded, twice decorated with the D.S.O., worked for a time as a butler in Long Island, his wife Misha as cook. They used to be invited out, as honored guests, to a neighboring mansion where lived the multimillionaire scion of a famous industrial family—the young man had served under Hamish with the American Field Service in Burma.

Bill Slim . . . Field Marshal the Viscount Slim, K.G., G.C.B., G.C.V.O., D.S.O., M.C., succeeded Monty as Chief of the Imperial General Staff, professional head of Britain's army; then became Governor General of Australia; is now retired in England —though technically still on the active list, as field marshals always are. He was the second and last Knight of the Garter from the Indian Army (Lord Roberts, Kipling's *Bobs Bahadur*, was the other). He is the same man, though, that he always was.

Pete Rees commanded the force on the India-Pakistan border during partition, a thankless and bloody task. Retired to England, the government appointed him administrator of a New Town in Wales, one of those garden communities designed to replace the old, appalling slums. He threw himself into the work with his usual fire, and took no more notice of a coronary than he had of Japanese snipers. In the winter of 1959 he dropped dead on the steps of the Home Office in London, aged sixty-one.

One other living organism, made of flesh and blood, whose spirit has illumined these pages from first to last—and, indeed, has caused them to be written—has ceased to exist: the 4th Prince of Wales's Own Gurkha Rifles have marched into history, with the Indian Empire of which they were both a foundation and an ornament. When the war ended the 1st Battalion had just left the 17th Indian Infantry Division, with which it had fought through all but the last scene of the Burma epic. (It was pulled back into rest after suffering nearly 100 per cent casualties at Imphal—over 100 per cent in officers.) The 2nd Battalion, re-formed after the disaster of the Cauldron, was approaching Venice. The 3rd Battalion, once Chindits, was preparing to invade Malaya. The 4th Battalion, which had taken Mandalay Hill, was standing by, with the rest of the Dagger Division, to execute Pete's next orders—whatever they might be.

But after 1947 the regiment did not really disappear; it merely underwent a small change—for the 4th Gurkha Rifles fills the same place in the army list of the new Indian Republic, and carries the same battle honors, and observes the same customs and traditions, and eats off the same plate and drinks out of the same silver, given by generations of us, first British, now Indian.

We of the old order are scattered to the ends of the earth— England, Scotland, Eire, Kenya, Malaya, Hong Kong, Australia, Canada. Some of us are still soldiers, some farmers, some oil tycoons, some diplomats, some civil servants. I am in the United States, a writer.

This spring Barbara and I attended the wedding of her daughter Liz to an officer of the Royal Navy, and helped weed and plant the garden of their tiny cottage in Dorset, not far from where my father and mother live. Mike, now twenty and about to go to Oxford, is spending the summer with us and our daughter and son here, where I write, at nine thousand feet above sea level in the Absaroka Range of Wyoming. I can see the Wind River peaks to the southeast and, when I climb the hill behind the cabin, the jagged tower of the Grand Teton to the west. Moose and elk and bear roam the forest and sometimes, between chapters, I walk up to the lakes below the cliff wall and catch a trout.

The hydrogen bombs remain, for the moment, in their subterranean lairs.

The road from Joshimath to the Diamond G Ranch, from English soldier to American author, has been as eventful and as important, at least to me and mine, as the road from Deir-es-Zor to Joshimath. Someday I hope to describe it.

Appendix

This appendix contains the Operation Order mentioned in the text, on page 162. I include it to show the sort of co-ordination that is necessary for an operation of this kind, and how that co-ordination is achieved—in other words, as a typical example of what we learned at the Staff College.

Apart from spelling out abbreviated words in full, omitting map references (useless without the maps), and the omission of one line at the request of British security officials, the order is exactly as issued on March 1, 1944, at Saiton Camp near Imphal, India. I have not, however, reprinted any of the ten appendices which went out with the order; they are of interest only to technicians.

I should add that the Order was followed, four days later, by an Operation Instruction dealing with the Brigade's battle tasks in Burma in the same way that this Order dealt with the job of getting the brigade into Burma; and that large parts of both the Order and the Instruction became useless and had to be rewritten when it was decided at the last minute to fly 111 Brigade into Chowringhee instead of Broadway and Piccadilly.

Destroy before emplanement   MOST SECRET
                                                Copy No......
                                                1 Mar 44

111 Indian Infantry Brigade Operation Order No. 1

Reference Maps sheets 83/H/NE, 83/H/SE, 92 D/NE, 92 D/SE at
scale of ½ inch to 1 mile; sheets 92 D/G 10, 11, 15 at scale of 1
inch to 1 mile; and sheet 92, at scale of 1/1,000,000

INFORMATION

1. This Operation Order will deal with the move of the brigade
    from present sites to its operational landing grounds, and an
    Operation Instruction will issue to cover details of move there-
    after, and information of the enemy.

2. *Enemy Air Forces.* General policy is to keep his air forces back
    in SIAM and only bring them forward to strips in BURMA
    for operations. Anti-aircraft field craft must be rigorously en-
    forced as it is impossible to guarantee immunity from air attack.

3. *Own troops*

    (a) 16 Brigade from LEDO 85 miles due north of SINGKA-
    LING HKAMTI cross the CHINDWIN near SINGKALING
    HKAMTI about 29 February, and are moving thence on IN-
    DAW via BANMAUK and the upper MEZA VALLEY.

    (b) 77 Brigade land columns by glider the night D/D plus 1,
    and build strips BROADWAY and PICCADILLY on which
    the rest of the brigade and stronghold troops will be landed by
    night, from D plus 1 to first light D plus 5. They are establishing
    a stronghold at PICCADILLY; Major R. Q. GAITLEY, Com-
    mander of 82 Column, is responsible for defence of BROAD-
    WAY until this is taken over by 111 Brigade; Colonel ROME
    will be in command of PICCADILLY throughout.

    (c) 49 and 94 Columns come under command of 77 Brigade
    forthwith. They will land by gliders and aircraft on CHOW-
    RINGHEE strip on the nights D plus 4/5 and D plus 5/6,
    thence operating against the enemy lines of communication
    EAST of the IRRAWADDY.

    (d) 6 Nigeria Regiment comes under command 2 March at
    LALAGHAT.

4. *Own air force*

    (a) Strategical Air Force, Tactical Air Force, Troop Carrier
    Command are in support of the operation.

    (b) 5318 Provisional Air Unit, USAAF, is under command of

3 Indian Infantry Division, with B Squadron, Light Plane Force, allotted in support of the brigade.

(c) The air plan includes disrupting enemy air operations by strategical bombing from D day, fighter sweeps over enemy airfields, night fighter attacks on airfields, bomber attacks on enemy ground concentrations, and direct air support as called for by columns, within the limit of resources available.

5. *Meteorological*

(a) Sun and moon tables issued to all columns and certain officers of brigade headquarters under this HQ L/225/G of 14 Feb 44.

(b) Chief R.A.F. Liaison Officer has cloud and ground mist charts of BURMA which Column R.A.F. officers will study before beginning of the operation.

INTENTION

6. 111 Indian Infantry Brigade will move by march and air from present camp sites into positions in BURMA from which it can carry out its operational role, completing by 0600 hrs D plus 7.

METHOD

7. *Outline*

(a) D day is 5 March 1944.

(b) Flying begins 9 March evening, ends 12 March morning.

(c) On the night 9/10 March 30, 40 Columns and advance parties of Brigade Headquarters, 26, 90, 41, 46 Columns move TULIHAL–BROADWAY in C.47s; same night, a detachment of the West African battalion moves LALAGHAT–PICCADILLY in C.47.

(d) On the night 10/11 March 41, 46 Columns and detachment of Brigade Headquarters move TULIHAL–BROADWAY in C.47s; detachment West African battalion moves LALAGHAT–PICCADILLY in C.47.

(e) On night 11/12 March 26, 90 Columns and a detachment of Brigade Headquarters move TULIHAL–BROADWAY in C.47s; West African battalion less detachments move LALAGHAT–PICCADILLY in C.47s.

8. *Dress, arms, and equipment:* Vide load-on-the-man tables issued under this HQ L/370/G of 22 Feb 44, and standard Column loads-weights given under Appendix B to this HQ letter L/225/G of 12 Feb. 44.

9. *March to Emplanement fields*

(a) West African battalion will make its own arrangements.

(b) For remainder, vide March Table, Appendix A to this Operation Order.

10. *Emplanement*

(a) Vide emplanement field diagram (Appendix B) and emplanement table (Appendix C) to this Operation Order.

(b) Final plane manifests, Appendix D to this Operation Order, will be completed and dealt with vide paragraph 13 below.

11. *Working parties*

Vide work table Appendix E to this Operation Order (not applicable to West African battalion).

12. *Action on deplanement*

Vide special orders, Appendix F, and deplanement field diagrams, Appendices G and H to this Operation Order.

13. *Loading manifests*

(a) A specimen completed manifest is attached as Appendix D to this Operation Order, and sufficient blank forms are sent herewith for completion by plane commanders.

(b) This manifest is to be completed by plane commander in triplicate at Forming Up Area before moving off to Ground Control Office. All three copies are to be handed in to Ground Control Office.

(c) "Commence emplaning" is the time at which the plane load is due to report to the Ground Control Office. "Complete emplaning" is ten minutes before take off.

(d) Weights of personnel, Column (b), will be altered to appropriate unit figure.

(e) Under heading of Column (c), after 800 lbs, add, "for small animals, 1000 lbs for large animals."

(f) Name of plane commander must be entered in remarks column.

(g) Remarks. IF ANYONE IN PLANE IS CARRYING CIPHER DOCUMENTS THEIR SOX NUMBERS MUST ALSO BE ENTERED.

(h) Sheet Number will be left blank.

14. *Air raids*

(a) May occur at any time during the move. The first battalion in camp at TULIYAIMA will dig its own slit trenches on arrival, other battalions will improve. Ground Control Office will arrange to dig slit trenches for 200 men in the Forming Up Area, and for all its own men.

(b) If air raid is signaled during emplanement, this will be broadcast on the Tannoy, and personnel in the Forming Up

Area will go to the slit trenches there; those on the strip to the irrigation ditch along the strip; all lights out. Emplaning will continue on Ground Control Office orders.

15. *Security of documents*
Before leaving the present camp a thorough search will be made of the entire brigade area for paper, which will be burnt. On reaching camp TULIYAIMA, all men will be searched, and all documents will be removed and burnt which give any of the following details:
(a) The identity of the brigade or the unit.
(b) Anything which concerns the general role of the brigade, or its immediate orders, except for very bare notes.
(c) Anything which concerns the equipment or armament of the brigade.
(d) All documents or manuals marked "This document must NOT fall into enemy hands."
(e) All maps which give detailed or general dispositions of our own or enemy troops.
(f) All pay books and identity cards. See Appendix J, paragraph 7.

16. *Security of personnel*
When on the march men will NOT be permitted to talk to villagers or personnel of other units, except in course of duty. On arrival at night harbor or the final emplaning area, units will be responsible for placing guards to ensure that nobody, civil or military, approaches the unit's area except in course of duty; that no man of the unit concerned leaves the unit area. In no circumstances whatever will any officer or man be permitted to go into local villages to purchase food etc. Anyone outside the brigade, whether civil or military, who acts in any way suspiciously or who asks unnecessary questions about the brigade will be arrested and sent to brigade headquarters.

17. *Security of equipment*
New weapons, such as the Lifebuoy, will be kept covered on the line of march.

18. *Air accidents*
Should an aircraft crash-land en route WEST of the ZIBYU-TAUNGDAN Range (passed 40 minutes after take off from TULIHAL/LALAGHAT) survivors will
(a) burn the aircraft.
(b) return to 4 Corps area, crossing the CHINDWIN between HOMALIN and YUWA.

If the aircraft crashes EAST of the ZIBYUTAUNG DAN survivors will burn the aircraft and march to PICCADILLY and report there to Headquarters 77 Brigade.

ADMINISTRATION

19. Administrative orders for the march to TULIHAL—see Appendix I.
20. Administrative orders for the start of operations—see Appendix J.
21. Administrative orders for personnel and stores not going into operations—see Appendix K.

INTERCOMMUNICATION

22. The Brigade commander will move with Group 1, ex SAITON camp on 7 March. He will fly with Wave 1, 9 March. An echelon of Advanced Brigade Headquarters will move with each of Groups 2 and 3.
23. Rear Brigade Headquarters will remain in present location throughout the move.
24. All reports will be made to the Ground Control Office, where a representative of Brigade Headquarters will be, who will relay by telephone and/or Dispatch Rider to Rear Brigade Headquarters. Rear Brigade Headquarters will arrange to provide two dispatch riders at the Ground Control Office for this purpose from 1200 hrs 9 March.
25. *Signal plan:* Vide Signal diagram attached as Appendix L to this Operation Order.

    All sets of Rear Brigade and Air Base will open full communications with effect from 1000 hrs 9 March. Column sets will open communications as soon as practicable after arrival target. Advanced Brigade sets will open communication immediately on arrival camp TULIYAIMA, and will march as follows:

    Group 1 set to CAMERONIANS net.
    Group 2 set to KING'S OWN net.
    Group 3 to 3/4 GURKHA RIFLES net.
26. Signal silence will be maintained by all Advanced Brigade and column sets from the hour of departure from SAITON until ordered to open vide paragraph 25 above.
27. *CIPHERS—Destruction in case of crash*

    Plane commanders will inform all personnel in the plane, before emplanement, if any man in the plane is carrying cipher documents. In the event of a crash which damages the wireless set beyond repair or kills the operators, the man carrying the ciphers, or the senior person present, will destroy cipher documents. The man burning the ciphers will note the details of the documents burned.

28. *Charging of batteries*

All batteries carried by columns will be fully charged before leaving SAITON camp. Final short gassing may be given at TULIYAIMA.

29. *Carrying of signal documents*

The non-commissioned officers in command of signal detachments will carry a copy of the signal diagram, frequencies, and code signs. Details will be issued by the Brigade Signals Officer.

30. *Transub cipher*

Phrases for the Transub cipher will be given to Column Staff officers by the Cipher Officer on 6 March.

31. *Synchronization*

All officers will synchronize watches on passage through the Ground Control Office before emplanement. The Ground Control Office will arrange to get AIR time.

ACKNOWLEDGE

Time of signature......   (*Signed*)   *J. Masters, Major*

Method of issue ....   Brigade Major.

DESTROY BEFORE EMPLANEMENT

About the Author

John Masters was born in India, the son of a captain in the 16th Rajputs. He was sent to England, his family's homeland, for his education.

After graduation from Sandhurst, the British West Point, in 1934, Mr. Masters returned to India to join the Indian Army. During World War II, he fought in Iraq, Syria, Iran, and Burma, being awarded the D.S.O., O.B.E., and a mention in dispatches. After the war, he was assigned to teach mountain and jungle warfare at the British Staff College in England.

After the Indian Emancipation in 1947, there was no longer a place for Masters in the Army and so, with his wife and children, he came to the United States. Today he lives in New City, New York.

His books have been published, praised, and widely read in many countries. They are: *Nightrunners of Bengal* (1951), *The Deceivers* (1952), *The Lotus and the Wind* (1953), *Bhowani Junction* (1954), *Coromandel!* (1955), *Bugles and a Tiger* (1956), *Far, Far the Mountain Peak* (1957), *Fandango Rock* (1959), and *The Venus of Konpara* (1960).